THE BEDSIDE
BACCALAUREATE

THE SECOND SEMESTER

EDITED BY DAVID RUBEL

AN AGINCOURT PRESS BOOK

STERLING
New York

STERLING
New York

An Imprint of Sterling Publishing
387 Park Avenue South
New York, NY 10016

AN AGINCOURT PRESS BOOK
© 2009 by Agincourt Press

ISBN 978-1-4549-0193-8 (paperback)
ISBN 978-1-4027-7253-5 (ebook)

Interior book design and layout: Jon Glick/mouse+tiger

For acknowledgments, see page 384.

Distributed in Canada by Sterling Publishing
c/o Canadian Manda Group, 165 Dufferin Street
Toronto, Ontario, Canada M6K 3H6
Distributed in the United Kingdom by GMC Distribution Services
Castle Place, 166 High Street, Lewes, East Sussex, England BN7 1XU
Distributed in Australia by Capricorn Link (Australia) Pty. Ltd.
P.O. Box 704, Windsor, NSW 2756, Australia

For information about custom editions, special sales, and premium and
corporate purchases, please contact Sterling Special Sales at 800-805-5489 or
specialsales@sterlingpublishing.com.

Printed in China

2 4 6 8 10 9 7 5 3 1

www.sterlingpublishing.com

PREFACE

THE DIFFERENCE BETWEEN THIS BOOK and a miscellany is the difference between knowledge and trivia. The appeal of a miscellany lies in its variety; but in achieving breadth, miscellanies often lack depth and fail to promote understanding. *The Bedside Baccalaureate* is more than a miscellany because it presents detailed, focused overviews of subjects with which any well-educated person would want to be familiar.

The goal of *The Bedside Baccalaureate* is not the simple accumulation of facts (some of which you may already know), but the placement of those facts within a framework of knowledge. The twenty courses that make up the book have been created by experts in their respective fields with the intention of making the subjects accessible to nonexpert readers. The interplay among these subjects is intended not merely to inform (and entertain!) but also to encourage the cross-pollination of ideas and to broaden the mind.

No doubt there will be occasions when you have questions that the text, given its brevity, doesn't answer. For this reason, the contributors have provided suggestions for further reading (beginning on page 382), which you can consult. That you'll want to read more should be expected, because learning is contagious; and once you get started, it can be difficult to stop.

HOW TO USE THIS BOOK

- The twenty courses are grouped, five at a time, into four sections, or "syllabi." These sections are easily viewed in the table of contents that follows.

- Each course consists of eighteen single-page lectures that maximize clarity without comprising the integrity of the ideas. The lectures are rotated, rather than clumped together, to add some variety to the reading experience and also to mimic the heady mix of subjects that one encounters in the world of the intellect.

- You can dip into an assortment of subjects by reading just a page at a time; or, if a course really grabs you, you can skip ahead. You'll find the lectures for each course on every fifth page, and roman numerals next to the lecture titles keep track of the sequence for you.

SYLLABUS

I

Art History
The Armory Show

18

KIRSTEN JENSEN

The 1913 Armory Show presented paintings and sculptures by such
leading members of the European avant-garde as Marcel Duchamp, Paul
Gauguin, Henri Matisse, and Pablo Picasso. The nonrepresentational styles
in which these artists worked—notably cubism and fauvism—shocked
critics and the public alike. The lectures in this course describe in detail
the circumstances of the Armory Show, how it came about, and why it
caused such a lasting sensation.

Social Sciences
Sigmund Freud

19

MARTHA HADLEY

Trained as a doctor, Sigmund Freud devoted his medical practice to the
treatment of patients suffering from illnesses for which there was no
discernible physical cause. In treating these patients, he made a profound
leap, recognizing that a large part of the human mind is unconscious, or
largely inaccessible to awareness. This course describes how Freud came
to make this breakthrough and how his theories developed over the course
of his career into the discipline of psychoanalysis.

English and Comparative Literature
Shakespeare's Tragedies

20

JESSE M. LANDER

This course examines Shakespeare's experiments with the genre of tragedy.
Attention is paid to classical and medieval precedents, but the emphasis is
on the developmental arc of Shakespeare's creative life—especially his
move from an early preoccupation with social fatalism (in such plays as
Romeo and Juliet and *Julius Caesar*) to the interest in human psychology
shown in the major tragedies *Hamlet*, *Othello*, *King Lear*, and *Macbeth*.

SYLLABUS

II

It is generally accepted that the Renaissance began in Italy and that the Italian Renaissance began in Florence. This course examines the question *Why Florence?* What was it about Florence during the fourteenth and fifteenth centuries that induced Niccolò Machiavelli to write that he loved the city "more than my very soul"? The answer can be found in two traditions, republicanism and humanism, that existed in other Italian city-states but nowhere else in the same remarkable combination.

This course offers a primer in the workings of the modern stock market. It looks at the different ways that businesses utilize the stock market, the various players involved, and how these parties interact to raise the capital necessary to fund corporate operations and expansion. Topics include the differences between fundamental and technical stock analysis, short-selling, arbitrage, stock options and indexes, mutual and hedge funds, and bubbles and crashes.

English and Comparative Literature
Literature of the Jazz Age
DELANO GREENIDGE-COPPRUE

The generation of American writers that emerged during the 1920s was deeply affected by World War I and expressed its reaction to the calamity of war in two profoundly different ways. This course describes both the Lost Generation, whose white members produced highly cynical works while leading notoriously hedonistic lives, and the Harlem Renaissance, whose black participants rejected the blue devils of modernism and instead created a new life-affirming culture based on the rhythms of jazz.

Physical Sciences
Electricity and Magnetism
RAMON E. LOPEZ

Beginning with the basic concepts of electric charge, electric force, and electric fields, the first half of this course explains the principles that allow utilities to generate the electric current that powers modern industrial society. The second half of the course presents corresponding concepts related to magnetism and then links the two phenomena together, as James Clerk Maxwell did with his famous electromagnetic wave equations.

Classics
The Epics of the Trojan War
DANIEL GREMMLER

At the foundation of the Western literary canon are the epic poems of ancient Greece and Rome—specifically, the *Iliad*, the *Odyssey*, and the *Aeneid*. These and other epic poems, now lost, tell the story of the legendary war between Greece and Troy for the return of the incomparably beautiful Helen, wife of the Greek king Menelaus. This course retells that story, paying particularly close attention to what it reveals about the worldview of the ancient Greeks and Romans.

SYLLABUS

III

Religion
The Protestant Reformation
CHARLES H. PARKER

By 1517, when Martin Luther composed his *Ninety-five Theses*, the problems of the Catholic Church—corruption, an overemphasis on ritual, a lack of ecclesiastical training—were already well known. Since the late twelfth century, numerous reformers had attempted to correct them, but all had failed. In this course, we learn why Luther succeeded and how his reforms changed the course of Western religious and political history.

Social Sciences
Issues in Feminism
A. REZ PULLEN

The fundamental premise of this course, and indeed of all feminist theory, is that a distinction exists between sex and gender, the former referring to one's biology and the latter to the social expectations that arise from sexual differences. After briefly reviewing the history of women's activism, this course describe such cutting-edge topics in feminist research as the Third Wave, intersectionality, womanism, intersex studies, and queer theory.

American History
The Roots of the Cold War
DAVID RUBEL

The roots of the Cold War reach all the way back to the Russian Revolution, but they are most firmly planted in the World War II alliance between the United States and the Soviet Union. This marriage of convenience succeeded in defeating Nazi Germany; but, as the lectures in this course make clear, disagreements over the conduct of the war in Europe and the withholding of information about the US atomic bomb project created a legacy of mistrust that pervaded postwar politics.

Math and Engineering
Game Theory
THEODORE TUROCY

This course introduces students to the basic principles of game theory, a branch of mathematics that uses modeling to help "players" think systematically about real-life situations. Essentially the science of strategy, game theory provides analytical tools that can be used to assess situations as though they were parlor games. When used properly, these tools provide best responses and dominant strategies that can help decision makers navigate the possibilities for conflict and cooperation in everyday life.

Environmental Science
Meteorology and Climate
ART DEGAETANO AND MARGARET M. DEGAETANO

Want to understand what makes the wind blow and the rain fall? This course tells you everything that the television weatherman leaves out, from the convective lifting that creates clouds to the various factors responsible for climate change. You'll learn how hurricanes and tornadoes form, the differences between warm fronts and cold fronts, and even the science of rainbows as you come to understand the interactions among temperature, pressure, and humidity that determine the weather outside your window.

SYLLABUS

IV

WALTER E. GRUNDEN

This course focuses on the three main stages of modern Chinese history: the failed effort at "self-strengthening" that characterized the late nineteenth century, the turmoil that followed the fall of the Qing dynasty in 1911, and the vicissitudes of the People's Republic that Mao Zedong established after the Communists defeated Chiang's Nationalists in 1949. An important theme throughout the course is China's relationship with the West and its ambivalent attitude toward technological modernization.

IAKOVOS VASILIOU

The intellectual activity known as philosophy began in ancient Greece during the sixth century BCE, reaching its height two centuries later with the work of Plato and his student Aristotle. This course examines the major components of Platonic and Aristotelian thought, including Plato's theory of forms, Aristotle's ideas about the most basic substance, and the different ways that each man conceived of the human soul.

Art History
Italian Renaissance Art

DENISE BUDD AND LYNN CATTERSON

This course makes sense of the transformation in style that produced the great artistic works of the Italian Renaissance. It begins with Giotto's resurrection of classical skills lost during the Dark Ages, continues with Brunelleschi's development of a system of linear perspective, and—moving from Florence to Milan and Rome—concludes with the masterpieces of Leonardo, Michelangelo, and Raphael.

Physical Sciences
Darwinian Evolution

ROB J. KULATHINAL

During the mid-nineteenth century, Charles Darwin developed the theory of evolution to explain the evidence of species change that he observed during his five years as a naturalist aboard the HMS *Beagle*. Darwin's theory proved to be highly controversial because it refuted nearly a millennium of Christian thought. This course discusses not only Darwin's ideas but also later developments in evolutionary theory such as heredity, population genetics, and the modern evolutionary synthesis.

Religion
The Origins of Judaism

MICHAEL PREGILL

This course answers the question *Who are the Jews?* by looking into the early history of the Jewish people. Although Judaism is most often associated with the belief in a single, sovereign God, an even more important concept predated Jewish monotheism—that is, God's covenant with Abraham. The lectures in this course describe the ways in which the idea of covenant subsequently shaped the history of the Jews, especially after the destruction of the Second Temple and the start of the Diaspora.

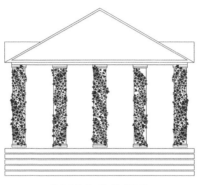

SYLLABUS

I

I. SALUTARY NEGLECT

DURING THE COLONIAL PERIOD IN AMERICA, the dominant economic philosophy in the Western world was mercantilism. Under the mercantile system, the goal of each nation-state was to accumulate as much capital (in the form of bullion) as possible. In general, this was done by maintaining a favorable balance of trade. When the value of a country's exports exceeded the value of its imports, the difference was made up in gold and silver, which the country hoarded in its national treasury.

An early coin minted in Massachusetts.

Because mercantilism held that nations could grow rich only at the expense of other nations, colonies were considered valuable assets. On the one hand, they could supply the mother country with raw materials; on the other, they were exclusive markets for the mother country's manufactured goods.

What the English Crown wanted from its colonies in North America was simple: economic obedience. But as time passed, many colonists became uncomfortable with this one-sided relationship, especially its presumption that colonies existed for no other purpose than to benefit the mother country.

Following the death of Oliver Cromwell and the restoration of Charles II in 1660, relations between the imperial government in London and the Puritans of the Massachusetts Bay Colony went from bad to worse. A Catholic sympathizer, Charles despised the extreme Protestantism of the Puritans and was offended by their attitude that they deserved to be free of English rule. Finally, in 1684, after having the colony's charter revoked, he imposed direct royal control.

The new royal governor, Edmund Andros, moved quickly to end representative government in Massachusetts and also began enforcing the Navigation Act of 1660, which the Puritans had largely ignored. This act had closed the colonies to all trade except that carried by English ships and required colonial exports of tobacco, sugar, cotton, and other commodities to pass through English ports so they could be taxed.

The hugely unpopular Andros found to his dismay, however, that consistent enforcement of the Navigation Act wasn't really possible. There were simply too many ships and too many ports for the small number of customs inspectors to cover. Meanwhile, a series of European wars distracted London's attention from the less-than-pressing problem of American smuggling. Finally, during the 1720s, British prime minister Robert Walpole settled on a policy of lax enforcement known as salutary neglect. Trade with America was flourishing, Walpole thought; so if the relationship wasn't broken, why fix it?

British law reflected the mercantilist view *that colonies should exist for the benefit of the mother country, but such laws were often easier to pass than to enforce.*

I. A NEW INFORMATION REVOLUTION

LET'S SAY THAT you need to research an obscure topic, such as the role of the turnip in English history. If you don't have Internet access, you'll have to travel to a research library, look up *turnip* in the *Readers' Guide to Periodical Literature*, and hope that one of the articles you find relates to English history. Of course, that's what everyone had to do before access to the Internet became widespread during the late 1980s and early 1990s. If you have Internet access, however, all you need to do is type the terms *turnip* and *English history* into a search engine and wait a few seconds for hundreds of results to come pouring in from libraries, publications, databases, and blogs all over the world.

This change in research methodology exemplifies a much broader and much more profound transformation that has taken place. We're in the middle of an information revolution; and like those of previous eras—involving the inventions of written language and the development of moveable-type printing—the current revolution has changed, and continues to change, our lives.

The term *Internet* refers generally to the mechanism that allows your computer to communicate with other computers elsewhere for a multiplicity of purposes—including sending and receiving email, browsing the World Wide Web, transferring files, and so on. The World Wide Web is, by contrast, much more limited. It refers only to the set of interlinked public documents commonly known as web pages. The relationship between the World Wide Web (or simply the web) and the Internet is that the web uses the Internet as its transport mechanism.

What follows in this course is a "peek under the hood," designed to identify the Internet's major components and explain how they work and interact. Before beginning, however, it's worth noting how the innovations of previous information revolutions have accumulated to make the current revolution possible. Johannes Gutenberg's invention of moveable type around 1450 made affordable the printing of scholarly journals, which in turn fostered the development of modern science and the scientific method. Scientists trained in this method made the theoretical and engineering breakthroughs that produced the Industrial Revolution, which encouraged the development of efficient methods of production. These methods are used today to produce the cheap, powerful computers that permit Internet access and manipulate all the information now available to us at our fingertips—as long as those fingertips are resting on a keyboard.

Access to the Internet *has produced a new information revolution in the tradition of written language and moveable-type printing.*

I. THE NATIONAL ACADEMY

The National Academy of Design at its nineteenth-century location.

BY 1913, the National Academy of Design in New York City had dominated the US art world for nearly a century. Founded in 1825, the National Academy was governed by established artists who fostered the development of American art by offering instruction based on European models. Like the French Académie des Beaux-Arts, the National Academy prescribed the study of nudes, copying from antique casts, and so on—while emphasizing the American preference for nature and landscape painting over figure painting.

The National Academy also served as a venue for annual exhibitions by members, faculty, and students. These exhibitions, like the Paris Salons, enhanced the institution's clout and helped shape the national taste, which for the second half of the nineteenth century favored landscapes. The trend began during the 1850s and 1860s with the Hudson River School, continued through the 1870s and 1880s with Barbizon-influenced paintings, and culminated with the impressionist and tonalist landscapes that remained popular through the first decade of the twentieth century. However, as more young artists returned from study in France, deeply impressed by what they had seen, figure painting began to rise in popularity.

Like its European counterparts, the National Academy celebrated tradition and viewed progress primarily as an extension of the past. Its exhibition juries reinforced this view with the selections they made. Overly progressive or modern ideas were generally discouraged, and artists whose work demonstrated tendencies that were deemed "subversive" (that is, overly modern) frequently found their canvases rejected—which meant that most of the public would never see them.

Shut out by the Academy, artists with different ideas about the direction American art should take sought out new ways to reach the critics and collectors who frequented the annual Academy shows. Around the turn of the twentieth century, they began to challenge the status quo by founding new organizations and holding separate exhibitions. Thus, by 1910, the American art world was primed for a revolt, and in 1913 it came. It was called the International Exhibition of Modern Art (more familiarly the Armory Show), and it brought modern styles to the forefront, transforming the American art establishment by presenting a direct and successful challenge to the hegemony of the National Academy of Design.

American art *during the first decade of the twentieth century was dominated, as it had been since 1825, by the National Academy of Design, which set the prevailing taste.*

I. THE PSYCHOANALYTIC VISION

AS THE FOUNDER OF PSYCHOANALYSIS, Sigmund Freud developed a theory of mind and a method of therapeutic practice that he used to treat some very human troubles that medical science couldn't yet explain or even comprehend. He spent his entire professional life over more than five decades creating, revising, and exploring new ways to resolve problems that had no discernible physical cause—problems such as hysteria, depression, obsession, anxiety, narcissism, and perversion.

Freud's ideas were based on his medical training, his clinical experience, and his extensive reading in other fields, from archaeology to philosophy. The theory of mind that he first proposed around 1900 had at its center the idea that a large part of the human mind is unconscious, or largely inaccessible to awareness. The maplike drawings that he used to illustrate this "topographic theory" suggest that the conscious mind is like the tip of an iceberg. Beneath the metaphorical waterline is a vast unconscious realm of drive energies, repressed emotions, conflicts, and forbidden wishes. Consequently, the sources of many of our responses and behaviors lie outside our conscious control. In fact, according to Freud, we are largely invisible to ourselves.

What Freud was saying defied deeply held Victorian beliefs in restraint, emotional control, reason, and the repression of sexuality; thus, his ideas about the unconscious generated controversy, skepticism, and a good deal of interest. Some people were eager to be analyzed by him so that they could understand the unconscious dynamics shaping their lives; others simply rejected his psychoanalytic ideas.

Rather than allowing himself to be buffeted by this admixture of admiration and scorn, Freud remained steady, writing and lecturing with increasingly clarity about the human condition, a wide range of human troubles, and his method for treating them. Out of this work, the psychoanalytic movement emerged.

More than a century later, Freud's ideas have become thoroughly ingrained in Western culture. His notion that people are moved to act by unconscious wishes and conflicts about which they are often unaware is now part of our daily discourse. Meanwhile, his theories and methods have produced not one but many different schools of psychotherapy, each of which takes a somewhat different approach to helping people suffering from psychological distress. Underlying all of these schools, however, is the insight that Freud had and the way in which he used his experience working with troubled patients to see humanity's unexplained struggles in a brand-new light.

Freud in 1922.

Freud's theory and method *of psychoanalysis followed from his realization that a large part of the mind is unconscious, or largely inaccessible to awareness.*

I. WHAT IS SHAKESPEAREAN TRAGEDY?

The title page of the First Folio (1623).

SHAKESPEARE'S MODERN REPUTATION rests most securely on his ten tragedies: *Titus Andronicus, Romeo and Juliet, Julius Caesar, Hamlet, Othello, King Lear, Macbeth, Antony and Cleopatra, Coriolanus,* and *Timon of Athens.* These plays are widely regarded as works of profound imaginative scope and unparalleled poetic power. Yet scholars remain troubled by the question of what precisely makes Shakespearean tragedy special. Is there a distinctive set of traits that defines Shakespearean tragedy; and, if so, what are they?

In large measure, the difficulty one has in answering this question stems from the slipperiness of the term *tragedy.* In its colloquial sense, *tragedy* refers to a painful event or inexplicable loss, but this usage has become so vague as to seem almost banal. When philosophers use the term *tragedy,* they generally mean the idea, originating with the German romantics, that existence itself may be essentially tragic—that individuals, thrust into a world not of their own making, experience a profound sense of homelessness, incapacity, and loss.

Even within the field of literary criticism—in which *tragedy* refers to a dramatic genre, defined by formal regularities—a stable definition is hard to come by, and critics dispute endlessly the constituent elements of a true or proper tragedy. In the words of critic Stephen Booth, "The search for a definition of tragedy has been the most persistent and widespread of all nonreligious quests for definition."

Searching Shakespeare's ten tragic plays for commonalities yields a few obvious features: All of the plays depict the death of the central character(s). All dwell on the theme of error (poor judgment) or the theme of mistaking (misperception). All depict excessive suffering. Taken together, these features may seem to provide a minimal definition of Shakespearean tragedy, but they are quickly overwhelmed by the significant differences among the plays that emerge upon closer examination. As one Shakespearean scholar has declared, "There is no such thing as Shakespearean tragedy, only Shakespearean tragedies."

While such a statement is not unreasonable, the ten plays do exhibit a family resemblance upon which some understanding of Shakespearean tragedy as a genre can be built. The best way to do this is to examine the plays individually in the order of their creation. This method allows us to look at the various ways in which Shakespeare engaged the genre of tragedy and chart how his approach developed over time.

The term *tragedy* *does not readily admit of definition, and* Shakespearean tragedy *is no less recalcitrant.*

II. THE FRENCH AND INDIAN WAR DEBT

DURING THE EARLY EIGHTEENTH CENTURY, Britain's most pressing concern in North America wasn't colonial smuggling but the machinations of its longtime rival France. Between 1689 and 1748, these two nations fought three long wars. For the most part, the fighting took place in Europe, but there were North American effects as well, with British colonists often taking up arms against their French counterparts, especially those living in Canada and the Ohio River Valley. During each of these wars, professional British soldiers fought alongside local colonial militias, and the British usually won, capturing more and more of New France.

The conflict that finally ended this competition began in the spring of 1754. During the previous winter, acting on behalf of Virginia governor Robert Dinwiddie, twenty-one-year-old militia major George Washington had delivered an ultimatum to the French living in the Ohio River Valley: Leave the land—which Great Britain claimed and colonial speculators coveted—or face the military consequences. When the French refused to go away, Washington returned the following May with 160 armed Virginians, initiating what came to be known in Europe as the Seven Years' War and in America as the French and Indian War.

George Washington leading troops during the French and Indian War.

Washington lost a third of his men at the outset and subsequently surrendered, giving the French an early advantage. But the course of the war changed in 1756, when William Pitt became the new English secretary of state and leader of the House of Commons. Before Pitt, the war effort had depended on the willingness of colonial assemblies to supply troops and funds. Pitt, however, assumed direct control of the fighting and for the first time committed large numbers of British troops to North America. The result was a victory so decisive that France had to surrender all of its remaining holdings in Canada.

In military terms, Pitt's strategy was completely successful, but it was also enormously costly, nearly bankrupting the Treasury. Thus, while Americans celebrated in the streets, basking in the glory of an empire at the height of its power, the British government debated how to pay off a £130 million war debt. To George Grenville, who had succeeded Pitt as leader of the House of Commons in 1761, it seemed obvious that the American colonies, for whom the money had been expended, should pay a fair share.

The British victory in the French and Indian War *was celebrated on both sides of the Atlantic, but a dispute soon emerged about who should retire the £130 million war debt.*

II. ANALOG AND DIGITAL INFORMATION

INFORMATION in the sense of *information revolution* refers to objective data: names, dates, lists, prices, images, sounds, and so on. In the natural world, such information generally occurs in a continuous form known as analog. An example would be the sound of a woman's voice. As the woman speaks, her voice transitions smoothly from one frequency level to another. If plotted on a graph, the curve representing her voice would be continuous, without any gaps or jumps.

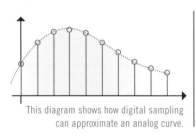

This diagram shows how digital sampling can approximate an analog curve.

By contrast, digital information (the kind that computers can process) is discrete. A digital recording of a woman's voice would dissect each second of sound into tens of thousands of individual data points, each of which would be assigned a set of numbers to represent a particular frequency. If you plotted these numbers, they would approximate the original sound curve. Obviously, the more slices you take per second (that is, the higher the sample rate), the closer the re-created curve will be to the original. However, digital representations can never perfectly represent analog data because they are inherently discontinuous.

Another way to think about digital representations of analog data is to consider what happens when you watch a movie in a theater. At normal projection speeds, the action in the film appears to be continuous. Yet if you were to slow down the projector, you would find that the action isn't continuous at all but rather composed of multiple discrete frames. As long as the sample rate remains high, the action will continue to appear smooth; but when projection speeds drop below sixteen frames per second, the resulting flicker becomes distracting. (Because early films were shown at projection speeds as slow as eight frames per second, they were nicknamed flicks.)

When analog data is digitized, there is always information loss because the process of assigning numbers to data points always involves rounding error. However, once this process is complete, the new digital information can be copied, stored, and transmitted with perfect accuracy—which can't be said of the original analog information. Think of the difference this way: If I take a photograph of a photograph, the copy will be fuzzier than the original. On the other hand, if I hear the winning lottery numbers on the radio and tell them to you accurately, you will have a perfect copy of the original information. Without this ability to manipulate digital information perfectly, there could be no Internet.

Unlike analog information, *which inevitably deteriorates when copied, digital information can be copied, stored, and transmitted with perfect accuracy.*

II. THE TEN

THE MOST INFLUENTIAL American artists at the turn of the twentieth century were The Ten, a group of painters who pioneered the closely related styles of impressionism and tonalism in the United States. The name of the group derives from their first joint exhibition, Ten American Painters, held at the Durand-Ruel Gallery in New York City in 1898. The founding members were Childe Hassam, John Twachtman, Julian Alden Weir, Frank Benson, Joseph De Camp, Thomas Dewing, Willard Metcalf, Robert Reid, Edward Simmons, and Edward Tarbell. William Merritt Chase was later added after the death of Twachtman in 1902.

At the time of the group's founding in 1897, each member was an established, successful artist. None lacked for critical or public acclaim, but all were bothered by the general absence of institutional support for impressionism, a leading-edge style in America at the time—especially in light of the unimaginative choices then being made by National Academy exhibition juries. Beginning with the Durand-Ruel show in 1898, The Ten's annual exhibitions proved so successful that they greatly amplified the popularity of impressionism and even forced the National Academy to recalibrate its taste. In fact, by the time the group put on its tenth-anniversary show in 1908, impressionism had become the dominant painting style in America.

Meanwhile, most of The Ten became leaders of the art establishment—which included membership in the National Academy, now a bastion of impressionism. This relatively rapid transformation of the New Guard into the Old Guard inspired some critics to chastise The Ten for losing their sense of innovation and openness to new ideas. One such critic, writing in the magazine *International Studio*, disparaged The Ten for moving in "too restricted a circle" and for being "positively unsympathetic, not to say hostile to the more recent manifestations of contemporary endeavor." By 1913, it was clear to many critics and artists that The Ten, along with the impressionist style they promoted, had served their purpose and were becoming part of the past.

Childe Hassam, *The Spanish Stairs* (1897)

The leading American artists *at the turn of the twentieth century were The Ten, a group of impressionists and tonalists who began as the New Guard and quickly became the Old Guard.*

II. FREUD'S CULTURAL AND HISTORICAL CONTEXT

FREUD'S IDEAS EMERGED, not coincidentally, within the historical and cultural context of fin de siècle Vienna. Originally a French phrase, *fin de siècle* refers to the literary and artistic climate of sophistication, world-weariness, and fashionable despair that characterized the close of the nineteenth century in Western Europe.

During this period, a great many extraordinary minds were present in Vienna, where Freud lived and worked. They were thinking remarkable, revolutionary thoughts about the arts, architecture, philosophy, and science. Yet, despite all the work being done and the progress being made, pessimism prevailed, and Viennese intellectual circles remained dominated by the idea that humanity was in decline.

A street in Vienna ca. 1899.

Meanwhile, the era of Victorian sexual repression was slowly coming to an end. Victorians have long been caricatured for their prudery, and with good reason. Believing that proper decorum required women's legs to be covered, some Victorians went so far as to eliminate the word *leg* from their vocabularies (using *limb* instead), while others covered the legs of their pianos with skirts so that indecent associations might be avoided. Yet many of these same people, in an all-too-human display of unconscious contradiction, purchased erotic literature, admired art that depicted nude bodies, and read scientific studies of sexuality of the sort being undertaken by Richard von Krafft-Ebing and others.

To some degree, Victorian morality protected as it controlled. Prior to the development of modern antibiotics, venereal diseases such as syphilis posed serious health threats, and no reliable methods of contraception existed short of abstinence. Nevertheless, as Freud later discovered, Victorian repression also caused problems. The social pressures that bound women to conventional values and to their roles as mothers, wives, and daughters could become so constraining that neurotic symptoms sometimes resulted.

A final aspect of late-nineteenth-century Vienna that affected Freud personally was the temporary decline in anti-Semitism that followed the emancipation of Austrian Jews in 1867. As Freud and others took advantage of new educational opportunities and entered the professions, they became quite assimilated. But this tolerance didn't last long. By 1897, a proposal to eliminate Jews from Vienna was gaining public support. Many Viennese Jews were thus placed in the difficult position of trying to accomplish great things while at the same time striving to fade into the background of a society that discriminated against them.

Freud's ideas were shaped *by the time and place in which he worked: fin de siècle Vienna.*

II. CLASSICAL TRAGEDY

SHAKESPEARE WAS STEEPED in the classics. His grammar school education would have included careful readings of classical texts; and from the many references to the works of Ovid and Virgil in his plays, we know that he was strongly influenced by these Roman poets. His exposure to classical tragedy, however, is more difficult to assess.

Certainly, he would have studied plays by the Roman tragedian Seneca, but there is little evidence that he read either Greek tragedy or Aristotle's analysis of the genre in the *Poetics*. Nevertheless, because Greek tragedy formed an important part of the classical canon revived during the Renaissance, Shakespeare would have known something of it. Aristotle's interpretation of Greek tragedy, in particular, was so well known in the Elizabethan literary world as to be unavoidable.

Greek tragedy flourished in Athens during the fifth century BCE—a period of intense cultural, social, and political transformation that witnessed the emergence of Athenian democracy and the beginnings of the Western philosophical tradition. Given this context, the austere tragedies of Aeschylus, Sophocles, and Euripides can be seen as attempts to resolve the ongoing conflict between old mythic modes of being and the new rational-legal world that was emerging.

This kernel of irrationality was rejected by Plato, who banished tragedy from his ideal republic because its presentation of inexplicable suffering called into question the rationality of the cosmos. Aristotle, however, sought to rehabilitate tragedy by pointing out that it serves the useful purpose of exciting and purging pity and fear—a process he called catharsis (from the Greek meaning "cleansing").

According to Aristotle, true tragedy shows neither the fall of a vicious person nor that of a virtuous person, because the former wouldn't provoke pity and fear and the latter would merely shock. Rather, successful tragedy depicts a protagonist who is "not eminently good and just, yet whose misfortune is brought about not by vice and depravity, but by some error or frailty."

An ancient Greek theater at Miletus.

The Greek word that Aristotle uses to describe this "error or frailty" is *hamartia*, which is often associated with the term *tragic flaw*. Such an association is problematic, however, because invariably it works to simplify and rationalize tragedy. Identifying Hamlet's tragic flaw as indecision illuminates nothing about the play yet makes its action seem explicable—thereby banishing the prospect of contingency, or unforeseen chance.

Shakespeare was strongly influenced by *the revival of classical learning, both directly in the case of Roman texts and probably indirectly with regard to Greek tragedy.*

III. THE SUGAR ACT

IN APRIL 1763, two months after the end of the French and Indian War, George Grenville became prime minister of Great Britain. Apparently, Grenville had such an unshakable faith in the virtues of a balanced budget that, it was said, he considered "a national saving of two inches of candle as a greater triumph than all Pitt's victories."

Determined that the war debt should be swiftly retired and that the American colonies should pay their share, Grenville persuaded Parliament to pass the American Revenue Act of 1764, which came to be known as the Sugar Act. The name is a little misleading, because the new law actually imposed tariffs on a wide range of goods; but the tax on sugar (in the form of molasses) was by far the most contentious.

To be fair, sugar had been taxed in the colonies since 1733, when the Molasses Act imposed an import tariff of six pence per gallon. The intention of the Molasses Act had been simply to regulate trade—that is, to raise the price of French West Indian molasses so that the colonists would have to buy exclusively from British West Indian suppliers. Instead, American rum distillers bribed customs officials and continued purchasing French molasses. The price difference was so great that they still came out ahead.

The Sugar Act had a different purpose, made clear by its preamble: "It is just and necessary that a revenue be raised...in America for defraying the expenses of defending, protecting, and securing the same." In Grenville's mind, the act was an equitable compromise: The tariff on molasses was halved to three pence per gallon, making its payment price-competitive with bribery. More importantly, it would now be enforced by the ten thousand British soldiers still deployed in North America.

Most of the colonial opposition to the Sugar Act came from merchants whose trade was directly affected. But there were others, an unlikely combination of intellectuals and rabble-rousers, who objected to the act on legal and philosophical grounds. The leaders of this group recognized Parliament's right to regulate imperial trade; and if import duties happened to generate a little extra revenue for the Crown, so be it. But direct revenue generation was another matter entirely. Whatever the costs of the French and Indian War had been, Parliament had no right to tax Americans, they said, because Americans had no representation in Parliament.

Grenville intended the Sugar Act to *raise money to pay off the French and Indian War debt, but some colonists objected, claiming that Parliament lacked the right to raise revenue in that way.*

III. URLS

ON THE INTERNET, names are important—especially their syntax, or the way they are written. The rules that govern Internet syntax are strict because computers are exact. If you're not precise, they won't be able to infer what you mean the way a human being could.

Different Internet naming systems serve different purposes. Consider, for example, the web page known as *http://www.irs.gov/charities/index.html*. Its name is a URL, which stand for Uniform Resource Locator. The URL naming system, to which all Internet uses must conform, is especially diverse and flexible because the first part of the URL indicates a particular scheme, and different schemes enable different functionalities. For instance, URLs that begin with *http://* bring users to web pages, URLs that begin with *ftp://* take users to remote files, and URLs that begin *mailto:* send emails. The US Post Office, by contrast, assigns postal addresses using a much less flexible system.

The syntax of the rest of the URL depends on the scheme chosen. With regard to the scheme *http*, URLs require two additional parts: the name of the host computer and the name of the resource to be accessed on that computer. (In the case of a web page, the resource would be the file containing the web page information.) Continuing with the example *http://www.irs.gov/charities/index.html*, the host would be *www.irs.gov*, and the resource would be *charities/index.html* (the file *index.html* in the folder *charities*).

The name of the host can be expressed either as a domain name (*www.irs.gov* being one example) or as an IP address. On the Internet, a computer's primary identification is its IP (Internet Protocol) address. Each IP address consists of four whole numbers separated by periods. Each number must be greater than or equal to 0 and less than or equal to 255. Therefore, 208.87.33.1 would be a valid IP address, and 208.87.331 would not (because it has only three numbers and also because the last number exceeds 255).

IP addresses are like telephone numbers. They simply make connections. The first three numbers of an IP address function in much the same way that telephone area codes do. That is, they typically identify a subnetwork (or subnet) of closely connected computers, usually located in the same office or building. Thus, computers with IP addresses between 208.87.33.0 and 208.87.33.255 can typically be reached using the same chain of intermediary routers (at least until the last hop).

The URL tells the Internet *where to find the resource, perhaps a web page or a file, that you want to access.*

III. THE EIGHT

AFTER THE TEN came The Eight, a group of innovative painters in whose work many critics saw the future of American art. The founding members of the group came together initially in Philadelphia, where most of them supported themselves as illustrators for the *Philadelphia Inquirer* in the days before newspapers printed photographs. They were Robert Henri (the acknowledged leader), John Sloan, William Glackens, Everett Shinn, and George Luks.

John Sloan, *Sunday, Women Drying Their Hair* (1912)

All of these artists painted in the realist style developed during the nineteenth century by Gustave Courbet in France and later Thomas Eakins in the United States. As an aesthetic, realism held that everyday people and events were fit subjects for painting. Given their experience as artist-reporters, the Philadelphia realists interpreted this to mean that they should be painting the gritty street life of modern Ameican cities, as opposed to the fashionable women and refined interiors being painted by The Ten. Unlike The Ten, whose impressionist works featured a light palette, the Philadelphia realists (whom critics called the Ashcan School because of their "ashy" paintings) preferred dark colors—especially blacks, browns, and dark greens. One critic dubbed them "the apostles of ugliness." Not only was their subject matter offensive to the Victorian sensibilities of the National Academy (and the public, too), but so were their bold, bravura brushstrokes, which flouted Academy dictates regarding careful shading and a smooth, polished finish.

Henri and the others eventually moved to New York City, the center of the American art world, where they became allied with three other painters working in equally progressive styles. These artists—Ernest Lawson, Arthur B. Davies, and Maurice Prendergast—were likewise frustrated with the National Academy's repressive approach to innovation. In 1908, the group held an independent exhibition at the Macbeth Gallery on Fifth Avenue. Eager for a revolution, critics called the show a "secession in art" (*New York Herald*) and an "outlaw salon" (*New York American*). Although reviews were mixed, the show was hugely successful because, as one critic wrote, The Eight had "escaped the blight of imitation." In response, the National Academy finally invited The Eight to participate in one of its annual exhibitions. All declined, confirming their status as champions of artistic independence and defiant nonconformity.

During the first decade of the twentieth century, *the members of The Eight fought back against the limitations of the National Academy and its taste for impressionism.*

III. FREUD'S FAMILY

SIGMUND FREUD WAS BORN on May 6, 1856, in Freiberg, Moravia—then part of the Austrian Empire, now part of the Czech Republic. His father, Jacob Freud, was a wool merchant; his mother, Amalia, was his father's second wife and twenty years younger. Sigmund was Jacob and Amalia's first child, but he had two older half brothers from his father's first marriage. These half brothers were, in fact, adults, quite close in age to his mother, and they had children of their own, who were Sigmund's nephews and peers.

Understanding this unusual family structure is important because it influenced the theories that Freud developed as a grown man. As many of his biographers have noted, the young Freud had a great deal of difficulty sorting out these relationships. He was troubled, for instance, by the obvious enjoyment his attractive young mother found in the company of his half brothers and by the lack of respect he sometimes felt for his father, who struggled economically and rarely fought back against anti-Semitic prejudice. These and other family dynamics resurfaced years later when Freud undertook his own analysis.

A sixteen-year-old Freud poses with his mother.

The family's minimal financial resources complicated life in the Freud household, which moved to Vienna in 1860 for financial reasons. Sigmund's needs, however, were always met. Amalia Freud idealized her eldest son and considered him a wunderkind. That he was brilliant soon became obvious to others as well. In 1873, he graduated first in his class from the prestigious gymnasium (secondary school) he attended. At home, despite limited space, he was given the privilege of having his own bedroom, and his younger siblings (all seven of them) were instructed to keep quiet while he was studying.

Freud went on to study at the University of Vienna, where he decided to pursue a career in medical research. Being Jewish, he was treated as an outsider, but he embraced the role willingly because he thought it promoted "a certain independence of judgment." Even then, detachment was an important part of his persona.

Freud had already spent five years working in the laboratory of Ernst Brücke, studying the nervous system of eels, when he received his medical degree in 1881. A year later, he left Brücke's lab for a job practicing medicine at Vienna's General Hospital. Financial considerations likely played a role in the move because earlier that year Freud had met Martha Bernays, the woman he would marry.

Freud's unusual family structure, *especially the closeness in age of his mother and half brothers, influenced his psychology and the theories he would develop as a grown man.*

III. MEDIEVAL TRAGEDY

IN ADDITION TO CLASSICAL TRAGEDY, Shakespeare was also influenced by medieval tragedy, which transmuted the legacy of the ancient Greeks and Romans into a form more suitable for the Christian Middle Ages. As defined by the Monk in Chaucer's

A portrait of Geoffrey Chaucer as a Canterbury pilgrim.

Canterbury Tales, "Tragedie is to seyn a certeyn storie, / As olde bookes maken us memorie, / Of hym that stood in greet prosperitee, / And is yfallen out of heigh degree / Into myserie, and endeth wrecchedly."

Several similarities between the Monk's view of tragedy and Aristotle's are immediately apparent. Like the Monk, Aristotle considered a reversal of fortune an essential element of a tragic plot. He also stipulated, as the Monk does, that the tragic hero must be "of heigh degree"—that is, greatly renowned and prosperous. But the Monk's notion of tragedy diverges from Aristotle's on several key points. First, the Monk sees tragedy as an ancient literary form to be found in old books rather than on the contemporary stage. Second, he thinks of tragedy as a narrative rather than a dramatic genre.

Aristotle's interest in the moral status of the tragic hero also disappears. In the Monk's tragic stories, the central characters are as likely to be blameless princes as despicable tyrants. The focus is instead on the characters' relentlessly downward trajectory. Especially important is the fickleness of Fortune, a Roman goddess taken up during the Christian Middle Ages as a symbol of contingency.

Stories about the punishment of bad behavior in high places suggested an inevitable comeuppance and thus reinforced the notion of a providential order. Depicting the fall of the blameless, on the other hand, made the point that one shouldn't trust prosperity, because worldly success is an illusion that distracts people from attending to the eternal.

Often referred to as de casibus tragedy—from Boccaccio's compendium of narrative tragedies *De casibus virorum illustrium*—medieval tragedy was, above all, a didactic genre designed to teach the fragility and impermanence of worldly felicity. Although it never became as fully developed as its classical predecessor, it nonetheless provided an important resource for Shakespeare because, unlike classical texts, it was readily available in English. Notable works in the de casibus tradition with which Shakespeare would have been familiar include John Lydgate's *The Fall of Princes* (1431–38) and *The Mirror for Magistrates* (1559), an enormously popular collection of verse that told the stories of many kings later featured in Shakespeare's history plays.

The focus in medieval tragedy *was invariably on the downward trajectory of the plot rather than on the moral status of the central characters.*

IV. THE STAMP ACT

GRENVILLE DISMISSED the colonists' no-taxation-without-representation argument as absurd. Of course Britain had the right to tax its colonies. Yet, as a politician, he realized that he had misjudged the situation. American public sentiment notwithstanding, the Sugar Act was a failure. Even after Grenville expanded the Royal Navy's patrols, the smuggling of French molasses continued, limiting Sugar Act receipts to just about twenty thousand pounds per year.

The war debt still had to be paid off, however, so Grenville asked Parliament to pass a new measure, the Stamp Act, which it did in March 1765. This new law, set to take effect on November 1, required Americans to purchase tax stamps for most forms of printed matter—including customs documents, marriage licenses, newspapers, and even playing cards. Grenville was confident that the Stamp Act would work because Englishmen were already paying a similar tax at home. However, as an additional sop, he had language inserted into the bill specifically allocating all revenue from the Stamp Act to "the defense of the colonies."

Two days after approving the Stamp Act, Parliament passed another law relating to the American colonies. Also recommended by Grenville, the Quartering Act obliged the colonial assemblies to provide housing and provisions for all British soldiers stationed in their jurisdictions. (None, however, were stationed in Boston.) Again, Grenville considered the measure absolutely reasonable: The troops were in North America for the benefit of the colonies; why shouldn't the colonists furnish room and board? Most colonists, however, considered the timing suspicious. Why should the Crown keep so many troops in America now that, after more than a century of conflict, the French threat was finally gone? Was it that the British government intended to use these troops against recalcitrant Americans?

Grenville wouldn't have denied that his government intended to change Britain's permissive approach to its American colonies. Yet he would certainly have challenged any characterization of what he was doing as a usurpation of colonial rights. He would have argued instead that Parliament was merely reestablishing the legitimate primacy of the mother country.

Whatever the merits of Grenville's argument, the practical effect of his effort to tighten the screws on America was an explosion of protest and retaliation exponentially worse than anything occasioned by the Sugar Act. Colonial opposition to the new Stamp Act was spontaneous, violent, and nearly universal.

With evasion limiting Sugar Act revenue, *Grenville looked for any way to tax the colonies. His next attempt was the Stamp Act, passed by Parliament in 1765.*

A British tax stamp.

IV. HTML

WHEN YOU TYPE A URL into a web browser, the first thing that your browser does is parse the URL. This means that it examines the syntax to find the punctuation marks that separate the URL's parts. Once your browser has identified the host computer's domain name or IP address (which your browser knows is the part that comes immediately after *http://*), it sends a message through the Internet to the host requesting the resource specified in the URL. In response, the host sends back a data packet containing instructions in a computer language known as HTML (hypertext markup language).

Following the rules of HTML, your browser then parses the web page code in order to determine what text, graphics, hyperlinks, and video it should place on your screen and where it should place them. (HTML can also be used to play sound files through your computer's speakers.) Finally, your browser translates these items into the tiny red, green, and blue lights (pixels) that produce the images on your screen.

The request sent by your browser would look something like *GET /home.html HTTP/1.0*. A simple response might be *<HTML>This is <I>italics</I>, and this is <B>boldface</B>.</HTML>*. The instructions that appear embedded in the text, bracketed by the less-than and greater-than signs, are the markup part of HTML. These instructions aren't displayed as written but rather tell your browser how to "mark up" the text that falls between them. The instructions *<HTML>* and *</HTML>* denote the beginning and the end of the web page. *<I>* turns on italics, while *</I>* turns italics off. Similarly, *<B>* and *</B>* instruct your browser to present the enclosed text in boldface. The HTML code for a typical web page contains many such instructions, which you can view using the Page Source feature of your browser.

The most important HTML instructions are *<a>* and *</a>*, which create the hypertext links (or hyperlinks) that reference other web pages. For example, the Google home page at *www.google.com* includes the hypertext *About Google*, clicking on which will take the user to the *About Google* web page. The HTML code used to create this link is *<a href="/intl/en/about.html">About Google</a>*, which means "display *About Google* as a link to the web page *http://www.google.com/intl/en/about.html*." Hypertext and hyperlinks are important because they're what make the web a web.

HTML is the computer language *that instructs web browsers how and where to display the elements of a web page.*

IV. DEVELOPMENTS IN EUROPE

WHILE THE GRITTY REALISTS of the Ashcan School spearheaded innovation in the United States, much more radical goings-on were taking place in Europe, where the avant-garde was beginning to work in revolutionary new styles that were distinctly nonrepresentational. In other words, the images that these artists were creating had little or no correlation to the natural, three-dimensional world.

At the 1905 Salon d'Autumn in Paris (not to be confused with the Paris Salons sponsored by the Académie des Beaux-Arts), a group of artists whom the critics soon began calling Fauves (wild beasts) made their first public appearance. The name was inspired by the dynamic, vivid colors and exaggerated brushstrokes that the Fauves used in their work, which seemed primitive and beastly. Unlike the bravura brushstrokes of the Ashcan School, which represented merely a refusal to hide the artist's technique behind a polished academic finish, the brushstrokes of Fauves such as Henri Matisse and André Derain were little more than great slashes of color, representing nothing other than the artist's emotional response to the world.

Belgian fauvist Rik Wouters,
Nel Wouters (1912)

The Fauves' color choices were similarly nonrepresentational—in fact, they were arbitrary. Natural features such as water, sky, earth, and trees could be rendered in a variety of hot, intense colors (reds, oranges, greens, blues, and yellows), because art was thought just to be art and needn't conform to reality. To the Fauves and other modern artists, a painting was just paint on a canvas. It could be whatever the artist wanted.

Nevertheless, in contrast with what followed, the Fauves were still quite representational. The tables in fauvist paintings, though simple in form, still looked like tables. Such was not the case with cubism, which first appeared in 1907 in the paintings of Pablo Picasso and Georges Braque. The radical nature of cubism, which broke entirely with the representational tradition, turned the Parisian—and soon the international—art world on its head. Unlike the Fauves, who emphasized color, Picasso and Braque minimized color in favor of structure, emphasizing the two-dimensional surface of the canvas and using geometric shapes to create form. The overriding principle of cubism was to present the visible world, but not to represent it.

Mounting its own revolution *at the turn of the twentieth century, the European avant-garde began experimenting with nonrepresentational styles such as fauvism and cubism.*

IV. THE SEDUCTION THEORY

FREUD WAS STILL WORKING for Brücke when he first met Josef Breuer, the physician who sparked his interest in hysteria. A frequent diagnosis during the Victorian era, hysteria was the name given to physical symptoms that had no apparent physiological cause. The hysterics, usually women, reported a wide variety of ailments—from tics, coughs, and headaches to fainting spells and even paralysis of body parts. No one denied that these symptoms existed, yet no one could explain what was causing them.

Breuer had several hysterics in his care, and it was while discussing their cases with Freud that the first hints of psychoanalysis began to emerge. Freud was especially interested in Breuer's use of hypnotic suggestion as a treatment. Finally, Breuer suggested to Freud that he travel to Paris to study with Jean-Martin Charcot, the master of medical hypnosis. After obtaining a grant, Freud did just that in 1885.

At the time, hysteria was considered a nervous disorder, and Charcot, being a neurologist, treated many hysterical patients. Based on this work, Charcot had developed a theory that linked hysteria with "traumatic neuroses," or neuroses caused by some trauma. (Neuroses are emotional disorders often accompanied by anxiety.)

Jean-Martin Charcot in his Paris clinic.

Freud was impressed; and when he returned to Vienna, he opened a medical practice specializing in hysteria and other nervous disorders. Meanwhile, he and Breuer continued their collaboration, exploring the possibility that releasing repressed, "unthinkable" memories could perhaps relieve hysterical symptomatology. The root cause of hysteria, they were beginning to think, was emotional rather than physiological.

As Freud pursued this idea, he became increasingly convinced that such troubling, repressed memories related to precocious sexual encounters, or seductions, experienced at a very young age and thus "unthinkable" to the girls involved. Breuer disagreed, and so did many in the Viennese establishment, medical and otherwise. In addition to being highly unconventional, Freud's "seduction theory" suggested that men associated with women who suffered from hysteria were somehow implicated in the sexual abuse of young girls. Not surprisingly, many took this suggestion as an affront to the honor of the families involved.

During the mid-1890s, Freud gave up his seduction theory after further evidence from his practice showed that inappropriate sexual encounters were not the only cause of hysterical symptoms. However, he continued to believe that hysteria, as well as similar neuroses, had their origins in repression, if not sexual trauma.

According to Freud's seduction theory, *the symptoms of hysteria were caused by the repressed trauma of sexual encounter experienced when a person was too young.*

IV. TRAGICAL HISTORY AND HISTORICAL TRAGEDY

DURING THE FIRST HALF OF his career, Shakespeare wrote mostly comedies and history plays. Although belonging to a genre of their own, the history plays nevertheless contributed to Shakespeare's developing interest in tragedy. After all, they described the fall of princes and thus readily conformed to the tragic model provided by Lydgate and others.

An early example, *Richard III*, tells the story of the rise and fall of the deceitful and malicious duke of Gloucester without the moral complications now commonly associated with tragedy. Richard III is simply a bad man: He gains and wields power for a time, puts several innocents to death, and then has his reign providentially cut short by Henry of Richmond, the progenitor of the Tudor dynasty, at which point order is restored.

What saves the character of Richard III from garden-variety villainy is his rich individuality. His famous deformities, which may or may not have been the invention of Tudor propagandists, function as the visible manifestation of his inner perversity. Thus, the play begins with a long speech by Richard in which he describes himself as having been "Cheated of feature by dissembling nature, / Deformed, unfinished, sent before my time / Into this breathing world, scarce half made up." Unable to tolerate a world at peace, he declares himself "determined to prove a villain." Richard then proceeds to assault the world with ruthless energy, all the while keeping the audience apprised of his stratagems with soliloquies and asides—a technique that invites the audience to understand, if not approve, his actions.

Richard II, which Shakespeare wrote several years later, is the most tragic of the history plays. Its protagonist is a king whose inflated sense of prerogative provokes a rebellion that leads to his overthrow and death. Richard himself locates his story within the de casibus tradition when he says, "For God's sake, let us sit upon the ground / And tell sad stories of the death of kings— / How some have been deposed, some slain in war, / Some haunted by the ghosts they have deposed, / Some poisoned by their wives, some sleeping killed, / All murdered." Yet as Richard's fortunes decline, his dignity unexpectedly increases. At the end—degraded, humiliated, and imprisoned—the once headstrong king finally becomes capable of self-reflection. In this way, the play takes up the subject of excessive suffering, especially mental suffering, and raises the possibility that such anguish may be transformative.

Edmund Kean as Richard III.

Although Shakespeare's history plays *belong to a separate genre, several are formally quite close to tragedy.*

V. THE SONS OF LIBERTY

THE TWO MOST OUTSPOKEN leaders of colonial opposition to the Sugar Act had been Bostonians Samuel Adams and James Otis. In fact, it was at a May 1764 town meeting organized by Adams that Otis had first given voice to the argument later distilled into the slogan NO TAXATION WITHOUT REPRESENTATION. When passage of the Stamp Act was announced in the spring of 1765, Adams and Otis were again in the forefront of the opposition, but this time they had a great deal more support.

Samuel Adams in a ca. 1770 portrait by John Singleton Copley.

Throughout America, Stamp Act riots erupted spontaneously in every major port city and inland as well, drawing in all economic classes and every political affiliation. In Boston, a newly organized underground group calling itself the Sons of Liberty began terrorizing the new stamp agents and destroying their stamps. On the night of August 14, 1765, for example, after hanging Massachusetts stamp master Andrew Oliver in effigy from the so-called Liberty Tree, members of the Sons of Liberty razed Oliver's new brick office and ransacked his home. Less than two weeks later, the home of Lt. Gov. Thomas Hutchinson was similarly plundered.

Obviously, something had to be done. Shaken by the violence, Gov. Francis Bernard called out the colonial militia, but the colonel in charge refused to act against his fellow citizens. To the contrary, he issued an order instructing his subordinates that any drummer attempting to sound the alarm should have his drum smashed. Boston thus passed out of Bernard's control.

In October, at the suggestion of the Massachusetts legislature, an intercolonial meeting was convened in New York City. Attended by twenty-seven delegates from nine colonies, the Stamp Act Congress drafted a petition to Parliament calling for the repeal of the Sugar and Stamp Acts and asserting the colonists' right to be taxed only by their own elected representatives.

The petition was important because it represented the colonies' first multilateral opposition to British policy, yet it was the mob violence that had the greater practical effect. Patriot groups, many now calling themselves Sons of Liberty, attacked stamp agents up and down the coast. Consequently, by November 1, when the new law took effect, there were no agents left to sell the stamps, and so the requirement was ignored.

The Sons of Liberty was a loosely organized federation *of local patriot groups that came together during the Stamp Act crisis to block, at times violently, enforcement of the new law.*

V. THE DOMAIN NAMING SYSTEM

THE DOMAIN NAMING SYSTEM (DNS) acts as a telephone directory for the Internet. Basically, it translates domain names, which make sense to people, into IP addresses, which make sense to computers.

Let's say that you want to place a telephone call to Jimmy Carter. You'd probably begin by calling directory assistance in Plains, Georgia, to ask for his telephone number. Now let's consider the analogous problem your browser faces when you ask it to take you to *www.jimmycarter.com*, which is the domain name of Jimmy Carter's website. How will your browser know where to find the necessary IP address?

The answer is that it consults an elaborate system of DNS servers scattered all over the Internet. (Servers are computers that provide services to other computers in the same network.) What happens specifically is that your browser sends an inquiry to a DNS server that it has been told about by your Internet service provider (ISP). In most cases, this first DNS server won't have the information your browser needs, but it will forward the request "upstream" to another DNS server in a different administrative district that might have the answer. If not, your request will continue to be forwarded.

Ultimately, if the answer isn't found sooner, your request will reach one of the handful of registrars with whom all domain names must be registered before they can be used. (This policy ensures the uniqueness of all domain names across the entire Internet.) The registrar with whom the domain name is registered will then forward your request to the DNS server directly supporting that domain, which will send your browser the definitive answer to its question. In the case of *www.jimmycarter.com*, the registrar is Network Solutions, which would forward your request directly to Jimmy Carter's hosting provider, BroadRiver Corp. The BroadRiver Corp. servers would then send your browser the correct IP address (216.24.170.159) for *www.jimmycarter.com*. The entire process would take only a few seconds, and all of the DNS servers contacted along the way would receive the same information, allowing them to process subsequent requests more expeditiously.

The operation of the domain naming system illustrates how the Internet can be decentralized and still work effectively. A single, centralized server handling all DNS requests might theoretically be more efficient; but as a practical matter, such an approach would create all sorts of problems, not the least of which would be overloading.

The domain naming system (DNS), *which processes your browser's requests for IP addresses, is the main enabler of Internet connectivity.*

V. AMERICAN IGNORANCE OF THE AVANT-GARDE

ALTHOUGH THE EIGHT continued working with other progressive American artists to build tolerance for new styles and develop new exhibition venues, they remained largely ignorant of the stylistic revolutions taking place in Europe. By 1910, the twin shocks of fauvism and cubism had transformed the Parisian art world; but in America, very few paid attention. In a country where the decades-old post-impressionism of Vincent van Gogh and Paul Gauguin was still obscure, the recent triumphs of the Fauves and the cubists weren't even reported.

An important exception to this general lack of awareness was the Photo-Secession Gallery in New York City. (Because the gallery's name was complicated, and because it was located at 291 Fifth Avenue, most people simply called it 291.) Operated between 1908 and 1913 by artist-photographer Alfred Stieglitz, who was ideologically

Arthur Dove, *The Lobster* (1908)

aligned with modernism and well connected in Europe, the gallery gave many artists of the Parisian avant-garde their first American exposure. At 291, Stieglitz displayed works by Matisse, Picasso, Paul Cézanne, Auguste Rodin, Henri Toulouse-Lautrec, and Henri Rousseau.

Stieglitz also promoted the paintings of young American artists then studying in Paris, whose styles were being strongly influenced by the developments taking place there. In 1910, 291 mounted the first group show dedicated to their work. The exhibition included canvases by Marsden Hartley, Arthur Dove, John Marin, Alfred Mauer, and Max Weber.

Eventually, European modernism crept into other venues as well. In 1912, for example, the American-Scandinavian Foundation organized a traveling exhibition that toured five cities in the United States. Among the paintings included in the exhibition were works by avant-garde artists such as the Norwegian Edvard Munch. However, as with Stieglitz's efforts, these showings received little or no attention in the mainstream press. The result of this lack of exposure to new artistic idea was a complacency that made what Americans were about to see in the Armory Show much more shocking than it otherwise would have been.

Because the works of the European avant-garde received little immediate exposure *in the United States outside Alfred Stieglitz's 291, most Americans remained ignorant of them.*

V. ANNA O.

STUDIES ON HYSTERIA (1895), cowritten by Freud and Breuer, presents accounts of their earliest cases. It also records their initial reflections on "hysterical phenomena" and documents their exploration of new approaches to treatment, some of which became the basis for psychoanalysis (a term that Freud began to use during the early 1890s).

Bertha Pappenheim (Anna O.) in 1882.

Perhaps the most famous case history in *Studies on Hysteria* is that of Breuer's patient Anna O. According to Breuer, she was healthy, imaginative, and intelligent. Her sexuality, however, was "remarkably undeveloped." She had never been in love and lived a "monotonous existence in an extremely puritanically minded family." She was especially close to her father, who became ill during the summer of 1880. As Anna O. devoted herself to his care, her own health declined. She had trouble eating, developed a nervous cough, and suffered from a "convergent squint" (double vision). These symptoms kept her bedridden for months, during which time she experienced additional symptoms including numbness of extremities, blurred vision, and a feeling that the walls of her room were falling in on her. None of these symptoms had any identifiable physiological cause.

Breuer was called in; and because of the extent of her symptoms, he visited her at home nearly every day. He used hypnosis to place her in trance states, during which she would speak with great emotion about the thoughts that had preoccupied her mind during the day—a process she called chimney sweeping because it cleaned out troubling feelings and memories. Day by day, as elements of Anna O.'s hidden mind became conscious, her behavior, which had been erratic, improved, and her symptoms began to abate. Breuer and Freud, who discussed her case often, referred to this new method of treatment as the "talking cure."

In his own practice, Freud noticed that the greatest benefit always came when the recollection of repressed events was accompanied by the release of related emotions. This observation led him to speculate that hysteria was caused by the repressed memories of events so traumatizing that the strong emotions associated with them threatened to overwhelm the individual. Freud considered repression or dissociation in the face of such trauma adaptive because it enabled the individual to protect herself from experiences that couldn't be endured or understood. An important clue was that the physical symptoms afflicting hysterics were often symbolically related to these repressed memories.

The case of Anna O. *was an important milestone in the development of the "talking cure," a method developed by Freud and Breuer to release repressed memories and emotions.*

V. TITUS ANDRONICUS

A ca. 1596 drawing of an Elizabethan theater.

SHAKESPEARE'S FIRST tragedy is a famously bloody example of the highly popular Elizabethan subgenre known as revenge tragedy. Revenge tragedies feature protagonists who suffer great wrongs and are denied justice by the prevailing authorities. As a result, they take on the role of revenger, imitate the original transgression, and become guilty of the very crime they seek to punish. Because Elizabethan playwrights rarely allow the wicked to flourish, the successful revenger invariably dies in the end.

Titus Andronicus is a Roman general who returns from a successful campaign against the Goths to find Rome in chaos and the late emperor's two sons, Saturninus and Bassianus, vying for the throne. Titus settles the dispute by supporting the elder brother, Saturninus. The newly elevated emperor then offers to marry Titus's daughter, Lavinia, but she is already betrothed to Bassianus—an engagement of which the embarrassed Titus is unaware. An insulted Saturninus spurns Titus and takes the general's prisoner, the Goth queen Tamora, as his new wife.

Because Titus has sacrificed Tamora's eldest son to appease the gods, the new empress plots to destroy Titus and his family. Her two younger sons murder Bassianus and rape Lavinia, afterward cutting off her hands and removing her tongue so that she can't identify them. Tamora's lover, Aaron, then frames two of Titus's sons for the murder and tricks Titus into believing that Saturninus will free the two boys if Titus cuts off his own hand and sends it to the emperor. Titus performs this grisly deed, but his hand is soon returned along with the heads of his sons. In the end, Titus captures Tamora's sons, bakes them into a pie, and serves them to their mother and stepfather. After killing Lavinia, he reveals what he has done and stabs Tamora. Saturninus then kills Titus, after which he is killed by Lucius, Titus's remaining son.

Throughout these gory goings-on, the passion of Titus remains at the center of the drama. Quoting Ovid, he observes that justice has fled the earth and that, consequently, human society is merely bestial. Meanwhile, Titus's agonies play out against the backdrop of a society on the brink of collapse. With barbarians at the gate and its fall imminent, the Rome of the play reeks of cultural decadence and inherited codes of conduct that now produce only violence and brutality.

Titus Andronicus **is a conventional Elizabethan revenge** *tragedy, steeped in gore and committed to the principle that all transgressors, including revengers, must be punished.*

VI. REPEAL OF THE STAMP ACT

THE STAMP ACT CRISIS created such a frenzy that a few colonial militants, notably Samuel Adams, began calling for independence, arguing that it was justifiable to overthrow a government that repeatedly violated citizens' rights. Such talk troubled the still-influential William Pitt, who became a strong advocate of Stamp Act repeal. "If we repeal the act," Pitt said, "we shall have all the sober part of America on our side, and we shall easily be able to chastise the few hotheaded republicans among them."

Another compelling rationale for repeal was a recent, steep decline in colonial trade. As part of the Sugar Act protests, many New Englanders had subscribed to nonimportation agreements. In other words, they had agreed to boycott imported British goods. The renewal and proliferation of these agreements during the Stamp Act crisis badly hurt the balance sheets of many British merchants and manufacturers, who also pressured Parliament to repeal the Stamp Act.

Already, in July 1765, King George III had dismissed George Grenville for poor handling of the Stamp Act and other matters as well. Grenville's replacement—Charles Watson-Wentworth, the marquis of Rockingham—was known as something of an appeaser. Like Pitt, the new prime minister strongly backed Stamp Act repeal; but the opposition in Parliament resisted, arguing emphatically that if the colonies couldn't be compelled to obey the Stamp Act, they soon wouldn't obey any parliamentary law at all. Rockingham finally got his way in March 1766, but it came at a price. On the same day that Parliament repealed the Stamp Act, it passed the vaguely threatening Declaratory Act, which affirmed its right to make laws for the colonies "in all cases whatsoever."

News of the Stamp Act's repeal elated the people of America, who proclaimed often their gratitude and loyalty to the Crown. For a time the contentment of 1763 seemed to have returned, primarily because most Americans chose to interpret the repeal as an admission by Parliament that only colonial legislatures could raise colonial revenue. But Parliament meant no such thing—and quite the contrary. The repeal of the Stamp Act was nothing more than an expedient retreat, and new taxes were already being planned. But this time, members realized, Parliament would have to move more carefully. As several royal governors had pointed out, the colonists had now learned that opposition could force concessions, so there would likely be more fractious behavior in the future.

Most Americans saw the repeal *of the Stamp Act as an admission by Parliament that it couldn't impose revenue-generating taxes. Actually, it was just an expedient retreat.*

A colonial caricature of a British tax stamp.

VI. DOMAIN NAME REGISTRATION

IN ADDITION TO FULFILLING requests for IP addresses, the DNS also regulates the syntax of domain names. It requires, for example, that all domain names consist only of letters, digits, and hyphens (not including the periods that separate the domain name parts). Even more importantly, the DNS requires that all domain names be unique. If domain names weren't unique—that is, if two websites could use the same domain name—DNS servers wouldn't know where to send your browser.

The uniqueness requirement does have some significant consequences, however. For one, it makes domain names precious. During the early days of the Internet, when anyone could register and own the rights to any domain name (such as *www.coca-cola.com*), some people practiced cybersquatting. This meant that, when possible, they registered for themselves domain names corresponding to the trade names of well-known companies. Later, when these companies realized that they needed a web presence, the cybersquatter who owned their name would sell them the rights to it for a disproportionate fee. DNS regulations now prevent most cybersquatting, and procedures are in place to resolve whatever disputes do occur.

Otherwise, it's still easy for anyone to register a domain name (though not so easy to find one not already in use). Suppose that you want to register the name *example.com*. You would go to the website of one of the registrars, make sure that the name is available, and pay a modest annual fee to control the rights to it. If you subsequently decide not to renew your registration, you would lose those rights, and the name would become available again to everyone else. (A surprising number of people and businesses neglect to renew their registrations and thus lose the rights to their domain names.)

In order to put your new domain name to use, you will need a hosting provider, who will also charge you a modest annual fee. In exchange, the hosting provider will set up email accounts for you (such as *info@example.com*) and also, if you choose, host a website for you at *www.example.com*. You (or someone you hire) will have to provide the content for the website in the form of HTML and resource files. (Numerous software programs exist that can help you create HTML files.)

Domain name registrars derive their authority from the Internet Corporation for Assigned Names and Numbers (ICANN), a California nonprofit corporation that now exercises the naming authority originally held by the US government.

The requirement that domain names *be unique makes them valuable. It also makes necessary a registration system so that uniqueness can be enforced.*

VI. THE REVOLUTION BEGINS

IN 1911, as part of the ongoing efforts of The Eight to develop new American exhibition venues, a diverse group of New York City artists formed the Association of American Painters and Sculptors (AAPS). Initially, the membership included both distinguished members of the profession and younger artists just beginning their careers. Less than a year into its existence, however, the organization began taking on a decidedly anti–National Academy attitude. Expressed openly in letters and interviews published in the newspapers, this posture caused many of the older, more conservative members (most of them members of the National Academy) to resign or at least distance themselves from the AAPS.

The leadership that emerged post-schism included Walt Kuhn; Walter Pach; Elmer MacRae; and Arthur B. Davies, a member of The Eight who became AAPS president. During the spring of 1912, the organization decided to mount a large exhibition of contemporary American and European art at the Sixty-ninth Regiment Armory on Lexington Avenue between Twenty-fifth and Twenty-sixth Streets. The International Exhibition of Modern Art, as the show was formally called, would run at the armory from February 15 to March 15, 1913, after which it would travel to Chicago and Boston. Immediately, because the schedule was already tight, Davies sent Kuhn to Europe to find suitable works by leading European modernists.

Arthur Davies, *The Mountaineers* (1915)

Kuhn's first stop was Cologne, where the Cologne-Sunderbund Exhibition was being held that summer. The show's displays of paintings by van Gogh, Gauguin, Cézanne, Picasso, Munch, and Matisse dazzled Kuhn, as did the way these works were arranged. In fact, Kuhn was so taken with the show's structure—specifically, its presentation of modern art as a logical progression from earlier styles—that the Cologne-Sunderbund Exhibition became the model for the Armory Show. From Cologne, Kuhn traveled throughout Europe, attending other exhibitions and meeting with artists and collectors. Joined along the way by Davies, he sought out the most experimental, cutting-edge art he could find Europe; and by the time he and Davies returned home in November, they had accumulated a collection of works that were guaranteed to shock the American art establishment.

In 1912, the maverick leadership *of the Association of American Painters and Sculptors decided to stage a show of modern art that would shock the American art establishment.*

VI. FREUD'S SELF-ANALYSIS

THE PERIOD THAT FOLLOWED the death of his father in 1896 was a difficult one for Freud—a time of mourning, moodiness, and reflection. It was also the moment in his life when he decided to undertake his own analysis, or "self-observation" (Freud's term for the process). His goal was to unearth his own repressed memories, emotions, and conflicts so that he could better understand their influence on his motivations and behaviors. Thus, he began scrutinizing his memories, feelings, and wishes—paying close attention to errors in writing; slips of the tongue; and, perhaps most important of all, his dreams.

Normally, when a patient undergoes analysis, he is able to work through feelings and conflicts by projecting them temporarily onto the listening, neutral analyst—a phenomenon that Freud later called transference. In self-analysis, however, there is no supportive, objective listener to offer help in interpreting and resolving what one remembers. This makes the process extraordinarily difficult; and as Freud struggled to muster the necessary self-discipline, he sometimes dreamed that he was "dissecting [his] own lower body."

Nevertheless, Freud's self-analysis enabled him to identify experientially important aspects of the analytic process that he was later able to recognize in his work with patients. He became particularly interested in the hidden or disguised meanings of dreams, especially the ways in which dreams "condensed" and reconfigured memories in order to defend the individual against the recall of painful emotions associated with long-repressed events.

The insights that Freud gained from his self-analysis, which is believed to have lasted about five years, profoundly influenced the future development of his psychoanalytic theories and method. During his self-analysis, he gained awareness, for example, of the love and strongly possessive feelings he had felt for his mother when he was young. Similarly, he came to recognize the hidden competitiveness that he had always felt toward his father, upon whom he had at times looked down. These personal insights contributed to Freud's awareness of the sexual dynamic that he later termed the Oedipus complex.

As Freud put himself through this challenging process of uncovering hidden memories, feelings, and conflicts, he became increasingly persuaded that the mind contained a vast unconscious realm relevant not only to the treatment of hysteria but also to the investigation of other neuroses, including some of his own.

Freud's self-analysis *enabled him to experience for himself and thus identify important aspects of the psychoanalytic process.*

VI. ROMEO AND JULIET

SHAKESPEARE'S SECOND TRAGEDY is a world removed from the decadence of *Titus Andronicus*. Like the Rome of *Titus*, the Verona of *Romeo and Juliet* is torn by civil strife, but the title characters speak with a lyricism that transcends mundane concerns. Upon first meeting, for example, Romeo and Juliet exchange lines of verse that together form a perfect sonnet.

Initially, the play conforms to the conventions of marriage-based comedy, in which a pair of young lovers must overcome obstacles, usually created by their parents. However, instead of delivering the victory of the young and the promise of social regeneration, *Romeo and Juliet* presents a series of mistakes and missed opportunities that combine to deprive the lovers of their future happiness. In the end, both commit suicide in protest against the senseless contingency of the world.

Although youthful impetuosity contributes to the downfall of both Romeo and Juliet, the action of the play turns more on the workings of destiny than on the impulsions of the characters. At the outset of *Romeo and Juliet*, a prologue delivered by a chorus describes "a pair of star-crossed lovers." Similarly, at the end of the play, Friar Laurence, who has unsuccessfully tried to help the two young lovers, can only conclude, "A greater power than we can contradict / Hath thwarted our intents."

The force of the tragedy comes from the sense that the world is in some way inimical to young love. Over the apparently dead body of Juliet, Romeo declares that he will never leave her tomb: "Oh, here / Will I set up my everlasting rest / And shake the inauspicious stars / From this world-wearied flesh." When Juliet awakens and discovers the dead body of Romeo, she refuses Friar Laurence's advice to bear the adversity and instead takes her own life as well.

Shakespeare celebrates the fearsome intensity of young love, but the play also offers some gentle criticism—as when Friar Laurence observes, "These violent delights have violent ends." Later, he warns Romeo to "love moderately," but Romeo proves incapable of accepting the advice. That we don't fault Romeo for this is a strong indication of the play's sympathetic portrayal of romantic love. As Lysander declares in *A Midsummer Night's Dream*, "So quick bright things come to confusion." Although incandescent love cannot last, it seems, the world would be a much poorer place without it.

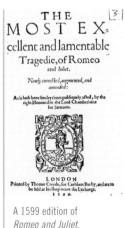

A 1599 edition of *Romeo and Juliet*.

Although **Romeo and Juliet** begins as *a conventional marriage-based comedy, it ends with the tragic recognition that the world is inimical to young love.*

VII. THE TOWNSHEND PLAN

ROCKINGHAM'S MINISTRY LASTED only twelve months. His primary antagonists were powerful British landlords who knew that less revenue from the colonies meant higher land taxes for them. After Rockingham, the king brought back an aging William Pitt, who turned out to be a poor choice. Pitt was already suffering from gout and soon declined mentally as well. Into this vacuum stepped Pitt's flamboyant

Charles Townshend in a ca. 1765 portrait.

chancellor of the exchequer (finance minister)—a clever, somewhat reckless man named Charles Townshend, whose nickname around London was Champagne Charlie.

Early on in his tenure, Townshend announced that land taxes would continue at their present (high) level, with perhaps a 25 percent reduction the following year. The landlords, finding this proposal unacceptable, persuaded Parliament that the reduction should take effect immediately. This move created a shortfall that had to be made up, so Townshend revisited the matter of colonial taxation.

During Parliament's deliberations on the Stamp Act, Benjamin Franklin, the colonial agent in London, had opposed the measure on the grounds that it was improper. In making his argument— an argument that was rejected—Franklin had emphasized the distinction between *external* tariffs (such as import and export duties), which Parliament had the right to impose to regulate trade, and *internal* taxes (such as the Stamp Act), which only the colonial assemblies could levy. Townshend thought this distinction meaningless; but, eager to avoid more problems with the colonies, he decided to honor it.

On its surface, Townshend's proposal seemed to be the Sugar Act redux. Its chief feature was the imposition of new duties on five prized colonial imports: glass, lead, paint, paper, and tea. But the plan, which Parliament approved in June 1767, went beyond these tariffs to reorganize the corrupt customs service. It created a new Board of Customs Commissioners, headquartered in Boston, to stop the rampant smuggling; it affirmed the legality of the writs of assistance (search warrants) that customs officials used to board and inspect suspect ships; and it established new admiralty courts in Boston, Philadelphia, and Charleston to try Americans found with contraband. (Regular colonial courts, especially those in Boston, typically freed even those defendants obviously guilty of smuggling.) Townshend also decreed that, henceforth, the salaries of all royal officials would be paid directly by the Crown, so that they wouldn't have to depend any longer on unfriendly colonial legislatures.

In addition to imposing new import duties, *the Townshend plan reformed the colonial customs service to make collection of those duties both more efficient and more certain.*

VII. PROTOCOLS

BASICALLY, all the Internet does is transmit sequences of numbers from one computer to another. The precise form that these sequences take is specified by a protocol, such as the Internet Protocol (IP) or the Transmission Control Protocol (TCP). Because IP and TCP are the leading protocols, the complete set of Internet protocols is often referred to as TCP/IP.

Beyond assigning addresses to computers, IP provides the basic method for routing data from one computer to another over the Internet. To make use of this functionality, your computer needs an IP address of its own, a netmask, and a default gateway. A netmask controls the IP addressing used by computers on the same directly connected local network. (It's through the netmask that your computer knows the IP addresses of its local neighbors.) A default gateway is the IP address of the router that your computer uses to reach other computers beyond your local network (that is, on the Internet).

Here's how the IP system works: When your computer sends an email, for example, it transmits data out of your computer and onto the Internet through your network's default gateway. The key to the IP system is that your network's default gateway has its own default gateway—and so on up the line. Utilizing these connections, the routers that make up the Internet transmit your data among themselves until your message reaches the destination computer, usually a few seconds later. In this way, the Internet connects your computer to other computers around the world.

TCP makes of use of IP for basic transport but adds a number of enhanced features—such as error checking and correction, delivery confirmation, and speed and congestion control. The data delivery that underlies email, web page access, and most other forms of Internet communication is usually handled by TCP.

All Internet protocols—and there are many besides IP and TCP—are based on voluntary standards. In other words, protocols are merely conventions upon which manufacturers, programmers, and other Internet professionals agree in order to make it possible for computers to exchange data with one another. These protocols are proposed by industry organizations, then debated, amended, approved, and published.

Sometimes, disputes over new protocols escalate into "standards wars" involving rival companies. Unfortunately, if one of these companies possesses a commanding market share, it often uses that commercial clout to contort the new standard into a self-serving form.

What makes the Internet an internetwork are protocols *such as IP and TCP that allow computers on one local network to communicate with computers on another local network.*

VII. THROWING A BOMB INTO THE ART WORLD

AAPS PRESIDENT ARTHUR B. DAVIES had always intended the Armory Show to effect a change of consciousness within the American art world. That's why he had sent Walt Kuhn to gather artwork that would jolt American academies, artists, and audiences out of what Davies perceived to be their collective aesthetic stupor. Even before the Armory Show opened in February 1913, newspapers were already describing the exhibition as an "invasion" of modern art. According to one headline, "It Will Throw a Bomb into Our Art World and a Good Many Leaders Will Be Hit." In other words, nearly everyone recognized the show for what it was: an assault upon the rigidity of what artist Oscar Bluemner called the "prune-faced authorities of the old regime"—that is, the National Academy.

Like the Cologne-Sunderbund Exhibition, the Armory Show emphasized the historical context of the works it presented. Even though Davies planned to shock visitors, he also wanted to explain the art to them, so he paid a great deal of attention to the physical arrangement of the exhibition. Consulting with Kuhn, he decided in the end to arrange the works chronologically—which, he believed, would make the prevailing trends much more understandable. Davies also chose to separate the American works from the European, thus creating two shows in one. In the European section, where French art predominated, the exhibition committee put together a fairly coherent progression from classicism through realism to modernism. In the American section, however, visitors found a jumble of traditions, reflecting the committee's rather poor understanding of native traditions.

Although typically omitted in accounts celebrating the success of the European section, the comparatively lackluster American section produced a great deal of bitterness among the artists whose work was exhibited. In their view (and the view of many AAPS members), the point of the Armory Show should have been to showcase modern trends in *American* art. They resented the large-scale inclusion of European artists, whose nonrepresentational work made their own representational art seem provincial and narrow-minded in comparison. Indeed, the critics generally ignored their work and chose instead to focus their attention—and vitriol—on the Europeans, particularly the cubists and the Fauves.

INTERNATIONAL EXHIBITION OF MODERN ART
ASSOCIATION OF AMERICAN PAINTERS AND SCULPTORS
69ᵗʰ INF'TY REG'T ARMORY, NEW YORK CITY
FEBRUARY 15ᵗʰ TO MARCH 15ᵗʰ 1913
AMERICAN & FOREIGN ART.

AMONG THE GUESTS WILL BE — INGRES, DELACROIX, DEGAS, CÉZANNE, REDON, RENOIR, MONET, SEURAT, VAN GOGH, HODLER, SLEVOGT, JOHN, PRYDE, SICKERT, MARIOL, BRANCUSI, LEHMBRUCK, BERNARD, MATISSE, MANET, SIGNAC, LAUTREC, CONDER, DENIS, RUSSELL, DUFY, BRAQUE, HERBIN, GLEIZES, SOUZA-CARDOZO, ZAK, DU CHAMP-VILLON, GAUGUIN, ARCHIPENKO, BOURDELLE, C. DE SEGONZAC.
LEXINGTON AVE.–25th ST.

The Armory Show catalog.

Arthur B. Davies wanted *the Armory Show to jolt Americans out of their artistic complacency, and it did just that.*

VII. THE PSYCHOANALYTIC METHOD

THE GOAL OF PSYCHOANALYSIS, according to Freud, was to reveal and understand the dynamics of the patient's unconscious mind, or "to make the unconscious conscious." As one might expect, the methods that Freud used to achieve this goal changed over time as he gained more knowledge and experience. By 1890, for example, his interest in hypnosis as a primary therapeutic technique had already begun to wane as he concluded that the contents of the unconscious were more easily accessed through talking, dreams, inexplicable forgetfulness, and slips of the tongue (Freudian slips) that revealed unconscious motivations and wishes.

Freud's working hypothesis was that these dynamics and the memories associated with them were rooted in repressed wishes, emotions, and conflicts dating from childhood. The way to access them was, generally, to talk about them in an unfettered way. The setting in which this talking took place was a private office where the patient lay propped up on a couch while the analyst sat just behind and to the side, out of the patient's sight. The analyst listened with "suspended judgment," never responding in a conversational way but commenting occasionally and asking questions designed to elicit hidden conflicts.

The original design of the analytic process gave authority to the analyst and encouraged the patient to surrender and let his or her mind wander. As patients spoke of their lives, recalling past episodes, memories emerged, and stories gradually unfolded. Working with this material, an analyst with an open mind could come to understand the patient's repressed unconscious conflicts and help him work them through.

For example, a child who competed with his father for his mother's attention and felt frustrated and ashamed by this would likely repress his wish, frustration, and shame. Later, as an adult, such a person might witness an older male employer showing preference for a female employee and experience a reaction (jealousy, anger, even physical symptoms) that would seem to others quite inexplicable and disproportionate to the incident. Freud believed that making such unconscious dynamics conscious led to the release of tension and the resolution of physical and psychological symptoms.

The art of clinical practice lay in piecing together from what was said an interpretation or narrative that elucidated the patient's repressed memories, long defended against, and explained the underlying dynamics of his condition. Yet "resistance" was inevitably a part of the work, because the dynamics of repression were powerful and slow to reverse.

The purpose of Freud's *psychoanalytic method was to bring repressed, unconscious material into consciousness so that it could be worked through.*

VII. JULIUS CAESAR

WHAT MAKES *JULIUS CAESAR* a political tragedy isn't simply the fact that its central characters are politicians engaged in political discord. More importantly, the play shows the political world to be essentially antagonistic and offers no solution. Instead, it merely depicts the consequences of conflict—in this case, between the imperialism of Caesar and the republicanism of those who conspire to assassinate him.

Although Caesar is the play's titular hero, the drama focuses on Brutus and the process by which this Roman noble arrives at his decision to resist Caesar violently. Like Richard II, Brutus is a study in tragic interiority: a good man who wishes to defend Rome's republican traditions, yet one who is also troubled by the prospect of taking Caesar's life. Early on, Brutus says, "Between the acting of a dreadful thing / And the first motion, all the interim is / Like a phantasma or a hideous dream."

The first "motion," or thought, of the assassination puts Brutus into a state of anguish that Shakespeare likens to a psychological civil war (analogous to the civil war that will follow Caesar's assassination). Brutus must choose between his affection for Caesar and his loyalty to the principle of Roman self-governance. In the end, he decides that Caesar must be killed in order to prevent his incipient tyranny.

Once committed to the assassination, Brutus recasts it as an act of piety— a sacrifice, rather than a murder. Acting idealistically, he spares the life of Caesar's close ally Mark Antony and even permits Antony to deliver a funeral oration, believing that the moral clarity of what he has done will be obvious to all and immune to misrepresentation. Antony, of course, sets aside the arid principles espoused by Brutus and instead exploits the emotions of his audience.

A drawing of Brutus falling on his sword from an Elizabethan text.

At the end of the ensuing civil war, a defeated Brutus commits suicide, and Antony unexpectedly commends his erstwhile enemy: "This was the noblest Roman of them all." According to Antony, Brutus, alone among the conspirators, was motivated by "general honest thought and common good." Yet the play leaves the audience with the powerful impression that Brutus was a man out of time, fighting historical forces that he didn't recognize and was powerless to oppose. As Brutus himself famously declares, "There is a tide in the affairs of men, / Which, taken at the flood, leads on to fortune."

Although not named for him, *the play* Julius Caesar *focuses on the character of Brutus, whose tragedy is that he must choose between two mutually exclusive ideals.*

VIII. THE QUARTERING OF BRITISH TROOPS

WHEN PARLIAMENT APPROVED the Townshend Act, it also looked again at the thorny issue of troop quartering. The Quartering Act of 1765 had required colonial assemblies to provide for British troops stationed within their jurisdictions. For the most part, this meant New York—where the army of Maj. Gen. Thomas Gage, commander in chief of all British forces in North America, was headquartered.

In the spring of 1766, soon after the repeal of the Stamp Act, Gage asked New York for the required support. The New York legislature, albeit with some misgivings, complied. The next year, however, when Gage made the same request, the leadership of the legislature refused, arguing that the burden on the colony was unfairly large. In London, some members of Parliament called for the arrest of the legislators on charges of treason, but cooler heads prevailed. Instead, Parliament passed the New York Restraining Act, which suspended the legislature until it agreed to comply.

In Boston, patriots rushed to support New York, announcing another boycott of British goods. Later, in February 1768, the Massachusetts legislature approved a circular letter, written by Samuel Adams, advocating resumption of the intercolonial nonimportation agreements. An irate Francis Bernard, still the royal governor of Massachusetts, ordered the legislature dissolved. He also began sending

British troops arrive at Boston in 1768.

secret messages to Parliament, asking for the immediate dispatch of British troops to Boston to support him in what had become a bitter struggle with the Sons of Liberty for control of the city's economic and political life. Adams and other patriot leaders were routinely using street mobs to coerce even pro-British colonists (known as Tories) into respecting the boycott of British goods.

Finally, in September 1768, acting on orders from London, Gage sent Bernard two regiments of infantry, and Boston became an occupied town. Regular patrols constrained what the Sons of Liberty could do, but the presence of so many British soldiers in Boston bound together and energized the various patriot factions as never before. The result was a political stalemate: Bernard and Lieutenant Governor Hutchinson were reluctant to enforce the new customs laws rigorously, fearing a general uprising; meanwhile the patriots, not yet ready for open rebellion, hesitated themselves. Both sides knew, however, that sooner or later an incident would take place that would spark a massive popular uprising against the British.

When Parliament suspended *the New York legislature for refusing to comply with the Quartering Act, Boston rose to New York's defense and soon had to quarter troops itself.*

VIII. DATA TRANSMISSION

COMPUTERS UNDERSTAND only two states: on and off. Either electric current is flowing through a semiconductor (on), or it isn't (off). Computers can process information only because these two states have been assigned numerical equivalents, 1 corresponding to on and 0 corresponding to off.

Thus, your computer "thinks" in base-2, or binary form. The letters of its alphabet, 0 and 1, are called bits (short for *binary digits*). Its words are called bytes. Each byte contains eight bits—accounting for 2^8, or 256, different possibilities ranging in base-10 value from 0 to 255. For example, the byte corresponding to the base-10 number 3 is 00000011, while the byte corresponding to the base-10 number 128 is 10000000.

The Internet is able to transmit digital information because, ultimately, all such information is made up of bits that can be represented electronically by the presence or absence of voltage. In fact, any device capable of turning on and off in a controlled manner can be used to send binary data. You could even use a flashlight. In practice, however, electronic devices are the most efficient because they can easily and accurately parse incoming transmissions carried by oscillating electrical current. After dividing the stream of current into precise time intervals, the electronic device examines each interval to determine whether the current was on (1) or off (0).

The most widely used medium for transmitting electronic data is copper wire—either the ordinary telephone lines that provide dial-up and DSL service or the Cat5 cables that connect computers to nearby routers. The most efficient way to transmit a high volume of data, however, is with fiber-optic cable. Although more expensive to install and maintain than copper wire, fiber-optic cable can carry so much more data that it becomes cost-effective for large-scale applications. A single fiber-optic cable is made up of dozens of strands of pure glass. Through each of these strands moves a beam of laser light whose photons provide an ideal medium for data transmission because they are tiny, massless, and fast.

Computers can also access the Internet wirelessly using systems such as WiFi. These work on the same principle as radio, using variations in electromagnetic radiation to transmit information. However, because wireless signals aren't contained in wires or cables, they spread out in space. This reduces their efficiency, but wireless systems are nevertheless competitive with copper wire and generally cheaper because there's no wire to install.

The Internet transmits data *in binary form through copper wire, through fiber-optic cable, and also wirelessly.*

VIII. POST-IMPRESSIONISM

BRITISH ART CRITIC ROGER FRY coined the term *post-impressionism* in 1910 to
categorize the various Parisian artists whose styles developed out of impressionism.
In contrast with the impressionists, whose paintings generally described reality, the
post-impressionists of the 1880s and 1890s favored dreamlike subjects that evoked
psychological or spiritual responses in the viewer. In other words, they preferred
subjectivity (the conceptual) to objectivity (the perceived).

Paul Gauguin,
Words of the Devil (1892)

By 1913, post-impressionism was a familiar style in
Europe; but in America, it was still largely unknown. For
this reason, Davies and Kuhn had made a last-minute
detour to attend Fry's Second Post-Impressionist Exhibition
at the Grafton Gallery in London, where they secured
additional works for their own exhibition.

Three of Gauguin's heavily symbolic Tahitian
paintings were hung in Gallery R of the Armory Show,
accompanied by translated excerpts from Gauguin's book
Noa Noa, which detailed the artist's primitive existence
among the people of Tahiti and his cohabitation with
native women. Critics found both the paintings and the
writing lewd and disturbing. Commenting in *Harper's Weekly*, artist Kenyon Cox,
who generously admitted to a bias against modernism, described Gauguin as a
"decorator tainted with insanity." Cox went on to criticize van Gogh and Cézanne—
whose work filled Gallery Q—for being, respectively, "too unskilled to give quality to
an evenly-laid coat of paint" and "absolutely without talent." Other critics dismissed
post-impressionist as "eccentric" and "negligible," worrying that its overindulgent
novelty would do nothing but harm to young, impressionable American artists.

Meanwhile, less judgmental critics argued that post-impressionism wasn't
well enough represented in the Armory Show to permit such authoritative verdicts.
Nevertheless, if opinions were to be offered, in their professional estimation Cézanne's
art was not all that revolutionary; van Gogh's expressiveness, though crude, could
be linked to earlier traditions; and Gauguin's paintings were actually good, both
visually interesting and intellectually stimulating.

The final word on post-impressionism came from the Metropolitan Museum
of Art, whose board of trustees voted (although not unanimously) to purchase from
the Armory Show Cézanne's *View of the Domain Saint-Joseph*, the first of the artist's
works to hang in an American museum.

Although post-impressionism was *three decades old by the time of the Armory Show, it was
nevertheless new to most Americans.*

VIII. THE INTERPRETATION OF DREAMS

FREUD'S APPROACH to dream interpretation, as described in his classic work *The Interpretation of Dreams* (1900), begins with the dreamer's memory of the dream's content, which Freud called its "manifest content." Because dreams are typically puzzling, like codes, the analyst then asks the dreamer to "free associate," or make connections to particular aspects of the dream without editing or feeling the need to make sense.

The idea of free association first occurred to Freud while he was treating Emmy von N., whose case history appears in *Studies on Hysteria*. According to Freud, Emmy became frustrated with his constant questioning of her and wanted him to let her "tell me what she had to say." Soon, Freud began suggesting to other patients that they speak freely, or free associate, while Freud listened and occasionally interpreted their associations. As a result, repressed memories and hidden feelings gradually moved into awareness.

Speaking freely about a dream can help to uncover its underlying meaning, which Freud called its "latent content." The purpose of the free association is to reveal the dream's unconscious significance and thereby decode its meaning. According to Freud, dreams are formed in the unconscious mind, where thoughts, memories, and feelings are compressed and distorted into symbols that both represent and hide the unconscious material being dreamed about. Freud called this process "dream work."

Most dreams are triggered by a recent event that reminds the dreamer unconsciously of some long-repressed memory or feeling. For example, a patient who feels guilty about a former marriage may well dream about apologizing to an old friend that he or she met only the day before because that old friend reminded the patient unconsciously of the former spouse. In this dream, the patient's repressed feelings about the former spouse are "displaced" onto the friend. The recent event, or "day residue," appears in the dream as a disguise for the troubling repressed feeling.

All dreams, according to Freud, are about "wish fulfillment" in that their purpose is to discharge the unconscious tension generated by repressed and forbidden wishes. In order to release this tension, the dreamer employs a sleight of hand, using dream work to protect the mind from directly experiencing its unconscious desires while simultaneously giving those desires free mental rein through displacement. The work of dream interpretation thus involves decoding the dream in order to reveal the patient's unconscious mind, which is why Freud called dreams "the royal road to the unconscious."

Freud called dreams *"the royal road to the unconscious" because decoding a patient's dreams reveals the workings of his or her unconscious mind.*

VIII. THE MAJOR TRAGEDIES

CRITICAL TRADITION HAS long separated out four of
Shakespeare's tragedies as particularly exemplary: *Hamlet,
Othello, King Lear,* and *Macbeth.* Bracketed by three earlier
and three later tragedies, this quartet of plays embraces
such an intense tragic vision that many critics have come
to treat them as the product of a peculiarly heartrending
period in Shakespeare's life. Written between 1599 and
1607, they all examine closely the nature of spiritual evil.

A posthumous portrait
of Shakespeare.

Their preoccupation with the metaphysical problem
of evil, however, is not their only commonality. The major
tragedies also share an especially high degree of craftsmanship, which elevates their
characters to three-dimensionality. In particular, the sense of tortured interiority
that Shakespeare launched with Richard II and developed with Brutus finds a new
and unprecedented maturity in Hamlet, Othello, Lear, and Macbeth.

Shakespeare's attention to consciousness in these plays was highly innovative,
and he didn't stop there, also introducing a deep awareness of the limits of human
knowledge. Tragedy invariably involves the mistaking of one thing for another, but
the major tragedies return repeatedly to the much more sophisticated problem of
what can be known. For example, the characters in these plays remark often on the
impossibility of knowing another person's mind.

In *Julius Caesar,* Shakespeare began to make use of the tragic potential of
betrayal—especially with the dying Caesar's interrogative accusation, "*Et tu, Brute?*"—
but it is not until the major tragedies that betrayal becomes endemic and inescapable.
Commenting on the inscrutability of the traitorous Thane of Cawdor, *Macbeth*'s
King Duncan says, "There's no art / To find the mind's construction in the face."
Hamlet similarly remarks that "one may smile, and smile, and be a villain." Even
more compellingly, Othello demands of Iago, "By heaven, I'll know thy thoughts."
To which Iago replies, "You cannot, if my heart were in your hand, / Nor shall not,
whilst 'tis in my custody."

This plumbing of new depths is profound and exhilarating, but it is accompanied
by the unsettling possibility that such depths may be inaccessible to us. The result is a
world that seems to lack reliable communication and resilient community. Macbeth,
in a moment of sadness, laments that he will never be able to enjoy the comforts of
old age. Instead, he can look forward only to "Curses, not loud but deep, mouth-
honor, breath / Which the poor heart would fain deny and dare not."

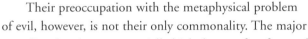

The four major tragedies *are distinguished by their remarkably fine characterization and
the ways in which they plumb new psychological depths.*

IX. THE BOSTON MASSACRE

ON THE WINTRY NIGHT of March 5, 1770, Pvt. Hugh White was on guard duty outside the Custom House in King Street when several young barber's apprentices began jeering him, provoking White to butt one of them in the head with his gun. As news of the incident spread, often exaggerated in the retelling, an angry crowd of perhaps fifty Bostonians gathered around White. They began throwing large chunks of ice at him and shouting, "Kill him! Knock him down! Fire, damn you, fire! You dare not fire!" The sentry shouted to a nearby military post for assistance.

The officer on duty that night, Capt. Thomas Preston, knowing what might happen if he called out the entire regiment, personally led a squad of seven men to rescue White. Despite the chaos of screaming men and barking dogs, Preston made it to the sentry post without incident. But when he tried to withdraw, the growing press of bodies in King Street blocked his path. Directing his men to form a defensive arc with their backs to the Custom House, Preston ordered the crowd, now numbering about four hundred, to disperse. The only responses he received were hoots and more snowballs.

As time passed and the crowd grew more emboldened, the distance between the line of soldiers and the line of civilians shrank to less than two feet. Suddenly, a club sailed through the air and struck Pvt. Hugh Montgomery. The impact knocked Montgomery to the ground. As he staggered to his feet and picked up his musket,

Paul Revere's engraving of the Boston Massacre.

the weapon went off—perhaps intentionally, perhaps not. Hearing this shot, which hit no one, members of the crowd lunged forward, swinging their clubs wildly. The soldiers fought back, fending off these blows with their bayonets; but during the next minute or two, a few other shots were fired.

The stunned Captain Preston neither ordered the shooting, nor halted it immediately once it had begun. When the first round of shooting stopped, the crowd continued to advance, and the soldiers parried more blows while reloading their muskets. Then a second round of shooting began—single shots again, fired sporadically over a period of one or two minutes. Finally, the shooting stopped again, and the crowd dispersed. In all, five Bostonians were killed and six wounded. It was a "massacre," Samuel Adams said.

On the night of March 5, 1770, *the taunting of a British private on guard duty escalated into a confrontation between soldiers and civilians that left five Bostonians dead.*

IX. THE EMAIL SYSTEM

EMAIL WAS CREATED during the 1960s by the developers of the university and governmental networks that later came together to form the Internet. Processing speeds were slow, and the community of users was small and well behaved. Thus, the initial standards were simple and even a little sloppy. Email caught on so quickly, however, that it became extremely difficult to implement new, more sophisticated standards. (The installed base of software was so large that people became resistant to change.)

In accordance with those original standards, which remain in place today, all email addresses consist of a local part and a host name separated by an @ sign. In the email address *info@example.com*, the local part is *info*, and the host name is *example.com*. The host name can appear either as a domain name or as an IP address enclosed in brackets.

Two kinds of software manage the email system: Mail User Agents (MUAs) and Mail Transport Agents (MTAs). MUAs, also known as email clients, are programs that aid users in creating and sending messages; they also interpret and display the messages that users receive. Popular email clients include Outlook, Mail (the Mac client), and Mozilla Thunderbird. The numerous web-based MUAs include Gmail and Hotmail.

MTAs carry messages created by MUAs across the Internet using a procedure called store and forward. Specifically, they receive and accept a complete copy of each email, which they store in a local file while attempting to forward it. If the forwarding doesn't take place immediately (because the next MTA in the chain is offline or busy), the message remains with the current MTA until forwarding becomes possible.

When you send an email, your client transmits the message to an MTA run by your email provider and known as your outgoing mail server. The outgoing mail server then forwards your message to another MTA in the same way that DNS servers pass on DNS requests. Eventually, the message should reach an MTA that accepts it for delivery to an inbox.

What current email standards most obviously lack are security features for the prevention of spam and email-based fraud. Two major obstacles exist. The first is that MTAs are required to accept and forward *all* messages. The second is that the burden of storing and filtering those messages falls entirely on the recipient, not the sender. Spam is widespread because the messages don't burden the sender, and the email system ensures their delivery.

Because most email standards *haven't been changed since they were first developed during the 1960s, email users remain vulnerable to spam and email-based fraud.*

IX. CUBISM

ALTHOUGH MANY AMERICANS were prepared to give post-impressionism the benefit of the doubt, the cubists were another matter entirely. True revolutionaries, they had invented a language that no American critic seemed able to understand—and

A caricature of Duchamp's *Nude Descending a Staircase, No. 2.*

because the critics couldn't understand it, they deemed it worthless. As a result, the cubists (along with the Fauves) were sensationalized in the press as freaks, quacks, degenerates, and anarchists.

Searching in vain for some semblance of reality in cubism's confusing, nonrepresentational forms, most Armory Show viewers found the style frustrating, jarring, and bewildering. After a short time, Gallery I, which held most of the cubist works, became known as "the chamber of horrors." New York critic Royal Cortissoz complained that the paintings seemed to be merely faceted shapes "thrown together in a heap." Cubism, he declared, was not art but "so many square yards of canvas, treated as though they were so many square yards of wallpaper."

Viewers were especially perplexed by the paintings' titles, which suggested recognizable forms but bore no apparent relation to the shapes on the canvas. Francis Picabia's *The Procession, Seville*, for example, looked nothing like a procession, nor like Seville. Similarly, Marcel Duchamp's *Nude Descending a Staircase, No. 2* appeared to contain neither a nude nor a staircase, yet it was so popular—as scandal, if not as art—that people had to push through crowds just to see it. Picasso, on the other hand, received little attention, largely because Davies and Kuhn had been unable to obtain any of his breakthrough works, and the artist was represented instead by earlier canvases.

Of the cubists, only Picabia undertook the long ocean journey to New York for the show. Thus, when the scandal broke, he became, by default, the movement's spokesperson in America. In an article printed in the *New York World*, he tried to put into words why the cubists had moved toward abstraction, explaining that art could no longer be purely visual or objective and had to relate instead to "qualitative conception." What Picabia meant was that art, because it was artificial and not representative of reality, could break down reality into component parts and then reconstruct it, piece by piece, like a building. Unfortunately, his article proved as unintelligible to Americans as his art and only muddied the waters further.

Most shocking to Armory Show viewers *were the nonrepresentational paintings that broke with traditional concepts of reality—especially those works produced by the cubists.*

IX. TRANSFERENCE

EARLY ON, both Freud and Breuer became aware that frequent sessions with a patient, during which strong emotions were recalled and expressed, produced in that patient strong feelings toward the physician. Anna O.'s treatment ended abruptly, for example, when she told Breuer that his "baby was coming." (Breuer immediately turned her care over to another physician and is said to have taken a much-needed vacation with his wife.)

Freud believed that the analyst should function as a "blank screen" onto which patients can project a variety of emotions, many of them conflicted. Often, these emotions are feelings that patients have about other important figures in their lives. Because patients *transfer* these intense, unresolved feelings of love, anger, shame, and frustration onto their analysts, Freud called the process transference.

According to Freud, transference aids patients in accessing deeply repressed and often highly conflicted feelings. For example, a patient who felt disliked as a child by a parent but isn't conscious of this feeling might experience an analyst's silence or innocuous gesture as rejection. Similarly, a patient who has always been competitive, perhaps because of an early urge to win the attention or affection of an unavailable parent, might find himself attempting to outsmart the analyst.

Initially, Freud believed that transference was useful merely because, like dreams, it provided important clues to the workings of the patient's unconscious. He reasoned that transferred feelings were expressions of the unconscious mind akin to the latent content of dreams and, therefore, could be interpreted usefully. By 1910, however, Freud had come to see transference as playing a much more central role in the resolution of a patient's problems.

Freud also came to recognize that transference stirred up feelings in the analyst as well (feelings known as countertransference). For example, the patient who felt rejected by a parent and now transfers that feeling onto the analyst might quickly come to seem annoying. In fact, an analyst might develop genuine feelings of dislike for such an insecure, needy patient. The key point, Freud maintained, was that the analyst should never give in to the countertransference. That is, under no circumstances should the analyst ever gratify the longings for love, anger, fear, and so on that patients transfer onto them. It is rather the role of the analyst to remain objective and a bit distant, interpreting the meaning and origin of these feelings but never engaging or satisfying them.

Transference is the process by which *patients project unresolved feelings they have about important people in their lives onto their analysts.*

IX. HAMLET AND REVENGE

EVERYONE KNOWS THAT HAMLET, the prince of Denmark, is troubled. The received wisdom is that he suffers from a neurosis that makes him endlessly introspective and incapable of action. This opinion, however, fails to take into account the extraordinary difficulty of Hamlet's situation. His father has just died, and his mother has swiftly remarried his uncle, Claudius, the new king.

A period engraving of Elsinore Castle, where *Hamlet* is set.

An already unpleasant situation is complicated by the appearance of a spirit claiming to be the ghost of Hamlet's father. He tells Hamlet that Claudius murdered him by pouring poison into his ear, and he demands that his son seek revenge. This setup suggests a conventional revenge tragedy, but Hamlet doesn't rise to the bait. Critics have described his hesitancy as inexplicable, but Hamlet's indecision really isn't that puzzling. As a result of the apparition's demand for revenge, Hamlet faces two quandaries. First, is the ghost telling the truth? Second, what should Hamlet's response be? In philosophical terms, these are difficult questions of epistemology and ethics.

Hamlet investigates the first question by arranging for actors to perform a play for Claudius in which the king is murdered by having poison poured into his ear. Claudius's alarmed reaction is proof enough of his guilt for Hamlet, yet the prince still refrains from killing Claudius because he fears that, having confessed his sins to God, Claudius will go to heaven. He wants to kill Claudius in the midst of some new sin so that Claudius's "soul may be damned."

Many critics view this reasoning as a rationalization of some fundamental inaptitude, but such an argument is needlessly clever. What Hamlet reveals here is not merely the remorseless logic of revenge but the degree to which revenge involves a usurpation of divine prerogative. In the endlessly quoted words of St. Paul, "Vengeance is mine. I will repay, saith the Lord." To pursue revenge is thus to assume blasphemously a divine prerogative.

The problem of delay is mitigated once we realize that Hamlet is not a conventional revenger who unproblematically accepts the project of revenge. The killing of Claudius that takes place at the end of the play happens when Hamlet himself has only moments to live. The murderous act is an almost reflexive response to his mother's poisoning and not a premeditated reprisal for the death of his father. *Hamlet* is not a revenge tragedy but a play *about* revenge tragedy.

Many critics view Hamlet as a neurotic, *incapable of action, but his hesitancy can also be interpreted as deep consideration of the ethical implications of revenge.*

X. THE MASSACRE TRIAL

AT 2 AM ON MARCH 6, the sheriff of Boston served an arrest warrant on Captain Preston, who surrendered an hour later. The eight soldiers in Preston's party were also imprisoned that night. All were charged with murder.

Later in the day, at a town meeting, Samuel Adams was chosen to lead a delegation of fifteen to Acting Governor Hutchinson (Bernard had resigned seven months earlier) to demand the removal of all British troops from Boston. Hutchinson capitulated, relocating both regiments to Castle William in Boston Harbor; but he refused to give in to demands for an immediate trial, fearing that the aroused state of the citizenry would dictate guilty verdicts no matter the evidence.

Eventually, all of Boston came to see that it was in everyone's interest for the proceedings to be fair. When Preston's trial began on October 24, among his prosecutors was Massachusetts solicitor general Samuel Quincy, a well-known Tory. Likewise, among his defense counsel were two prominent patriot lawyers, Josiah Quincy (Samuel Quincy's brother) and John Adams (Samuel Adams's cousin).

A parade of witnesses told first the civilians' and then the soldiers' version of events, after which the lawyers made their closing arguments. Prosecutor Robert Treat Paine, a patriot sympathizer, absolved the Bostonians and blamed the soldiers, pointing out that members of the crowd couldn't be held "answerable for the rude speech of every person that happens to be near them." In his turn, John Adams countered that the shooting was surely justified because the soldiers had been attacked—but not by patriots. "The plain

John Adams in ca. 1766 portrait.

English is," Adams said, "most [of the mob was] probably a motley rabble of saucy boys, negroes and mulattoes, Irish teagues, and outlandish jack-tars."

At trial's end, the jurors were instructed that if they were satisfied "that the sentinel was insulted and that Captain Preston and his party went to assist him," then the homicides were "doubtless excusable...if not justifiable." Under such circumstances, Judge Edmund Trowbridge continued, "any little spark would kindle a great fire, and five lives were sacrificed to a squabble between the sentry and Piemont's barber's boy." On October 30, the jury returned a verdict of not guilty. A month later, the eight remaining defendants were tried as a group. Six were acquitted. The other two, Montgomery and Pvt. Matthew Killroy, were each found guilty but merely branded on the right thumb.

The soldiers involved in the Boston Massacre were prosecuted by *a Tory and defended by patriots because it was in the interest of both sides that the trials be thorough and impartial.*

X. EMAIL MESSAGES

AN EMAIL MESSAGE is essentially a structured block of text—composed of letters, numbers, punctuation marks, and blank spaces. It has two parts: a header and a body. The header, like any other form of Internet communication, has its own special syntax. The body is simply a block of text—although it may have additional parts, such as files, which are commonly called attachments. In order to be transmitted through the email system, a message needs to be encoded by an MUA before it's sent and then decoded by another MUA after it's received.

Headers are much more complicated than most people think. When you view an email using your MUA, it shows you only a truncated version of the header—usually just the sender's name, the recipient's name, the date and time the message was sent, and the subject line. By changing the view settings of your email client, however, you can see the message's complete header.

The full header shows the message's entire path from the sender's outgoing mail server to the recipient's incoming mail server, including all the stops along the way. For this reason, header information can be very useful in tracing email problems. However, because of the email system's lack of security features, there's no way to tell whether the header information in an email is authentic. Purveyors of spam take advantage of this weakness, creating fabricated headers in order to disguise the sources of their emails. MTAs accept these fabrications as genuine because that is what they're programmed to do.

Spammers also cover their tracks by sending messages to nonexistent email accounts at specific MTAs—placing in the header, in the space reserved for the sender's address, the email address of the intended target. Because the message is undeliverable, the MTA will generate an error report and send it, along with the original message, to the "sender" (that is, the spammer's target).

With regard to the body of an email message, clients usually display the complete text but handle different attachments in different ways. Some clients will display the contents of a JPEG or PDF file; others will merely indicate the presence of attachments with icons. If you find that you can't open an attachment, the most likely problem is that your MUA isn't able to recognize the format in which the file was created. It may also be that your computer lacks the software necessary to manipulate files in that format.

Email messages have two parts: *a header that shows the path the message has taken and a body that contains text and possibly attached files.*

X. THE FAUVES

BECAUSE THE WORKS OF THE CUBISTS were so radically nonrepresentational, they were relatively easy for American critics to lampoon and dismiss. The works of the Fauves, however, especially those of Matisse, were close enough to what had come before that they evoked not condescension but wrath among critics and artists associated with the National Academy establishment.

Amadeo de Souza Cardoso's *The Leap of the Rabbit* (1911) was among the fauvist works shown at the armory.

Other Fauves had works in the Armory Show, but Matisse drew most of the rage because he was obviously the star. In fact, Matisse was the most thoroughly represented artist in the entire exhibition with sixteen canvases. Furthermore, unlike the relatively minor works chosen to represent Picasso and cubism, the Matisse selection included five of what are now recognized as his greatest paintings: *The Blue Nude*; *Le Luxe, II*; *Goldfish and Sculpture*; *Nasturtiums and the Painting "Dance," II*; and *The Red Studio*.

Matisse's paintings were so provocative because they seemed to deny long-held academic standards. Most critics acknowledged that he had talent, but they couldn't understand why he had chosen to undermine so blatantly every traditional form of art: the nude, the still life, the portrait, and so on. In Matisse's work, form and perspective were distorted, and color was laid down in seemingly erratic patterns. The result was incomprehensible to American critics and viewers alike. At best, paintings such as *The Blue Nude*, lent to the show by Leo and Gertrude Stein, were attacked as examples of the overindulgent individualism that seemed to pervade the modernist movement. More typical, however, was the response of the critic who referred to Matisse paintings simply as "hideous monstrosities." To many, Matisse's primitivism seemed not merely childlike but depraved and offensive—a degeneration of centuries of knowledge, rather than an advancement in art.

Matisse was in Paris when he learned of the vituperation his paintings were causing in America. Granting an interview, he said, "Oh, do tell the American people that I am a normal man, that I am a devoted husband and father, that I have three fine children, that I go to the theatre!" But these words did little to moderate the storm of criticism casting Matisse's work as nothing less than an assault upon Western civilization.

Because fauvism maintained some ties to representationalism, *critics perceived it as a much greater threat to prevailing academic standards than cubism, which seemed merely foolish.*

X. THE PSYCHOPATHOLOGY OF EVERYDAY LIFE

IN HIS 1901 BOOK *The Psychopathology of Everyday Life*, Freud described the ways in which unconscious conflicts and wishes find expression in everyday behavior. The book became quite popular because it described experiences familiar to readers and explained their psychological significance—documenting and discussing the inability to recall a fact or a name; psychological "blocks" that defy conscious will; and, most notably, the errors in speech that have since come to be known as Freudian slips. Freud's general theory was that these phenomena were produced by repressed thoughts and feelings that occasionally rose up from the unconscious to interfere with daily life. Thus, they were meaningful and could be interpreted.

The Psychopathology of Everyday Life presents many examples of this sort of behavior, including this one related to Freud by his colleague Carl Jung:

> *A Herr Y fell in love with a lady; but he met with no success, and shortly afterwards she married Herr X. Thereafter, Herr Y, in spite of having known Herr X for a long time and even having business dealings with him, forgot his name over and over again, so that several times he had to enquire what it was from other people when he wanted to correspond with Herr X.*

The conflicted, probably resentful feelings that Herr Y obviously had toward Herr X—feelings that Herr Y repressed because he couldn't express them directly—interfered with his ability to recall Herr X's name. Of course, it could be argued that people forget names all the time, but Freud didn't believe that lapses such as this were accidental. Why Herr Y's name, and why so consistently? According to Freud, there were no accidents: Everyday errors of this sort always had unconscious significance.

The Psychopathology of Everyday Life also included this example of a classic Freudian slip:

> *You probably still recall the way in which the President of the Lower House of the Austrian Parliament opened the sitting a short while ago: "Gentlemen: I take notice that a full quorum of members is present and herewith declare the sitting closed!" His attention was only drawn by the general merriment, and he corrected his mistake.*

Freud's interpretation was that the president "wished he was already in a position to close the sitting." His slip merely revealed this unconscious wish.

According to Freud, *certain everyday behaviors such as errors in speech (Freudian slips) are not accidental but rather have great unconscious significance.*

X. HAMLET'S CONSCIENCE

HAMLET'S REPUTATION for introspection is not undeserved. With four major soliloquies, he spends more time unfolding his thoughts than any other Shakespearean character. The most famous of these soliloquies—beginning "To be or not to be"—engages directly the play's existential themes. Although critics commonly describe this soliloquy as being "about" suicide, the question of taking his own life occupies only a small part of Hamlet's reflection.

The opening line, however, does pose existence against nonexistence, and Hamlet initially sees death as a respite from the travails of life. This leads him to a consideration of "what dreams may come" in "that sleep of death"—which, he decides, is an unpleasant prospect, sufficiently so as to make people bear the "whips and scorns of time" rather than kill themselves. "The dread of something after death" thus has a corrosive effect on action. "It puzzles the will," Hamlet says, and makes us "rather bear those ills we have than fly to others we know not."

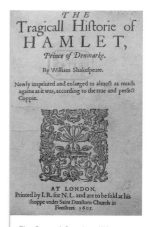

The Second Quarto edition (1604) of *Hamlet.*

> *Thus conscience does make cowards of us all;*
> *And thus the native hue of resolution*
> *Is sicklied o'er with the pale cast of thought,*
> *And enterprises of great pitch and moment*
> *With this regard their currents turn awry*
> *And lose the name of action.*

Conscience—the internal moral compass that distinguishes right from wrong—inhibits our natural tendency to act, because any attempt to evaluate the ethics of an action yields too many possibilities and too many potential pitfalls. Careful ethical scrutiny is thus a disease that stops us in our tracks.

In his final soliloquy, Hamlet revisits this conclusion when he asks, "What is a man, / If his chief good and market of his time / Be but to sleep and feed?" Such animal behavior is unbecoming for humans, who have been endowed with memory and the ability to plan as well as "godlike reason"—all capacities that must be used. Yet Hamlet's revenge remains unaccomplished, and he worries that he is hampered either by "bestial oblivion" or "some craven scruple of thinking too precisely on th'event." In this sense, "godlike reason" becomes self-defeating, while consciousness and reflection show us so much that we lose the capacity to act.

In addition to ethics, Hamlet *also focuses on thought itself, suggesting that conscience and introspection work to inhibit action.*

XI. THE BOSTON TEA PARTY

IRONICALLY, the day of the Boston Massacre—March 5, 1770—was also the day that Parliament repealed the Townshend Act. The economics of the repeal were simple: Between the nonimportation agreements and the smuggling, the new import duties raised just £295, while enforcement costs totaled £170,000. For the sake of British pride, however, the new prime minister—Frederick, Lord North—insisted that one duty remain as a symbol of parliamentary supremacy: the import tariff on tea.

Once most of the duties passed away, so did the nonimportation agreements, and the colonies resumed a lively trade with Great Britain. Even in Boston, where outrage over the "massacre" was still deeply felt, merchants bought and sold British goods rather than lose out to competitors in other colonies. As a result, by the time the massacre trials ended in December 1770, the patriot cause had lost a great deal of momentum.

To revive it, Samuel Adams and others persuaded the Boston town meeting in November 1772 to create a "committee of correspondence," which would articulate and publicize opposition to British rule. Similar committees were soon established in other towns and colonies. But, as always, it was the British themselves who did the most to revive the patriot cause.

In May 1773, Parliament passed the Tea Act, granting the financially strapped East India Company permission to sell its tea in the colonies without paying any import duty. This deal allowed the East India Company to charge less than the usual colonial middlemen and still earn a sizable profit. But rather than applaud Parliament for lowering tea prices, Americans denounced the deal because of its long-term implications: If Parliament could eliminate one profitable colonial trade, why not another? No aspect of American commerce would be safe from British interference.

An engraving of the Boston Tea Party.

Abetted by the committees of correspondence, opposition to the Tea Act spread. In New York City and Philadelphia, royal authorities, fearing violence, turned back ships bearing East India Company tea rather than allowing them to land and unload. Bostonians tried to turn back three such ships in December 1773, but their effort failed and the ships entered Boston Harbor. Undeterred, 150 members of the Sons of Liberty, crudely disguised as Mohawks and surrounded by a large crowd of onlookers for protection, boarded the ships on the night of December 16 and dumped their cargo of tea chests overboard.

Although repeal of the Townshend Act quieted Boston for several years, *the Tea Act reminded colonists of past grievances and led to the most rebellious protest yet: the Boston Tea Party.*

XI. CODES

TRANSFORMING SOME TYPES OF information into numbers is almost effortless. Letters, for example, can easily be rendered as numbers using simple substitution codes. Using a code that maps *a* to 1, *b* to 2, *c* to 3, and so on, the word *cat* can be rendered quickly as the sequence 3, 1, 20.

Computers are particularly dependent on a similar substitution scheme known as ASCII, which stands for the American Standard Code for Information Interchange. ASCII maps each of the symbols found on a standard computer keyboard to a specific number between 0 and 127. For example, an open parenthesis maps to the number 40, an uppercase *A* maps to the number 65, a lowercase *t* maps to the number 116, and so on. In ASCII, the word *cat* is rendered as the sequence 99, 97, 116. (Several alternatives to ASCII have since been created to handle non-English alphabets.)

For a message to travel through the email system, it must be encoded in ASCII. This doesn't pose a problem for headers or body text (as long as they're written in English), but it does complicate the transmission of non-English alphabets and nontextual attachment such as sound and image files. MUAs get around this problem by using MIME (Multipurpose Internet Mail Extensions) encoding. What MIME encoding does is convert the digital information in a JPEG or MP3 file into sequences of symbols borrowed from the ASCII alphabet, which can then be sent the usual way. Because MIME makes use of 64 different ASCII characters and thus functions as a base-64 system, it's both efficient and compact.

Computers also make use of error-correcting codes (ECCs). Although digital information is perfectly reproducible in theory, in practice tiny errors sometimes creep in because of unreliable communications or faulty storage media. ECCs use extra or redundant information to confirm the accuracy of data and, if necessary, correct any errors. A primitive ECC might create three copies of every ASCII character in an email message. When the message is received, these characters would be checked; and if one differed from the others, a simple two-out-of-three determination would reveal the correct value.

Hard drives make similar use of ECCs to compensate for defects in their physical media. Even human DNA uses error correction to compensate for genetic mutations. In general, error correction allows engineers to build devices that are more reliable than their component parts.

ASCII is a simple substitution code *that converts standard keyboard characters into digital information that can be transmitted via email.*

XI. EUROPEAN SCULPTURE AT THE ARMORY SHOW

THE PAINTINGS OF the cubists and the Fauves weren't the only radical breaks with tradition present at the Armory Show. The European sculptures on display in Galleries H and I similarly challenged audiences with their less-than-representational forms. For most Americans in 1913, "modern" sculpture still meant works in the style of French realist Auguste Rodin—a style that had been revolutionary when it debuted in the 1870s, but not since and certainly not in Europe. The modernist sculptors whose works Davies and Kuhn collected for the Armory Show—Constantin

The Duchamp brothers (Marcel, Raymond, and Jacques) ca. 1912.

Brancusi, Wilhelm Lehmbruck, Raymond Duchamp-Villon, and Alexander Archipenko—had moved well beyond realism, and their pieces (along with a few by Picasso and Matisse) showed Americans just how far the European avant-garde had progressed.

The works of Brancusi, a pioneer of modernism in sculpture, baffled the critics most of all. The Armory Show included three of his most famous pieces—*The Kiss*, *Sleeping Muse*, and *Mlle. Pogany*—all of which simplified natural form to the point of abstraction. *Mlle. Pogany*, in particular, was described by one critic as "a hard-boiled egg balanced on a cube of sugar."

Viewers found Lehmbruck's work nearly as enigmatic. His piece *Kneeling Woman* still showed some links to representationalism, but the manner in which Lehmbruck attenuated the woman's natural form and exaggerated her gestures made the sculpture an easy target for caricature. In a magazine article titled "A Layman's View of an Art Exhibition," Theodore Roosevelt compared *Kneeling Woman* to a praying mantis. The former president also scolded Archipenko, a Russian who later immigrated to the United States, for the lack of realistic proportion in his work and his tendency toward abstraction.

Yet, even as they found elements to ridicule, most critics admitted also to finding a certain charm in the work of these sculptors. One cited the "singular and penetrating power" of Lehmbruck's emotionally expressive style; and even though the reviews of Duchamp-Villon's slightly cubist pieces were mostly unfavorable, he nevertheless sold three of his four works on display. His brothers Marcel Duchamp and Jacques Villon performed even better, however, selling all of their exhibited works.

In 1913, most Americans still associated *modernity in sculpture with the realism of Rodin; thus, they were unprepared for the abstractions they saw at the Armory Show.*

XI. THE WEDNESDAY PSYCHOLOGICAL SOCIETY

AS FREUD'S THEORIES BECAME more widely known, some colleagues expressed interest in learning more about them. During the fall of 1902, they began meeting regularly at Freud's apartment. Because the meetings took place on Wednesday nights, the group called itself the Wednesday Psychological Society. Its members included Alfred Adler, Wilhelm Stekel, Otto Rank, and later Karl Abraham, Carl Jung, Sándor Ferenczi, and Ernest Jones—the founders of what became the psychoanalytic movement.

As later described by Freud, the Wednesday Psychological Society was a small group of "young physicians gathered around me with the declared intention of learning, practicing, and disseminating psychoanalysis." The meetings had a regular format: One member would present a paper; then—after a break for coffee, cake, and cigars—a discussion would follow. New members were added only by a unanimous vote of the existing membership. By 1906, the membership had expanded to seventeen, with at least a dozen members attending on any given night. Two years later, the group renamed itself the Vienna Psychoanalytic Society.

While most of the original members were physicians, Freud encouraged other educated people to join as well. Meanwhile, the movement spread beyond Vienna. Abraham, for example, lived in Berlin, while Ferenczi lived in Budapest. (Both men traveled regularly to Vienna, however.) Later, through Abraham, with whom he had worked at the Burghölzli Mental Hospital outside Zurich, Jung also joined the group.

Freud with colleagues during his 1909 trip to the United States.

As the circle expanded, tensions developed, especially with regard to the competition for Freud's attention. Letters written by various parties living in different cities document these struggles. Most of the members aspired to gain Freud's friendship and approval. Some, such as Jung and later Ferenczi, even jockeyed to succeed him as he grew older. Freud, however, was hardly willing to step aside, and when one of his followers chose to back a different view regarding the course psychoanalysis should take, that person was often expelled from the inner circle. The most famous instance concerns Jung's break with Freud.

Freud was adamant that psychoanalysis should be a science with no religious associations. Jung, however, had a more spiritual vision. His conflict with Freud over this issue, recorded in a remarkable correspondence between the two men, led to Jung's retreat to Zurich and the founding of his own school of psychoanalysis.

The early psychoanalytic movement *emerged from the regular meetings at Freud's apartment of a group of young physicians who called themselves the Wednesday Psychological Society.*

XI. OTHELLO

OTHELLO IS A LOVE TRAGEDY that begins with the elopement of the title character, a Moorish general working for Venice. The father of Othello's bride, Desdemona, is a Venetian senator who objects strenuously to the match—for racial, among other, reasons—but Venice is being threatened by the Turks and so requires Othello's services.

After eloquently defending their marriage, Othello and Desdemona relocate to the Venetian garrison on Cyprus, where the couple's happiness is threatened by Iago, whom Othello has passed over for promotion and who now seeks revenge. Othello's marriage gives Iago an opening; and through insinuation, duplicity, skillful stage management, and blind luck, he persuades Othello that Desdemona has been cheating with Michael Cassio, Othello's chief lieutenant and Iago's main rival. Othello kills Desdemona only to discover that he has been tricked. In his grief, he kills himself.

Uta Hagen and Paul Robeson as Desdemona and Othello in a 1940s Broadway production.

Othello's status as an outsider—both racially and as a foreigner—makes him especially vulnerable to Iago's manipulations. But Shakespeare isn't making the conventional point that like should marry like or that marriages between partners of different backgrounds always come to grief.

When Desdemona declares "I saw Othello's visage in his mind," she means that she was attracted to Othello not by his physical appearance but by his personality. For his part, Othello reports, "She loved me for the dangers I had passed, / And I loved her that she did pity them." In other words, Desdemona finds his life story captivating; and he, in turn, delights in her intimate and sympathetic response, which military honors cannot afford.

What makes the unraveling of their love so excruciating is that they are both good people. Even Iago admits this. Of Othello, he says, "The Moor is of a free and open nature," and regarding Desdemona he schemes to "turn her virtue into pitch, / And out of her own goodness make the net / That shall enmesh them all."

In the final act, Othello wants to believe that Iago is some sort of devil; but Shakespeare, by freeing the play of supernatural elements, doesn't permit this excuse. Alternatively, Othello asserts that he has "loved not wisely but too well." This equally poor attempt at self-exculpation does, however, contain a bitter truth: The very elements of imagination and fantasy that are central to the experience of love are also implicated in its collapse.

Although Othello wants to believe *that he has "loved not wisely but too well," the play suggests love can never overcome the barriers that separate one mind from another.*

XII. THE INTOLERABLE ACTS

OUTRAGED BY THE AUDACITY of the Boston Tea Party, Parliament responded with a quartet of laws designed to punish Massachusetts and, more generally, to tighten its hold on the American colonies. Known as the Coercive Acts in Britain and the Intolerable Acts in America, these laws included the Boston Port Act, the Massachusetts Government Act, the Administration of Justice Act, and a new Quartering Act.

The Boston Port Act closed Boston Harbor to all commercial traffic until restitution was made for the spoiled tea. The Massachusetts Government Act converted

A sympathetic 1774 British satire titled *Bostonians in Distress.*

almost every public office in the colony into a royal appointment, ending self-rule there. The Administration of Justice Act, passed with the Boston Massacre in mind, authorized the royal governor to transfer capital cases involving royal officials to Great Britain if he believed that the accused couldn't get a fair trial in Massachusetts. The final Intolerable Act amended the Quartering Act to require the opening of private homes to soldiers if the barracks provided by colonial legislatures were inadequate.

Although many Bostonians considered the Tea Party unacceptable vandalism, the Intolerable Acts scared them, angered them, impoverished them, and ultimately forced them to choose a side. A few wealthy conservatives remained loyal to the Crown, but nearly everyone else rallied around the Sons of Liberty.

Elsewhere, the reaction was much the same. Lord North had thought that disciplining radical Massachusetts would isolate it from the other colonies, but this wasn't so, and his policy instead drew the colonies closer together.

As during the Stamp Act crisis, an intercolonial meeting was held in September 1774. Calling themselves the Continental Congress, fifty-six delegates from twelve colonies (all but Georgia) met at Carpenter's Hall in Philadelphia to discuss what common action they might take in response to the Intolerable Acts. Although some conservative delegates initially hoped to persuade Massachusetts to repay the East India Company, all soon realized that appeasement was no longer a workable course. Seven weeks of often-heated debate followed, at the end of which the delegates approved a set of resolves demanding, among other things, the repeal of the Intolerable Acts and the recall of British troops posted to Boston. To back up these demands, a boycott of British goods was resumed. Finally, the delegates agreed to reconvene the following spring if Parliament hadn't complied.

Parliament responded to the Boston Tea Party *by passing the punitive Intolerable Acts, the colonial response to which was debated at the First Continental Congress.*

XII. PUBLIC-KEY ENCRYPTION

IN ADDITION TO CODES that enable transmission, save space, and correct errors, there are also computer codes designed to conceal. Without such codes, many of the most popular Internet uses, especially commerce, wouldn't be possible. All of these codes, known as encryption systems, are based on a breakthrough made during the 1970s called public-key encryption.

Letter-substitution codes, while easy to use, are also easy to break. So encoding your credit card number using ASCII won't protect it. There are sophisticated codes available that are nearly impossible to crack; and if you use one of these, no doubt your credit card number can be transmitted safely. But would the person receiving your transmission know how to decode it? If you were sending the number to your mother, to whom you had previously entrusted the key, there might not be a problem. But what if you need to send your credit card number to the server at Amazon.com, which doesn't have your key?

This problem was solved in 1977 by Ronald Rivest, Adi Shamir, and Leonard Adleman, who invented the first practical public-key encryption system (known as the RSA method for the first letters of each of their last names). The essential feature of public-key encryption is that the encoding and decoding keys are separate and kept apart. Otherwise, knowledge of how to encode a message would enable a clever code breaker to determine (through reverse engineering) how to decode a message. Consequently, the encoding key can be disclosed publicly (so you can order from Amazon.com) without compromising the secrecy of the decoding key.

The separation of encoding and decoding keys is accomplished in a highly complex way that involves a great deal of advanced mathematics (which is why it took mathematicians a few thousand years to develop). The basic principle, however, is that the encoding is done using "noninvertible," or "one-way," functions that can't be reversed. As a result, knowing the encoding instructions doesn't help at all with the decoding.

Here's how public-key encryption works in practice: When you place an order with Amazon, your web browser obtains from the Amazon website Amazon's public key, which your browser uses to encode your order. By keeping the decoding key secure, Amazon ensures that no one but Amazon will be able to decode your order. (You won't be able to decode it, either; but you already know what it says because you wrote it.)

The essential feature of public-key encryption *is that the encoding key remains separate from the decoding key, and thus the encoding instructions don't reveal the decoding process.*

XII. THE OLDER AMERICAN ARTISTS

ALTHOUGH ONE WOULDN'T KNOW it from the reviews, which focused everyone's attention on the European modernists, more than half of the artists on display at the Armory Show were Americans. A large number, not surprisingly, were older, established artists associated with Robert Henri and the Ashcan School, whose realism may have seemed cutting edge in America but was already old news in Europe. Even though most visitors to the Armory Show didn't know this before they arrived, the historical arrangement of styles in the galleries of the European section made the datedness of realism obvious to all. When viewed in the company of works by the European modernists, even the socially and politically powerful paintings of John Sloan seemed tame and provincial in comparison.

The biggest difference between the American realists and their European peers was the continuing American belief in narrative representational art—that is, pictures with a *meaning*—as opposed to nonrepresentational art, which most Americans considered merely "decorative" (a pejorative term in this sense). Although some of the American realists who participated in the Armory Show—Sloan, Eugene Higgins, Jerome Myers, and George Bellows— would go on to have significant artistic impact during the 1930s, in 1913 their work seemed hopelessly out of touch.

Maurice Prendergast, another established artist, was one of the few American post-impressionists on display at the show. Prendergast had studied in Paris during the mid- 1880s, when post-impressionism was just beginning to take hold, and his

Maurice Prendergast, *Landscape with Figures* (1913)

exposure to the developing movement profoundly affected his own work. Although a member of The Eight, he had little in common stylistically with the realist members of the group. Specifically, he approached a painting as a flat surface to be covered with contrasting patches of luminous color. As in a mosaic, these tiny patches combined to create larger forms. As Prendergast matured, his canvases—such as *Landscape with Figures*, which hung in Gallery C of the Armory Show—became even more flattened and abstract in the manner of European artists such as Georges Seurat.

The work of older, established American artists *was well represented at the Armory Show but seemed provincial and dated in comparison with the works of the European modernists.*

XII. SEXUALITY

FROM THE START, Freud's work aroused controversy because of its strong emphasis on instincts, drives, and especially sexuality. For example, his initial seduction theory held that hysterics suffered from repressed memories of sexual feelings and/or encounters experienced too early in childhood to be processed properly, if at all. It was this emphasis on the sexual etiology of hysteria, in fact, that led to Freud's break with Breuer in 1895.

Later, after giving up his seduction theory, Freud came to believe that hysterics were imagining many of the traumatic memories they reported because they suffered from a repression of their natural drive energies, which manifested as physical symptoms. Eventually, Freud came to the conclusion that such repression was at the source of most neuroses. More generally, he believed that the expression of sexuality and aggression and the redirection of these drives toward more personally useful goals (a process that he called sublimation) played an integral role in human development and was part of the human condition.

Freud was especially interested in the ways that sexuality, a biologically based drive, was shaped and thwarted by civilization. Being one himself, Freud was well aware that Victorians weren't allowed to act on, or even freely express, their sexual desires. The public display of bodily pleasure was forbidden, and even feelings of love for a mother or father were constrained.

The central emotional event in every child's life, according to Freud, takes place sometime between the ages three and a half and four, when the child experiences a strong desire (not genital but nevertheless impassioned) for his or her opposite-sex parent. The expression of this desire can be as simple as the statement *When I grow up, I'm going to marry Daddy*. Amused adults usually take such wishes in stride, but children soon learn, to their dismay, that social norms exist to thwart these desires. The way that children resolve—or fail to resolve—their longings has, Freud wrote, a powerful influence on their future adult relationships.

Freud described this dynamic, which he believed to be universal, as Oedipal and the time frame in which it occurred as the Oedipal period. The struggle that takes place during the Oedipal period between the powerful wishes of the individual and the prohibitions of society has, Freud wrote, a lifelong impact on the ways that people experience jealousy, intimacy, and other aspects of interpersonal relationships.

Freud believed that sexual repression was *part of the human condition, and he studied closely the ways in which civilization thwarted and redirected sexual and other instinctual energies.*

XII. THE SUFFERING OF KING LEAR

KING LEAR, SHAKESPEARE'S BLEAKEST TRAGEDY, tells the story of an aging English monarch who plans to divide his realm among his three daughters. Unfortunately, the divestment ceremony goes grievously wrong when Lear's most beloved daughter, Cordelia, inexplicably refuses to give him the declaration of love he demands. This causes Lear to banish her, leaving him at the mercy of his two despicable daughters, Regan and Goneril.

Meanwhile, a subplot unfolds involving the earl of Gloucester; his legitimate son, Edgar; and his bastard son, Edmund. Jealous of Edgar, Edmund plots successfully to have his half brother disinherited and condemned as a criminal. Disguising himself as a mad beggar, Edgar escapes but finds himself homeless—which is also now the state of Lear, who has been cast out by his daughters.

When Gloucester attempts to help Lear, Regan's husband puts his eyes out. Later, Lear wanders exposed on a heath during a terrible rainstorm, losing his mind but then regaining his wits when he is rescued by Cordelia, who has returned at the head of a French army.

Yet just when a happy ending seems possible, Cordelia's army is defeated by forces under Edmund, who secretly orders the execution of both Cordelia and Lear. The still-disguised Edgar then challenges Edmund to single combat and wounds him mortally, at which point Edmund reveals what he has done, once again presenting the possibility of recovery. However, before Edmund's order can be reversed, Cordelia is murdered, and Lear dies of a broken heart.

It's difficult not to dwell on the unmitigated suffering in *King Lear*, which depicts not only the collapse of families but also the disintegration of society in general. Not surprisingly, the characters in the play often debate the role of the gods and the possibility of human justice. One of the starkest assessments comes from Gloucester, who says, "As flies to wanton boys are we to th' gods; / They kill us for their sport." Edgar attempts to rebut his father's pessimism, declaring, "The gods are just, and of our pleasant vices / Make instruments to plague us." But the play's brutal ending, following upon so much false hope, hardly confirms Edgar's viewpoint. The bad characters are punished, but so are the good. Lear and Gloucester, who suffer excessively, are at least guilty of pride and moral blindness, but what of Cordelia? Because she is blameless, her death contradicts the divine economy of justice that Edgar proffers.

King Lear presents a world characterized by suffering *that is excessive, senseless, and absurd.*

XIII. THE MILITARY OCCUPATION OF BOSTON

Thomas Gage in a 1768 portrait.

DURING THE COURSE of its deliberations, the First Continental Congress often discussed the volatile situation in Massachusetts. In May 1774, a new military governor, Thomas Gage, had replaced the civilian governor, Thomas Hutchinson. Gage's job was to enforce the Boston Port Act, and he was supported by the deployment of four thousand British troops to Boston.

From the Crown's point of view, Gage was the perfect man for the job. He had nearly twenty years' military experience in the colonies and saw the situation clearly. In 1770, Gage had written, "America is a mere bully, from one end to the other, and the Bostonians by far the greatest bullies." But Gage's first year as governor sobered him considerably. He had sufficient troops to occupy Boston but not nearly enough to control the countryside, which was highly aroused.

Realizing that warfare was probably imminent, local militias began purging Tories from their ranks and forming special units that drilled two or three times a week. Trained to be ready at a moment's notice, these companies were known as minutemen. (The British soldiers, who dressed in fashionable red uniforms, were known as redcoats or lobsterbacks.)

Because Gage was committed to force, he began searching out and confiscating patriot armaments. Meanwhile, his superiors in London, refusing to accept that the colonies were turning against them, subscribed to a bad-apple theory. At the heart of the problem, they believed, were agitators such as Samuel Adams and John Hancock. Adams, of course, had long been America's most inspiring and effective radical, while Hancock, a wealthy Boston merchant (and likely a smuggler), was known to be a chief source of patriot funds. In late January 1775, Lord Dartmouth, the secretary of state for the colonies, wrote to Gage ordering him to arrest the "principal actors and abettors," believing this would pacify the populace.

By then, neither Adams nor Hancock was living in Boston. Gage had made the city too hot for them, so both had relocated to the countryside. Nevertheless, there were still plenty of Sons of Liberty in Boston to keep a close watch on the comings and goings of Gage's men. The general's soldiers repeatedly mounted raids, hoping to locate caches of militia weaponry, but the patriots' early-warning system ensured that few of these were successful.

Once Gage and his four thousand troops *moved into Boston, the British became irrevocably committed to a policy of government through force.*

XIII. BACKBONE AND LAST-MILE CARRIERS

IN SOME WAYS, the Internet operates like a highway system. Analogous to the interstates are the trunk lines that large corporations, known as backbone carriers, build and maintain. Connecting to these fiber-optic interstates are the smaller local roads that are the ISPs. The ISPs, which are also known as last-mile carriers, collect the data traffic generated by individual users and funnel it into the backbone system.

All of the big telephone and cable television companies have become Internet carriers. Some specialize in backbone connections, some in last-mile connections, and many in both. In some ways, the big investments they make give them near-monopoly control over the course of Internet development. For this reason, they remain subject to government regulation, especially with regard to "net neutrality." According to this principle, Internet carriers that are paid to transmit data shouldn't be tampering with the flow of that data in any way, either to expedite some transmissions or to impede others. The fear is that a large backbone carrier also in the business of providing cable television service might degrade the video feeds being sent to its Internet customers by one of its corporate rivals. (The purpose for doing so would be to persuade potential cable television customers not to patronize online sources of movies and television.)

In recent years, these larger players have bought up nearly all of the small companies that once provided last-mile connections. At the same time, however, a number of small companies have been entering the carrier business as wireless service providers (WISPs). The capital investment required to establish wireless service is much less than that required to build a wired network, so WISPs have found a market niche bringing high-speed Internet access to poorly served communities in remote or sparsely populated areas.

Last-mile carriers such as ISPs and WISPs are basically resellers of Internet connectivity. They buy connectivity at wholesale prices from backbone carriers and sell it to individual users at a higher retail price. Until recently, the nominal capacity that an ISP sold to its users was typically twenty or more times greater than the capacity it purchased wholesale. ISPs could do this because their customers tended to use the Internet moderately and intermittently. However, as people continue to access bigger and bigger files containing movies and television shows, the last-mile business model will have to change.

Issues of competition, monopoly power, fairness, and government regulation are probably inherent in the structure of the privately funded Internet, and thus will probably be recurring subjects of debate and struggle.

Backbone carriers build and maintain *the trunk lines of the Internet, while last-mile carriers (the ISPs) provide backbone connectivity to individual users.*

XIII. THE YOUNGER AMERICAN ARTISTS

WHILE THE OLDER GENERATION of American artists seemed largely out of touch at the Armory Show, this wasn't true of the younger generation, many of whose members had recently been students in Europe. Marsden Hartley, Arthur Dove, John Marin, and Alfred Mauer had already taken part in Alfred Stieglitz's 1910 group show at 291, and they were joined now by other young Americans, including Charles Sheeler, Morton Schamberg, Samuel Halpert, and Oscar Bluemner. Although these young artists were little known at the time, even in New York City, their Armory Show work evidenced a sophisticated understanding of post-impressionism, cubism, and fauvism. Even so, few of the European-obsessed critics bothered to notice.

Viewers who took the time, however, could see in the paintings of Schamberg, Mauer, and Bluemner the influence of both Cézanne and Matisse. For Schamberg, in particular, a 1910 trip to Paris had proved transformative, directing his work away from what he had learned at the Pennsylvania Academy of the Fine Arts and moving him toward nonrepresentational form. In an interview that he gave just prior to the Armory Show, Schamberg asserted, "It is not the business of the artist to imitate or represent nature. Art is creative, or rather, interpretive…[It] has only to do with sensuous pleasure—that which is pleasurable to the sense of vision." Although Schamberg and his friend Sheeler were once protégés of impressionist William Merritt Chase, when they began moving toward abstraction, the dismayed Chase stopped speaking with them.

Another former student of Chase who took part in the Armory Show was Patrick Henry Bruce. After traveling to Paris in 1904, Bruce was so taken with

Alfred Maurer, *Woman with a Blue Background* (1907)

the French capital that he decided to remain there. By 1907, his work had already turned decidedly modernist; and the following year, he began studying with Matisse, completing his transition from representation to abstraction. Referring to Bruce's four canvases in the Armory Show, Samuel Halpert observed that Bruce was "the only American painter considered [i.e., acknowledged] by French artists."

Most critics were too obsessed *with Matisse and Duchamp to notice that the Armory Show also presented works by young American artists well schooled in European ways.*

XIII. THE IMPACT OF WAR

ONCE WORLD WAR I BEGAN in August 1914, Freud wrote very little, but the little that he did write showed clearly the impact that the war was having on his thinking. Freud's letters to friends and relations from this period often express his frustration with the international situation as they describe his family's struggle to endure wartime hardships. Freud was particularly worried about two of his sons who spent most of the war on the front lines. Meanwhile, in Vienna, the Freud family, like nearly everyone else, found it difficult to obtain food, coal for heating, and even writing paper. According to his daughter Anna, Freud once asked a journal for whom he had written an article to pay him in potatoes instead of cash.

Beyond the fighting, flu epidemics also took many lives, both during the war and immediately afterward, among populations weakened by cold and malnutrition. In 1920, Freud's daughter Sophie, who was living in Hamburg with her husband and two young children, perished in such an epidemic. Her death devastated both Freud and his wife, but they weren't able to attend her funeral because there was no train service then between Vienna and the German coast.

Freud with daughter Sophie.

The first of two important papers that Freud wrote during these years appeared in 1915. "On Narcissism" described the means by which libido (the psychic energy integral to sexual drive) could turn inward and foster self-absorption. The resulting condition, narcissism, made the establishment of satisfying relationships with other people nearly impossible and often produced defensiveness and aggression. Freud's underlying motivation in writing this paper was clearly to explain a psychological dynamic that could cause people to become destructive and engage in warfare.

Two years later, he published "Mourning and Melancholia," a very personal work in which he explored the idea that the process of mourning can also turn inward so that "the shadow of the [lost] object falls upon the ego." The resulting melancholia— a condition characterized by negativity, self-hatred, and despair—is essentially mourning gone wrong. Freud believed that for proper mourning to take place, mourners must completely let go of the person (or situation) they have lost. If they don't, their anger at the loss can become internalized, leading to negative feelings about aspects of themselves that can close them off to life and hamper future relationships.

The worry and hardship that preoccupied Freud (and the rest of Europe) *during World War I found expression in two famous papers, "On Narcissism" and "Mourning and Melancholia."*

XIII. LOVE, LOYALTY, AND SYMPATHY IN KING LEAR

OFFERING LITTLE CONSOLATION, *King Lear* tests the endurance of its characters and its audience. Indeed, many have found the play too excruciating to bear. There is no sense that society, having purged itself of evil, will now flourish, nor are we left with the impression that Lear and Cordelia are passing on to a heavenly afterlife.

On the other hand, the play does offer the possibility of human virtue. Cordelia and Edgar, for example, never waver in their love for their fathers; and Lear and Gloucester, who are both guilty of withdrawing their love from loyal children (and suffer extremely for it), nevertheless come to a new self-knowledge through their suffering.

Encountering each other on the cliffs at Dover, the blinded Gloucester and the still-mad Lear discuss the relationship between sight in the optical sense and sight in the sense of insight. Previously, Gloucester has condemned the rich man who "will not see because he does not feel," suggesting that suffering and enlightenment are linked. Now, at Dover, Lear observes that, even without eyes, Gloucester can nevertheless "see how this world goes." "I see it feelingly," Gloucester replies, meaning that he perceives the world through a sympathetic act of understanding.

Both powerful men now humbled by circumstance, Lear and Gloucester are forced to recognize that the trappings of wealth and prestige are contingent—a realization that inspires in them an urgent sense of social injustice. Lear, for example, castigates himself for failing to protect the poor: "Take physic, pomp; / Expose thyself to feel what wretches feel." His exposure to the storm is the "physic," or medicine, that cures him of his arrogance and reminds him of the frail humanity that he shares with the wretched of the world. Indeed, when the once proud and peremptory Lear is reunited with Cordelia, he declares, "I am a very foolish fond old man."

Returning to his senses, Lear recognizes that Cordelia is his daughter and also that she has moral worth. More than enough reason exists for her to despise her father, and yet she denies this—"No cause, no cause"—indicating that her love for Lear transcends the mechanical logic of cause and effect. Just as the hard hearts of her sisters remain a painful mystery, so the durability of Cordelia's love defies explanation. The fact that it exists at all mitigates the terrible cruelty that otherwise dominates the world of the play.

Although *King Lear* offers little consolation *of the usual sort, the play does mitigate its oppressive cruelty with the possibility of human love, loyalty, and sympathy.*

XIV. PAUL REVERE'S RIDE

BY THE SPRING OF 1775, Gage was under considerable pressure to pacify Boston so that trade could be resumed. In early April, one of his intelligence officers learned that a large cache of munitions was being maintained in Concord, eighteen miles away. Gage decided to seize it; but knowing that a single misstep could set off a shooting war, he moved cautiously. First, he relieved elite light infantry and grenadier units of garrison duty; then he secretly re-formed them into a strike force of 750 men under Lt. Col. Francis Smith. On the night of April 18, under cover of darkness, Smith's battalion set off by longboat across the Charles River, headed for Concord.

Gage was counting on the element of surprise, but patriots in Boston had noticed immediately the change in unit routine. In fact, on April 15, their leader, Dr. Joseph Warren, had sent silversmith Paul Revere to warn Adams and Hancock, then holed up in Lexington. On his return, Revere had paused in Charlestown— where, according to his own report, he "agreed with a Colonel Conant…that if the British went out by water, we [in Boston] would show two lanterns in the North Church Steeple; and if by land, one as a signal."

Paul Revere in a 1768 potrait by John Singleton Copley.

About ten o'clock on the night of April 18, after Smith's men were seen marching down to the common, Warren again called for Revere. The doctor had already sent William Dawes to warn Lexington and Concord by the overland route across Boston Neck. Now he dispatched Revere by the quicker "sea" route, which the British themselves were taking. Pausing only long enough to arrange for two lanterns to be hung in the North Church steeple, Revere hastily set out across the Charles River with two oarsmen.

Reaching the Charlestown side about eleven o'clock, he was met there by several patriots who had seen the North Church signal. They gave him a fast horse, and he immediately raced away, alarming the local minutemen as he went.

It was nearly midnight when a breathless Revere reached the home of the Rev. Jonas Clarke in Lexington, where Adams and Hancock were lodging. As the story goes, one of the men guarding the house told Revere to keep quiet lest his noise wake those sleeping inside, but Revere couldn't be contained. "Noise!" he thundered. "You'll have noise enough before long. The regulars are coming out!"

Although Gage attempted to conceal the raid *that he was planning, patriots in Boston noticed the change in military routine and sent warnings to Lexington and Concord.*

XIV. PROBLEMS

ONE OF THE DEFINING CHARACTERISTICS of the Internet is that its growth, like its use, has been unmanaged. This lack of foresight has produced some pleasant surprises but also many unhappy ones. For example, consider the growing scarcity of certain Internet resources. In addition to the shrinking availability of domain names, IP addresses are running out. Because they consist of four parts, each with 256 possible values, there are more than four billion possible IP addresses. This sounds like a sufficiently large number until one realizes that it's two billion less than the current world population. The next system, which will feature IP addresses made up of eight parts, has already been designed, but many people believe that it won't be implemented soon enough because not enough thought has been put into a workable transition strategy.

Another problem that has recently developed—again, largely because of unmanaged growth—involves capacity of a different sort. Many of the newest Internet applications involve real-time interaction. The most popular of these include "streaming" video (watching television in real time), Internet phone service (talking back and forth in real time), and remote control protocols (turning on house lights or panning a webcam in real time).

Because the Internet wasn't designed to support real-time responsiveness, it doesn't do it very well. The problem isn't just bandwidth, which refers to the amount of data that can flow at one time through a given connection. Other aspects of the problem include IP, which permits the dropping of data packets. Because retransmission soon follows, this quirk doesn't materially affect your email service, but it does make watching a movie online difficult. To support real-time applications properly, the Internet needs both higher-quality equipment and more sophisticated protocols.

Still other problems derive from the natural inclination of large companies to resist jointly devised standards. Because of their hefty market shares, large companies tend to believe that they can do whatever they want, and generally they can. (The history of Microsoft is a case in point.) As the company's idiosyncratic ways become increasingly the de facto industry standard, it has plenty of incentive to crush other potential standards, whatever their merits may be, because all represent threats to its market share. If the company's proprietary methods do become the industry standard, then it can thwart all competitors simply by invoking its patent rights or using obfuscation to ensure that only its products function properly within the new environment it has set.

The unmanaged growth *of the Internet has produced problems relating to limited capacity, vanishing resources, and poorly devised standards.*

XIV. WOMEN AT THE ARMORY SHOW

BOTH THEN AND NOW, most accounts of the Armory Show focus on the men who were involved: the male AAPS officers who put on the show, the male artists whose paintings were displayed, the male critics who voiced their opinions, and the male collectors who bought the works. The truth is, however, that many important women also took part in the show as patrons, critics, and artists. For instance, of the three hundred artists whose work was exhibited, nearly fifty were women.

Among the American paintings in Gallery D were several by Marguerite Zorach and Kathleen McEnery, both of whom exhibited a fearless dedication to modernism in art. More so than their male colleagues, these women had to be courageous, because American social sensibilities were still highly Victorian, and women had much more to fear from being called degenerate.

Marguerite Zorach,
Man Among the Redwoods (1912)

In 1908, after studying for a time with Robert Henri, McEnery moved to Paris, where she became influenced by the work of Cézanne. Her two Armory Show paintings were both female nudes, a subject still considered daring for a woman painter in 1913. Zorach, who also studied abroad, was taught by the Fauve-inspired British painter John Duncan Fergusson to compose like Matisse—taking a nonrepresentational approach to figure and using bold colors, unmixed, straight out of the tube. Zorach's Armory Show entries included an untitled figure study that became one of the few American works to draw a critical rebuke. According to the *New York American*, "The pale yellow eyes and the purple lips of her subject indicate that the digestive organs are not functioning properly."

Women were also among the leading patrons at the Armory Show. Some participated as lenders—including Katherine Dreier, Sarah Sears, and Gertrude Stein—and others took part as buyers. Lillie P. Bliss, one of the most important collectors at the exhibition, bought two paintings and eighteen prints. Meanwhile, Eliza G. Radeke, president of the Rhode Island School of Design, purchased a Matisse drawing and two watercolors by French post-impressionist Paul Signac. Radeke's purchases were especially significant because, as the head of a prestigious art school, she had to consider the consequences of breaking ranks with the rest of the American academic establishment.

Although the men involved in the Armory Show *received nearly all of the attention, a number of important women also took part as artists and patrons.*

XIV. BEYOND THE PLEASURE PRINCIPLE

AFTER WORLD WAR I, like many other Europeans, Freud tried to come to terms with what he had seen. The mass destruction and relentless killing had disturbed all of Western society, but to Freud these horrors posed an additional and specific problem. The highly aggressive and harmful ways in which individuals and entire nations had behaved challenged Freud's existing theories about human motivation. Previously, he had hypothesized that humans were primarily motivated by the "pleasure principle," or the desire to seek gratification while avoiding pain and deprivation. (The reality principle, by contrast, explained why mature adults could defer gratification and endure pain if the situation warranted.) But the pleasure principle alone clearly wasn't sufficient to explain all that had happened during the war.

By 1920, Freud had been working as a clinician for more than thirty years; and during that time, he had come across many patients who had felt compelled to repeat painful, often self-destructive patterns in their lives. For example, patients in abusive relationships might manage to leave those relationships, only to find themselves sometime later caught up in similar dynamics with entirely different people. Another example would be the dreams of a traumatized person, in which the same frightening experience is relived over and over.

The human condition, Freud knew well, was replete with examples of these "repetition compulsions." He also knew that, in such cases, his technique of making the unconscious conscious had little effect, because the patients were already aware of the patterns and their causes.

In *Beyond the Pleasure Principle* (1920), Freud presented a revised and extended theory of mind based in part on his experience of World War I and in part on his accumulated clinical experience. He now proposed two opposing instincts, which existed at odds with each other in the human psyche. The first, Eros, was the life instinct. The second, Thanatos, was the death instinct. Unlike Eros—which encouraged survival, creativity, and sexuality and found its expression in the pleasure principle—Thanatos relentlessly pulled the individual toward aggression and destructiveness. Within each person's psyche, the struggle between these two instincts was continuous and unending.

Freud's new dualistic view of the mind—and of life itself—accounted for repetition compulsions by associating them with the darker, disorganizing death instinct. Trauma, whether experienced in childhood or later in life, empowered Thanatos and enabled it to prevail over Eros, with unfortunate consequences for the traumatized individual.

In ***Beyond the Pleasure Principle***, *Freud attempted to explain why individuals return again and again to the same painful experiences and patterns of behavior.*

XIV. MACBETH

WHAT MAKES THE CHARACTER MACBETH distinctive is his knowing choice of evil. What makes the play *Macbeth* distinctive is that, even though its hero has chosen evil, the audience never entirely loses sympathy for him.

As the play begins, Macbeth, a loyal subject of King Duncan, returns to court after successfully defending Scotland against rebellion and invasion. Along the way, he and his companion Banquo meet three weird sisters who predict that Macbeth will become king and Banquo the progenitor of kings. Macbeth is stunned, but quickly his mind turns to the horrible possibility of murdering Duncan. He temporarily rejects the idea but then is persuaded by his wife to commit regicide and cast the blame on Duncan's two sons, Malcolm and Donalbain. The deed is done, the implicated princes confirm their "guilt" by fleeing, and Macbeth assumes the throne.

Macbeth encounters the weird sisters in an illustration from Shakespeare's principal source for the play.

Macbeth thus returns to the challenge of *Richard III*: the depiction of a mind given over to criminality. But while Richard doesn't experience the pangs of guilt until the night before his death (and then only briefly), Macbeth is immediately tortured by his conscience. Admittedly, he becomes even more brutal in his attempt to preserve the crown that has cost him so dearly, but he never loses sight of what his actions have cost him in human terms. His mind becomes "full of scorpions," and his life no better than "a fitful fever."

But even as Macbeth reveals an astounding capacity for criminal violence, he also shows himself capable of stunning poetry. As A. C. Bradley has written, "This bold ambitious man of action has, within certain limits, the imagination of a poet." Macbeth's imaginative ability, along with his remarkable facility with words, are what guarantee him his hold upon the audience.

However one assesses the role played by Lady Macbeth in persuading her husband to act, it is clear that Macbeth loves her dearly and that hers is the society that matters most to him. She is his "dearest partner of greatness;" and when she dies, his world loses its meaning, becoming "a tale told by an idiot, full of sound and fury, signifying nothing." Yet Macbeth is resolute. Abandoned by his followers, assailed by the forces of Malcolm, his grand ambitions shattered, Macbeth refuses to yield. Although we understand that he must die, we cannot help but admire his heroism, perverse though it may be.

Macbeth's criminality makes him an unlikely object *of sympathy, yet his stunning poetry ensures that he never entirely loses his hold on the audience.*

XV. THE SHOT HEARD 'ROUND THE WORLD

SMITH'S CONCORD-BOUND BATTALION landed in a marsh, which slowed its advance. Upon reaching dry land, it tarried further in a futile effort to dry off. As a result, Maj. John Pitcairn's advance party didn't reach Lexington until dawn on April 19. Waiting there were about seventy minutemen under Capt. John Parker. More defiant than threatening, Parker's men stood by the side of the road in homespun breeches as Pitcairn's nattily dressed column approached. The redcoats could have simply marched past, but Pitcairn stopped and ordered the minutemen to disperse. A shot was fired. (No one knows by whom; each side later blamed the other.) Pitcairn's men responded with a fusillade.

Amos Doolittle's 1775 engraving of the battle of Lexington.

The fighting was over within minutes, as the outgunned patriots withdrew. But in that time, eight Americans were killed and ten wounded, while one redcoat was injured. Not far away, Adams and Hancock were leaving Lexington in a coach when they heard the gunfire. Realizing its significance, Adams proclaimed, "What a glorious morning for America!"

The British continued on to Concord, where they discovered that the arms cache had been moved. Smith ordered a house-by-house search. Meanwhile, having received intelligence that additional stores were hidden at a farm north of town, he sent a detachment across the North Bridge to find and destroy them. A little later, militiamen, aware of what had happened in Lexington, attacked the soldiers left behind to guard the bridge. Three redcoats died in the skirmish—the first British fatalities of the Revolutionary War.

During the next two hours, Smith regrouped his command, attended to the dead and wounded, and prepared to return to Boston. All the way back to Lexington, however, his troops were harassed by hundreds of militiamen hiding along the road behind buildings, stone walls, fences, and trees. Flanking parties generally kept these snipers at a comfortable distance; but when the road narrowed, forcing in the British flanks, the Americans were able to pick off several score of the easily visible redcoats.

About 2:30 PM, with the ranks of the minutemen increasing rapidly, Smith reached Lexington. There, he was joined by a thousand reinforcements under Hugh, Lord Percy; but even with these reinforcements, the British were still outnumbered by about two to one. Had Percy not brought some cannon with him, he and Smith might not have made it back to Boston.

On their way to Concord, *the British passed through Lexington, where they needlessly engaged about seventy defiant but unthreatening minutemen.*

XV. INTERNET SECURITY

A COROLLARY TO THE INTERNET'S history of unmanaged growth is its damn-the-torpedoes attitude toward security issues. In the rush to expand, those who have built the Internet have left open many doors through which evildoers can exploit users for fun and profit. In general, there are two categories of Internet security issues: those relating to the Internet itself and those relating to the vulnerabilities of personal computers connected to the Internet.

Among the first category, the most prevalent crime is fraud, and the most prevalent fraud is phishing. Phishing is the attempt to acquire sensitive information (such as bank account data) by tricking users into believing that they are revealing the information to a legitimate entity (such as the bank holding the account). Phishing attacks typically arrive in emails directing the user to a website via a hyperlink. The body of the email attempts to persuade the user to click the link, often by informing the user that there is an urgent problem with his account. The problem seems plausible, and the hyperlink does say *First National Bank*, but the link doesn't take the user to the real First National Bank website. Rather, it takes him to a "spoofed" First National Bank site (that is, a facsimile of the real site created by, and controlled by, the phisher). Using account numbers and passwords obtained in this way, the phisher can commit lucrative identity fraud.

The most common attacks directed against personal computers are viruses. Before Internet access became widespread, viruses could enter your computer only through floppy disks or your local network. Now that systems are much more interconnected, your computer's vulnerability to virus attack is exponentially greater. This is because viruses, once installed, can use your computer's resources to send copies of themselves to other users (such as everyone in your email address book) and infect their computers as well.

An interesting and surprisingly common form of virus attack takes place when a "worm" (or some other piece of intrusive, pernicious software) gains entry into your computer and commandeers it. A group of computers controlled in this way is called a botnet (short for "robot network"). Botnets are often used to initiate mass mailings of spam because the spam is traceable only to the compromised computers. Cleverly designed botnets create so little activity on compromised systems that usually they go unnoticed.

Internet security issues fall into two categories: *those that relate to the Internet itself (such as phishing) and those that exploit the vulnerabilities of personal computers (such as viruses).*

XV. THE CRITICAL RESPONSE

THE BATTLE WAS JOINED as early as November 1912, when articles began appearing both for and against the modernist works that would soon be exhibited in the Armory Show. Everyone wanted to stir up the public: The AAPS organizers knew that scandal would boost attendance; the academicians who opposed modernism thought that, if they could persuade people that modernist art was aberrant, no one would attend; and the newspapers wanted to sell more newspapers.

All told, the sensational coverage drew more than seventy thousand visitors to the Armory Show, and the European modernist galleries were always filled with people tutting and gaping. One day, opera star Enrico Caruso added to the circus atmosphere by drawing caricatures of the modernist paintings on postcards and handing them out to delighted passersby.

A commentary on the press response to the Armory Show.

For as long as the show lasted, the pages of daily newspapers in New York City and elsewhere were filled with reports from the armory; and even after the show moved to Chicago, the drumbeat continued. The newspapers published inflamed diatribes, caricatures, jokes, and doggerel of varying degrees of quality and creativity. In order to encourage as much ridicule as possible, artists associated with the National Academy mounted spoof exhibitions, such as the Post-Mortem Exhibition, which was advertised to contain works by "the Neurotic, Psychotic, and Paretic Schools." All of this the press covered gleefully.

A good deal of serious art criticism was also published, of course; but these efforts were limited by the lack of a suitable aesthetic vocabulary to describe the new art. One critic attempting to describe Duchamp's *Nude* wrote that it looked like a "dynamited suit of armor." Another called it an "academic painting of an artichoke." A third famously described it as "an explosion in a shingle factory." These responses all reflected an inability to see the work on its own terms, without reference to objects or ideas present in the natural world.

Forward-looking critics such as Harriet Monroe and D. W. MacCall tended to refrain from commenting on the social aspects of cubism and fauvism and whether these styles might have a negative effect on the viewing public. Instead, they tried to focus attention on the art *as art*, without the use of analogies or comparisons. These efforts, although often lost in the sensationalism, had a significant effect on the development of modern art criticism.

While most critics and commentators sensationalized what they saw *on the walls of the armory, a few worked hard to develop a new aesthetic vocabulary that could explain modernism.*

XV. THE EGO AND THE ID

IT WAS IN THE FINAL CHAPTERS of *The Interpretation of Dreams* that Freud first articulated his "topographic theory of mind." According to this theory, the mind was like an iceberg. The part that was visible above the waterline was the conscious mind. Below this was a thin layer called the preconscious, which functioned as an interface for the retrieval of thoughts and memories. Beneath the surface, however, inaccessible to the individual, lay the far greater domain of the unconscious mind, populated with repressed instinctual drives and conflicted thoughts and feelings.

As Freud's ideas about the mind deepened, however, he became aware of a number of problems with his topographic theory. It didn't describe, for example, the way that the conscious mind and the unconscious mind work together in the process of repression; nor did it explain how forbidden impulses and disturbing feelings are identified before they become conscious. The implication was that some unconscious process must also be taking place.

In a small but important book titled *The Ego and the Id* (1923), Freud advanced a new, more complex hypothesis that came to be known as his structural theory. The structure of mind to which this name refers was made up of three components: the id, the ego, and the superego. The id, according to Freud, is the part of the mind where the individual's instincts and drive energies are located. The superego, often in conflict with the id, is where the social mores that a person internalizes during childhood reside. (The superego thus functions as a conscience.) The ego mediates between the id and the superego—that is, between instinctual drives and social realities—while orienting the individual to reality and maintaining good relations with the external world.

It is the ego's job to keep conflicts between the id and the superego unconscious, where they won't threaten a person's equanimity. The ego does this, in part, by keeping the id in check while sufficiently satisfying its drive energies so that they don't cause problems (such as hysteric symptoms or destructive behavior). The ego also acts as a reality tester and as an editor, screening difficult memories and feelings from the conscious mind.

All three of these components—id, ego, and superego—develop together during childhood, with the child's specific experiences, relationships, and social world determining their eventual makeup and relation to one another. Thus, uncovering the early history of the individual became an even more important aspect of successful analysis.

Freud's structural theory posited an id, where drive energies *are located; a superego, where social mores reside; and an ego, which negotiates between the other two parts of the mind.*

XV. ANTONY AND CLEOPATRA

THE SUFFERING PORTRAYED IN *Antony and Cleopatra* is certainly pitiful but not nearly of the same magnitude as that found in the four major tragedies. Taking place during the historical period immediately following the death of Julius Caesar, the action of the play is lightened considerably by the dignity and grandeur of the title characters.

Like *Romeo and Juliet*, *Antony and Cleopatra* tells the story of two ill-fated lovers. Unlike Romeo and Juliet, however, Antony and Cleopatra are conspicuously mature. Romeo knows nothing but youthful spontaneity, whereas Antony is a "triple pillar of the world," one-third of the triumvirate that rules Rome. He is accomplished and experienced yet abandons his prudence to follow his heart. Cleopatra, meanwhile, embodies an allure that far surpasses even the considerable charms of Juliet. According to Antony's lieutenant, Enobarbus, "Age cannot wither her, nor custom stale her infinite variety."

As the play opens, Antony is recalled from Egypt by news of civil war in Rome and the death of his wife. Back in Italy, he secures his political alliance with Octavius Caesar by agreeing to marry his sister. Unfortunately, Octavia is of "a holy, cold, and still conversation"—the very opposite of the mercurial and erotic Cleopatra. Unable to resist his feelings for the Egyptian queen, Antony abandons his new wife and returns to Egypt, where the two lovers deliberately reject the pragmatic and make a doomed stand against the forces of the ruthlessly rational Octavius.

Not surprisingly, the love between Antony and Cleopatra is full of slights, manipulations, betrayals, and misunderstandings. Ultimately, Antony is tricked into believing that Cleopatra has killed herself and so gives himself a mortal wound. He lives long enough, however, to enjoy a parting kiss with his "sweet queen," who determines to deprive Caesar of the glory of conquest by killing herself as well. Yet before committing suicide, she delivers an astounding elegy for Antony, whom she celebrates as "past the size of dreaming." Despite the obvious hyperbole of her words, her loyalty and resolution are admirable; and as she dies, she imagines herself reunited with Antony, whom she now calls "husband." The deaths of Antony and Cleopatra are thus extremely moving, but one cannot help feeling that the world they have left behind is dominated by political calculation and inhospitable to passionate love.

Antony and Cleopatra revisits many of the questions posed by Romeo and Juliet *but considers them from a much more mature, world-weary perspective.*

XVI. THE SECOND CONTINENTAL CONGRESS

THE BRITISH CASUALTY FIGURES for the battles of Lexington and Concord were 73 dead, 174 wounded, and 26 missing. The American totals were 49 dead, 40 wounded, and 5 missing. But these statistics don't convey the full measure of what took place on April 19 and its effect on Gage's situation. As news of the fighting spread around New England, militiamen from all over the region (and some from as far away as New York and Pennsylvania) descended on Boston, trapping the British there.

To have called these armed men "soldiers," however, would have been charitable. They were untrained and ill equipped, dressed in plain clothes, and lacking both proper discipline and proper officers. Yet they were exceptionally high in morale; and by the time the Continental Congress reconvened in Philadelphia on May 10, this "army" was well on its way to numbering sixteen thousand people.

A meeting of the Second Continental Congress in Philadelphia.

The delegates to the Second Continental Congress, confronted now with the unalterable reality of armed conflict, considered what to do. Initially, some tried to debate further what Silas Deane of Connecticut called "the old affair of the right of regulating trade." It wasn't too late, they argued, to seek reconciliation with Britain by affirming Parliament's authority in this regard. Aware that public opinion outside New England was still somewhat mixed, cautious delegates from the Middle Colonies, notably John Dickinson of Pennsylvania, worried that Massachusetts radicals were forcing rebellion on the rest of the colonies. In fact, they already had—a state of affairs that soon became clear to everyone. Meanwhile, the urgent need to plan a military defense quickly propelled the delegates beyond talk of accommodation into active preparation for war.

The most pressing task was the chartering of an American army and the selection of its commander in chief. Although John Hancock clearly craved the position, he was too closely identified with Massachusetts radicalism to be a strong consensus choice. Even his Massachusetts colleagues understood this—which is why John Adams, eager to promote interregional solidarity, nominated the French and Indian War veteran George Washington of Virginia. Active in the patriot cause since the Stamp Act Congress, Washington was a modest yet compelling man whose appointment to lead the new Continental army was unanimously approved on June 15.

The Second Continental Congress began with more debate about the regulation of colonial trade, but it soon became obvious to the delegates that Massachusetts radicalism had forced rebellion on the rest of the colonies.

XVI. INTERNET-BASED ALTERNATIVES

CONTENT PROVIDERS EARN money by selling access to information that is otherwise privileged, usually by virtue of copyright protection. Whether these companies offer their content in the form of reference books, newspapers, music CDs, or movie DVDs, their existence depends on their ability to control access to the information they are selling. The current information revolution has made this task more challenging.

For example, many well-established print resources are now being replaced by Internet alternatives. Dictionaries, encyclopedias, and atlases are all available now online, often in versions created by the same companies that produced the original print volumes (and often free of charge, paid for in theory by advertising). The advantage of such online access is obvious; the difficulty is creating a business model that makes economic sense for the content providers.

Another example of an old way of doing business being radically revised by the Internet involves the stock market, where traditional retail brokers are being supplanted by online brokerages that allow customers to make their own trades. These online brokerages charge low fees but earn high profits when they grow large enough to match buy and sell orders within their own systems. When this happens, the online companies pocket the spread (the difference between the bid and the ask) that they would normally pay to the stock exchange.

In the entertainment industry, many companies are moving toward making Internet download their primary means of content distribution. Already a great deal of music is being delivered this way, and television shows are becoming increasingly available online. Because such a change would eliminate the need to manufacture and transport physical media such as CDs and DVDs, this trend is unlikely to be reversed.

The telephone business is also changing. Because its voice signals represent merely another form of data transmission, telecommunications is, like the Internet, an information-carrying enterprise. However, by today's technological standards, traditional landline telephone service is both inefficient and relatively expensive. Largely, this is because telephone companies rely on old, low-grade copper cable that's high in cost relative to its information-carrying performance. A new Internet alternative is VoIP (Voice over Internet Protocol), which encodes voice signals for transmission over the Internet. Using headphones or special telephone adapters, users can make and receive VoIP calls at a much lower cost.

Many old ways of doing business *are now being replaced by Internet-based alternatives.*

XVI. THE ARMORY SHOW IN CHICAGO AND BOSTON

FROM THE SIXTY-NINTH REGIMENT ARMORY, the International Exhibition of Modern Art traveled to the Art Institute of Chicago, which was initially reluctant to host such "radical" paintings and sculpture. The modernist art in the show, it was thought, might have a negative effect on the institute's students; the institute's board of trustees, however, was eventually persuaded of the show's educational merits.

There was indeed cause for concern. The Art Institute of Chicago wasn't a rented hall but a nationally famous museum. Its decision to display works of art conferred on that art a certain legitimacy, which didn't escape the notice of the Chicago press. As in New York City, the pages of Chicago's daily newspapers became filled with stories about the new "degenerate" art on display at the Art Institute, inciting the public to action. Upright Chicagoans, mostly clergymen and society ladies, shocked by what they saw, insisted that the police shut down the "indecent" exhibition; but the head of the vice squad, even though he didn't like the art either, saw nothing illegal in it.

Paintings and sculpture from the Armory Show on display at the Art Institute of Chicago.

Despite all this furor, the Art Institute continued to see the show as an educational opportunity, and it organized lectures and gallery tours designed to explain the basic tenets of modernist art. These programs were generally filled to capacity; and because of all the publicity, more people attended the show in Chicago than had in New York.

After Chicago, however, Boston was an anticlimax. Perhaps because of "Armory fatigue," Bostonians turned out to be largely uninterested in modernism, and the city's newspapers found it difficult to whip up much enthusiasm one way or the other. Additionally, because the rented venue (Copley Hall) was quite small, no works by American artists were shown, and the exhibition was also stripped of its European historical section. The bomb that the AAPS organizers had wanted to drop into the American art world had gone off as planned in New York and Chicago; but in staid Boston, it ended as a dud.

The public reaction in Chicago turned out to be *even more vitriolic than it had been in New York. In Boston, however, there wasn't much reaction to modernism at all.*

XVI. CIVILIZATION AND ITS DISCONTENTS

IN ONE OF HIS LAST and best-known works, *Civilization and Its Discontents* (1930), Freud moved beyond the workings of the individual psyche to look at civilization as a whole. Undoubtedly influenced by Freud's wartime experiences, this pessimistic book focuses on the tension between the needs of the individual and the demands of society.

Although people certainly need one another, Freud wrote, living in society necessitates obedience to rules and the acceptance of cultural norms that limit one's ability to fulfill personal wishes and desires. Children learn to follow civilization's rules early in life because they fear punishment and want to please their parents (or at least avoid being punished by them). This early socialization gradually becomes internalized and, in accordance with Freud's structural theory, forms the core of the adult superego.

The ways in which different cultures set these rules vary, as do the ways in which individuals adapt to them, but the universal fact that all cultures set limits profoundly shapes human lives and psyches. The result is a human condition replete with conflict, guilt, and discontent. The guilt derives from both the actual breaking of rules and the mostly unconscious desire to fulfill forbidden wishes, especially those relating to sexuality and aggression. The discontent follows from the conflict, guilt, and frequent lack of fulfillment.

How do we cope? Freud's answer is love and work: love structured within the social order, experienced in the context of family and friends; and work that permits the effective sublimation of repressed wishes.

Within this discussion of how to manage the unhappiness of life, Freud also considered the role of religion. Previously, he had criticized religion as a collective neurosis, writing that religious belief provides an illusion of salvation because it enables the believer to feel connected to something larger than himself. In *Civilization and Its Discontents*, Freud (an avowed atheist) developed this idea further, describing the ways in which religion creates a sense of community around a shared set of beliefs. The specifics of those beliefs don't matter, as long as they offer hope and solace to the believer. The psychological price paid for such illusory solace, according to Freud, is subordination to the church and even greater limitations on one's individual longings.

In **Civilization and Its Discontents**, *Freud looked beyond the individual psyche to civilization as a whole and the ways in which it produces conformity along with conflict, guilt, and discontent.*

XVI. CORIOLANUS

CORIOLANUS is the last of Shakespeare's Roman tragedies. Its title character is the Roman general Caius Marcius—who, after defeating the Volscian general Aufidius and sacking the city of Corioles, is honored with the surname Coriolanus. Returning home in triumph, he is encouraged to become the new consul (chief magistrate of the Roman republic), but first he must present himself to the people and gain their approval. Fiercely proud, Coriolanus resists humbling himself in this way and submits to the process only grudgingly. Initially, he receives the people's consent, but this is soon rescinded after the tribunes (officials who protect the citizenry from magisterial abuse) persuade the public that Coriolanus is not their friend. Enraged by the turn of events, Coriolanus declares his contempt for the people, and the situation threatens to devolve into civil war.

Although the tribunes demand Coriolanus's execution, the general's patrician friends arrange for his banishment instead. In Antium, Coriolanus forms an alliance with the Volsci and agrees to lead their army in an assault upon Rome. Bent on revenge, he ignores the pleas of his friend and mentor Menenius; but when his wife, son, and mother—all still residents of Rome—entreat him on the eve of battle to withdraw, he cannot deny them. So Coriolanus returns to Antium, where he is accused of treason and murdered by Aufidius.

The tragedy of *Coriolanus* is that its hero cannot recognize his own humanity. Imagining himself to be a perfect killing machine, the general doesn't anticipate the effect that his family's entreaty will have on him. At the same time, *Coriolanus* is also a sharply political tragedy that dwells on the relationship between martial heroism and political reality. By the time Shakespeare wrote this play, Elizabethan optimism about the renewal of chivalry had given way to a profound Jacobean pessimism about the prospects for heroism.

The autonomy of the hero who stands apart from the mass of ordinary people is here transformed into a perverse inhumanity. As Aristotle wrote, "He who is unable to live in society, or who has no need for it because he is sufficient for himself, must be either a beast or a god." Coriolanus believes that he can repudiate Rome because "there is a world elsewhere." But he is wrong, because there is no world that can accommodate him—an indictment not only of Coriolanus's refusal to compromise but also of a world that can't tolerate greatness.

Coriolanus's heroism *sets him apart from the rest of the population and ensures, ironically, that he has no place in the world.*

XVII. THE BATTLE OF BUNKER HILL

IN LATE MAY 1775, three British major generals—John Burgoyne, Henry Clinton, and William Howe—joined Gage in Boston. Howe immediately devised a plan for the storming of the American encampment at Cambridge. Learning of this, the Americans decided to respond by fortifying Bunker Hill on the nearby Charlestown peninsula.

With George Washington still in Philadelphia, the American forces at Cambridge lacked a unified command. As a result, authority was shared among several people—including Col. William Prescott of the Massachusetts militia; Maj. Gen. Israel Putnam of the Connecticut militia; and Richard Gridley, a Bostonian with nearly two decades of service in the British army as a military engineer.

About 9 PM on June 16, Prescott arrived on the Charlestown peninsula with twelve hundred men. Putnam and Gridley met him with several wagonloads of picks and shovels. But before work could begin, the three officers had a lengthy discussion about whether to entrench on Bunker Hill, as their orders stated, or on Breed's Hill, which was closer to Boston. The back-and-forthing lasted for about an hour before Putnam overruled Gridley, insisting that Breed's Hill be the one fortified.

When first light revealed the Americans' position, Gage and the others agreed that the colonials would have to be removed. Clinton suggested landing troops near Charlestown Neck to cut off an American retreat; but Howe quickly trumped this plan, proposing a direct assault featuring beautifully straight firing lines of the sort so admired by military tacticians of the eighteenth century.

Howe's assault force landed on Charlestown peninsula in the early afternoon and soon began marching up Breed's Hill, slowed somewhat by long grass and the sixty-pound packs they were carrying. In order to conserve precious musket balls and powder, Putnam ordered his men, "Don't fire until you see the whites of their eyes." When the redcoats finally came close enough, the patriots fired decimating volleys into the neat British lines.

Howe regrouped his men and sent them up the hill again, with much the same result. Finally, during a third British assault, the Americans ran out of ammunition.

At this point, the fighting turned hand to hand, and Prescott ordered a retreat. Thus, the British took the hill, but at a pyrrhic cost: The Americans killed or wounded more than a thousand of Howe's twenty-six hundred men, while suffering only half as many casualties themselves.

The battle of Bunker Hill *(which actually took place on Breed's Hill) was a pyrrhic victory for the British, who suffered casualties of nearly 50 percent.*

A drum used during the battle of Bunker Hill.

XVII. NEW PARADIGMS

THE INTERNET HASN'T merely introduced new ways to accomplish old, familiar tasks; it has also encouraged the development of new paradigms that have changed the way information is organized and disseminated. The first of these new paradigms was the search engine. The protocols of the World Wide Web made information posted on web pages *potentially* available to all users; but as a practical matter, if you didn't know where to look for a particular web page (or even that such a page existed), the access was useless. Search engines changed all that.

Using software programs called web crawlers or spiders, search engines scan the web continuously, visiting pages and recording the words and phrases they find there. All of this information is then compiled and indexed so that when you type a request into a search engine, it responds quickly with links to various websites containing matching information.

Without search engines, researching the role of the turnip in English history would be nearly impossible, and you would be better off in a library. On the other hand, the growth of search engine power has produced some unanticipated and unfortunate consequences, among them a considerable loss of privacy. Type your name into a search engine, and you may be surprised to see the sort of personal information that appears.

Another new and influential paradigm made possible by the Internet is the wiki, which is based on the principle of collaboration. A wiki is a collection of web pages designed so that users can easily contribute to or modify the content. The exemplar of this growing phenomenon is Wikipedia, the Internet-based encyclopedia with more than two million articles written and edited (often repeatedly) by users. Containing much less inaccuracy than one might suspect, Wikipedia offers—in addition to the expected articles on Plato, postmodernism, and primates—a surprising abundance of advanced and highly technical information written by experts for a narrow, specialized audience.

Finally, anyone with an Internet connection can now become a published author simply by posting an essay on one of the public websites known as blogs (short for "web logs"). Although the potential audience for these articles is as vast as the web itself, bloggers and their readership tend to focus on specific topics, most notably politics. Political blogs such as the Daily Kos attract millions of readers and have become respected sources of news and opinion with a prominence and credibility that few would have predicted.

The growth of the Internet *has encouraged the development of new paradigms relating to the organization and dissemination of information.*

XVII. THE LIMITATIONS OF THE ARMORY SHOW

LIKE ALL ART EXHIBITIONS, the Armory Show had limitations, some of which were merely a reflection of Arthur Davies's personal taste. For example, several important contemporary European styles, notably German expressionism and Italian futurism, were left out of the show because Davies considered them minor offshoots of cubism and fauvism.

Stanton MacDonald-Wright, *Abstraction on Spectrum (Organization 5)* (1914–17)

Other limitations were logistical. Because Picasso declined to submit any entries, he was represented only by works on loan from collectors. Unfortunately, this selection didn't reflect his current style or his most significant work to date. Similarly, by 1913, Duchamp and Picabia were already moving toward what would become Dada, but none of this work appeared in the Armory Show, either.

The show's most important limitation, however, was intentional. Davies wanted to start a revolution, so he and Kuhn made some decisions not for aesthetic reasons but to further that goal. Most importantly, they chose American works that were less than current in order to emphasize the contrast between the American and European galleries. These choices, while increasing the show's impact, misrepresented the many American artists already exploring modernism in 1913.

The mission of the AAPS had originally been to promote American artists; yet the way the Armory Show developed, this mission became subordinate to the goal of provocation. Davies was determined to show everyone how backward the National Academy and the rest of the American art establishment were. To have included current American modernism in the Armory Show would have blunted this point, so Davies didn't include any—or at least not much.

Marsden Hartley, for example, had already begun working in an abstract style by 1913, but Davies and Kuhn chose instead to display two of Hartley's earlier, Fauve-inspired works, explaining in a letter written by Kuhn that "no American has done this kind of thing and [the earlier works] would serve [Hartley] and the exhibition best at this time." Similarly, Stanton MacDonald-Wright and Morgan Russell, among the first American artists to paint nonrepresentationally, had invented in 1912 a new style called synchromism. Based on the premise that painters can create harmonies of color in the same way that composers create harmonies of sound, synchromism was the first American avant-garde movement to gain widespread international recognition—yet it wasn't included in the Armory Show, either.

The most important limitation of the Armory Show *was its intentional misrepresentation of the state of American modernist art.*

XVII. THE END OF FREUD'S LIFE

FREUD'S SEVENTY-FIFTH BIRTHDAY in May 1931 was marked with celebrations in Vienna, London, New York, and other cities where psychoanalysis had caught on. Freud himself received letters of congratulation from students, colleagues, and admirers such as Albert Einstein, who wrote that he was reading Freud's work and discussing it weekly with a friend. The approbation was certainly well deserved. Since the publication of *Studies on Hysteria* thirty-six years earlier, psychoanalysis had evolved from a method of treating hysteria into a framework within which the human condition could be contemplated and understood. Moreover, by 1931, Western culture had internalized many of psychoanalysis's most important concepts and made its terminology part of the common cultural vocabulary.

Yet Freud's sense of achievement was offset by personal struggles. His lifelong love of, and addiction to, cigars had finally caught up with him in 1923, when he was diagnosed with cancer of the mouth. The cancer later spread to his jaw, requiring more than thirty surgeries. Although often in pain, Freud never stopped writing, and he continued to see patients and train students, if on a more limited basis.

Freud was also becoming more and more concerned over the growing social unrest in Europe, especially the rise of Nazism in Germany and the effect that this was having on Austria. In a letter to his nephew written in late 1930, Freud reported that "General conditions are especially dreary in Austria...Things are going from bad to worse." When Adolf Hitler became chancellor of Germany in 1933 and ordered the burning of degenerate books, Freud's were among those tossed onto the fire. Many Jewish psychoanalysts left Germany for the United States and South America, and Freud was urged by friends and colleagues to join them before it was too late.

German troops march into Austria in March 1938.

Like many Viennese Jews, Freud was reluctant to leave; but after witnessing the March 1938 Anschluss (the German annexation of Austria), he knew that he wanted "to die in freedom." Because of his fame and many influential friends, he was able to obtain an exit visa and in early June departed London, where he continued his struggle with cancer but otherwise lived comfortably with his daughter Anna, who had become an eminent psychoanalyst in her own right. Freud died on September 23, 1939, three weeks after the start of World War II.

Although Freud was celebrated *internationally as the father of psychoanalysis, his final years were diminished by his poor health and anguish over the rise of Nazism.*

XVII. TIMON OF ATHENS

TIMON OF ATHENS is Shakespeare's most unloved and unlovable tragedy. Its title character is an ancient Greek aristocrat who showers others with gifts until he has bankrupted himself—at which point he learns that none of those he has helped are willing to help him. Transformed by this experience into a bitter misanthrope, Timon abandons Athens for a cave near the sea, where he discovers buried gold. Several Athenians subsequently visit him, urging his return to society. These people have various motives—some want his gold, some merely his company—but Timon remains unreconciled and dies alone.

Although the appearance of these visitors provides the occasion for a great deal of corrosive debate about the fundamental nature of humanity, the character of Timon lacks the sort of psychological complexity that makes other Shakespearean heroes compelling. His gift-giving isn't inspired magnanimity but a sort of foolish recklessness; and when he is forsaken in his time of need, only the naive and prodigal Timon is surprised.

The shock is so great that it transforms entirely Timon's worldview. Once he conceived of the universe as a beautifully orchestrated system of reciprocity; now it seems to him that the universe operates according to the principle of theft:

> *The sun's a thief, and with his great attraction*
> *Robs the vast sea; the moon's an arrant thief,*
> *And her pale fire she snatches from the sun.*
> *The sea's a thief, whose liquid surge resolves*
> *The moon into salt tears. The earth's a thief,*
> *That feeds and breeds by a composture stol'n*
> *From gen'ral excrement. Each thing's a thief.*

Sounding like Lear in his madness, Timon implores the earth to "Ensear thy fertile and conceptious womb; / Let it no more bring out ingrateful man!" But unlike Lear, he never returns to his senses and never recognizes a need for other people. Rather, Timon displays an extreme rigidity like that of Coriolanus but without the positive characteristics that make Coriolanus, for all his fierce severity, sympathetic.

In his rejection of Athens, Timon rails against commerce, which he claims is but a thin veil for violent forms of appropriation. Thus, both *Timon of Athens* and *Coriolanus* seem to set themselves against the quickening pace of modern life—especially in the city, where both commerce and politics prevail.

Timon of Athens is an unloved and unlovable play because its corrosive satire lacks a countervailing sense of human dignity and power.

XVIII. THE BRITISH LEAVE BOSTON

AFTER THE BATTLE OF BUNKER HILL, King George III relieved Gage of his command, declared the colonies to be in "open rebellion," and issued a proclamation closing all American ports to imperial trade. Meanwhile, George Washington had other problems with which to contend. When the general arrived in Cambridge after a twelve-day journey from Philadelphia, he found morale high. But as summer slipped into fall and winter, spirits among the members of the new Continental army waned. Lacking sufficient artillery, Washington could do little but poke at the British. Thus, beyond the occasional skirmish, there was little to do but loiter around camp. Army life became so monotonous that many men quit as soon as their six-month enlistments were up. As a result, by February 1776, Washington had fewer than half of the troops promised him by the Continental Congress.

George Washington in his Continental army uniform.

An even more formidable problem was discipline. Many of the new recruits were unruly libertarians aroused by the language of the patriot cause but possessing little respect for authority, British or American. Washington had to turn these men into obedient soldiers, while organizing the disparate units into a coherent army.

He also had an immediate goal to accomplish— driving the British out of Boston—but to do so, he needed heavy cannon, and none seemed to be available. Finally, in February 1776, Washington learned that several artillery pieces had been captured at Fort Ticonderoga the previous May. Immediately, he sent bookseller and amateur artillery expert Henry Knox to upstate New York to retrieve them.

Knox's mission wasn't easy. Eighteenth-century technology wasn't up to the job of transporting such heavy, unforgiving objects over mountains (the Berkshires) during the coldest part of winter. Yet somehow Knox managed the feat. Thus, when spring came, the British awoke one morning to find their own cannon pointing at them from atop Dorchester Heights.

Recognizing that Boston was now lost to him, Howe (who had replaced Gage) proposed a deal: Washington's promise of safe passage in exchange for Howe's promise not to burn Boston. When Washington agreed, Howe loaded nearly nine thousand troops onto 125 transports and sailed away on March 17—his destination Halifax. Washington, thinking Howe would head to New York City instead, began moving his own troops south.

It took Washington nearly nine months to force the British *out of Boston—a goal he accomplished only with the help of cannon hauled from Fort Ticonderoga by Henry Knox.*

XVIII. THE IMPACT OF THE INTERNET

ALREADY THE INTERNET HAS PRODUCED—and surely will continue to produce—fundamental changes in our society, a great many of which have served to empower the individual. For example, by eliminating the need for a storefront, the online marketplace eBay has enabled a huge number of small merchants and craftspeople to sell their goods to customers all over the world. Similarly, blogging now allows individuals with complaints about large and powerful interests to air their grievances in a way that can quickly generate attention and results. A related phenomenon is that minorities of all sorts now enjoy a more level playing field. Disabled people, for example, can access resources through the Internet that might otherwise be beyond their reach. Just as importantly, they can interact with other users without any need to reference or be mindful of their disabilities.

By empowering the individual, the Internet also serves to undermine the social control practiced by totalitarian regimes. Dictatorships, for example, have historically sought to control the flow of information to the public because information supports thought and thought leads to action. With unlimited access to the Internet, however, such information control becomes impossible. By the same logic, some historians have attributed the collapse of the Soviet Union to the proliferation of the fax machine, which allowed dissident citizens to create effective message networks. To prevent the same sort of destabilization from taking place in China, the Chinese government has set up far-reaching censorship systems to block citizens' access to websites containing content that the government finds objectionable. Even so, savvy Chinese Internet users have developed various methods (such as the use of proxy servers and encrypted connections) to circumvent these blocks.

The future, especially with regard to technology, is notoriously difficult to predict. The history of the Internet is replete with authoritative, well-reasoned predictions that turned out to be dead wrong. In 2004, for example, Microsoft chairman Bill Gates predicted that "two years from now, spam will be solved." Even more embarrassing was the prediction made in 1977 by Digital Equipment Corporation cofounder Ken Olsen, who declared that "there is no reason for any individual to have a computer in his home." So the best approach to anticipating the future probably isn't to make predictions but rather to expect change and to be ready and willing to deal with what comes.

The overall impact of the Internet *has been to empower individuals in their relationships with large and powerful entities such as corporations and governments.*

XVIII. THE LEGACY OF THE ARMORY SHOW

BECAUSE THE ARMORY SHOW clearly succeeded in shaking up the art world, it's generally considered a pivotal moment in American art history. The exhibition was, as historian Milton Brown has written, "both a culmination and a beginning, an effect as well as a cause."

Initially, its impact on American artists was mixed. Some, including many of the show's organizers, simply continued to work in their previous styles. Others experimented with modernism—some later returning to earlier approaches, some not (such as Joseph Stella). For those Americans already working in modernist styles, however, the Armory Show legitimized what they were doing and greatly upgraded their status. Before 1913, they had been denizens of the fringe; now they found themselves moving into more dominant roles.

For example, after the Armory Show, the National Academy's hold on American art loosened considerably. Even though much of the press coverage had been negative, its sheer volume had demonstrated that modernism was relevant in a way that the American art establishment was not. As a result, people began thinking about art in a different way, and modernist galleries soon opened to capitalize on the vogue. Meanwhile, institutions such as the National Arts Club, the Cosmopolitan Club, and the Gamut Club, which had previously excluded modernist works from their exhibitions, now opened their doors to the new styles. By the early 1920s, even the museums were joining the bandwagon, with the Pennsylvania Academy of the Fine Arts leading the way.

Much of this action was driven by the serious collectors who snapped up modernism at the Armory Show and pursued it thereafter. In a short time, several amassed significant holdings that later became the bases of important museum collections. Lillie P. Bliss's purchases, for example, became the nucleus of the Museum of Modern Art, founded in 1929.

While it wouldn't be accurate to credit the Armory Show with all that followed in twentieth-century American art, it would be fair to say that the show put into motion forces that, over time, transformed the character of American art, causing it to become much more abstract and leading eventually to the emergence of the New York School and Jackson Pollock.

An exterior view of the Sixty-ninth Regiment Armory during the show.

As its organizers had hoped, *the Armory Show had a profound, long-lasting impact on the artists, collectors, and institutions of the American art world.*

XVIII. PSYCHOANALYSIS AFTER FREUD

Freud in 1938.

THE PSYCHOANALYTIC MOVEMENT that Freud fathered has grown and changed dramatically since his death in 1939. A conversation of sorts has taken place since then involving many different people who have variously critiqued, revised, and expanded upon Freud's original ideas and methods. At times, this conversation has become heated, and participants have sometimes walked away to pursue radically new psychoanalytic ideas.

The three aspects of psychoanalytic theory that have changed the most since Freud's day are his characterization of early-childhood psychosexual stages, his explanation of gender development, and his views on the shaping of a person's internal world. Freud saw infantile sexual development largely in terms of the Oedipus complex, but modern psychoanalysts have moved beyond this focus, no longer believing the condition to be universal. Regarding gender development, Freud emphasized the influence of castration anxiety for boys and penis envy for girls, but psychoanalysis has since left behind such sharp gender stereotypes and placed more emphasis on the development of individual identity. Similarly, as to the ways in which a person's early experiences shape his or her internal world, modern analysts give important recognition to culture, class, race and other aspects of the human condition that Freud never contemplated.

Yet Freud's original work endures. The unconscious mind, though understood somewhat differently, remains central to psychoanalytic thought, as does a person's family life. The "talking cure" also continues to be practiced, with analysts still mindful of the benefits and pitfalls of transference and countertransference.

Significantly, though, the position of the analyst has become less authoritative with the recognition that neutrality and objectivity are not possible in a therapeutic relationship that involves mutual influence. Even though analysts are trained to contain and reflect on their feelings, those feeling cannot be entirely denied.

Psychoanalysis now takes place less formally and less frequently than it did a century ago, and analysts speak with patients more than they once did. But, for the most part, the basic terms of the relationship remain unchanged: Analysts strive to listen to and accept without judgment what a patient has to say, building a working alliance. They then use this therapeutic relationship to help the patient learn to reflect and develop the insight and self-knowledge necessary to resolve his or her troubles and find new ways to relate.

Although some of Freud's ideas are now considered obsolete, *others have been retained and revised in accordance with contemporary knowledge and ways of life.*

XVIII. THE TRAJECTORY OF SHAKESPEAREAN TRAGEDY

SHAKESPEAREAN TRAGEDY is best understood within the developmental arc of the playwright's intellectual and creative life. Because Shakespeare's thinking about tragedy was always in motion, his early focus on social fatalism eventually gave way to a later questioning of minds and motivations. *Titus Andronicus*, for example—set in a late-imperial Rome that has run out of options—is full of suffering from which there seems no possibility of escape. Similarly, the young lovers in *Romeo and Juliet* hope to establish a private erotic space outside the social constraints and endemic feuds of Verona, but their enterprise is doomed from the start.

With *Hamlet*, on the other hand, Shakespeare turns toward interiority. The social world continues to matter, of course, but there is a new emphasis on human psychology. Shakespeare's careful depiction of individuals under great stress is what led critic A. C. Bradley to isolate the four major tragedies and focus on character as the hallmark of Shakespearean drama. However, this extraordinary attention to psychology carries with it the dark shadow of solipsism (the theory that knowledge of other minds is impossible and that the only real object of knowledge is the self). Ultimately, with his final three tragedies, Shakespeare retreats from the dramaturgical magnification of interiority and moves back into the social world.

All the while, Shakespearean tragedy remains dark and inexplicable. It speaks of things that shouldn't have happened and of the fragility of goodness as well as the terror of unmerited suffering. Far from uniform, it pushes relentlessly against the limits of the genre. The result is a body of work that paradoxically makes plain the shortcomings of human life while at the same time attesting to the possibility of astounding artistry, profound vision, and deep sympathy.

One often comes across the phrase *an almost Shakespearean tragedy* in theater and film reviews, as well as in descriptions of contemporary events, because Shakespeare's ten tragedies have long since supplanted the works of the ancient Greeks as the benchmark of tragedy in the popular understanding. Such shorthand references to the complex qualities of Shakespearean tragedy may have their place, but they nonetheless fail to describe the passionate love, admirable heroism, and profound sense of loss that the most accomplished of Shakespeare's tragedies effortlessly convey.

Shakespearean tragedy moved from an early *focus on social fatalism to a later emphasis on human psychology as it pushed insistently against the limits of the genre.*

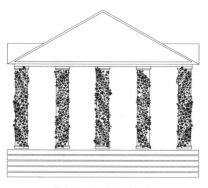

SYLLABUS

II

I. WHY FLORENCE?

A map of fifteenth-century Florence.

FLORENCE IS COMMONLY REGARDED as the cradle of the Italian Renaissance. Between 1250 and 1550, masterpieces of art, architecture, and literature were created there (and elsewhere by Florentine expatriates). Individually as well as collectively through their civic institutions, Florentines glorified their city in histories and poems and beautified its environs. Florentine humanists, who immersed themselves in the literature of ancient Greece and Rome, compared Florence's republican government favorably to its vaunted Roman predecessor. According to Florentine humanist Leonardo Bruni, Florence's republican form of government, established in 1293, permitted its citizens to take part in civic life and thereby encouraged the development of their talents, artistic and otherwise.

But why did the Renaissance emerge in Florence and not somewhere else? The economic, social, and political forces that impacted Florence were certainly felt in other Italian city-states. Venice, Milan, and Genoa benefited similarly from the expansion of European trade that made Florence an important commercial center.

What made Florence different was its self-image. Although one may reasonably question the extent to which the city's government was actually a republic, there can be no doubt that Florentines considered themselves republicans—a view enthusiastically supported by the city's substantial assembly of humanists.

Florence was not the only republic in Italy. Republican governments held sway in Venice, Siena, Lucca, and Perugia and from time to time in Genoa and Bologna. Yet the strong humanist presence in Florence made its citizens much more conscious of the city's republican ideology.

Because Florence had one of the highest literacy rates in Europe, its humanists were able to disseminate their ideas widely; and because the city lacked a strong university tradition, those ideas went largely unchallenged by other intellectual viewpoints. Thus, the humanists' laudatory assessment of Florentine republicanism became deeply embedded in the civic psyche.

Humanism thrived elsewhere, but humanists in the employ of lords tended to reinforce the legitimacy of their employers, appealing to Roman imperial rather than Roman republican history. The powerful Medici family that came to dominate Florentine politics may have ruled in effect as lords, but the Medicis wisely chose never to challenge publicly the institutions of republicanism that Florentines held so dear.

A deeply rooted republican self-image, *supported by a strong humanist presence, set Florence apart from other Italian city-states and made it the cradle of the Renaissance.*

I. CAPITAL MARKETS

ALL BUSINESSES NEED CAPITAL to fund their operations. Generally, they raise it in one of three ways: They borrow money from a bank, issue bonds, or issue stock. Each of these methods has its own advantages and disadvantages, so companies tend to use a combination of all three.

Borrowing money from a bank would seem to be the simplest approach, but the process is actually complicated and laborious. Because both sides want to include specific terms to benefit and protect themselves, loans have to be customized by teams of lawyers and accountants. This customization comes at a cost, making bank capital expensive.

If a company chooses not to borrow from a bank, it usually turns to the capital markets, which are the mechanisms by which securities (stocks and bonds) are issued. Because securities are offered to large numbers of investors rather than to a single bank, customization is much less of an issue. Therefore, the issuing of securities— presuming that investors are willing to buy them—offers companies not only a lower cost of capital but also a more broadly based (and thus more stable) capital structure.

If investors were forced to hold on to their securities in the same way that most banks hold on to the loans that they issue—that is, for the duration—investors might not find securities so appealing. But securities needn't be held because capital markets are highly liquid. (Liquidity refers both to the supply of cash in a market and to the ease with which assets can be converted into cash.) The opportunity to buy and sell securities at will is important because it permits investors to increase or decrease their exposure to a specific company as the situation warrants.

When a bank makes a loan that it knows will stay on its books for a long time, it demands a hefty premium for assuming so much risk. This translates into a higher cost of capital for borrowers. Purchasers of securities, on the other hand, will usually provide capital at a lower cost as long as they are assured that they can sell those securities later on in the capital markets.

National economies with strong capital markets have a substantial advantage over other economies because the depth and liquidity of their markets attract capital, increasing its supply and lowering its cost. The more money there is sloshing around in a market, the more competition there will be for investment opportunities, and the lower the returns to competing investors.

Capital markets are the means by which *companies raise capital through the issuance of securities (stocks and bonds).*

I. THE AUTOBIOGRAPHY OF AN EX-COLORED MAN

THE DESIRE TO ESCAPE ONE'S PAST has been an important thread in the American social fabric ever since the first European colonizers arrived at the start of the seventeenth century. As a result, part of the process of becoming an American has been to cast off one's personal history in order to create a new identity.

James Weldon Johnson

James Weldon Johnson (1871–1938) was just such an American. Born into the Jim Crow South, where nine out of ten African Americans lived at the time, Johnson attended Atlanta University, taught high school, studied law, and then reinvented himself as a songwriter, penning hits for the Broadway stage and (as a favor to Booker T. Washington) Theodore Roosevelt's 1904 campaign song, "You're All Right, Teddy." After Roosevelt's reelection, the president rewarded Johnson with an appointment as US consul to Venezuela.

In 1912, four years before becoming the NAACP's first full-time field secretary, Johnson published anonymously *The Autobiography of an Ex-Colored Man*, which tells the story of a light-skinned biracial musician who crosses the color line to live as a white. Initially, the book was thought to be a factual autobiography, and it caused quite a stir. Only later did readers come to understand that the *Autobiography* is fiction.

The *Autobiography* is, in fact, a bildungsroman in which the nameless protagonist, a cultural orphan at the crossroads of race, uses music to establish his identity. Although classically trained, he makes his living playing ragtime. A forerunner of jazz, ragtime began in the black community around the turn of the twentieth century before spreading quickly to the white, becoming a racial hybrid (as jazz later would). "No one who has traveled can question the world-conquering influence of ragtime," Johnson wrote, "and I do not think it would be an exaggeration to say that in Europe the United States is popularly known better by ragtime than by anything else it has produced in a generation. In Paris they call it American music."

Like ragtime, Johnson's *Autobiography* predates the Jazz Age, yet its blending of cultures so captured the spirit of the 1920s—especially the mingling of music, race relations, and nightlife—that the novel was republished in 1927 and thereafter hailed as a classic.

The blending of race, *music, and nightlife in James Weldon Johnson's* The Autobiography of an Ex-Colored Man *set the tempo for the artistic, social, and intellectual tensions of the Jazz Age.*

I. ELECTRIC CHARGE

ELECTRIC CHARGE IS a fundamental property of matter. It determine how objects interact with the rest of the universe. The human ability to manipulate electric charge (and the forces associated with it) has been as transformative to civilization as the taming of fire or the development of agriculture.

All matter is made up of atoms, which consist of protons and neutrons (in a nucleus) surrounded by orbiting electrons. Neutrons have no charge, while protons and electrons have charges that are equal in magnitude—specifically, 1.67×10^{-19} coulombs—but opposite in polarity. The charge carried by electrons is negative, while the charge carried by protons is positive. Because atoms generally have the same number of protons and electrons, most matter has no net charge.

Electric charge can neither be created nor destroyed, but it can be transferred. If you rub a balloon against your hair, some of the electrons in your hair will be transferred to the balloon. When the number of protons and electrons in an object becomes unbalanced, it acquires a net charge. In this example, your hair would acquire a net positive charge and the balloon a net negative charge. *Static electricity* is the term used to describe the buildup of unbalanced charge in an object. It's easily observable because electric charges exert forces. Like charges repel, whereas unlike charges attract.

If, after rubbing the balloon against your hair, you held it close to a pile of paper scraps, the balloon's negative charge would repel some of the electrons in the scraps, creating a net positive charge in the scrap ends closest to the balloon. Because unlike charges attract, the balloon would pick up the scraps by their positive ends. Manipulating uncharged objects in this way to produce positive and negative areas is called charging by induction.

Sometimes when an object has a net negative charge, the electric forces acting on that object become so strong that excess electrons begin to jump to other objects. We see these electron jumps as electrical sparks. For example, if you walk down a long carpeted hallway, you will probably transfer enough electrons to your body (by the action of your shoes rubbing against the carpet) to create a spark when you touch a neutrally charged object, such as a doorknob. A similar process takes place during thunderstorms, creating lightning.

Lightning strikes the Eiffel Tower.

Electric charge is a fundamental property of matter. *There are two types: positive charge and negative charge. Like charges repel, whereas unlike charges attract.*

I. THE EPIC GENRE

THE EPIC POEMS *Iliad* and *Odyssey* are the oldest known works of ancient Greek literature and thus the oldest known elements of the Western literary canon. Epics are long narrative poems that recount the deeds of legendary or historical heroes. Originally, bards composed and sang them to the accompaniment of musical instruments, often lyres (hence the term *lyric poetry*). The *Iliad* and the *Odyssey* were both composed in this oral tradition and only later—sometime around 700 BCE—set down in writing.

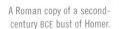

The poet Homer, to whom both works are traditionally attributed, is believed to have lived during the middle of the eighth century BCE, at the start of the Archaic era in ancient Greek history. This period coincided with the onset of political stability in the Peloponnesus and the expansion of Greek trade. It lasted until 505 BCE, when the establishment of democracy at Athens began the Classical era.

A Roman copy of a second-century BCE bust of Homer.

Although attribution of the *Iliad* and the *Odyssey* to Homer dates back to Classical Greece, modern scholars remain unsure whether the same person wrote both poems. It's fairly certain, however, that no matter who originally composed these epics, their texts shifted during the Archaic era and didn't become stable until the fifth century BCE.

By then, Greek poets were composing works in a world increasingly dominated by written discourse. As a result, the musical accompaniment began to drop away, yet poets continued to write in the epic tradition and use the Homeric meter of dactylic hexameter (as compared with Shakespeare's iambic pentameter).

The ascent of Rome during the first century BCE transformed the Mediterranean world; however, other than the shift of language from Greek to Latin, the new regime had little effect on the substance or popularity of the epic genre. Virgil's *Aeneid*, for example, was commissioned by the emperor Augustus as a Roman national epic, yet its plot and meter owe much to Homeric poetry.

Much of what we know about Greek and Roman mythology comes to us from epic poems. Some of our knowledge comes directly from the few epics that have survived. (Most, sadly, have been lost.) The rest comes indirectly from mythographers (such as Apollodorus and Proclus), whose prosaic accounts summarized the stories presented in the epics, and from historians (such as Herodotus and Diodorus of Sicily), whose works discussed the epics skeptically yet authoritatively.

The epic is the oldest known form of Western literature. *The first epics were sung poems that didn't come to be written down until the eighth century BCE.*

II. THE FLORENTINE GUILDS

FLORENCE HAD LONG BEEN identified with its wool industry. During the thirteenth century, however, the city also became famous for its commercial brokerage services; and its bankers, who mastered the complex credit-and-exchange system then prevalent in Western Europe, became internationally prominent as well.

Yet Florence's new prosperity was threatened by regular infighting among the nobility who ruled the city. Noble clans, known as *consorterie*, constructed fortified towers within urban territories, from which they fought with other *consorterie*. Because these struggles for political control often became deadly, Florentine merchants and tradesmen increasingly banded together for protection. Among the associations they formed were guilds, which united practitioners of like trades, and neighborhood societies, which organized guildsmen living in the same district into armed companies.

Guilds were self-governing entities founded on the principle that all members were entitled to equal rights and privileges. Through the guilds, members regulated their trades, exposing fraudulent practices and adjudicating disputes. Guilds even set the days and hours of the workweek and decided where in the city certain trades, such as the butchering of animals, could be practiced.

The earliest of the guilds, the Calimala, was founded during the late twelfth century. It encompassed a variety of trades and eventually splintered along occupational lines. During the thirteenth century, a number of new guilds were founded, but the overall trend was toward consolidation. The doctors' guild merged with the apothecaries' guild and later the shopkeepers' guild. Other guilds were simply disbanded, so that by the end

An Italian apothecary ca. 1300.

of the century, the twenty-one guilds that remained active were strong and stable. Total membership was about eight thousand, or nearly one in three adult males.

Guilds, however, didn't offer membership to all workers in the industries they controlled. In the wool industry, for example, which served as the industrial backbone of Florence, different workers managed different stages of production, often at different work sites. Some workers, especially women, spun wool thread in their homes; others, such as wool cleaners and combers, toiled in shops, using tools owned by the wool merchants who employed them. Of these people, only the merchants were granted membership in the wool guild. All of the other wool industry workers fell under the jurisdiction of the guild but were permitted no voice in its deliberations.

The thirteenth-century guilds founded by Florentine merchants *and tradesmen were initially intended for mutual protection, but they soon came to dominate Florentine industry.*

II. STOCKS AND BONDS

EVEN WHEN ISSUED BY the same company, stocks and bonds appeal to very different categories of investors because they have very different risk and return characteristics. Bonds are essentially large loans that have been divided up into many small pieces. Typically, the nominal (face) value of a bond is one thousand dollars. The contract that governs the rights and obligations of issuer and purchaser is called the indenture.

The interest paid on a bond (known as its coupon) is sometimes fixed and sometimes floating. (An example of a floating rate would be LIBOR plus 2 percent—where LIBOR is the London Interbank Offered Rate, or the rate at which a group of influential banks lend money to one another.) Coupon payments are usually made semiannually until the bond matures, at which point the principal is also due.

A zero-coupon bond is a bond that pays no interest but is sold at a discount (that is, for less than its face value). At maturity, however, purchasers receive the full face value. Thus, the buyer of a five-year zero-coupon bond issued at seventy-five cents on the dollar will earn at maturity an amount (twenty-five cents on the dollar) equal to 5 percent annual interest on the face value of the bond or 6.7 percent annual interest on the original investment.

Bonds are sometimes backed by specific assets, in which case they are said to be secured. Otherwise, bonds are merely general obligations of the issuing company, although some are entitled to repayment before others. Bonds at the end of the repayment line are said to be subordinated.

Stock, on the other hand, represents an ownership interest in the issuing corporation. Theoretically, the interests of shareholders are represented by the company's board of directors. In practice, however, shareholders are severely limited in their ability to influence company management. Almost all publicly held companies place limitations on the percentage of stock any single investor can own, and few allow shareholders to nominate outsiders for board membership.

So why would an investor forgo guaranteed (on pain of bankruptcy) coupon payments for the uncertainty and limitations of being a shareholder? The appeal, of course, is the potential for unlimited gains. Although bonds can be sold at a premium when their coupons exceed the prevailing interest rate, these profits don't compare to the gains enjoyed by stockholders when the companies they own succeed in the marketplace.

Bonds are loans that have been divided up *into many small pieces, while shares of stock represent ownership interests in the issuing company.*

II. OUT CAME JAZZ

INTO THE MUSICAL POT OF NEW ORLEANS during the early 1900s was poured not only ragtime but also blues, religious music, military marches, minstrel tunes, opera, and other ingredients too numerous to mention. For about a decade, this music cooked in the nightclubs and whorehouses of the overheated Storyville district. Eventually, out came jazz. Its leading practitioners were piano player Jelly Roll Morton, cornetists King Oliver and Louis Armstrong, and clarinetist Johnny Dodds.

The Original Dixieland Jazz Band in 1917.

In 1917, five white men from New Orleans calling themselves the Original Dixieland Jazz Band began making records that became wildly popular. The Dixieland jazz that they played was much more raucous than the music of their black counterparts. Its message, according to one early practitioner, was, "Let's all get loaded and see how nutty we can sound."

Players such as Oliver and Armstrong, however, were much more concerned with musicianship. After World War I, both men joined the migration of black southerners up the Mississippi River to Chicago, where they took up residence on the city's South Side and began playing in its nightclubs. The "hot" jazz that Oliver and Armstrong creatd was much more improvisational than Dixieland and attracted a new generation of young white musicians. Among those who crowded into the Lincoln Gardens during the summer of 1923 to hear Oliver and Armstrong play were Hoagy Carmichael and Bix Beiderbecke. When Armstrong launched into "Bugle Call Rag," Carmichael recalled, "I dropped my cigarette and gulped my drink. Bix was on his feet, his eyes popping…'Why,' I moaned, 'why isn't everybody in the world here to hear that?'"

With the rise of jazz, African Americans gained increased prominence in the broader American culture. In New York City, for example, the Cotton Club, located at 644 Lenox Avenue in the heart of Harlem, became the most celebrated nightspot in town, featuring black jazz musicians but catering exclusively to a moneyed white clientele. Owned by bootlegger Owney Madden, the Cotton Club featured as its house band from 1927 until 1931 Duke Ellington's Washingtonians. About the same time that Ellington began playing regularly at the Cotton Club, the fledging CBS radio network began broadcasting five nights a week from the Harlem hot spot. These broadcasts helped Ellington and the other bandleaders build national followings that crossed the color line—an extremely rare occurrence in the racially polarized United States of the 1920s.

During the 1920s, *jazz music, shaped by African American culture, became the dominant American musical form.*

II. THE ELECTRIC FORCE

THE ELECTRIC FORCE that two charged objects exert on each other depends on several factors. Think again about the balloon. It needs to be very close to the paper scraps in order to pick them up, so distance is obviously one factor, with decreasing distance producing an ever stronger force. Also, the longer you rub the balloon against your hair, the more paper scraps it will pick up; therefore, the amount of charge also matters, with greater charge corresponding to a stronger force. The third factor is polarity, with unlike charges producing an attractive force and like charges creating a force that repels.

These relationships are described mathematically in the formula known as Coulomb's Law,

$$F = \frac{kq_1q_2}{r^2}$$

where F is the force on charge q_1 from charge q_2, r is the distance between the two charges, and k is a constant. If one uses standard units of measurement—coulombs (C) for the magnitude of the charges, meters (m) for the distance between them, and Newtons (N) for the magnitude of the force—then k is 9×10^9 Nm^2/C^2. Because negative charges are represented by negative numbers, positive values for F represent repulsion, whereas negative values for F indicate attraction.

Like the gravitational force, the electric force is inversely proportional to the square of the distance between the two objects. The magnitude of the electric force, however, is much greater than the magnitude of the gravitational force. The electric force that exists between two protons in an atomic nucleus, for example, is 10^{36} times greater than the corresponding gravitational force. In fact, one of the great mysteries of the universe is why the gravitational force is so much weaker than the electric force.

If the electric force is so strong, why doesn't it dominate the universe? One reason is that most objects are uncharged; thus, they exert no electric force and remain unaffected by electric force unless a charged object is nearby. Another reason is that the forces exerted by charged objects, because they are both positive and negative, tend to cancel one another out on the largest scales.

Coulomb's Law states that *the electric force exerted by one charge on another depends on the magnitude and polarity of the charges and on the distance between them.*

II. THE TROJAN WAR CYCLE

BY FAR THE MOST POPULAR EPICS in ancient Greece were those that told the story of the Trojan War. According to Hesiod, the Trojan War was fought at the end of the Age of Heroes, but modern scholars aren't sure whether such a war actually took place. Archaeologists have found considerable evidence to suggest that Troy was destroyed by conflict sometime around 1200 BCE, but nothing they have found indicates the scale of fighting described by Homer.

Of the eight Trojan War epics, only the *Iliad* and the *Odyssey* have survived. Both are complete works, yet each tells only a part of the story. The six epics that have been lost are believed to have been written by various authors at least fifty years and perhaps more than a hundred years after the completion of the Homeric texts. The episodes they describe are known only through secondary sources.

The Trojan War Cycle begins with the *Cypria*, which describes the origins of the conflict. The most important event in the *Cypria* is the Judgment of Paris, which provides the Achaeans with their casus belli and brings their fleet to Troy. (Homer often used the term *Achaeans* to describe the Greeks collectively. It refers to the Peloponnesian prince Achaios, a mythological ancestor of the Greeks who fought in the Trojan War.)

Next in narrative order comes the *Iliad*, which takes place during the last year of the ten-year war. Its focus is on the rage of the Greek hero Achilles, the consequences of that rage, and its subsequent abatement. The two works that follow the *Iliad*, the *Aithiopis* and the *Little Iliad*, chronicle the deaths of the Amazon warrior Penthesileia; Memnon, son of the goddess Eos; and Achilles himself, over whose armor the Achaean heroes Ajax and Odysseus feud.

As its title suggests, the *Sack of Ilion* describes how the Achaeans conquered Troy, whose ancient name was Ilion. The *Returns* and the *Odyssey* concern the struggles that various Achaean heroes endured on their journeys homeward.

Virgil's *Aeneid*, the only surviving Latin epic, tells the story of Aeneas, whose escape from Troy led to the founding of a Trojan colony in Italy and ultimately the establishment of Rome. Although the *Aeneid* wasn't part of the Trojan War Cycle (a strictly Greek creation), Virgil did consciously draw from and emulate the Homeric form.

Of the eight epics *that originally made up the Trojan War Cycle, only the* Iliad *and the* Odyssey *survive.*

A page from the *Virgilius Romanus*, one of the oldest Virgil manuscripts.

III. GUILD REPUBLICANISM

THE FLOURISHING OF THE GUILDS encouraged new political ambitions among the merchants, tradesmen, and artisans known collectively as the *popolo*. Their middle-class interests conflicted with those of the nobility, just as their desire for political inclusion conflicted with the nobles' ideology of privilege. Eventually, the *popolo* became sufficiently emboldened to challenge the nobility for power. Strongly supported by bankers with international connections who wanted a stable business environment, the *popolo* subdued the nobility in 1293 and established a new republican government in Florence. Its officials were all required to be guildsmen.

The twenty-one guilds that made up the Florentine guild federation in 1293 were divided into three tiers. There were seven upper guilds, five middle guilds, and nine lower guilds. Each of these guilds was given political representation in the new government and expected to offer its members equal access to public office. But the most elite members of the upper guilds (six hundred or so of the eight thousand Florentine guildsmen) quickly realized that their personal interests were more closely aligned with those of the nobility than with those of their guild peers. Consequently, these powerful merchants, bankers, and lawyers began using their considerable social and economic influence to exclude middle and lower guildsmen (and even nonelite upper guildsmen) from political power.

Goldsmiths in fourteenth-century Italy.

For the most part, the nonelite members of the upper guilds went along with the rest of the *popolo* in accepting the hegemony of the elite upper guildsmen. As long as business remained good and the political elite offered the occasional concession, the government remained stable. However, in 1343, when the economy faltered, the nonelite members of the upper guilds joined the greater guild community in toppling the government.

After subduing the political elite, the greater guild community elevated to government office numerous guildsmen whose families had never before served. The political elite didn't stay down long, however. In 1348, when the Black Death struck Florence, the resurgent elite created a powerful new government committee, the *balìa*, and used it to purge the names of "foreigners" from the lists of candidates for public office. This tactic denied representation to the many middle and lower guildsmen not native to Florence and returned control of the city to the elite.

Although the new Florentine guild republic *was supposed to be broadly representative, its institutions came quickly under the control of a narrow political elite.*

III. THE VALUE OF A SHARE OF STOCK

UNLIKE A BOND, which obligates the issuer to make coupon payments, a share of stock has no intrinsic value. The dividends that some stocks pay impart a modicum of value, but the main reason to buy a stock is because the buyer believes that, in the future, someone will pay him more for the stock than he paid. This is called the greater fool theory.

Because stocks have no intrinsic value, it's very difficult to valuate them. Even in the special case of a takeover bid, the amount offered in cash to shareholders doesn't establish share value. What really matters is the total price being paid for the company. Only part of that price is paid to shareholders. Another part (often a disproportionate amount) goes to management as an inducement to approve the transaction, and the rest goes to the buyer—who, having the option to build a new company, usually buys only at a discount.

In 1934, Columbia Business School professors Benjamin Graham and David Dodd described in their book *Security Analysis* a strategy that would later come to be known as value investing. A value investor is someone who looks to buy a dollar's worth of assets for fifty cents. (By contrast, a growth investor is someone who believes that a stock is worth buying because its prospects are good, regardless of its current cost.)

Graham and Dodd's strategy makes sense, of course, but how can one tell that a share is selling for less than its worth if that worth can't be determined? In extreme cases, investors have been able to find stocks selling for less than the company's net cash on hand. Almost as good is a stock selling for less than the company's liquidation value. Yet even in these extreme cases, extracting the value of the assets means liquidating the company—a difficult and messy undertaking.

For example, at the end of the Internet bubble (which peaked in March 2000), hundreds of public companies saw their businesses disappear overnight. But some were left with a great deal of cash on hand, raised through initial public offerings of stock (IPOs). When their stock prices fell below the level of their net cash, investors began buying the stock. In only a few cases, however, were these investors able to force the distribution of the cash. For the most part, management made use of its legal protections to spend that money as it saw fit until all of it was gone.

Unlike a bond, *a share of stock has no intrinsic value. Rather, it's worth only what someone else will pay for it.*

III. THE JAZZ AGE

THE TERM *JAZZ AGE*—usually credited to F. Scott Fitzgerald, author of the 1922 short-story collection *Tales of the Jazz Age*—refers to the period between the end of World War I in 1918 and the collapse of the stock market in 1929. Before World War I, the United States was but a minor player on the global stage; afterward, with Europe ravaged, the nation quickly assumed a position of prominent international leadership.

The cover of the February 18, 1926, issue of *Life* magazine.

It was thus with a new sense of its own economic and political might that the United States roared into the 1920s. The recent introduction of the airplane and the skyscraper made it seem that the sky was literally the limit to what Americans could accomplish. Advances in mass production heightened this sense of civic euphoria, making automobiles and other consumer goods much more affordable to working-class families. Fueled by a range of speculative economic practices, the United States was quite literally a nation on the move.

Not surprisingly, the postwar boom also produced a number of significant social side effects. The new mobility, for instance, shattered the repressive Victorian morality that had governed American public behavior since the mid-nineteenth century. Women, in particular, took advantage of the new liberality to toss aside their restrictive corsets and even bob their hair. The Jazz Age was thus founded on a buoyant confidence in the future, but its optimism was also driven by a corresponding desire to escape the past.

Life in the United States began moving at a much faster pace, and from this frenzy emerged the consumerism that has since come to dominate American life. The popular music was, of course, jazz; and the sky-scraping notes of King Oliver's Creole Jazz Band, Jelly Roll Morton's Red Hot Peppers, and Louis Armstrong's Hot Five filled the illegal speakeasies, cabarets, and private parties that sprang up in the wake of the Eighteenth Amendment (1919), which began the era of Prohibition. Forbidding alcohol, of course, only increased its desirability, which in turn led to a great deal of excess. The literature of the Jazz Age teems with gin joints, champagne parties, and bootleggers; and to the chief chroniclers of the period, especially Fitzgerald, the decade must have seemed like one long party.

The postwar economic boom that propelled *the United States to international leadership also created a faster-paced, consumer-driven lifestyle fed by a sense of buoyant optimism.*

III. ELECTRIC FIELDS

THE CONCEPT OF A FIELD is essential to physics. Fields are sets of values that vary according to position and time. A field is expressed mathematically as $f(x, y, z, t)$, where x, y, z, and t are space–time coordinates. Consider the example of Earth's temperature field. The magnitude of the field (that is, the temperature value) at sea level in Rio de Janeiro on a midsummer day is different from the magnitude of the field at the top of Mount Everest on a midwinter night.

Physicists define an electric field (E) as the electric force exerted on a charge q at the space–time coordinates (x, y, z, t) divided by that charge. Mathematically, this is expressed as $E = F/q$. Electric forces, however, also have direction, indicating attraction of repulsion, so electric fields are vector fields. (A vector is a mathematical quantity that indicates both direction and magnitude. A car traveling at fifty miles per hour would represent a scalar quantity. The same car traveling at the same speed due north would represent a vector quantity.) By convention, when E is expressed graphically, it points away from positive charges and toward negative charges.

Electric fields are important because they can affect the kinetic energy of charged objects, By definition, kinetic energy (the energy of motion) is equal to $\frac{1}{2}mv^2$, where m is the mass of the object and v is its velocity. If a force acts on an object in the direction in which the object is already traveling, the object will speed up (accelerate), and its kinetic energy will increase. If, however, the force acts in the opposite direction, the object's speed and kinetic energy will decrease. The amount of change in the object's kinetic energy will be equal to the magnitude of the force multiplied by the distance over which the force acts.

So, a stationary charge q placed in an electric field E will feel an electric force F and accelerate, thus gaining kinetic energy. The amount of energy gained will be equal to the force acting on the charge multiplied by the distance over which the charge travels, or Fd. Rewriting the electric field equation above, we can see that the electric force is equal to the electric field multiplied by the magnitude of the charge ($F = qE$). Therefore, the amount of kinetic energy gained by the charge can also be expressed as qEd.

The electric force *can be described in terms of an electric field that causes charges to gain or lose kinetic energy.*

III. THE JUDGMENT OF PARIS

ACCORDING TO THE *CYPRIA*, the origins of the Trojan War are to be found in the jealousy of Eris, the goddess of strife, who becomes upset when she fails to receive an invitation to the marriage of the goddess Thetis and the mortal Peleus. In retaliation, Eris resolves to spark a quarrel among Athena, Aphrodite, and Hera. She creates a golden apple on which she inscribes the words FOR THE MOST BEAUTIFUL; then she deposits this apple in a grove where the three goddesses are sure to find it.

Of course, each goddess assumes that the apple is for her, and they fight over it. To settle the matter, they turn to Zeus, but he craftily sends them to Mount Ida— where, he tells them, the mortal shepherd Paris will judge their dispute. (Paris is actually a prince of Troy, but at his birth it was foretold that he would bring about Troy's destruction, so he was exposed; but a servant saved him and raised him as a shepherd.)

Each goddess offers Paris her eternal love in exchange for the apple. Athena promises Paris victory in battle. Hera offers him wealth and dominion over Asia and Europe. Aphrodite offers him the incomparably beautiful Helen, mortal daughter of Zeus. Unfortunately, what Paris doesn't realize is that whatever judgment he renders, along with his prize he will also earn the eternal enmity of the two goddesses he disappoints.

A Greek vase depicting the Judgment of Paris.

Because Paris can't resist his desire for Helen, he awards the golden apple to Aphrodite, thus setting in motion the chain of events that leads ultimately to war—the destiny that neither the Greeks nor the Trojans can avoid. Thus, we glimpse again the tragic fatalism that lies at the heart of Greek epic: Humans don't understand the significance of their actions; only the gods do.

Helen is already married to the Spartan king Menelaus, but Aphrodite casts a spell over her so that when Paris comes to collect her, she leaves with him willingly. Together, they travel to Troy, where Paris is welcomed as King Priam's son. The rest of the *Cypria* details the anger of Menelaus and his allies at the kidnapping of Helen, their assembly of a fleet, and its voyage to Troy. Upon the Achaeans' arrival in Asia Minor, they send an envoy to Priam demanding the return of Helen. When they are refused, they besiege Troy while sacking several of the city-state's allied neighbors.

The Judgment of Paris *exemplifies the precarious relationship between human will and divine agency—which Greek mythology teaches us is the essence of the human condition.*

IV. THE ORIGINS OF HUMANISM

HUMANISM BEGAN AS AN EDUCATIONAL PROGRAM that emphasized the study of the humanities, including literature, philosophy, history, grammar, and rhetoric. Most thirteenth- and fourteenth-century humanists were professional men—university-educated notaries and teachers, trained in the Roman law that informed current legal practice, who had become more generally interested in the history and culture of the ancient world. They focused their attention, in particular, on classical Greek and Roman texts, which were only then beginning to find their way back into intellectual circulation. The early humanists collected as many manuscripts as they could find, translated them, and produced thoughtful critical exegeses.

A Florentine translation of a work by Plotinus.

But humanism was more than simply an intellectual movement; it had a political aspect as well. Reading the works of ancient Roman politicians, the Florentine humanists couldn't help but compare the political culture of republican Rome with the conditions prevailing in their own city. Moreover, as humanism expanded its reach, members of the *popolo* found in the values of republican Rome (adherence to the rule of law, peaceful relations among the citizenry, nobility of birth not an entitlement to power) an expression of their own political longings. Although fully aware of the differences between their contemporary society and the ancient past, the Florentine humanists regularly cited ancient precedent to express their own civic ideals and criticize the power of the noble elite.

In 1266, the notary Brunetto Latini used the works of the Roman historian Sallust and the Roman politician Cicero to justify the *popolo*'s demand for a government of elected representatives committed to civic peace and bound by the rule of law. (During the late thirteenth century, the nobles who ran Florence routinely disregarded legal norms and were quick to raise arms.)

After the founding of the Florentine republic in 1293, the city became even more deeply immersed in humanist culture. Although the egalitarianism of the ancient Roman republic would seem to gainsay the new rulers' oligarchic tendencies, the political elite easily justified their practices by selectively emphasizing civic responsibility and the rule of law. Furthermore, by the early fifteenth century, even the elite had come to embrace humanism and considered their children's study of humanist curricula a sign of their superior civility. By then, Florence had become the center of humanism in Europe.

The Florentine humanists *called attention to ancient Roman republican precedents that the thirteenth-century* popolo *used to justify their own political longings.*

IV. FUNDAMENTAL ANALYSIS

EVEN THOUGH STOCKS ARE essentially impossible to value, investors keep trying to value them anyway so that they can rationalize their investment decisions. The methods that analysts use to assess share value are commonly divided into two broad categories: fundamental analysis, which looks at the performance of the underlying company; and technical analysis, which looks only at the performance of the stock.

Fundamental analysis begins with a company's balance sheet and income statement. The balance sheet lists all of the company's assets and liabilities at a point in time; the income statement shows all of the money flowing into and out of the company (primarily sales and expenses) over a period of time. The US government requires all publicly held companies to provide this information in quarterly and annual statements audited by an outside accounting firm and signed by management.

Fundamental analysts also research the industry within which the company is operating and the company's position within that industry. Important factors include the ownership of valuable patents or proprietary technology, the strength of the company's brands, ancillary assets such as real estate, the competence of the company's management, and so on. From this base, analysts attempt to project the company's future earnings. They can't do this, of course, without also taking into account the future of the industry and that of the national economy as well.

One of the most common measures used by fundamentalists is the price-to-earnings (P/E) ratio, which expresses the relationship between a company's share price and its current annual earnings (net profit) per share. Although a company's P/E ratio (also known as its multiple) is nearly meaningless by itself, it becomes useful when compared with the P/E ratios of other companies in the same industry and to the market as a whole. Fundamentalists also use their future-earnings projections to create "forward" P/Es, which can be compared with current P/Es. All of these comparisons help analysts make judgments about whether a stock's current price is too high or too low.

In the end, however, the multiple that the market assigns to a stock is basically arbitrary. For example, fast-growing companies are usually assigned higher multiples because their stocks are hotter. But a fast-growing company with a multiple of 150 may or may not be a better buy than a stable, slow-growing company with a multiple of 3. It all depends on whether the low-multiple company has a significant upside.

Fundamental analysis attempts to value stock *by looking at a company's financial position (its balance sheet and income statement), as well as its position within its industry.*

IV. THE LOST GENERATION

BECAUSE THE UNITED STATES DIDN'T enter World War I until the fighting was three-quarters over, and because none of the fighting took place on American soil, it was relatively easy for most Americans to put the unprecedented carnage of the Great War behind them. Veterans, however, found it much more difficult to forget what they had seen. Most had no outlet for the suffering and loss they had experienced, but a few were eventually able to transform their alienation into enduring works of art.

Stretcher bearers on a French battlefield.

The "return to normalcy" promoted by Warren Harding during his successful 1920 presidential campaign seemed to these people but a thin mask concealing the corrosive materialism then consuming the country, so many of them left—becoming expatriates in Paris, where they wrote, caroused, and discussed bold ideas. The center of their universe was the Left Bank salon of the American-born avant-garde writer Gertrude Stein (1874–1946). One day, when Stein took her Ford into a French garage for a repair, she overheard the owner dismissing a young apprentice's entire age group as "*une génération perdue.*" Stimulated by the metaphor, she translated the phrase into English and applied it to the cohort of young disillusioned Americans then living in Paris.

The members of the Lost Generation shared, most of all, an avid disdain for the values of their parents' generation. In their view, these values had produced the Great War and its accompanying devastation. Their reaction was to rebel, but this rebellion took the form of living life as a candle burning at both ends. "It will not last the night," poet Edna St. Vincent Millay wrote. "But ah, my foes, and oh, my friends— / It gives a lovely light!" The longer-term result of their hedonism, however, was sadness and despair.

The ranks of the Lost Generation read like a Who's Who of twentieth-century American literature. Along with F. Scott Fitzgerald, the group included Ernest Hemingway, Hart Crane, E. E. Cummings, John Dos Passos, Sherwood Anderson, Ezra Pound, and William Faulkner. The works of these authors, whose heyday was the 1920s and early 1930s, used the backdrop of postwar prosperity to show that money and happiness shared little connection. In Fitzgerald's *The Great Gatsby* (1925), for example, the character Daisy Buchanan speaks for all when she says, "Well, I've had a very bad time…and I'm pretty cynical about everything."

The Lost Generation *was a group of young expatriate writers who, disillusioned by their experiences during World War I, fell into lifestyles of hedonism and despair.*

IV. VOLTAGE

VOLTAGE EXPRESSES the difference in electric field strength between two points. Consider two points separated by the distance d. The voltage difference between them (V) is defined as Ed, where E is the average field strength along the line between the two points.

Now let's assume that the voltage difference between these two points happens to be zero—in other words, that the average electric field (E) multiplied by the distance between the points (d) is zero. In this case, $V = 0$. Therefore, because d is not zero, E must be. This is why birds can safely perch on high-voltage electrical lines. The line may have a voltage of 150,000 volts (V) relative to the ground, but if both of the bird's feet are resting on the line, then V is zero. However, if the bird were to remove one foot and place it on the ground (whose voltage is zero by convention), then the resulting V would be the full 150,000 volts.

Recall that the kinetic energy gained by a charge q moving in an electric field is qEd. Therefore, by substituting V for Ed, we find that the gain in kinetic energy experienced by a charge moving between two voltages is equal to the magnitude of the charge multiplied by the difference in the voltages, or qV, where V is defined as the initial voltage minus the final voltage. Therefore, positive charges ($q > 0$) gain energy when moving from a high voltage to a low voltage ($V > 0$), and negative charges ($q < 0$) gain energy when moving from a low voltage to a high voltage ($V < 0$).

Moving a charge from low to high energy takes work in the same way that rolling a boulder up a hill does. Once atop the hill, the boulder represents potential energy that can be released by rolling the boulder down the hill again. The same is true of charges at high energy, such as those in a battery. The rating (in volts) of a battery expresses the difference in voltage between the battery's two terminals.

If you were connect these terminals with a wire, electric charges would begin moving through the wire from the high-energy terminal to the low-energy terminal. It is this energy, derived from the motion of the charges, that powers electrical devices. The battery eventually dies as the stored energy is used up and the movement of charges stops.

Voltage describes the potential energy *gained by moving an electric charge from a position of low energy to one of high energy.*

IV. THE RAGE OF ACHILLES

AMONG THE CENTRAL FIGURES of the *Iliad*, which takes place during the tenth and final year of the Trojan War, are Achilles and Agamemnon. Brother to Menelaus, Agamemnon is the king of Mycenaeans and the *primus inter pares* (first among equals) of the Achaean army. The warlord Achilles is the child of Thetis and Peleus—to whose wedding Eris was not invited. Thus, Achilles is mortal yet endowed with certain superhuman traits.

Achilles eats a meal in his tent during the siege of Troy.

When the Achaeans sack Troy's neighbor Chryse (prior to the action in the *Iliad*), they capture as war prizes two maidens, Briseis and Chryseis, whom the army awards to Achilles and Agamemnon, respectively. Agamemnon, however, is forced to relinquish his prize by Apollo (because Chryseis's father turns out to be a priest of Apollo). An angry Agamemnon decides to soothe his seething spirit (*thumos*) by using his power as commander in chief to reclaim Achilles's prize for himself. Although within his power, Agamemnon's action is considered abusive by most Achaeans, and it sends Achilles into the rage that drives the plot of the *Iliad*.

In the war of words that follows, Achilles and Agamemnon each complains of the other's savage nature while failing to recognize the savagery within himself. They both feel justified in their actions—Agamemnon in his taking of Briseis, Achilles in his rage—yet neither is right. Nestor, the old and wise king of Pylos, warns, "And you, Achilles, never hope to fight it out with your king, pitting force against his force." Always the voice of reason, Nestor also rebukes Agamemnon for abusing his power. But neither hero gives ground.

This brings up a recurring theme in the *Iliad*: the tragedy of the human condition. Even Achilles, the greatest of heroes, and Agamemnon, the greatest of kings, are doomed to error (*hamartia*) and death (*thanatos*). Moreover, because Achilles is partially divine (by virtue of his mother's immortality), his actions are always magnified. When he fights, he does so with a skill and ferocity that no purely mortal man can match. Likewise, when he mourns, his grief is beyond all measure; and when his *thumos* is stirred, it rages beyond reason or appeasement.

The *Iliad* begins, "Rage, sing goddess the rage of Achilles, murderous, doomed, that cost the Achaeans countless losses, sending many great souls of heroes down to Hades and making their bodies feasts for dogs and birds." The rage of Achilles thus frames the story from the start.

The *Iliad* tells the story of *the implacable rage of Achilles brought on by Agamemnon's seizure of his war prize.*

V. THE GROWTH OF HUMANISM

ALTHOUGH THE HUMANIST MOVEMENT was well under way when Francesco Petrarch (1304–74) was born, he is considered by most scholars the father of humanism because he popularized the movement. Petrarch's enthusiastic recovery of ancient texts,

revival of ancient genres, and promotion of ancient writers encouraged many other Florentines to take up humanism; and the large group of followers he amassed—including Giovanni Boccaccio (1313–75), author of the *Decameron*—carried on his work well into the next century.

What's especially interesting about Petrarch is his rejection of humanism's political implications. An accomplished poet, Petrarch shunned politics and instead advocated a life of study and contemplation. He was thus unhappy to discover that his hero, Cicero, whose moral philosophy he so admired, had written letters to a friend, Atticus, describing in detail his own extensive political machinations. Even so, Petrarch happily took up the genre and used it to express his most intimate thoughts.

Francesco Petrarch

This was significant because, before Petrarch, medieval letter writing served a purely functional purpose. After Petrarch, the expression of personal opinion and feelings became an integral part of Renaissance humanism.

The humanists who followed Petrarch became interested in other ancient genres, such as the dialogue and the oration, which they adapted to suit the circumstances of contemporary life. They also shared Petrarch's love for ancient texts, uncovering and translating many Roman works that had been hidden away for centuries in old monasteries and private libraries. Meanwhile, the works of Homer, Sophocles, Herodotus, and other ancient Greeks became available for the first time in manuscripts imported from the Byzantine Empire.

The popularity of humanism grew in Florence until the city's elite families began hiring humanists to educate their children—which meant that the elite soon started producing humanists from within their own ranks. As a young man, Cosimo de' Medici, the founder of the Medici dynasty, studied under the humanist Roberto de' Rossi. Later, he used his great wealth to assemble a fabulous library of ancient texts. In this way, humanist learning became increasingly associated with high social status. As the Medicis consolidated their power, however, members of the previous regime who had been displaced ironically began calling for greater political access using the same humanist arguments that the *popolo* had previously championed.

Following Petrarch's lead, *Florentine humanists promoted the study of literature, history, and philosophy, eventually becoming instructors to the children of the city's elite.*

V. TECHNICAL ANALYSIS

THE ESSENTIAL PREMISE of technical analysis is that history repeats itself across industries, markets, and eras. While fundamental analysis focuses on a stock's underlying value, technical analysis dispenses entirely with notions of cheap or expensive and looks only to a stock's trading history. Once technicians discern a pattern in that history, they buy or sell based on the assumption that the pattern will continue.

The foundation of all technical analysis is the price chart, which shows the fluctuations in a stock's price over time. From there, technical systems can become dizzyingly complex, and the number of different systems in use is vast. However, there are some commonalities. Trend-following systems, for instance, look for stocks that are likely to continue moving in a particular direction, either up or down. These systems generally use trailing average prices as a starting point and then make adjustments of one sort or another.

The trailing average price is the average of a stock's closing prices over a specified period of time. To calculate the 150-day trailing average for a stock, you would add together the stock's closing price on each of the last 150 days and divide by 150. This average changes every day, of course, as the latest close replaces the earliest close in the average. Values for these averages are then plotted and compared. One trend-following system might generate buy orders every time the graph of the 10-day trailing average crosses the graph of the 150-day trailing average from underneath with rising volume.

Other common technical systems are called oscillators because they attempt to identify ranges in which trades should and should not be made. These systems seek to identify stocks that are shifting from a basing phase, during which the stock remains within a relatively narrow price band, to a trending phase, when it begins to move outside that band. Stocks that rise out of such bands and continue moving upward are referred to as breakouts.

Despite the claims of their inventors, no technical system has yet been shown to be consistently and meaningfully profitable. This is not to say, however, that all aspects of technical analysis are useless. For example, it has been demonstrated statistically that, in the medium term, stocks do hold to trends: Those that begin to go up generally continue to go up, and those that begin to go down generally continue to fall.

The purpose of technical analysis is *to forecast future stock prices based on where the stock has been in the past.*

V. THE WASTE LAND

BORN AND RAISED IN ST. LOUIS, T. S. Eliot (1888–1965) graduated from Harvard in 1910, after which he traveled to Europe, where he spent a year in Paris studying at

the Sorbonne. The experience converted him from a student of literature into one of philosophy, and in 1911 he returned to Harvard to begin a doctoral program in philosophy there. During the summer of 1914—prior to matriculating at Merton College, Oxford—Eliot visited Europe again but was forced to cut short his trip to Germany because of the impending war. Three years later, *The Egoist*, a magazine of the English avant-garde, published his first collection of poems, *Prufrock and Other Observations*. The book—made possible by the silent financial support of another American expatriate, Ezra Pound—included as its centerpiece "The Love Song of J. Alfred Prufrock," which established Eliot's reputation as a poet of great merit. Its elegiac

T. S. Eliot in his twenties.

style and unflinching exploration of disillusionment also served as harbingers of what was soon to come from the Lost Generation.

In 1922, Eliot published *The Waste Land*. This 434-line poem begins in London and ends in the Himalayas, allowing the author to guide the reader on what becomes a pilgrimage of renewal and regeneration. The poem's famous opening phrase— "April is the cruellest month, breeding lilacs out of the dead land"—echoes the opening of Chaucer's *Canterbury Tales*—"When April with his showers sweet with fruit…" But the cheerfulness and promise apparent in Chaucer's words are clearly absent from Eliot's, prefiguring the bleak austerity of *The Waste Land* as a whole. Nevertheless, while the landscape of Eliot's poem is unwelcoming, its theme of spiritual renewal in a world of material decay is surprisingly hopeful.

Eliot's central metaphor—civilization as a wasteland—would later shape many Jazz Age novels, including Fitzgerald's *The Great Gatsby* (1925) and Hemingway's *The Sun Also Rises* (1926), both of which are set against worlds gone to pieces. The poem also influenced writer Ralph Ellison, who was studying music composition at Tuskegee when he first read *The Waste Land* in 1935. The poem, he later said, caused him to change his major from music to literature. Reflecting on his initial encounter with *The Waste Land*, Ellison observed, "Somehow its rhythms were often closer to those of jazz than were those of the Negro poets, and even though I could not understand then, its range of allusion was as mixed and as varied as that of Louis Armstrong."

T. S. Eliot's epic poem The Waste Land *transformed modern poetry and gave the Lost Generation a dominant metaphor for postwar life: civilization as a wasteland.*

V. ELECTRIC CURRENT

CONNECTING A WIRE to the terminals of a battery causes charges to move through the wire because the difference in the field strength at the terminals creates a net electric force. The motion of these charges, called electric current, is measured in amps (A). Amps express the number of coulombs of charge that move past a given point in the wire each second.

In theory, both positive and negative charges can generate electric current; in practice, however, current almost always refers to the motion of negative charges. One reason is that negatively charged electrons are nearly two thousand times lighter that positively charged protons, which means that they accelerate faster when a force is applied. Another reason is that electrons orbiting in the outer shells of atoms have a much greater freedom of movement than protons trapped in the nucleus. Because the nuclear forces that bind protons together are much stronger than the electric force, electric fields aren't powerful enough to pry protons free and push them through a wire. Some electrical devices, such car batteries, make use of liquids in which positively and negatively charged atoms move about freely in solution; but in solid materials such as wire, electric current is carried by electrons.

By convention, electric current is said to flow against the motion of the negative charges. Therefore, if you attach a wire to the two terminals of a battery, the electrons will flow from the negative (low-voltage) terminal to the positive (high-voltage) terminal, but the current will flow from the positive terminal to the negative terminal.

What if you attach a wire to only one terminal of a battery? Because the wire itself has a voltage of zero, charges would begin moving into the wire; but the current would quickly cease as the charges piled up in the wire, raising its voltage to the voltage of the battery. On the other hand, if the wire is attached to both terminals, a circuit is created in which the voltage difference (or potential energy) provided by the battery maintains the current flow.

Now think again of the bird on the high-voltage wire. As long as it keeps both feet on the wire, it's safe; but if one foot touches the ground, creating an enormous voltage difference between its two feet, the equally enormous current will begin moving through the bird, depositing enough energy to fry it instantly.

Electric current is *the motion of electric charges through a circuit.*

V. YOKED BY NECESSITY

AFTER BRISEIS IS TAKEN from him, Achilles withdraws from the fighting. Meanwhile, his mother, Thetis, persuades Zeus to honor her son by favoring the Trojans in battle. Zeus's help is hardly significant, except that it provokes Athena to come down from Olympos and fight beside the Achaean hero Diomedes, who uses the strength she provides to dominate the field.

To save Troy, Paris proposes that he and Menelaus fight a duel to the death, the winner receiving Helen along with a suitable tribute. Because both armies are weary of war, they embrace the idea enthusiastically and proclaim a truce. When the duel begins, Menelaus gains the upper hand; but before he can deliver the death blow, Paris is whisked away to Troy by Aphrodite.

Paris's sudden disappearance startles everyone. Declaring victory for Menelaus, Agamemnon demands the immediate surrender of Helen and Paris. Having witnessed Paris's defeat in fair combat, the Trojans are willing to comply, but the prince is nowhere to be found. Finally, Athena tricks the Trojan archer Pandarus into shooting an arrow at Menelaus, breaking the truce. Thus, the fighting resumes; and humans are shown once again to be responsible for, though not entirely in control of, their actions.

The gods' near-constant manipulation continues when Aphrodite orders Helen to treat Paris's wounds and make love to him while he recuperates. Protesting, Helen laments her fate. She complains that Aphrodite deluded her into leaving Sparta with Paris, and she chides Paris for being such a weakling and a coward. But the goddess will hear none of it, and she forces Helen to attend to Paris, warning her not to become hated by all parties (the Trojans as well as the Achaeans).

Helen does what she must, just as all humans in the *Iliad* do what they must. Despite their inability to determine willfully the consequences of their actions, humans must nevertheless make choices and act upon them. Recall the Judgment of Paris: There is no good choice for the Trojan, because whatever choice he makes, two powerful goddesses will despise him eternally. Yet Paris must choose and suffer consequences. The Greeks called this predicament being "yoked by necessity."

The Greek and Trojan armies are likewise yoked by necessity. They cannot escape fighting the Trojan War, during which great deeds will be done by heroes who will be remembered for all eternity. But the tragic price of such glory is suffering, pain, and death.

Although attempts are made *to end the war, the fighting continues because the Greeks and the Trojans are "yoked by necessity" to fulfill destinies beyond their control.*

VI. THE BLACK DEATH

IN APRIL 1348, the Black Death struck Italy; and Florence, like other cities, endured its ravages. The plague killed indiscriminately—infecting young and old, male and female, rich and poor. According to contemporary accounts, Florence lost two-thirds of its population in a matter of months.

Boccaccio, who witnessed the plague's arrival, described the resulting chaos in his *Decameron*, which recounts in horrifying detail how husbands deserted infected wives and parents abandoned infected children. So many people died, Boccaccio wrote, that Florentines began leaving the corpses on public thoroughfares. These accumulated in great piles until they were carted off and dumped in mass graves.

A scene of the Black Death from a Bible illustrated in 1411.

The Black Death returned to Florence seven more times before the end of the century, making population recovery slow. There were new births, of course, but more importantly there was significant immigration from the countryside. Many of Florence's rural parishes emptied completely as survivors moved to the city in search of opportunity. Even so, the recurrence of plague kept the population down. In 1427, when the first census was taken, there were still only 38,000 people living in Florence, compared with about 120,000 a century earlier.

The severity of the population decline made Florentines especially anxious about marriage and reproduction. The city's convents emptied as families steered their daughters toward childbearing; and the Florentine government supported this trend by establishing a fund to subsidize the dowries of young women. Not surprisingly, Florentines also became preoccupied with death. Wealthy men, in particular, became interested in commemorating themselves and their lineages. Many endowed private chapels within churches, while others commissioned funerary artifacts (such as candlesticks, chalices, and sacred paintings) emblazoned with their family's coat of arms.

The nineteenth-century Swiss historian Jakob Burckhardt famously promoted the idea that the Italian Renaissance ushered in modernity because the "Renaissance man" was the first to express his individual personality without reference to family or lineage. The evidence of Florentine testaments, however, proves otherwise. During the years following the Black Death, many Florentines began specifying how their family property would be held, used, and transmitted through living and future heirs, obligating succeeding generations to abide by their wishes.

The Black Death that struck Florence *in 1348 killed an estimated two-thirds of the population and dramatically transformed Florentine attitudes toward family, society, and memory.*

VI. MARKET TRANSPARENCY AND EFFICIENCY

THE ROOTS OF THE MODERN STOCK MARKET can be traced back to the coffeehouses of eighteenth-century London, beyond that to the tulip exchanges of seventeenth-century Amsterdam, and even farther back to the market fairs of medieval Europe. In all of these cases, the basic purpose of the market was the same: to bring together as many buyers and sellers as possible.

Investors have since learned that financial assets attain their greatest value when traded in active, liquid markets. Thus, in modern times, stock markets have come to embrace those qualities that promote activity and liquidity—specifically, transparency and efficiency.

Transparency ensures that neither buyer nor seller will be at an information disadvantage. When trades are openly displayed, buyers are more willing to pay high prices, because they know that no better deal is available; and sellers are less likely to withhold inventory, because there is little chance that an uninformed buyer will pay more than the current market price.

Efficiency is especially important when it relates to the transmission of price-moving information. In efficient markets, this information moves nearly instantaneously. For example, if an aggressive buyer enters an efficient market, his actions will become immediately apparent in the movement of the stock price. Even if the buyer is careful, his purchases will change the stock's trading pattern and alert watchful sellers.

Transparency and efficiency thus directly promote activity and liquidity, making it easier for all market participants to trade. Furthermore, because liquidity tends to attract more liquidity, successful markets tend to prosper at the expense of their competition. Over time, large, active exchanges drive out smaller ones. In the United States, for example, the New York Stock Exchange (NYSE) and the NASDAQ have taken away all of the business from regional exchanges in Boston, Philadelphia, and Denver.

Like stock markets of old, however, modern exchanges are run by insiders. The practice of restricting membership used to be justified by the claim that it maintained the integrity of the exchange. Ostensibly, the practice weeded out people of low moral character who might be tempted to manipulate prices or transactions. Today, no such moral claims are made, but members remain privy to inside trading information. When they use this information to facilitate public trades, they are doing their jobs. When they use the information for private gain, however, they are guilty of illegal insider trading.

Transparency and efficiency, *the hallmarks of the modern stock market, promote the activity and liquidity that make modern markets successful.*

VI. ERNEST HEMINGWAY

ALTHOUGH HIS PRIMARY RESIDENCE was the Chicago suburb of Oak Park, Ernest Hemingway (1899–1961) spent most of his boyhood summers hunting and fishing with his father in northern Michigan. In high school, he wrote articles for the school newspaper as well as some poetry about football. Following his graduation, because he had no interest in college, the eighteen-year-old Hemingway took a job as a cub reporter for the *Kansas City Star*. Meanwhile, the United States having finally entered World War I, he tried to join the army but was rejected because of poor eyesight. Rebuffed but not deterred, he soon found his way into the war as a volunteer ambulance driver for the American Red Cross.

Although Hemingway spent just six months on the staff of the *Kansas City Star*, the lessons he learned there about succinct prose guided him throughout his writing life. The newspaper's stylebook included 110 rules, but the first was the most important: "Use short sentences. Use short paragraphs. Use vigorous English. Be positive, not negative [i.e., state matters directly]." These and other directives, such as the rule warning against the excessive use of adjectives, later formed the basis for what Hemingway called his iceberg theory of writing: "If a writer of prose knows enough about what he is writing about he may omit things that he knows and the reader, if the writer is writing truly enough, will have a feeling of those things as strongly as though the writer had stated them. The dignity of movement of an iceberg is due to only one-eighth of it being above water."

On July 8, 1918, three weeks after his arrival at the Italian front, Hemingway was distributing cigarettes at a forward observation post when a mortar shell exploded overhead, sending 227 pieces of shrapnel into his legs. As he hobbled away with a wounded soldier on his back, he was shot twice more by an Austrian machine-gunner. After recovering from his wounds in a Milan hospital, Hemingway returned to

Ernest Hemingway recuperates at a Red Cross hospital in Milan.

the United States in January 1919, receiving a hero's welcome. By December 1921, however, he was married (to Hadley Richardson) and back in Europe—working in Paris as a foreign correspondent for the *Toronto Star* because a fellow Chicagoan, short-story writer Sherwood Anderson, had told him Paris was the place for a young writer to be.

Ernest Hemingway's six months *on the staff of the* Kansas City Star *taught him how to write, but it was his experience of World War I that made him a writer.*

VI. RESISTANCE

MATERIALS IN WHICH ELECTRONS can move about easily are called conductors because they permit an easy flow of electric current. Metals, for example, are particularly good conductors because their outer electrons can move about anywhere in the material, which becomes a sea of mobile, current-carrying charges. Materials whose atomic structure inhibits the flow of current are called insulators. Air, for example, is an excellent insulator because it takes very strong electric fields to strip electrons from its atoms. (When this does happen, we see the result as sparks or lightning.)

Electrons that flow through conductors routinely collide with atoms in the material. During these collisions, kinetic energy is transferred from the electrons to the atoms, causing them to vibrate. We experience these vibrations as heat, which is also a form of energy. Thus, electrons moving in a current gain energy by traveling across a voltage difference but also lose energy through heat-producing collisions (such as those that generate the heat of a hair dryer).

Materials that are prone to these collisions dissipate more energy through heat and therefore require higher voltages to maintain the same level of current. Electrical resistance, which measures how well or poorly a material resists the flow of current, is defined as the voltage difference across the material divided by the amount of current flowing through it.

Most, but not all, materials have a constant resistance to current flow. When this is the case, the relationship among voltage (V), current (I), and resistance (R) can be expressed using the simple equation $V = IR$, known as Ohm's Law.

Power, measured in watts (W), is related to resistance, measured in ohms (Ω), because power expresses the amount of energy used per time and this amount depends on the level of resistance in a circuit. Recall that the kinetic energy gained by a charge moving across a voltage difference V is qV. If that energy gets used up overcoming the resistance in a circuit, then the power required to overcome the resistance is IV, because I is an expression of q per time.

Therefore, if you plug a 600-watt hair dryer into a 120-volt outlet and turn it on, the current flow through the hair dryer will be 5 amps (because 5 x 120 = 600). Using these values, we can then manipulate Ohm's Law to calculate the hair dryer's resistance. If $V = IR$, then $R = V/I$, or 120/5, or 12 ohms.

Resistance measures the degree to which the atomic structure *of a material inhibits the flow of current. Ohm's Law expresses the relationship among resistance, current, and voltage.*

VI. THE EMBASSY TO ACHILLES

AFTER PANDARUS'S ARROW wounds Menelaus in the leg, Zeus fills the Trojan army with fighting spirit. Led by Hector, heir to the enfeebled Priam, the Trojans drive the Achaeans all the way back to their ships. It is only then, with his army facing annihilation, that Agamemnon concedes the folly of his dispute with Achilles and resolves to end it. Knowing that his own presence will only inflame the situation, he sends three warriors dear to Achilles—Odysseus, Phoenix, and

A detail from a ca. 520 BCE wine jug showing Agamemnon.

Ajax—to persuade him to rejoin the battle. Agamemnon offers not only the return of Briseis but also land, treasure, servants, and his daughter's hand in marriage.

Odysseus speaks first, pleading with Achilles to accept Agamemnon's offer. But Achilles refuses, stating that nothing can repair the breach. Warriors risk their lives in service to their leaders. The rewards for their valor are honor (*timē*) and fame (*kleos*). During their lifetimes, this fame is measured in the trophies and honors they receive. Like the deeds that produce it, *kleos* cannot be undone. Therefore, Agamemnon's conduct toward Achilles has shown him to be an untrustworthy giver of gifts and thus an unworthy leader.

Phoenix then attempts to change Achilles's mind by telling him the story of a prince who was called upon to defend his city but refused because he was having a feud with his mother. The queen implored the prince again and again to come to the city's aid, promising him great trophies; but it wasn't until he saw the carnage outside his own window that he took up arms and drove the invaders off. Because his heroism came only after much destruction, however, he was denied the honors initially offered him. The implication is clear: Achilles will ultimately act to defeat Hector; but if he waits too long, he will be denied the honors otherwise due him. Achilles replies by offering Phoenix a place on his ship, implying that he won't act to prevent the other Achaean vessels from being burned.

Finally, Ajax chides Achilles for having "turned his great heart savage." Civilized people, Ajax explains, agree to laws that mitigate their strife. When a man kills another, for instance, he pays legal compensation to the victim's family and thereafter lives on in the community without fear of retribution. "Everything you say is after my own mind," Achilles acknowledges, but he still can't bring himself to make amends with Agamemnon.·

When Agamemnon realizes that *the Achaeans are about to be defeated, he sends an embassy to Achilles, offering him lavish gifts in exchange for his return to the battlefield.*

VII. THE REVOLT OF THE CIOMPI

EVEN BEFORE THE BLACK DEATH decimated the city, the Florentine economy had lost much of its thirteenth-century dynamism. By the early 1340s, several major banking firms had collapsed, there were food shortages, and the government found itself hard pressed to pay its creditors. When the plague struck, production fell precipitously, and prices immediately shot up, especially for food.

Once people got back to work, however, the resulting depopulation produced a brief golden age for wage earners. Because of the severe labor shortage, these normally marginalized workers were able, for a time, to set the terms of their employment; and their incomes more than doubled. Yet even though high mortality rates continued to favor labor for the next hundred years, changes in both the Florentine economy and government policy gradually made life precarious again for much of the city's workforce.

Despite the high wages they earned and the relatively low prices they paid (because of the steep decline in demand), urban workers found it increasingly difficult to meet their obligations, especially their tax obligations. During the last quarter of the fourteenth century, the government's military budget ballooned; and under Florence's arcane system of taxation, citizens with the means to pay were forced to make loans to the government to cover any shortfalls. Given the government's poor financial condition, these loans were rarely, if ever, repaid. Previously, the laboring classes (*ciompi*) had been excluded from such assessments because of their low earning power. By the 1370s, however, that situation had changed.

In 1378, with forced loans rapidly draining away their increased income, the *ciompi* petitioned the government for the right to establish their own guild, for access to public office, and for more equitable taxation. When the government failed to go far enough in meeting their demands, the workers staged an armed uprising known as the Revolt of the Ciompi. Although this insurrection was quickly put down, the specter of armed laborers in the streets haunted the guild community for generations to come.

The decline of the Florentine wool industry also hurt the city's unskilled labor force. Because of increased competition from England, Florentine wool merchants shifted their business into the manufacture of silk, which required highly skilled artisans. For these workers and the entrepreneurs who employed them, the Florentine economy of the early fifteenth century offered rich opportunities for profit; but for the unskilled laborers who had worked for generations in the wool industry, the economic possibilities dwindled.

Although depopulation temporarily improved the lot of the laboring classes, *heavy taxation and changes in the Florentine economy eventually widened the gap between rich and poor.*

VII. REGULATING THE MARKETPLACE

WITHIN THE LARGER FINANCIAL MARKETPLACE, transparency is enforced through regulation. The United States prides itself on having the most extensive and complex regulatory system in the world. Its overriding mission is to compel disclosure—because the more investors know about their investments, the lower their risk will be, and the lower the cost of their capital to businesses. Transparency also promotes market discipline, because informed investors will reward competent managers (usually through higher stock prices) and punish inept ones. Sometimes, however, the purpose of a regulation and its practical effect don't match. An interesting example is the poison pill. When a hostile investor buys more than a specified percentage of a company's stock (usually 15 to 20 percent), the company's board of directors can issue additional stock to *every other shareholder* at a very low price (often pennies per share). This "pill" is "poisonous" to the hostile buyer because it drastically dilutes the value of his stake in the company.

Poison pills were created during the takeover boom of the 1980s by the Chancery Court of Delaware. (Most large US businesses are incorporated in Delaware because the state maintains a business-friendly environment and its body of corporate law is the most highly developed in the country.) The purpose of the poison pill was to give companies whose market value was low a way to fend off corporate raiders whose takeover bids were financed by high-risk, high-yield junk bonds.

It may sound unjust that a company should be forced into a coercive sale simply because its stock price is low, but poison pills dramatically undercut shareholder rights. Most importantly, they entrench poor management. If well-run companies can't force the sale of poorly run companies—in other words, if the only way to dislodge management is at management's own discretion—then what has become of market discipline?

Canada permits a so-called dissolving pill, which a Canadian board can institute when it receives a bona-fide takeover offer. But the dissolving pill lasts only long enough (usually forty-five to fifty days) for the board to organize either a defense or a sale process. Ultimately, the shareholders decide whether to accept the bid or support the management plan. The British go even farther in safeguarding shareholder rights. They disallow pills altogether and prohibit boards from taking any "frustrating action," such as selling a major company asset or buying another business in order to increase company debt.

Although most market regulations are *designed to promote disclosure, which benefits investors, some forms of regulation (such as poison pills) undermine shareholder rights.*

VII. THE SUN ALSO RISES

HEMINGWAY ARRIVED IN PARIS with a letter from Sherwood Anderson introducing him to Gertrude Stein, into whose circle he was quickly absorbed. As Hemingway would later recall, he would stand at his window and look out over the rooftops of

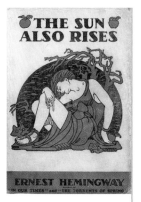

The first edition of
The Sun Also Rises.

Paris, thinking to himself, "'All you have to do is write one true sentence. Write the truest sentence that you know.' So finally I would write one true sentence, and then go on from there."

Hemingway's first novel, *The Sun Also Rises* (1926), chronicled the bohemian lifestyle of the Lost Generation. It was also an attempt to create meaning in a world that evoked in Hemingway mostly cynicism and disbelief. Narrator Jake Barnes is, like Hemingway, a journalist seeking to become a novelist. He's also a Great War veteran who has been rendered impotent by an unspecified injury. The main action of the plot is a pilgrimage that Jake and his friends make to Pamplona to see the bull fights. Because of his impairment, however, Barnes remains an outsider in the world he describes.

Eschewing the poetic flourishes found in the works of other Lost Generation writers such as Fitzgerald and Faulkner, Hemingway employed simple words and even simpler sentence structure. (Faulkner once remarked that one never needed a dictionary to read Hemingway.) Characters in *The Sun Also Rises* speak in clipped sentences and respond to questions usually with just one or two words. As one character tells Jake, "And you claim you want to be a writer, too. You're only a newspaper man. An expatriated newspaper man. You ought to be ironical the minute you get out of bed. You ought to wake up with your mouth full of pity." The incongruity, of course, is that Hemingway himself cast aside irony in favor of simple, direct truth.

As the novel progresses, it becomes clear that, for Hemingway, the most apposite metaphor for writing is bullfighting. Both practices require skill, discipline, and sacrifice. In fact, although Jake is the central character, the novel's moral focus is star matador Pedro Romero. Romero's independence, fidelity, and commitment to his craft stand in stark contrast with Jake's own behavior; and when Barnes describes Romero's technique, he might as well be describing Hemingway's: "Romero never made any contortions, always it was straight and pure and natural in line. The others twisted themselves like corkscrews." Much like Romero, who killed bulls without wasting motions, Hemingway wrote sentences without wasting words.

In *The Sun Also Rises*, *Hemingway searches for meaning in the postwar world while simultaneously questing for what he calls the "true sentence."*

VII. DIRECT AND ALTERNATING CURRENT

A CURRENT THAT FLOWS in only one direction, such as from the positive to the negative terminal of a battery, is called direct current (DC). The electric current that runs through the wires in your home takes a different form, called alternating current (AC). In AC systems, the current reverses direction at a fixed rate. In the United States, this rate is 60 cycles per second, or 60 hertz (Hz). The rest of the world typically uses 50 Hz systems.

The first generating station to produce centralized power began operating in 1882. It was built in New York City by Thomas Edison to provide electricity for his new electric lightbulb. Several years later, Nikola Tesla, a former Edison employee, invented an AC system, which he developed with George Westinghouse to compete with Edison's DC generators.

A nineteenth-century direct-current dynamo (generator).

Alternating current eventually prevailed over direct current because voltage and current could be changed much more easily in Tesla and Westinghouse's system than in Edison's system. Using a device called a transformer, the operator of an AC system could increase the voltage in its transmission lines while simultaneously decreasing the current, thereby minimizing the energy loss due to heat in the wires. As a result, AC systems transmitted electricity much more efficiently (and over longer distances) than DC systems—an important competitive advantage. (Transformers couldn't be used in DC systems because they require changes in the current direction to work.)

Today, utility companies still use transformers to step up the AC power they produce to very high voltages and very low currents before distributing it through their transmission lines. When this power finally reaches a customer's house, other transformers step it down to the 110 V required by most US appliances. Many electrical devices—lightbulbs, for example—run on both AC and DC. Some devices, however, such as laptop computers, run only on direct current. These devices use rectifiers to convert AC power into DC power. When a laptop runs off its DC battery, no conversion is needed, but the power adapter you plug into the wall contains both a transformer and a rectifier to produce the proper voltage and current for the computer.

The electric current produced by a battery is direct current *because it flows in only one direction— from the positive to the negative terminal. The electric current produced by utilities is alternating current because its direction changes at fixed intervals.*

VII. THE HEROIC IDEAL

IN A FAMOUS MONOLOGUE, Homer uses the character Sarpedon, a Lycian prince and ally of Troy, to illustrate the heroic ideal. Sarpedon begins the speech by asking his compatriot Glaukos, "Why is it you and I are honored before others in Lycia?" Answering his own question, Sarpedon says, "It is our duty to stand at the forefront of the Lycians in battle so that others might say, 'Indeed, these are not unworthy lords of Lycia, these kings of ours who accept all the choicest meats and wine that we offer them. There is valor in them because they fight in the forefront of the Lycians.'"

Sarpedon thus puts into words the generally unspoken code that bound ancient warriors to their leaders. But there is more: "Supposing you and I, escaping this battle, would be able to live on forever [that is, become immortals]? I would not continue to fight at the forefront, nor would I urge you into the fighting where men win *kleos*." What Sarpedon means is that immortals have no reason to fight as men do on the battlefield because only mortal warriors can win *kleos*. This is because only mortals risk their lives in battle. Immortals, who risk nothing, can't prove their greatness in the same way.

Kleos in this sense transcends a hero's death. Once he is dead, a hero loses his possessions, but his *kleos*—that is, the fame and glory of his deeds—cannot be taken away from him nor tarnished in any way. For this reason, as Sarpedon points out, the sacrifice of a hero's life is paradoxically the means by which he obtains immortality. By giving up his life, he wins *kleos*, which ensures that he will be remembered forever.

Sarpedon's own fate is especially important in the *Iliad* because, like Achilles, Sarpedon has a divine parent. His father is none other than the omniscient Zeus, who knows that his son is fated to die. Certainly Zeus can save him—he has the requisite power—but to do so would mean defying fate and thus distorting the order of the universe. This dilemma highlights Zeus's ambiguous role in the *Iliad*'s cosmic order: He consults with fate and often plays a prominent role in its enactment, but he doesn't write the script himself. Although Zeus wants to rescue Sarpedon, his decision is never really in doubt. In the world of the ancient Greeks, even the mightiest gods can be yoked by necessity.

Sarpedon represents the heroic ideal *to which all Homeric warriors aspire. His eventual death suggests that even Zeus is not beyond the yoke of necessity.*

A detail from a Greek vase showing Sapredon's death.

VIII. THE PRICE OF FLORENTINE EXPANSION

DURING THE EARLY FOURTEENTH CENTURY, like many other Italian city-states, Florence began to push beyond its borders, absorbing the territory of smaller, weaker neighbors. Such behavior led to wars of expansion and defense, necessitating the mustering of much larger armies than the city had previously maintained. Just as importantly, the composition of those armies changed over time. In 1260, the Florentine militia numbered about seven thousand citizens and peasants, supplemented by about two hundred mercenaries. During the next hundred years, however, that ratio steadily inverted until by the 1360s, the army had become entirely mercenary.

There were several reasons for this transformation, but the pressing need was manpower. Worried about losing their political control, the elite upper guildsmen who ran the city disarmed the neighborhood societies that had been set up during the thirteenth century to defend commoners against warring nobility. Therefore, the government had to turn elsewhere for men under arms. The obvious solution was to hire mercenaries—who were, after all, much better suited than untrained militiamen to fight Florence's wars of expansion.

Yet the use of mercenaries did pose some problems. For one, mercenaries were expensive; and as city-states began to compete for their services, their wage demands became exorbitant. For another, professional soldiers tended to shift their allegiances rather easily, even in the midst of battle. To retain the loyalty of its prized captains, Florence offered citizenship and a lifetime exemption from taxes. Some mercenaries received even higher honors. In 1436, for example, Paolo Uccello was commissioned to paint a funerary portrait of the English mercenary John Hawkwood for a wall in the Florentine cathedral.

Uccello's portrait of John Hawkwood.

This total reliance on mercenaries meant heavy taxation, of course, which in turn transformed Florentine politics. Three costly wars against Milan, fought during the 1390s and early 1400s, imposed enormous financial strains on the government, causing it to assess an unprecedented number of forced loans. When even these failed to meet the need, the government began arranging short-term loans at high rates of interest. Meanwhile, as the political elite became increasingly dependent on the city's wealthiest citizens to subsidize Florence's military adventurism, those citizens began demanding—and receiving—more and more political power, leading ultimately to the political elite's decline and the rise of the Medicis.

Florence's desire for expansion *and the hiring of mercenaries to achieve this goal led to high taxation, the undermining of the government, and the rise of the Medicis.*

VIII. PRICES AND SPREADS

BECAUSE MODERN STOCK EXCHANGES ARE highly liquid, they maintain continuous two-way trading in the stocks that they list. The price at which a buyer is willing to buy is called the bid. The price at which a seller is willing to sell is called the ask or offer. The difference between the bid and the ask is the spread. Spreads are necessary if there is to be continuous two-way trading because they account for (and price) the risk that market participants assume when they put up their capital. You can also think of the spread as the fee charged by the exchange to the ultimate buyer and seller.

For many years, the standard spread on the New York Stock Exchange for stocks trading over five dollars a share was one-eighth of a point (dollar), or 12.5 cents. An eighth of a point was also the minimum increment in which stock prices moved up and down. Therefore, if the spread on a stock was 35 to 35 ⅛, an NYSE member who bought the stock at the bid and sold it at the ask made 12.5 cents per share, or 0.36 percent of the capital he put at risk. Under competition from foreign markets, exchanges in the United States have since tightened their spreads, and the NYSE now offers spreads denominated in pennies (or even fractions of a cent) rather than in eighths of a dollar.

The size of the spread depends on several factors—including the liquidity of the stock, its price, and the rules of the exchange. A lot of action in a stock brings in more people and more money, lowering the risk assumed by short-term traders who decide to take positions in the stock. If these traders can easily sell their shares should the price move against them, they will demand a smaller profit on each trade, making up the difference in volume. Therefore, the more liquid a stock is, the narrower its spread will be.

The spread is also affected by the share price. Stocks with higher share prices generally have proportionately greater spreads so that the ratio of the spread to the share price remains fairly constant. AT&T, with a share price in the range of $40, usually has a two-cent spread (equal to 0.05 percent of the share price). On the other hand, Google, a $650 stock, usually trades with a twenty-five-cent spread (equal to about 0.04 percent of the share price).

The spread is the difference between *the bid (what a buyer is willing to pay) and the ask (what a seller is willing to accept).*

VIII. F. SCOTT FITZGERALD

MINNESOTAN F. SCOTT FITZGERALD (1896–1940) entered Princeton University in 1913, attracted more by the social scene than by the academics. In fact, he spent so much of his time writing lyrics for the musical comedy productions staged by the Triangle Club that he was forced to withdraw from the university in the middle of his junior year because of poor grades. Fitzgerald returned to Princeton in the fall of 1916 but left again in October 1917 to join the army as a second lieutenant. The war ended before he could

F. Scott Fitzgerald in a 1937 portrait by Carl Van Vechten.

be sent overseas, however, and he served out his time as an aide-de-camp to the commanding general at Camp Sheridan in Montgomery, Alabama—where, at a country club dance, he met his future wife, Zelda Sayre, the debutante daughter of an Alabama supreme court judge.

In November 1917, as Fitzgerald went on active duty, he began writing a novel that he called *The Romantic Egotist*. Three months later, he finished the first draft and submitted it to Charles Scribner's Sons, which rejected it. Meanwhile, he became engaged to Zelda Sayre and, upon his discharge from the army in February 1919, moved to New York City. Fitzgerald's plan was to work for an advertising agency while trying to break into magazine fiction. He didn't do well enough for Zelda, however, who—unconvinced that Fitzgerald could support her—broke off the engagement.

Moving back into his parents' St. Paul home, Fitzgerald rewrote his novel under the guidance of Scribner's editor Maxwell Perkins, eventually producing *This Side of Paradise*. The novel was published in March 1920, and a month later Scott and Zelda Fitzgerald were married. *This Side of Paradise* told the largely autobiographical story of Amory Blaine, a Princeton University student who neglects his studies for musical comedy and has a series of romances that leave him disillusioned. Selling forty thousand copies during its first year, *This Side of Paradise* marked Fitzgerald's arrival on the Manhattan literary scene. "When I returned six months later the offices of editors and publishers were open to me, impresarios begged plays, the movies panted for screen material," Fitzgerald recalled. "To my bewilderment I was adopted not as a Middle Westerner, not even as a detached observer, but as the very archetype of what New York wanted."

Twenty-three-year-old Princeton dropout F. Scott Fitzgerald *became the toast of Manhattan when he transformed the events of his young life into the popular novel* This Side of Paradise.

VIII. MAGNETIC FIELDS AND FORCES

MAGNETISM IS A COMMON PHENOMENON, and almost everyone has had some experience with it. Yet few people realize how closely related magnetism is to electricity.

In the same way that charges create electric fields (which in turn exert electric forces), magnets create magnetic fields (which in turn exert magnetic forces). Like electric forces, magnetic forces vary inversely with distance from the source of the field. But in most other ways, magnetic fields are much more complicated.

The most important distinction between electric and magnetic fields is that magnetic fields form closed loops. Because this is so, one never encounters an isolated north pole or an isolated south pole. Every north pole has a south pole, and vice versa, with the magnetic field pointing out of the north pole and in toward the south pole.

In addition, the magnetic forces created by magnetic fields act not only on magnets but also on moving electric charges. (They have no effect on stationary charges.) Furthermore, magnetic fields produce magnetic forces only when the motion of the charge is perpendicular to the direction of the field. (The motion of a charge parallel to a magnetic field produces no force at all.) Finally, the magnetic force exerted by a magnetic field acts in a direction perpendicular to both the magnetic field *and* the direction of the charge's motion. For example, if a charge is moving along the *x*-axis of a coordinate space, and the direction of the field corresponds to the *y*-axis, then the force exerted by the field will deflect the charge along the *z*-axis.

The way in which Earth's magnetic field deflects high-energy cosmic particles illustrates these principles. Because the particles consist entirely of atomic nuclei without electrons, they are positively charged. Therefore, when most of these particles enter Earth's magnetic field, a magnetic force is exerted on them, deflecting them at a right angle away from the planet. At the equator—where Earth's magnetic field runs roughly parallel to the surface—incoming cosmic particles, moving nearly perpendicular to the direction of the field, receive maximum deflection. Near the

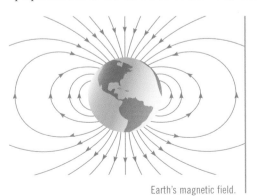

north and south magnetic poles, however—where Earth's magnetic field points directly down or up, respectively—the charged particles move roughly parallel to the magnetic field and thus feel little or no magnetic force.

Magnetic fields exert magnetic forces *on electric charges moving perpendicular to the direction of the field.*

Earth's magnetic field.

VIII. THE HEART OF A HERO

AJAX'S COMPLAINT that Achilles has "turned his great heart savage" is emblematic of a growing problem in the *Iliad*. Initially, there is civility on the battlefield; but as the story proceeds, restraint is abandoned, and heroic action and bestial behavior become increasingly intermixed.

In the original Greek text, the word that Ajax uses to describe Achilles's "heart" is *thumos*. Also translated as "spirit," *thumos* refers to the seat of human emotion—which is often manipulated by external, supernatural (*daimonic*) forces. Achilles's reply to Ajax implies as much: "Everything you say is after my own mind. Yet still the *thumos* in me swells with rage." When Achilles subsequently sees one of the Achaean ships burning, he feels sympathy for his companions, but his *thumos* remains subject to the *daimonic* forces influencing him. He does, however, allow his best friend, Patroklos, to join the fighting; and soon Patroklos kills Sarpedon, claiming the Lycian prince's armor as his prize.

Possession of an opponent's armor was considered significant because it perpetuated the *kleos* of one's victory. Typically, the corpse also brought a ransom from those family or friends who wished to give it an honorable burial. The fighting over Sarpedon's corpse, however, is of a particularly savage nature because Patroklos wants to mutilate the body and leave it unburied as food for beasts.

Achilles bandages an injured Patroklos.

This sort of antiburial is a constant threat in the *Iliad*, and it's associated with the overwhelming desire to annihilate one's enemy for all time—that is, even in death. Such an outcome denies the fallen hero the *kleos* he would otherwise have received from a proper funeral. This principle is so important that Zeus eventually intervenes to rescue Sarpedon's body and return it to Lycia.

A similar fate awaits Patroklos—who, after securing the Achaean ships, attempts to storm Troy. Although Achilles has ordered him not to do so, Patroklos's *thumos* has clearly taken charge of his reason—which is part of Zeus's new plan to draw Achilles back into the fray. A slap from Apollo (who is the patron god of Troy) knocks off Patroklos's armor and leaves him dumbstruck, permitting an otherwise unimportant Trojan to spear him. Hector then finishes Patroklos and claims his armor, thus accepting responsibility (of a sort) for Patroklos's death. As for Patroklos's corpse, Hector wants to impale the head on a spike, but the Achaeans recapture Patroklos's body before Hector can carry it away.

The *thumos* of a Homeric hero *is a metaphysical organ of emotion that gods manipulate to drive the conflict beyond human control.*

IX. CIVIC HUMANISM

IN 1402, when Milanese troops threatened to overrun Florence, the city's leading humanists, especially Leonardo Bruni and Matteo Palmieri, rushed to defend their homeland, with words if not with arms. Rejecting Petrarch's dictate that humanists should avoid political entanglements, Bruni, Palmieri, and others praised the freedom inherent in Florence's ostensibly republican form of government and castigated the tyranny of principalities, such as the duchy of Milan. Their rhetoric served both to promote patriotic participation in the war effort and to neutralize, through the guise of patriotic unity, the lingering political ambitions of the *popolo*.

The civic humanists, as this new crop of intellectuals came to be known, believed that it was the height of virtue to engage in public affairs. They argued that while royal forms of government restricted civic participation and stifled intellectual inquiry, republics were uniquely suited to bring out the best in a populace. Viewing Florence as the modern heir to the ancient Roman republic, the civic humanists reinterpreted Roman history to vilify Caesar and ennoble his assassin, Brutus, for acting faithfully to preserve republican liberty. Bruni later claimed, somewhat grandiloquently, that in resisting Milan, Florence was merely fulfilling its historical obligation (as heir to the Roman republic) to save Italy from tyranny.

It's difficult to know the extent to which civic humanists consciously crafted their rhetoric to serve the ruling political elite. Historian Hans Baron has shown, however, that the posture of some Florentine humanists certainly changed with the onset of the Milanese threat. Bruni, for example, wrote two different versions of his *Dialogues to Pier Paolo Vergerio*. In the first, written before 1402, he disparages several early Florentine writers, including Petrarch and Boccaccio; but in the second, written after 1402, he praises these same writers in order to extol the greatness of Florence.

Like their predecessors, the civic humanists often used classical sources to justify their changing political views. Bruni, for example, shielded the city's wealthy families from criticism by explaining that, according to the ancient philosophers, all that mattered morally was how the wealthy spent their money. Similarly, when the government faced increasing dissent, Palmieri appealed to an ancient Roman sense of paternalism, arguing that the average Florentine should defer to the judgment of the city's experienced politicians—a great leap from the fourteenth-century humanist ideal of government as a broadly based fraternity of equals.

The civic humanists of the fifteenth century *disregarded Petrarch's injunction to avoid politics and instead used their classical learning to justify contemporary social and political practice.*

IX. PRICE RANGES

UNTIL RECENTLY, the New York Stock Exchange was dominated by specialists, each of whom controlled all of the activity in a particular stock. Specialists were obligated to commit their own capital in order to facilitate trades and maintain a fair and orderly market. They did this by purchasing stock from sellers at the bid and selling stock to buyers at the ask, retaining the spread for themselves as compensation.

This system has now become obsolete. Specialists currently handle less than half of NYSE volume, and their share is shrinking. They are being replaced by electronic trading systems that allow customers to manage their orders minutely. The fantastic speeds of these computerized systems have allowed for an explosion of statistically based trading strategies and a corresponding increase in trading volume.

All of the world's major stock exchanges now utilize electronic systems; but even as they converge technologically and merge corporately, exchanges have retained a certain measure of individuality. For example, most exchanges have a preferred range within which their stocks usually trade. In the United States, the typical stock trades around $35 per share. In the United Kingdom and Italy, on the other hand, share prices tend to hold in the $3–4 range, while in Switzerland they are usually much higher. Swisscom, for example, trades around $350 per share, while Telecom Italia, a similarly sized company, trades around $2.25 per share.

There is no reason why this should be, other than market psychology, because share price is basically an arbitrary number. What really matters is a company's market capitalization, which is the total value of all its stock (the share price multiplied by the number of shares). The US stock Berkshire Hathaway sells for $120,000 per share. In comparison, the UK stock Vodafone sells for about $3.50 per share. But there are only one million shares of Berkshire Hathaway outstanding, compared with fifty-three billion shares of Vodafone. Thus, both companies have similar market capitalizations.

When share prices rise too high for market comfort (usually above one hundred dollars per share in the US), the stock usually splits. When companies split their stocks, shareholders receive two new shares for each old one. Stock splits thus double the number of shares, reducing the value of each by half. Once the share price is lowered in this way, the stock can continue to rise unhindered by psychological resistance to high share prices.

Although the share price of a stock is *essentially an arbitrary number, different markets tend to prefer (for largely psychological reasons) stocks that trade within certain high or low ranges.*

IX. THE GREAT GATSBY

IN APRIL 1924, the Fitzgeralds began an extended trip to France and Italy. In Paris, they became acquainted with members of the American expatriate community, notably Ernest Hemingway, whose work Fitzgerald later recommended to Maxwell Perkins.

While in Europe, Fitzgerald began work on the novel that would become his masterpiece and, in the opinion of many critics, the finest novel of the Jazz Age. Like *This Side of Paradise*, *The Great Gatsby* (1925) had strongly autobiographical elements. The title character, Jay Gatsby, is a former military officer who has come into exceptional wealth, which he uses to host notoriously lavish parties at his mansion on Long Island, where the Fitzgeralds themselves lived (and partied) from the fall of 1922 until their departure for France. The story of Gatsby's effort to regain his lost love, Daisy Buchanan, is told to the reader by Nick Carraway, another young Great War veteran who rents a small cottage bordering Gatsby's property. Like Jake Barnes, Nick is essentially an outsider, witnessing the tragic events that lead to

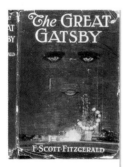

The dust jacket of the first editon of *The Great Gatsby*.

Gatsby's fall. As Nick observes, "I was within and without, simultaneously enchanted and repelled by the inexhaustible variety of life."

The weekly parties that Gatsby throws are, Nick tells us, spectacles for the eyes. Lights bloom and flicker; forms emerge and vanish; consumption is conspicuous; and the soundtrack is unmistakably jazz. Like the bootleg whiskey and automobiles that also figure prominently in the book, the music conveys the speeding-up of American life that Fitzgerald saw all around him. Gatsby's is a life, according to Fitzgerald, of "purposeless splendor" amid a cultural wasteland of the sort that Eliot had recently described. Yet, like Eliot, amid the despair, Fitzgerald still manages to capture the persistence of dreams of renewal and rebirth that could make life seem purposeful again.

Imagining Long Island before the first European settlers arrived, Fitzgerald writes, "Its vanished trees, the trees that had made way for Gatsby's house, had once pandered in whispers to the last and greatest of all human dreams; for a transitory enchanted moment man must have held his breath in the presence of this continent, compelled into an aesthetic contemplation he neither understood nor desired, face to face for the last time in history with something commensurate to his capacity for wonder." The greatness of *The Great Gatsby* is that the novel evokes anew this "capacity for wonder" in a world so lately and brutally ravaged by war.

Steeped in the prevailing jazz culture, The Great Gatsby *captures the hedonism and cynicism of the Lost Generation as well its dreams of regeneration and renewal.*

IX. MAGNETIC FIELDS AND ELECTRIC CURRENTS

BECAUSE ELECTRIC CURRENTS are composed of moving charges, magnetic fields will exert forces on them, provided that the direction of the current is perpendicular to the direction of the field. Interestingly, this relationship is reciprocal, in that electric currents will also create magnetic fields perpendicular to the direction of the current. To determine the direction of the induced magnetic field, physicists use the right-hand rule, which works this way: Point your right thumb in the direction of the current and let your other fingers curl around as though they were forming a fist. These fingers point in the direction of the induced field.

The simplest magnetic field, known as a dipole field, can be produced by running electric current through a circle of wire. The term *dipole* refers to the two poles, north and south, that are created. (Like magnetic poles repel, whereas unlike poles attract.) If the loop of wire is lying flat on a table with the current moving counterclockwise when viewed from above, then the north pole of the induced magnetic field can be found in the center of the loop slightly above the plane of the table. Similarly, the south pole can be found in the center of the loop slightly below the plane of the table. Using the right-hand rule, we can see that the magnetic field lines at any point in the loop pass up out of the loop (thus emanating from its "north" side), travel around the outside of the loop, and then head back into the loop from its "south" side.

The right-hand rule.

Earth's magnetic field is basically a dipole field with single north and south magnetic poles. According to a complex mathematical model known as dynamo theory, this field is created by the motion of molten metal in Earth's core. A similar process generates the magnetic fields that surround the Sun, other stars, and planets such as Jupiter. If the rotation of the molten metals should stop, however, as it has within Mars's frozen core, then the magnetic field would slowly dissipate.

Confusingly, Earth's geographic and magnetic poles are unrelated. Earth's south magnetic pole is actually located near its north geographic pole. The planet's magnetic field thus points away from the Southern Hemisphere and toward the Northern Hemisphere. Compass needles point north because they are actually the north magnetic poles of tiny bar magnets and are therefore attracted to Earth's south magnetic pole, which is located in Canada.

Electric currents create magnetic fields, *the direction of which can be determined using the right-hand rule.*

IX. THE RESOLUTION OF ACHILLES'S RAGE

WHEN ACHILLES LEARNS of Patroklos's death and intended beheading, his *thumos* is moved, and the focus of his rage shifts from Agamemnon to Hector. Achilles's *thumos* still drives the events in the *Iliad*, but its redirection marks a major turning point in the plot. Whereas Achilles's rage has thus far kept him off the battlefield, now his every thought is bloody; and with his return to the fighting, rivers literally run red with the blood of the unburied dead.

Civilization, according to the Greek worldview, is founded on reason, which the Greeks considered the defining distinction between humans and animals. Without reason, there is only the savagery of the jungle. In the *Iliad*, however, Achilles's actions are governed not by his reason but by his *thumos*, which is associated with the source of passions and cannot be reasoned with. The greatest hero at Troy thus comes to represent the pinnacle of savagery, which is made clear when Achilles comes upon the Trojan prince Lykaon.

Instead of fighting Achilles, Lykaon begs him for mercy, to which Achilles replies, "Before Patroklos met his doom, it was the way of my heart to be sparing. Now there is not one who can escape death, if the gods send him against my hands here at Troy." Then Achilles slays Lykaon and throws his body into a river, thereby denying him the possibility of a decent burial. Until this point in the *Iliad*, such savagery has been merely threatened. Now it becomes all-consuming.

Achilles (left) lunges forward to kill Hector.

Eventually, Achilles finds Hector and mortally wounds him. As Hector dies, he entreats Achilles to ransom his body back to Troy. The still-enraged Achilles refuses, proclaiming, "I wish only that my spirit and fury would drive me to hack your meat away and eat it raw for the things that you have done to me."

Explicitly likening himself to an animal, Achilles has now clearly moved beyond the pale of civilized human behavior. He picks up Hector's body and drags it back to his camp. There, he is visited by Priam, father of Hector and king of Troy, who sneaks into Achilles's hut with the help of the messenger god Hermes and pleads with Achilles for the return of his son's body. Because Priam reminds Achilles of his own father, Achilles relents and accepts Priam's ransom. At last, Achilles's rage is resolved, and he is reintegrated into society—at which point the *Iliad* ends.

The surrender of Hector's body *to Priam marks the end of Achilles's uncivilized rage and his reintegration into society.*

X. THE RISE OF THE MEDICIS

BY THE EARLY FIFTEENTH CENTURY, the political ambitions of the *popolo* had dissolved entirely. Meanwhile, the political elites who had manipulated Florence's republican institutions for most of the fourteenth century began competing with one another for power. The winners of this struggle were the Medicis, who became the preeminent family in Florence.

Although the Medici family was one of the oldest in Florence, it didn't rise to prominence until 1411, when Giovanni di Bicci de' Medici (1360–1429) became banker

A posthumous portrait of Cosimo the Elder.

to the pope. Giovanni's son Cosimo (1389–1464), also known as Cosimo the Elder, subsequently expanded the family bank, opening branches in other European cities and creating a financial empire.

Meanwhile, Cosimo also became politically active. During the 1420s, when Florence was fighting costly wars with Milan (1424–28) and Lucca (1429–33), Cosimo made a series of bridge loans to the government that greatly enhanced his influence. But as Cosimo's power grew, so did his opposition until there were just two parties left in Florence: the Medicis and the anti-Medicis, led by the Albizzi family.

Cosimo's great advantage was the network of supporters he built up both within and without Florence. He acquired some of these allies by arranging advantageous marriages—not only for his sons but also for kinsmen, friends, and neighbors. Within the city, he acted as a patron, cultivating clients to whom he offered favors and lent money so that they could pay their taxes and remain eligible to hold public office. In the countryside, where the Medicis owned several estates, he similarly patronized the local rural population, which became for him a base of armed support. But the asset that truly set Cosimo apart from his Albizzi rivals was his banking empire, which enabled him to develop allies in other Italian states.

The Albizzi party, fearful of the Medicis' growing strength, managed to have Cosimo exiled from Florence in late 1433 after accusing him of prolonging the war with Lucca for personal profit. For Cosimo, however, this was merely a temporary setback. Much to the Albizzis' dismay, Florence's most important ally, Venice, backed Cosimo, and he was soon recalled.

Less than a year after his exile, Cosimo returned to Florence with a host of armed peasants. During the next two months, his allies within the nine-member Signoria (the executive committee of city government) banished more than seventy members of the Albizzi party, consolidating Medici control over the city.

Cosimo de' Medici's ability *to lend money to the government facilitated his rise, but it was his vast network of local and foreign allies that set him apart from his rivals.*

X. SELLING SHORT

WHEN A TRADER SELLS SHORT, he agrees to provide stock that he doesn't own. Instead, he borrows the necessary shares from a "long" (someone with an established position in the stock) and pays the long a fee for the privilege. Later, sometime before the loan comes due, he purchases the necessary shares and conveys them to the lender.

In general, short-selling falls into two broad categories: hedge trades and speculative trades. When making a hedge trade, short sellers are usually looking to eliminate price fluctuation as a risk factor in their investments. A common hedge trade is the relative value trade (a subset of the more general category of pairs trading). In a relative value trade, the investor goes long on a stock that seems undervalued while selling short another stock in the same industry that seems overvalued. In this way, by being both long and short, he mitigates his exposure to the vagaries of the market. To the extent that either the industry or the broader market moves up or down, the gains and losses caused by this market movement will offset.

Even more importantly from the point of view of the market, relative value trades help bring stock prices back into line. Selling an overvalued stock short temporarily increases its supply, satisfying excess demand and thereby reducing the overvaluation. Meanwhile, going long on the undervalued stock temporarily increases demand, thereby reducing its undervaluation.

Speculative short-selling, on the other hand, is all about taking risks. Speculators sell short when they think that a stock is overpriced, because they want to profit from its fall. If the stock price rises, of course, speculators can quickly get into trouble. So disreputable ones will sometimes go beyond spreading bad news about a company to malign its management, allege accounting fraud, and promote other rumormongering. Such behavior is one of the reasons that short-selling has a poor reputation.

Another reason is the bear raid. This term refers to the once common practice of using short-selling to dump large amounts of a stock onto the market in order to depress its share price. Bear raids came to an end when the practice of naked short-selling (selling short without borrowing the stock necessary to cover the sale) was made illegal. Because there is only a limited amount of stock available to borrowers, bear raiders can no longer accumulate enough to move the stock price meaningfully.

Selling short is the practice of selling shares *of stock that one doesn't own but has only borrowed (for a fee).*

X. EUGENE O'NEILL

BORN IN A BROADWAY HOTEL ROOM, Eugene O'Neill (1888–1953) grew up around the theater. His father was a touring actor who traveled back and forth across the country with his family in tow. When O'Neill was old enough, his family sent him to boarding schools in New York City and Connecticut, and in 1906 he entered Princeton. But, like Fitzgerald, he was soon asked to leave because of poor grades. During the next five years (1907–12), he worked as a seaman while living as a heavy-drinking denizen of the docks. Finally, after contracting tuberculosis, he settled down in 1913 to begin writing plays. While visiting Provincetown, Massachusetts, during the summer of 1916, he joined a group of writers staging one-act plays in a shed on the town wharf. In the fall, the group moved to New York City, where it opened the tiny Playwrights' Theatre in Greenwich Village.

Eugene O'Neill in a 1921 studio portrait.

Before O'Neill, except for the occasional European import, the American stage was dominated by farce and contrived melodrama. O'Neill, however, believed—as modern European playwrights did—that the stage was capable of handling the same literary topics and themes that had generally been reserved to the novel.

O'Neill's *The Emperor Jones* debuted in November 1920 at the Playwrights' Theater, later moving to the Neighborhood Playhouse on Broadway, where it became the first Broadway production to feature a racially integrated cast. The title character, Brutus Jones, is a Pullman porter who kills a friend while arguing over a dice game. Arrested for the crime, he is put to work on a chain gang, but he escapes on a steamer, jumps ship in the West Indies, and swims to a nearby island. Through a combination of fast talking and brute force, he exploits the natives and becomes their emperor. The action of the play takes place after Jones has become emperor, and it concerns the natives' eventual rebellion. Their increasing displeasure with Jones is heard in the beat of a tom-tom, which grows louder and more insistent as the play progresses.

Through flashbacks, O'Neill offers his audience glimpses of modern African American life, indicating how the dominant white culture perceived blacks at the time. In much the same way that painter Paul Gauguin depicted Tahitians, O'Neill focused on the idea of the "primitive," and his play reflected a growing white interest in African Americans, reaffirming James Weldon Johnson's belief that black culture was worthy of a grand stage.

Eugene O'Neill, *who gave the American theater a new seriousness, captured in* The Emperor Jones *the country's growing fascination with African American culture.*

X. MAGNETIC MATERIALS

AS DISCUSSED PREVIOUSLY, all atoms consist of positively charged nuclei surrounded by negatively charged electrons. Because these electrons have angular momentum, we often speak of them as "orbiting" the nucleus—as though they were moving along closed paths, which they don't. The way things really work on the atomic level is much more complicated and bizarre, but that is the province of quantum mechanics. For our purposes, we need only think of electrons moving about a nucleus, creating an electric current that generates an associated magnetic field.

In most materials, the total magnetic field generated is zero because the individual atomic magnetic fields cancel one another out. (Like electric fields, magnetic fields are vectors; therefore, fields of equal magnitude and opposite direction add up to zero.) However, in some materials, such as iron, the rules of quantum mechanics cause clusters of aligned atoms (called magnetic domains) to form. Because the atoms in these clusters are aligned, the tiny magnetic fields they produce combine to form a single, stronger magnetic field.

Even so, as long as the domains themselves remain unaligned, their cumulative fields will tend to cancel one another out, just as unaligned atomic fields do. On the other hand, if you were to take an iron bar and place it within an external magnetic field, the force exerted by that field would act to align the domains in the bar in the direction of the external field, as though the domains were freely moving compass needles finding north.

If this happens, the magnetic fields produced by the domains will combine, and the iron bar will become magnetized. You can make a magnet in this way by simply placing an iron bar parallel to Earth's magnetic field and striking one end with a hammer. The blow will jostle the magnetic domains; and as they settle down, they will tend to realign in the direction of the magnetic field. Materials that are able to permanently retain this sort of alignment are called ferromagnetic materials.

If you were to wrap a wire around a ferromagnetic rod and run a current through it, the current in the coils of the wire would create a magnetic field parallel to the axis of the rod. This magnetic field would align the magnetic domains in the rod, thus amplifying the magnetic field created by the current. Such a device is called an electromagnet.

All atoms generate magnetic fields, *but only in some materials will these tiny fields line up to create the strong permanent fields associated with magnets.*

X. THE TROJAN HORSE

BOTH THE *Aithiopis* and the *Little Iliad* take place after the rage of Achilles has subsided. The *Aithiopis* begins with the arrival of Penthesileia, an Amazon warrior who comes to the defense of Troy following the death of Hector. She faces many Achaeans and slaughters them all until she meets Achilles in battle and is killed by him. This pattern is repeated with the Ethiopian warrior Memnon, who arrives to assist the Trojans after the death of Penthesileia and is also killed by Achilles.

By now, it's clear that Achilles dominates the battlefields; and after routing the Trojans once more, he attempts to storm the city's walls. This effort fails when an arrow shot by Paris and guided by Apollo kills Achilles. Because Paris delivers this blow from afar, he can't claim Achilles's fabulous armor, forged by the smith god Hephaestos, and the Achaeans are able to rescue Achilles's corpse. The *Aithiopis* concludes with the burial of Achilles and also, according to the mythographer Proclus, "a conflict...between Odysseus and Ajax over the armor of Achilles."

The *Little Iliad* begins with Thetis's declaration that her son's armor should go to the greatest remaining Achaean warrior. In terms of physical strength, this would be Ajax, who was widely considered the most powerful Achaean after Achilles. Odysseus, however, while not as strong as Ajax, was craftier. Ultimately, the Achaean warlords decide to award the armor to Odysseus—at which point Ajax becomes crazed and slits the throats of cattle, believing them to be the throats of Agamemnon, Menelaus, Odysseus, and others. When he realizes what he has done (under a spell cast by Athena), he kills himself rather than endure the shame.

Soon thereafter, Paris is slain by Philoctetes; yet the war continues because Deiphobos, another Trojan prince, chooses to marry Helen rather than surrender her to the Achaeans. Eventually, Athena suggests to Odysseus that he manufacture a giant horse in honor of the "horse-breaking Trojans," whom the Achaeans couldn't conquer. The Achaean fleet should then pretend to sail away, but not before Odysseus and several other Achaean heroes hide themselves within the horse. At night, after the Trojans have brought the horse into the city, the Achaeans can sneak out and open the city gates so that the rest of the army can enter Troy. The *Little Iliad* ends after the construction of the horse but before the ruse can be tried.

*The **Aithiopis** and the **Little Iliad** chronicle the continuing cycle of pain and suffering at Troy from which both the Achaeans and the Trojans are unable to extricate themselves.*

XI. THE CONSOLIDATION OF MEDICI POWER

GREAT WEALTH and widespread patronage had allowed Cosimo de' Medici to seize power in Florence, but these assets alone, he knew, wouldn't hold that power. He needed a way to control the Florentine government absolutely without surrendering the facade of republicanism that kept the *popolo* pacified. In two intermittently convened committees, the *balìa* and the *accoppiatori*, he found the mechanism he needed. Because these committees possessed extraordinary powers, they were traditionally constituted only for short times during periods of crisis. Under Cosimo, however, the tenures of these committees were extended from a few days to years at a time. Filled with Medici partisans, they allowed Cosimo to manipulate the electoral process to ensure that only Medici partisans held seats in the Signoria.

The Palazzo della Signoria is visible in the background of this ca. 1485 fresco.

Within the Florentine government, the Signoria proposed new legislation to be approved or rejected by legislative councils made up primarily of middle-class guildsmen. The role of the renewed *balìa* was to consider Signoria legislation relating to government finance or the election laws. As discussed previously, the *balìa* was also charged with preparing lists of candidates eligible to serve in the Signoria. These lists were passed on to the *accoppiatori*, who vetted them (in a process called a scrutiny) and placed the names of approved candidates in a pouch (one pouch per scrutiny). Every two months, names were drawn from one of these pouches to fill the seats in the Signoria. Cosimo was able to maintain control of the Signoria by controlling these committees and thus the names in the pouches.

The political instability of 1433–34 gave Cosimo sufficient cover to reconstitute the *balìa* and the *accoppiatori*, and the wars of expansion that continued until 1454 justified their regular renewal. With the cessation of hostilities, however, the guildsmen on the legislative councils joined ranks with the anti-Medici elite to abolish the *balìa* and cancel the appointments of the *accoppiatori*. In response, the Medicis instigated a crisis in 1458, persuading Florence's other elite families that the *popolo* were politically resurgent. Frightened, these families agreed to call a *parlamento*—that is, a legislative assembly made up of the entire citizenry. Once the *parlamento* was called, the duke of Milan sent troops to Cosimo, who stationed Milanese soldiers around the main public square to intimidate the *parlamento*. The tactic worked, and the *parlamento* subsequently approved all of the measures proposed by the Medicis, including renewals of the *balìa* and the *accoppiatori*.

While maintaining a republican facade, *the Medicis ruled Florence through the* balìa *and the* accoppiatori, *also employing intimidation when necessary.*

XI. OPTIONS

AN OPTION IS A CONTRACT that confers upon the owner the right—but not the obligation—to buy or sell a specified amount of stock at a specified price during a specified time period. The stock covered by the option is called the underlying, the price at which the underlying is to be bought or sold is called the strike, and the date at which the right terminates is called the expiration. An option that confers the right to buy is known as a call; an option that confers the right to sell is known as a put. In exchange for whichever right is purchased, the buyer of the option pays the seller (the writer) a fee known as a premium.

Options can be either covered or uncovered. A call option is said to be covered when the writer of the option is long in the underlying and can deliver the stock that may be called without having to purchase it elsewhere. A put option is considered covered when the writer has sold the underlying short and has the cash to pay for the stock that may be put to him.

The buyers of calls are usually traders looking to make as much money as possible from an expected rise or fall in the price of a particular stock. Let's say that a trader believes a stock currently selling at $90 will rise within the next three months. He can simply buy shares of that stock for $90 each, or he can buy for $1 each three-month call options with $100 strikes. For the trader to make money on these options, the share price has to rise above $101 (the strike price plus the premium paid). However, should the share price rise to $105 before the expiration, the trader can make a killing.

Investing $90 in a single share would yield $15 in profit. However, investing that same amount in call options on ninety shares would produce $360 in profit ($4 per option). Thus, the use of options can leverage a 17 percent move in the underlying into a 400 percent return on investment. Of course, if the share price rises only to $99—an increase of "merely" 10 percent—then the options become worthless, and the trader loses what he has paid for them. This, however, is the limitation of the option buyer's risk. The writer, on the other hand, accepts risk that is potentially unlimited.

Options, *which confer the right to buy or sell a particular stock at a particular price, allow traders betting on that stock's rise or fall to leverage capital and maximize their profit.*

XI. WE RETURN FIGHTING

AFRICAN AMERICAN CULTURE was itself changing rapidly during the 1910s and 1920s. As early as the 1890s, black sharecroppers in the South had begun moving north to cities such as New York, Detroit, Cleveland, and Chicago in search of better-paying industrial jobs. When World War I began, the demand for industrial labor spiked, and this process accelerated, becoming known as the Great Migration.

At the same time, many African Americans patriotically joined the armed forces; and though they were sent overseas in segregated units, they had experiences that put the lie to southern claims that racial separation was "natural." Because the French typically made no distinctions among white and black Americans, many black veterans returned home optimistic about the future of race relations in their country.

A wounded Harlem Hellfighter pauses during the February 1919 parade.

On February 17, 1919, a million people turned out to watch the 369th Colored Infantry, newly returned from France, parade up Fifth Avenue. Known as the Harlem Hellfighters, the regiment had introduced jazz to Paris; and when its parade entered Harlem, the music shifted from a military march to "Here Comes My Daddy Now."

The image of black men wearing uniforms and carrying weapons became an important source of racial pride to African Americans, and the veterans themselves, with a personal confidence bred of combat, expected better treatment than they had received before proving their valor on the battlefields of France. What they found instead was that the wartime atmosphere of cooperation and tolerance soon yielded to the status quo antebellum. According to Benjamin Mays, the future president of Morehouse College, "Negro soldiers were told, 'Take off those uniforms and act like a nigger should.'" Those who obeyed were left alone, while those who resisted were subjected to murderous reprisals. The lynching rate, which had been in decline, more than doubled, and race riots broke out all over the country during the particularly violent summer of 1919.

"It was right for us to fight," W. E. B. Du Bois wrote in the May 1919 issue of *The Crisis*, the NAACP magazine. "But by the God of Heaven, we are cowards and jackasses if now that that war is over, we do not marshal every ounce of our brain and brawn to fight a sterner, longer, more unbending battle against the forces of hell in our own land. We return. We return from fighting. We return fighting."

Unlike the disillusionment that overcame the Lost Generation, *the African American experience of World War I was generally uplifting, with military service becoming an important source of racial pride.*

XI. THE TELEGRAPH

THE KNOWLEDGE THAT ELECTROMAGNETS can generate strong magnetic fields was put to use early in the nineteenth century by the inventors of the telegraph, the world's first electromagnetic communications technology. A simple telegraph consists of nothing more than a battery, an electromagnetic sounder, and a switch (known as a key), all connected by wire. When the key is depressed, the circuit is closed, and the current from the battery runs through the wire and into the electromagnet, producing a strong magnetic field. This field exerts a force on the sounder's ferromagnetic crossbar (usually a piece of iron), causing the crossbar to become attracted to an anvil attached to the electromagnet. As the crossbar strikes the anvil, it makes a clicking sound. When the key is released, interrupting the flow of current to the electromagnet, a spring attached to the crossbar returns the crossbar to its original position.

To send messages, telegraph companies used to string wire between stations. This wire was insulated from the ground, usually by being hung on wooden telegraph poles. A battery controlled by a key was then attached to one end of the wire, and an electromagnetic sounder to the other end. Both ends of the system were then grounded (that is, attached to metals rods driven deep into the ground). This completed the circuit, because it allowed the current that traveled through the wire to return to the battery through the ground. Telegraph operators would then communicate with one another by toggling the key to create Morse code. Clicks with short intervals between them were transcribed as dots and clicks with longer intervals as dashes.

It's difficult for people today to realize what an enormous impact the telegraph had on nineteenth-century life and commerce. Important news could now be sent almost instantaneously over great distances, and information about prices in various part of the country became widely available, leading to the formation of national stock and commodities markets. By the time of the Civil War, generals, politicians, and newspapers were all highly dependent on the technology, indicating that the transformation of human society through the use of electromagnetism had already begun.

The telegraph made use of *the fact that electromagnets generate strong magnetic fields to become the world's first electromagnetic communications technology.*

XI. THE SACK OF TROY

ALTHOUGH THE *Sack of Ilion* is one of the six lost Trojan War epics, our knowledge of its contents is significantly supplemented by Virgil's *Aeneid*, which also concerns the fall of Troy. The *Sack of Ilion* begins with the Trojans' discovery of the giant horse left behind by the apparently departed Achaeans. After some discussion, they decide to keep the horse in honor of Athena (or sometimes in honor of Poseidon, depending on the source). Once the Trojans bring the horse inside the city, however, Odysseus and the others hiding within its belly creep out, overpower the unsuspecting gatekeepers, and signal the Achaean army, which has been hiding nearby. The Trojans are then slaughtered, and many atrocities are committed, including the desecration of temples.

Many Trojans properly claim sanctuary within these temples, but the Achaeans, caught up in a blood rage, kill them anyway. This is, of course, highly uncivilized behavior, and it has consequences. Both Athena and Poseidon, for example, reconsider the steadfast support they have given the Achaeans thus far in their long war with the Trojans, and they resolve to punish the Achaeans for their sacrilegious brutality.

Meanwhile, all the commotion awakens Aeneas—the child of Aphrodite and her mortal lover Anchises, a prince of Dardania (a Trojan ally). Quickly, Aeneas

A Renaissance Italian depiction of Aeneas fleeing Troy.

dons his armor and prepares for death in battle, but his mind is changed to flight when his immortal mother appears before him and orders him to save his family and some sacred items from the royal household so that he might preserve and continue the Trojan heritage elsewhere. The faithful Aeneas obeys his mother, collects the sacred items, assembles what few survivors he can, and leads them to safety outside a city that is now fully ablaze. Famously, Aeneas carries his geriatric father out of Troy on his shoulders.

The rest of Aeneas's story is told in the *Aeneid*, discussed later in the course. For now, let us simply note the strong contrast meant to be drawn during the sack of Troy between the sacrilegious behavior of the Achaeans and the dutiful conduct of Aeneas.

The Achaeans sack Troy with *a savage exuberance that includes the defiling of temples. For this impious behavior, they will later be punished by the gods.*

XII. PATRONAGE OF THE ARTS

BETWEEN 1434 AND 1494, three Medicis—Cosimo the Elder, his son Piero, and Piero's son Lorenzo—ruled Florence through the agency of a few select partisans. As a result, affluent Florentines who had previously sought social status through politics had to look elsewhere. Mostly, they turned to the ostentatious consumption of luxury goods, such as expensive clothing and furnishings, and patronage of the artists we now commonly associate with the Renaissance in Florence.

While the Medicis ruled Florence, nearly a hundred new palaces were built or remodeled. These monumental structures were often so large that entire blocks of housing had to be razed to make room for them. As one might expect, Cosimo de' Medici set the standard when he commissioned the architect Michelozzo to construct a new palace for the Medici family, begun in 1444 and completed in 1460.

Another noteworthy trend was the construction and lavish decoration of private family chapels. Some were built into palaces; others were constructed as additions to existing public churches. All celebrated the lineage of the patron and expressed his personal aesthetic taste.

Private wealth also funded a great deal of civic beautification—but not necessarily for civic purposes. In 1456, Giovanni Rucellai commissioned architect Leon Battista Alberti to design a new facade for the church of Santa Maria Novella. To ensure that everyone in Florence understood who had paid for the work, Rucellai had Alberti inscribe his name into the frieze below the new pediment. The inscription read: IOHAN[N]ES ORICELLARIUS PAUL(LI) F(ILIUS) AN(NO) SAL(UTIS) MCCCCLXX ("Giovanni Rucellai son of Paolo in the year of salvation 1470").

Even so, no Florentine patronage could

The inscription to Giovanni Rucellai on the church of the Santa Maria Novella.

be compared to that of Cosimo de' Medici and his brother Lorenzo, who jointly commissioned masterworks of art and architecture on a scale never before attempted by private individuals. The brothers took on projects such as the reconstruction of the Dominican convent of San Marco, which stood a few blocks north of the new Medici palace. (Interestingly, this project included the construction of Florence's first public library to house books and ancient texts collected by Cosimo's late friend Niccolò Niccoli.) By placing symbols of their family on all such commissions, the Medicis asserted their dominance over Florence and its surrounding territory.

As opportunities for political participation *declined in Medicean Florence, wealthy families began seeking social status in patronage of the arts.*

XII. PRICING AN OPTION

IN PRICING AN OPTION, three basic factors must be taken into account: the duration of the option, the price of the strike relative to the current share price of the underlying, and the volatility of the underlying. Although the mathematics of option pricing can get very complicated very quickly, by focusing on these three factors the value of most options can be reasonably assessed.

With regard to duration, longer always costs more. The reason is fairly obvious: The longer an option lasts, the greater the chance that the price of the underlying will hit the strike and move "into the money."

With regard to strike price, options that are struck close to the current trading price are more valuable than options struck far away. For options that are struck out of the money—which includes most options—the only important consideration is how soon the option will move into the money—that is, how soon it can be exercised profitably. The sooner that appears to be, the more the buyer will have to pay.

Some options have strike prices that are already in the money. For these, too, paradoxically, the closer to the current trading price they are, the more expensive they are relative to their intrinsic value. The reason is that as an option moves farther into the money, its intrinsic value crowds out its value as leverage. Options that are less in the money cost less and tie up less capital, making them more valuable to traders looking for leverage. Therefore, buyers will pay relatively more for options that are in the money only a little so that they can control more stock with the same capital investment. For example, a call that is $7 in the money may be priced at $9, while a similar call that is $15 in the money may be priced at $16.

With regard to volatility, more costs more. This is because a more volatile underlying is more likely to hit the strike during one of its price swings than an underlying that hardly moves at all. However, the time scale of that volatility has to be taken into account. Stocks that jump around from day to day may hold to a specific price range from month to month or year to year. Therefore, when pricing an option, a trader needs to match the volatility period of the underlying to the duration of the option.

The price of an option depends *primarily on its duration, the strike price relative to the current share price of the underlying, and the volatility of the underlying.*

XII. THE HARLEM RENAISSANCE

WHILE THE MEMBERS OF the Lost Generation struggled in Paris to find meaning in their sense of loss, the writers most closely associated with the Harlem Renaissance found themselves working with much more positive emotions: excitement, exuberance, and optimism.

Alain Locke in 1926.

The Harlem Renaissance is the name given to the artistic movement of the 1920s, centered in Harlem, through which African American culture developed a much more sophisticated sense of self-awareness. Among the movement's landmark documents is *The New Negro* (1925), an anthology compiled by Howard University philosophy professor Alain Locke. Having studied the influence of African culture upon Western civilization, Locke began encouraging black artists to seek subjects in contemporary Negro life, not only to increase their self-respect but also to feed their creativity. In *The New Negro*, he gave important exposure to works of fiction, poetry, drama, and essays by such emerging talents as Langston Hughes, Claude McKay, Countee Cullen, and Rudolph Fisher. Immediately, the anthology was acclaimed for demonstrating what could indeed be accomplished when African American writers wrote about African American subjects.

Above all else, Locke wanted to revise the ways in which both white and black Americans perceived black culture. By presenting works of art expressive of black humanity, he hoped to overcome the limitations that racial prejudice had placed upon blacks. "In the last decade," Locke wrote in his introduction to *The New Negro*, "something beyond the watch and guard of statistics has happened in the life of the American Negro and the three Norns who have traditionally presided over the Negro problem have a changeling in their laps. The Sociologist, the Philanthropist, the Race-leader are not unaware of the New Negro, but they are at a loss to account for him." The Norns to which Locke refers are the goddesses of Norse mythology equivalent to the three Greek Fates. The reason that Locke's metaphorical Norns can't "account for" the New Negro is that he has grown beyond prewar racial stereotypes.

For Locke, art was strongly linked to social responsibility. To achieve excellence in art was to express one's excellence as a person and thus combat the racism one faced in everyday life. In the process of creating such art, the writers and intellectuals of the Harlem Renaissance pursued a deeper understanding not only of themselves but also of their heritage.

During the Harlem Renaissance, *African Americans began exploring their cultural roots through literature and the arts.*

XII. CHANGING MAGNETIC FIELDS

LET'S CONDUCT A THOUGHT EXPERIMENT: Imagine you are sitting in a room with an instrument that measures the strength of the magnetic field around you. Suddenly you notice that the magnetic field spikes. Any number of circumstances could have caused this. Perhaps someone in the room turned on an electromagnet. Perhaps Earth suddenly entered a region of space with a steady magnetic field produced by some galactic current. Sitting in the room, you don't know; all you do know is that you are now experiencing a magnetic field that wasn't there before.

Now consider this physical experiment: If I take a conductor—a wire loop, for example—and move it perpendicular to the direction of a magnetic field, the electrons in the loop will feel a force due to their motion relative to the magnetic field. That force will act in a direction perpendicular to both the motion of the loop and the direction of the field, causing the electrons in the loop to begin moving. Moving charges, of course, constitute an electric current. Therefore, moving a conductor through a magnetic field produces an electric current in the conductor.

Finally, let's put these two experiments together: One of the fundamental principles of relativity is that the laws of physics remain unchanged whether an observer is said to be moving relative to one fixed point or stationary relative to another. Sitting in a room, your speed relative to the room is zero; however, relative to the Sun, you and the room are hurtling through space at tens of thousands of miles per hour. These frames of reference are very different; but whichever you choose, it won't affect the behavior of the magnetic field you're experiencing in the room.

Similarly, a perfect equivalence exists between the case of a moving conductor passing into an existing magnetic field and the case of a stationary conductor experiencing a newly generated magnetic field. As far as the conductor is concerned, the magnetic field changes, and that's all that matters.

Taking this line of reasoning one step farther, recall that electric currents are driven by differences in voltage. Therefore, a magnetic field that changes must be creating a voltage difference (because it causes a current). This conclusion is known as Faraday's Law. Furthermore, because voltage differences imply the existence of electric fields, Faraday's Law tells us that changing magnetic fields produce electric fields without associated electric charges.

Changing magnetic fields *create current and therefore voltage and therefore electric fields.*

XII. THE RETURNS

WITH THE SACKING OF the city, the Achaeans finally punish Troy for sheltering Paris. In the course of their uncivilized rampage, however, they incur the wrath of the gods whose shrines are desecrated. This is never a good thing, and the *Returns* records the gods' vengeance.

The setting is the Achaeans' voyage home. In counsel with Athena, Poseidon creates a powerful storm that sinks many of the Achaean ships and scatters the rest. Numerous Achaeans are drowned, and the rest are forced to struggle for their survival. However, different Achaeans suffer widely different fates.

Diomedes and Nestor, for example, leave Asia Minor before the rest of the Achaeans and reach home safely. The implication is that they are spared because they didn't take part in the sacrilege at Troy. Menelaus, who did take part, loses most of his ships, but he and Helen (with whom he is now reunited) manage to survive. However, they are blown all the way down to Egypt and require Egyptian aid in order to return to Sparta.

Menelaus with Helen (center) and Aphrodite on a Greek vase.

Although the flagship bearing Agamemnon becomes separated from the rest of the fleet during the storm, it nevertheless arrives home without further incident. This is a mixed blessing because Agamemnon is soon murdered by his cousin Aegistheus aided by his own wife, Clytemnaestra, who despises Agamemnon for having sacrificed their daughter Iphigenia to propitiate the goddess Artemis before setting sail for Troy.

An even more unusual case is that of Achilles's son, Neoptolemos, who didn't arrive at Troy until after his father's death. Although he takes part in the desecration, Neoptolemos escapes the fate of the fleet because his grandmother Thetis warns him not to sail home. Instead, he and Achilles's former mentor Phoenix set off for home by land through Thrace. The journey is more arduous than a successful sea voyage would have been, and Phoenix dies along the way, but Neoptolemos returns safely home in the end.

Nevertheless, the most famous of the return stories by far is the tale of Odysseus, which Homer tells in the *Odyssey*. Although most of Odysseus's ships survive the storm, he and his men are blown so far off course that it takes Odysseus years to find his way back home again to Ithaca. During that time, he has many legendary adventures at sea.

Because of their impious conduct *during the sack of Troy, the Achaeans suffer as divine punishment a catastrophe at sea.*

XIII. LORENZO THE MAGNIFICENT

WHEN PIERO DE' MEDICI (1416–69) took control of Florence upon Cosimo's death in 1464, some of his father's supporters resisted the idea of a hereditary dynasty. Piero, however, still enjoyed the support of Milan and many Florentine peasants, so

challenging him would have meant arming the guildsmen and the laborers—which the anti-Medicis, recalling the Revolt of the Ciompi, lacked the nerve to do.

When Lorenzo de' Medici (1449–92) succeeded his late father in 1469, he faced similar opposition from the political elite. But Lorenzo, although only twenty, was a much stronger leader, and he responded aggressively to threats to his authority. When some of Piero's closest associates publicly challenged his wishes, the Medici known as Il Magnifico (the Magnificent) called on the support of Milan, whose troops quickly cowed all opposition.

A bust of Lorenzo created during his lifetime.

Even so, Lorenzo continued to fear reprisals, and so he held his power closely. Increasingly, he governed through fungible bureaucrats, chosen for their lack of ties to members of the political elite. Isolated from other sources of patronage, these men were loyal to Lorenzo and did only his bidding. Such a system proved troublesome after Lorenzo's death, because it was inherently unstable; but during his lifetime, it permitted Lorenzo to disenfranchise the political elite and limit their opportunities for intrigue. When Lorenzo's stranglehold forced his rivals to seek allies outside the city, Il Magnifico retaliated with intimidation and violence.

In 1478, members of the Pazzi family conspired with Pope Sixtus IV, the duke of Urbino, and others to murder Lorenzo and his brother Giuliano. On April 26, the assassins caught the brothers off guard in the Florentine cathedral. Giuliano was killed, but Lorenzo escaped and afterward relentlessly avenged his brother's death. In the end, more than eighty conspirators, alleged conspirators, and friends of the conspirators were hunted down and killed.

During the 1480s, with Florence firmly under his control, Lorenzo began expanding his family's influence outside the city—acquiring in 1489 the post of cardinal for his second son, thirteen-year-old Giovanni. Lorenzo's foresight in placing his son within the church paid off for the family in 1513, when Giovanni became Pope Leo X. Lorenzo also arranged marriages between his other children and notable Italian families, further advancing Medici power beyond Florence.

The regime of Lorenzo the Magnificent *represented the pinnacle of Medici authority, yet in Lorenzo's ruthless and suspicious nature one can also find the seeds of Medici decline.*

XIII. ARBITRAGE

ARBITRAGE IS THE simultaneous purchase and sale of the same security or commodity in two different markets between which a price disparity exists. A classic example would be purchasing gold in New York at $100 an ounce and selling it simultaneously in London, where the market price is $105 an ounce. The only limitation on the profitability of this arrangement would be the amount of capital you have with which to buy gold in New York.

When performed properly, arbitrage produces an immediate profit without compelling the arbitrageur to assume any market risk. However, as communications technologies have improved, the opportunities for classic arbitrage have steadily declined; and electronic trading has dampened the business further, reducing the duration of arbitrage opportunities to seconds and their profitability to pennies per share.

This is as it should be. In efficient, transparent markets, arbitrage opportunities shouldn't arise very often; and when they do, sufficient capital should be attracted to close them immediately. As a result, only the most efficient traders, operating with a low cost of capital and sophisticated computer-driven systems, can still play the arbitrage game successfully.

For example, there are several Canadian companies listed on both Canadian and US exchanges. As their stock prices fluctuate during the day, the price on one exchange may drift away from the price on the other. Let's say that the US price goes up while the Canadian price goes down. When the disparity becomes sufficient to make arbitrage economical, the arbitrageur's computer will immediately send simultaneous orders to both exchanges, buying stock in Canada and selling the same amount in the US. Meanwhile, the computer will also send an order to a bank hedging the two currencies. (Without the currency hedge, the arbitrageur might lose his riskless profit if the US dollar, in which he is now long, falls in value relative to the Canadian dollar.)

Throughout the trading day, many such programs constantly monitor markets around the world. Rarely are arbitrage trades available for more than a few hundred shares, but over time and the course of many thousands of trades, the profits add up.

In terms of market discipline, these programs provide the important ancillary benefit of keeping prices aligned. Because arbitrage quickly eliminates all price differentials, traders can use whatever market or currency they like for their trades, knowing that all of their choices are essentially equivalent.

Arbitrage operates on the price disparities that occasionally arise *across different markets. Properly handled, it produces riskless profit while keeping market prices closely aligned.*

XIII. JEAN TOOMER

Jean Toomer in college.

JEAN TOOMER (1894–1967) was born and raised in Washington, DC, where he grew up in a racially mixed middle-class neighborhood. Although white by appearance, Toomer was actually biracial by virtue of his maternal grandfather, P. B. S. Pinchback, a Union officer during the Civil War and later a Reconstruction-era governor of Louisiana. Although Pinchback was himself light-skinned enough to pass for white, he insisted that his grandson attend black schools so that he could learn how to live in both worlds. After Toomer's graduation from high school in 1914, he studied at six different colleges before finally settling down as a writer and literary intellectual in New York City.

Early on, Toomer eschewed racial classifications, desiring to live neither as a white nor as a black but as an American. His work during this period tended to bridge the gap that existed between the black writers living in Harlem and the white writers living in Greenwich Village. Toomer's poems caught the attention of James Weldon Johnson, who wanted to publish them in his 1922 *Book of American Negro Poetry*. Not wishing to be racially categorized even by Johnson, Toomer declined; yet he couldn't quite escape the alienation he continued to feel as a man living on the cusp between two polarized racial worlds.

During the fall of 1921, Toomer spent several months in Sparta, Georgia, working as interim principal of the Sparta Agricultural and Industrial Institute. Living in the South as an African American allowed him to recover the Negro roots that had been obscured by his ambiguous racial upbringing. The sights and sounds he encountered in Georgia stimulated his racial consciousness, and he found himself overflowing with poems and short stories about his African American heritage. These writings became the basis for his 1923 masterpiece, *Cane*.

Like its author, *Cane* defies easy categorization. Consisting not only of poetry and short fiction but also of playlike dialogue, it reigns as one of the most important works of the Jazz Age. Some critics have suggested that its innovative treatment of African American characters and culture sparked the Harlem Renaissance; others, because of the book's experimentalism and critique of postwar values, have associated it with the Lost Generation. Either way, Toomer's work captures the irony experienced by Great Migration blacks as they sought the Promised Land only to find in the North different yet equally intense forms of racism.

Jean Toomer's 1923 masterpiece, Cane, *one of the formative works of the Harlem Renaissance, represents the biracial author's rediscovery and celebration of his African American roots.*

XIII. ELECTRIC GENERATORS AND MOTORS

NOW THAT WE KNOW that a changing magnetic field can produce an electric current in a conductor, we can use this principle (called induction) to generate electricity. All we have to do is spin a magnet. The spinning magnet creates the changing magnetic field, which induces the current, which flows through the conductor.

But there's a hitch: The current creates its own magnetic field in a direction opposite to that of the changing magnetic field that induced it (a principle known as Lenz's Law). In practice, if we place a spinning magnet near a conductor, the induced current in the conductor will create a magnetic field that pushes back on the spinning magnet, slowing it down and eventually stopping it. When the magnet stops spinning, of course, the induced current disappears. In order to keep the current flowing, we need to keep the magnet spinning. To do this, we need to attach a motor of some kind. The resulting device is called a generator.

Generators convert the mechanical energy used to spin the magnet into electric current that can be used to power electrical devices. The typical generator has two parts: an outer shell to which magnets are affixed and an inner coil of conducting wire, which rotates in the magnetic field created by the external magnets. (Remember that, because of relativity, it doesn't matter whether the magnetic field or the conductor moves as long as one moves relative to the other.) As the coil spins, the magnetic field relative to the coil changes, inducing a current that flows out of the generator and into the circuits that power our cities. Furthermore, because the direction of the wire coil relative to the magnetic field changes with each half spin (moving up for half a revolution and then moving down), the electric current produced is alternating current.

So a generator converts mechanical energy into electrical energy. But what happens if you push electric current into a generator? You get a motor, which converts electrical energy back into mechanical energy.

As current flows through the wire coil inside a motor, it creates a magnetic field. This field pushes against the motor's fixed magnets, causing the coil (which is free to rotate) to spin. A motor is thus a generator in reverse. Spin a generator, and you get electricity; feed electricity into a generator, and you get a motor.

Generators use the principle of induction *to convert mechanical energy into electrical energy. Motors are generators acting in reverse.*

XIII. THE SAVAGE WORLD

THE STORM THAT SCATTERS the Achaean fleet blows Odysseus's twelve ships into a part of the world populated by mythological creatures and divine beings—that is, outside the normal human spheres of family (*oikos*) and the city-state (*polis*).

In need of supplies, Odysseus cautiously puts to shore at an island where he detects signs of habitation, specifically smoke. Picking twelve men to accompany him, he orders the rest to remain hidden until he can "find out what those men are like, wild savages with no sense of right or wrong or hospitable folk who fear the gods."

What Odysseus finds is that the island is inhabited by a cyclops named Polyphemus, whose solitary life in a cave stands in stark contrast with the social world of Odysseus and his men. (The Greeks believed that living together in a community is an essential part of civilization.)

The description of Polyphemus's circumstances emphasizes the distinction between civilized human norms and the frightening primordial world in which Odysseus now finds himself. According to Odysseus, who narrates most of the *Odyssey* in the past tense, "We came to the land of the Cyclopes, lawless savages who leave everything up to the gods. These people neither plow nor plant." For

Oydsseus and Polyphemus.

Homer, agriculture and the rule of law are both important because they distinguish human civilization from wild nature. Polyphemus recognizes neither, yet he does tend a flock of sheep, which he shelters in his cave at night.

Using a giant boulder, Polyphemus traps Odysseus and his men in his cave and begins to eat them raw as the mood strikes him. Mounting a rescue, the hidden sailors sharpen a large tree branch and at night, while Polyphemus is sleeping, drive it through his single eye. Although the cyclops can no longer see to take vengeance, Odysseus and his men remain trapped in the cave with Polyphemus's sheep. However, when Polyphemus eventually moves the boulder so that his sheep can leave to graze, Odysseus and his men escape by clinging to their bellies.

This pattern is repeated when Odysseus, stopping at another island, sends two heralds to a town populated by giants called Laestrygonians. The queen picks up one of the heralds and swallows him whole, at which point the other herald races back to warn his companions. The ships immediately set sail, but before they can travel out of range, the giants—who, like the cyclops, don't cultivate crops—destroy every ship but Odysseus's.

The contrast between human civilization and *wild nature is a central theme of the* Odyssey.

XIV. LAY PIETY

SUPPORTING JAKOB BURCKHARDT'S interpretive emphasis on Renaissance individualism was his view of Renaissance Italians as the progenitors of modern secularism. During the Middle Ages, according to Burckhardt, people necessarily saw the world through a lens of religion. During the Renaissance, however, as faith in religion became enervated, a more objective perspective emerged.

Certainly, the Renaissance church had numerous problems; but modern scholars no longer accept Burckhardt's interpretation because it fails to take into account significant evidence of intense piety among Renaissance Italians.

For most of the fourteenth century, there was no pope in Rome. Because of political unrest there, Pope Clement V had moved the papal capital to Avignon in 1309. Gregory XI returned the papacy to Rome in 1377, but a faction of French cardinals resisted the move, installing a rival "antipope" in Avignon and beginning the Great Schism, which lasted until 1417.

Once reestablished in Rome, the Renaissance popes generally focused their attention on high living and the recovery of territory lost to the papacy during its exile in Avignon. Perhaps no pope embraced these ambitions more than Julius II (1503–13), who hired Michelangelo to create an elaborate tomb for his final resting place and who dressed in full armor so that he could personally lead his papal troops into battle. Such unseemly behavior greatly diminished popular respect for the church and also for the clergy, among whom simony and nepotism were rampant.

Although numerous attempts to reform the church failed because of a lack of institutional support, the Franciscan and Dominican movements of the thirteenth century had a profound effect on lay piety. Advocating a return to the poverty and proselytizing that characterized the early church, these orders gained large followings and, eventually, papal sanction. Cities subsidized the construction of huge basilicas to accommodate the massive crowds they attracted; and religious confraternities developed, in which laypeople joined together for such devotional practices as praying, singing lauds, and performing charitable work.

Individual piety increased as well. Because of the spread of humanism, vernacular editions of the Gospels and the Psalms became more readily available, as did other works of devotional literature. All had a considerable effect on Renaissance culture. The diffusion of devotional literature, for example, generated interest in the stories of the Bible and encouraged wealthy patrons to commission artists to represent biblical stories in paintings and sculpture.

Although Jakob Burckhardt popularized the *association of Renaissance achievement with a decline in religious devotion, the period actually saw a significant rise in lay piety.*

XIV. WHAT IS A STOCK INDEX?

INVESTORS ARE OFTEN interested to learn how the stock market has performed over a given period of time, such as the last trading day or the last five years. But *How did the market do today?* is a difficult question to answer because stocks don't move in one direction all at once. Technology stocks may generally move up on a day when Microsoft announces a strong quarterly profit, but the stocks of Microsoft's direct competitors will likely go down.

Nevertheless, the desire to track market performance is so strong that even crude measures find an audience—which is why the stock index was invented. A stock index is a mathematical tool that measures the performance of a group of stocks chosen to represent a particular sector of the stock market or the market as a whole. In theory, if the component stocks are chosen correctly, the direction and magnitude of changes in the index will reflect the direction and magnitude of changes in the sector or market being measured.

Indexes are typically created and owned by publishing companies, which use them to generate sales and licensing income. They are designed, therefore, to attract attention and satisfy the needs of the publisher's customers.

One of the most important decisions that the creator of a new index must make is whether or not to weight the stocks that the index will track. Indexes created during the early twentieth century tended not to be weighted, but newer indexes typically make use of sophisticated mathematical tools to represent as closely as possible the composition of the broader economy. These indexes are usually weighted both by sector and by market capitalization. Without such weighting, stocks with high share prices would move the index more readily than stocks with low share prices—even though, as we have seen, share price is a rather arbitrary measure.

Another important consideration is how to manage the index over time in order to maintain its value. Usually, the owner establishes a committee to review periodically the list of companies being tracked so that some can be removed and others added. This process keeps the index current. For example, as new media comes to replace old media, the owners of a media-sector index would be well served to replace some of declining print companies it tracks with a few new Internet companies—and so on.

Stock indexes track the performance of *a group of representative stocks that serve as a proxy for either a particular sector of the market or the market as a whole.*

XIV. LANGSTON HUGHES

Langston Hughes ca. 1924.

THERE IS NO MORE IMPORTANT poet of the Harlem Renaissance than Langston Hughes (1902–67). Hughes was born in Joplin, Missouri, but spent most of his boyhood in Lawrence, Kansas, where he lived with his maternal grandmother while his mother searched for work and a new husband. (Hughes's father, James, abandoned the family shortly after Langston's birth.) Following his grandmother's death in 1915, Langston went to live with his mother and her new husband in Lincoln, Illinois, and then Cleveland. About this time, he began writing poetry, his chief influences being Walt Whitman, Carl Sandburg, Paul Laurence Dunbar, and Claude McKay. Following his high school graduation in 1920, he spent a year living with his father in Mexico, attempting to persuade the elder Hughes to pay for his tuition at Columbia University. Finally, James Hughes relented on the condition that, rather than pursue a career in poetry, his son study engineering. Langston agreed and maintained a B⁺ average at Columbia but dropped out after his freshman year because he found the arts scene and nightlife of Harlem more to his taste.

During the next three years, Hughes traveled the world as a seaman, gaining life experience that he fashioned into poems, some of which appeared in *The New Negro*. Hughes's first book of poetry, *The Weary Blues*, appeared in 1926. As the collection's title suggests, music had a strong influence on Hughes, whose poems often took the structure of a twelve-bar blues. The most famous poem in the collection, "The Negro Speaks of Rivers," links together the Euphrates, Congo, Nile, and Mississippi. In doing so, the poem shows the influence of Whitman's "Crossing Brooklyn Ferry," which similarly connects a wide range of themes across space and time. In Hughes's hands, of course, the result is uniquely reflective of the African American experience. With *The Weary Blues* as his calling card, Hughes gained immediate entrance into the innermost literary circles of the burgeoning Harlem Renaissance.

Unlike Jean Toomer, who attempted to transcend race, Hughes believed that black artists could achieve liberation only when they allowed race to define their work. In his famous 1926 essay "The Negro Artist and the Racial Mountain," Hughes described the black artist's struggle to fit within white modes of expression as an obstacle, or mountain, that had to be overcome. The only way to do this, Hughes explained, was to embrace "racial individuality" so that artistic freedom might emerge.

African American music, *especially blues and jazz, had a profound impact on Langston Hughes, whose poems and critical essays championed racial pride.*

XIV. INDUCTION DEVICES

THE PRINCIPLE OF magnetic induction has inspired much modern technology, such as the induction brakes used in some automobiles. A typical disc brake consists of a pad mounted on a caliper operated by the brake pedal. When the driver steps on the pedal, the caliper squeezes the brake pad against the disc, which is attached to the end of the car's axle. The resulting friction slows the car down.

Instead of friction, induction brakes makes use of magnetic forces. When the driver presses down on the brake pedal in a car equipped with induction brakes, he turns on an electromagnet that surrounds the disc in the same way that the magnets of a generator surround its spinning coil. As the spinning disc (a conductor) moves through the magnetic field of the electromagnet, a current is induced in the disc. This current, in accordance with Lenz's Law, produces its own magnetic field, which pushes back on the field created by the electromagnet, slowing the car down. (In some hybrid and electric cars, the current induced in the disc is shunted into the battery so that the energy can be stored for later use.)

Another popular application is the induction cooktop. Most electric stoves work by passing a current though a high-resistance heating element, which converts the electrical energy into heat. Induction cooktops use rapidly varying currents to create changing magnetic fields, which in turn induce currents in the pots and pans sitting on top of the stove. The induced currents heat the pots and pans directly because the pots and pans act as resistors in the induced circuit.

Induction cooktops are much more efficient than other electric stoves because they lack the intermediary heating elements that contribute to energy loss. Induction cooktops also respond instantly, but they work only with ferromagnetic cookware.

Devices built on the principle of magnetic induction *are typically more energy-efficient than devices that convert mechanical or electrical energy directly into heat.*

XIV. THE DIVINE WORLD

DURING HIS WANDERINGS, Odysseus meets not only savages (such as the Cyclopes and the Laestrygonians) but also several divinities, most famously the sea nymph Circe. Odysseus's constant need for food and other supplies forces him to stop at Circe's island, where he learns that the divine places of the world are no more suitable for humans than the savage.

When Odysseus sends heralds to Circe's lodge, she drugs them and transforms them into pigs. When more of Odysseus's men come looking for the missing heralds, she transforms them into pigs as well. Finally, Odysseus is forced to investigate. With the help of Zeus and Hermes, Odysseus avoids Circe's drugs and overpowers her, after which she swears an oath of friendship to him and returns his men to human form.

Circe offers a drink to Odysseus.

After about a year on Circe's island, Odysseus's men grow homesick, and he asks Circe for her consent to leave. She gives it because she knows that Odysseus is fated to continue searching for his home on Ithaca. Advising him to seek the counsel of the shade (ghost) of Tireisias, once a great prophet of Apollo, Circe explains to Odysseus that he can find Tireisias "across the river Ocean."

When Odysseus crosses the ocean and reaches the edge of the world, he sacrifices two sheep, whose blood attracts the shades of the Underworld. (When drunk, the sheep's blood gives a shade the power of speech.) Odysseus carefully guards the blood until the shade of Tireisias appears and drinks it. Then Tireisias explains why the gods are persecuting Odysseus (because of his sacrilege at Troy) and what he must do in order to appease them.

Odysseus converses with other shades as well. He speaks, for instance, to Elpenor, who died on Circe's island but wasn't given a proper funeral. Elpenor makes Odysseus promise to return to the island and give him a proper burial so that his soul can be at peace. Odysseus also speaks with the shade of a gloomy Achilles, whom Odysseus tries to console by describing the *kleos* Achilles still has among the living. Achilles declares, however, that he would rather be "a slave to the poorest dirt farmer than lord it over all the dead." This conversation suggests a darker view of war than that presented in the *Iliad*, which holds that the greatest prize any warrior can obtain is a glorious death in battle.

Circe's island and the Underworld *are divine parts of the world where living humans such as Odysseus and his men have no place.*

XV. THE INDIVIDUAL IN RENAISSANCE FLORENCE

WHEN JAKOB BURCKHARDT described the Italian Renaissance as the point of transition between the Middle Ages and the modern era, he was referring in particular to the idea that Renaissance Italians were the first Europeans to see themselves solely as individuals—set apart from any group, institution, or family. Shorn of these bonds, Burckhardt's "Renaissance man" acted primarily under his own guidance.

Modern social historians , however, have identified a multiplicity of bonds that united and obligated Renaissance Florentines. In the aftermath of the Black Death, for example, parents became much more attached to their children, and family life became a major concern. This is evident in the proliferation of parenting manuals written by such famous humanists as Matteo Palmieri and Leon Battista Alberti. Meanwhile, kinship remained an important social factor, as relatives continued to form business ventures together, support one another's political careers, and serve as counselors or mediators in times of conflict.

The emblem of the wool guild of Florence.

Those Florentines unable to call on extended families for support often found effective substitutes in guilds and other social organizations. Even the laboring classes, who remained excluded from the guilds, met in neighborhood social groups known as *potenze*. Especially under the patronage of Lorenzo the Magnificent, these groups flourished and played a leading role in city festivals (as part of Lorenzo's plan to cultivate popular support and project the image of a beneficent leader). Religious confraternities based in parish churches similarly enhanced neighborhood ties by bringing together men, women, and youth of various social backgrounds.

Social bonds were also forged in less structured ways. For instance, in selecting godparents for their children, Florentines were able to establish important connections with their neighbors. Asking a neighbor to become a godparent was a meaningful act, and it created an intimacy that would have been difficult to achieve through other means.

Burckhardt's view notwithstanding, Renaissance Florentines saw themselves not as individuals but as members of many different communities—all interconnected by family, business, neighborhood, and religious ties. In fact, the personal interests of most Renaissance Florentines, on which Burckhardt placed his emphasis, were in many ways determined by the social networks to which each person belonged.

Contrary to Burckhardt's claim that *individualism defined Renaissance life, Renaissance Florentines were bound by complex social networks that often determined their personal interests.*

XV. THE LEADING STOCK INDEXES

THE MOST CLOSELY WATCHED stock indexes in the United States are the Dow Jones Industrial Average (DJIA) and the Standard & Poor's 500 Index (S&P 500). Each tracks the stock market in a different way, reflecting a different indexing philosophy.

The DJIA was created in 1896 by Charles Dow, cofounder of Dow Jones & Company, which publishes the *Wall Street Journal*. It consists entirely of blue-chip stocks. These are the stocks of large, well-established companies that enjoy high public confidence in their worth and stability. The term *blue chip* is said to have been coined during the 1920s by a journalist comparing the high share prices of DJIA stocks to high-denomination poker chips.

At the time the DJIA was created, a company's share price was thought to be an indication of its quality. Because it was Dow's intention to track only the most trustworthy companies—not the market as a whole, nor the national economy— he selected twelve stocks that were well regarded and thus had high share prices. Of these, only General Electric remains part of the current average, now composed of thirty companies.

Because of this narrow focus on blue chips, the usefulness of the DJIA as an economic indicator is rather limited. Its principal virtues are its simplicity and its longevity. In terms of mathematics, the DJIA couldn't be simpler: It's merely an average of the share prices of the stock of its constituent companies, adjusted for splits. (Note that, because the DJIA isn't weighted, high-priced stocks have a greater influence on the index than high-capitalization stocks.) As for its longevity, the DJIA has benefited greatly from its focus on corporate giants. The *Wall Street Journal* maintains a committee that periodically reviews and adjusts the list of companies that make up the DJIA, but changes are rare because the companies are so stable. As a result, market analysts can use the DJIA as a consistent baseline when studying long-term trends.

By contrast, the S&P 500 is a rigorously defined index that makes use of much more sophisticated mathematical tools. For example, while the static DJIA has no specific rules for including or excluding companies, the S&P Index Committee routinely publishes the criteria that it uses to rebalance the index, which it does on a regular basis to adjust to changing economic conditions. For this same reason, the S&P Index Committee also weights the 500 Index by sector and by capitalization in order to model the broader economy more effectively.

The leading stock indexes in the United States, *the Dow Jones Industrial Average and the Standard & Poor's 500 Index, reflect very different indexing philosophies.*

XV. ZORA NEALE HURSTON

Zora Neale Hurston in 1938.

ZORA NEALE HURSTON (1891–1960) was born in Notasulga, Alabama, to highly literate parents, a preacher and a schoolteacher, who taught her an appreciation for words that lasted her entire life. While she was still a toddler, her family moved to Eatonville, Florida, one of several all-black towns founded in the South after the Emancipation Proclamation freed the slaves in Union-held territory. The Eatonville of her youth was, according to Hurston, "a city of five lakes, three croquet courts, three hundred brown skins, three hundred good swimmers, plenty guavas, two schools, and no jailhouse." However, following her mother's death in 1904 and her father's hasty remarriage, her childhood became less than idyllic. Her relationship with her father soured, and she left home in 1905. Twelve years of wandering later, she finally returned to high school in Baltimore but had to lie about her age, pretending to be sixteen, in order to qualify for public financing. For the rest of her life, she maintained the fiction that she was ten years younger than her actual age.

In the fall of 1918, Hurston entered Howard University, where she met Alain Locke and began publishing short stories in *The Stylus*, the school's literary magazine. Supporting herself as a waitress and manicurist, she attended Howard part-time for the next six years until a lack of funds forced her withdrawal. In the meantime, with Locke's help, she began submitting stories to *Opportunity*, a magazine of Negro life launched in 1923 by the National Urban League. Following the December 1924 publication of her story "Drenched in Light," Hurston moved to Harlem, where she attended in May 1925 an awards dinner sponsored by *Opportunity*. There, she met and impressed philanthropist Annie Nathan Meyer, who arranged for her to attend Barnard College in the fall. The first black woman to obtain a degree from Barnard, Hurston studied anthropology and later became a folklorist.

After producing two volumes of southern folklore, Hurston traveled in 1936 to the Caribbean, where she intended to study religious practices but instead found herself wrestling with a spiritual crisis of her own. The resolution can be found in *Their Eyes Were Watching God* (1937), which Hurston wrote in Haiti in just seven weeks. "It was dammed up in me," she later explained, "and I wrote it under internal pressure." The novel's protagonist is Janie Mae Crawford, a biracial woman who struggles to blend her individual pride with her racial pride.

Hurston moved easily between the worlds of *white academia and black literature, her work always celebrating both individual and racial pride.*

XV. CHANGING ELECTRIC FIELDS

WE HAVE SEEN THAT changing magnetic fields produce electric fields, but what happens when electric fields change? To investigate this question, let's begin with the capacitor, which is a device that stores electric charge.

Capacitors are made of two small conductive plates with a gap (usually filled with an insulator) between them. When a capacitor is added to an electric circuit, current flows into it, building up on one of its plates. This is how the capacitor stores electric charge. At the same time, however, current flows out of the capacitor from the other plate. This outflow takes place even though the insulator prevents charges from crossing the gap between the plates. In fact, the current stops only when the inflow plate becomes "full" and no more charge can be pushed onto it. How can this be?

The answer has to do with the capacitor's changing electric field. As charge builds up on the inflow plate, it creates an electric field that grows stronger as the charge increases. Once the capacitor becomes fully charged, the electric field stops increasing, and the current stops flowing. Notice the connection here: The current flows only as long as the electric field keeps changing. This is the clue that led Scottish physicist James Clerk Maxwell to solve the puzzle.

So far, we've thought of current only as a stream of moving charges, such as electrons. These electrons are material (that is, they take up space), and they create electric fields. But remember that changing magnetic fields, which are not material, also create electric fields. Maxwell's great insight was his realization that current could just as easily be created by something nonmaterial. The changing electric field in the capacitor, he concluded, is simply a different form of current.

A current carried by the motion of charges is called a conduction current. A current carried by a changing electric field is called a displacement current. Both types of current are equally real, and thus both produce magnetic fields. Because a displacement current produces a magnetic field, it follows that a changing electric field produces a magnetic field, just as a changing magnetic field produces an electric field. The symmetry of this relationship indicates that electricity and magnetism are both expressions of the same fundamental force: electromagnetism.

Electric and magnetic fields have a symmetrical relationship *because electricity and magnetism are both aspects of the same fundamental force: electromagnetism.*

XV. THE POWER OF FATE

AFTER BURYING ELPENOR'S body properly, Odysseus leaves Circe's island again on a course that Circe warns will take him past three great dangers: the Sirens, the giant whirlpool Charybdis, and the Scylla. The Sirens are half-human, half-avian creatures who sing enchanting songs that lure sailors to their deaths on the rocky shores where the Sirens live. Forewarned by Circe, Odysseus escapes by stuffing his crewmen's ears with wax. Meanwhile, Odysseus forgoes the earplugs but has himself tied to the mast so that he can hear the Sirens' song without endangering the ship.

The next two dangers arrive in tandem, because the Scylla, a huge monster descended from the gods, lives on the shoreline of the strait that contains Charybdis. Odysseus decides to steer around Charybdis, but this maneuver will bring the ship perilously close to the Scylla. Odysseus decides not to warn the crew about the Scylla

A third-century BCE Roman mosaic of Odysseus and his men salining past the Sirens.

because, being immortal, the Scylla cannot be bested in battle and because Odysseus's men would likely become fearful and lose their focus in the rough water of the strait, causing the ship to wreck. Odysseus and the crew successfully avoid the whirlpool; but as they pass the Scylla, it plucks six of them off the ship.

The winds then die, and Odysseus and his men have to put ashore on Thrinacia, where they remain stranded for days. Having foreseen this eventuality, both Tireisias and Circe warned Odysseus not to harm the cattle that graze on the island, because they belong to the sun god Helios. When the crew's food runs out, however, the men slay and eat some of the cattle. Almost immediately, a strong breeze strikes up, and they set sail again. But Helios begs Zeus to punish the cattle thieves, and Zeus complies, destroying the ship. Only Odysseus survives, clinging to the mast.

These episodes point out the gap that exists between human and divine knowledge and also the irresistible power of fate. Being a goddess, Circe has access to divine knowledge; but even with this knowledge, Odysseus and his men cannot escape their fates. Knowledge of the Scylla doesn't prevent the loss of the six crewmen, nor does knowledge of the cattle's ownership prevent the destruction of the ship. It's no coincidence, for example, that that Odysseus and his men are stranded on Thrinacia just long enough to drive them to slaughter the cattle.

Despite his access to divine knowledge, *Odysseus still can't navigate the dangers of Charybdis, the Scylla, and Helios's cattle unscathed.*

XVI. SAVONAROLA

LORENZO DE' MEDICI'S UNEXPECTED DEATH IN 1492 exposed the downside of his strategy to rule through intimidation. Initially, Il Magnifico's place was taken by his eldest son, Piero; but the resentment felt by elite families excluded from power for so long came crashing down on Piero in 1494, when Charles VIII of France marched an army into Italy to stake his claim to the Neapolitan throne.

When Charles's army approached Florence, Piero met with the French king and, without the support of the Signoria, tried to appease him by relinquishing several important Florentine strongholds. Learning of this, the Signoria banished Piero and his brothers, Giuliano and the cardinal Giovanni, from the city. It then sent its own ambassadorial party to the French, headed by the Dominican friar Girolamo Savonarola, whom Il Magnfico had brought to Florence shortly before his death.

Savonarola was chosen for this mission because he had prophesied correctly that Charles would invade Italy. His goal now was to persuade the French king to leave Florentine territory—which he did by agreeing that Florence should pay Charles off and let him keep the fortresses until the end of the Neapolitan campaign. Savonarola also let slip that God had plans for Charles that wouldn't be fulfilled if he kept hanging around Tuscany.

Savonarola's success greatly elevated his standing; and when disputes broke out among elite families and guildsmen concerning who should run post-Medici Florence, the friar assumed an important mediatory role. At his suggestion, a single, much larger body—modeled on the Great Council of Venice—supplanted previous legislative councils. The nobility went along, believing they could exercise control through an executive committee like the Venetian Senate. But Savonarola was an egalitarian, and under his leadership more Florentines became eligible for public office than ever before.

Girolamo Savonarola ca. 1498.

Meanwhile, urging a return to Christian fundamentals, Savonarola called for a rejection of wealth and economic inequality that struck at the heart of the Florentine elite's lifestyle and artistic patronage. He organized gangs of boys to go about the city harassing citizens wearing extravagant clothes and sponsored a "bonfire of the vanities" in which lewd books, paintings of nudes, and luxury items were burned. These initiatives appealed to a broad swath of Florentines—including the artist Sandro Botticelli, who burned several of his own paintings in the 1497 bonfire.

The charismatic preacher Girolamo Savonarola *helped restore republican government to Florence after six decades of increasingly authoritarian Medici rule.*

XVI. MUTUAL FUNDS

A MUTUAL FUND IS a company formed for the purpose of investing shareholder capital jointly. Funds typically contract with outside managers to provide them with investment advice, execute trades on their behalf, and handle their accounting. Most but not all funds offer shares to the public. Those that do are regulated by the Securities and Exchange Commission (SEC).

Mutual funds can be either actively or passively managed. The managers of active funds frequently readjust their portfolios in order to maximize shareholder profit. The managers of passive funds, such as index funds, simply follow clearly defined rules that require no independent judgment. The managers of the Vanguard 500 Index Fund, for example, merely watch and follow the actions of the S&P Index Committee. The underlying S&P 500 Index, however, is run like an actively managed mutual fund, with the Index Committee continually researching and reevaluating its "holdings."

Mutual funds are especially attractive to investors because they take advantage of huge economies of scale. Securities analysis is a highly labor-intensive activity. Whether one is visiting factories or back-testing technical strategies, the research involved is cumbersome and time-consuming. Most importantly, the analysis required to make a sound investment is the same whether one buys five shares of a company or five million shares. Therefore, mutual funds with enough capital to buy five million shares have much lower per-share research costs.

The absolute size of mutual funds is also important because large funds regularly use their huge buying power to negotiate better deals with brokers. As a result, they enjoy lower commissions and greater access to the brokers' own analysis, which can be useful because analysts at brokerage houses tend to have close relationships with the companies they cover. Companies also respect the huge buying power that mutual funds represent, often permitting their analysts greater access to company management.

Some mutual funds are closed-ended, which means that they issue a fixed number of shares in an initial public offering, after which all shares are bought and sold on an exchange as though they were shares of stock. Open-ended funds, on the other hand, continually issue shares to investors who want to buy while redeeming shares owned by investors who want to sell. Both issuance and redemption take place at the fund's net asset value (NAV) as of the close of the trading day.

Mutual funds invest shareholder capital jointly *in order to take advantage of economies of scale and the benefits of massed buying power.*

XVI. CARL VAN VECHTEN

AS A YOUNG MAN, Carl Van Vechten (1880–1964) developed an interest in music and theater that he found difficult to satisfy in his hometown of Cedar Rapids, Iowa. At the University of Chicago, however, which he attended from 1899 until 1903, he became steeped in both subjects and began writing about them. His first job out of college was as a reporter for the *Chicago American*; and in late 1906, he moved to New York City, where he became assistant music critic at the *New York Times*. Beginning in 1915, he worked

A 1934 self-portrait of Carl Van Vechten.

as a freelance writer, publishing several volumes of critical essays; then, in 1922, he turned his hand to the writing of novels.

Like F. Scott Fitzgerald, Van Vechten had a special feel for the elegant decadence of the Jazz Age. While his early novels typically concern New York City's white artistic elite (of which Van Vechten was a member), his most famous work, *Nigger Heaven* (1926), explores life in Harlem. The title refers to the theater balconies in which blacks were forced to sit while whites occupied the more desirable orchestra seats below. In Van Vechten's novel about a librarian and an aspiring writer whose love is stifled by racism, this vantage point becomes a metaphor for life in Harlem, the uptown neighborhood to which blacks are restricted while the more prosperous whites enjoy life downtown. Implied in the metaphor, however, is the suggestion that blacks, stationed above whites, might also be socially superior.

As a man about town, Van Vechten frequented the Cotton Club and other fashionable Harlem nightspots; yet his interest in Negro life and culture extended well beyond that of the dilettante. Often, he invited members of the Harlem literati to parties at his Fifth Avenue apartment, and a famous caricature of the period by Miguel Covarrubias shows Van Vechten with dark skin. Nevertheless, Van Vechten's depiction of African American characters and his use of the word *nigger* proved highly controversial among both whites and blacks who wondered whether Van Vechten had gone too far in crossing the color line.

Although criticized by many as sensationalist, *Nigger Heaven* bridged the gap between the Lost Generation and the Harlem Renaissance, asserting that the struggle for artistic integrity in a decadent world transcends the color of one's skin. After reading the novel, James Weldon Johnson praised it, insisting, "The book and not the title is the thing."

As a music and theater critic, *Van Vechten had his finger on the cultural pulse of the Jazz Age, hence his ability to link the values of the Lost Generation with those of the Harlem Renaissance.*

XVI. ELECTROMAGNETIC WAVES

AS WE HAVE SEEN, although electric fields are typically created by electric charges, they can also be created when no charge is present by a changing magnetic field. Similarly, although magnetic fields are typically created by moving electric charges, they can also be created in the absence of moving charges by a changing electric field. Combining these phenomena mathematically, James Clerk Maxwell showed that, in general, electric and magnetic fields can exist without the involvement of electric charges at all. They can simply create each other by changing in time. The type of equation that Maxwell used to describe this behavior is known as a wave equation.

Wave equations are common in physics. Mechanical waves, which propagate in material media such as air or water or guitar strings, describe disturbances that change the media's position over time. Consider the mechanical wave produced by dropping a pebble into a pond. The wave causes the level of the water at a given point in the pond to rise and fall (that is, change its position) over time (that is, as the wave passes). An equation written to describe a wave therefore has to include variables for both time and position.

Sound is another type of mechanical wave; and because it's a mechanical wave, it requires a medium (air) in which to propagate. That's why sound can't be heard in a vacuum. But electromagnetic waves do travel through vacuums because they aren't mechanical. The changes in time and position that they produce don't involve atoms in a medium but electric and magnetic fields. This is how an electromagnetic wave propagates: A changing magnetic field produces a changing electric field nearby. That changing electric field then produces a changing magnetic field around the changing electric field—which in turn produces even more nearby changing electric fields, and so on.

The speed of a mechanical wave generally depends on the characteristics of the medium in which it travels. The vibration of a guitar string, for example, is a type of mechanical wave. Its wave equation takes into account the density of the string, how tightly it's stretched, and so on. But the wave equation for electromagnetic radiation, which doesn't require a medium to propagate, is much simpler. When solved, it shows that all electromagnetic waves traveling in a vacuum move at a constant speed—the speed of light, which is itself an electromagnetic wave.

Unlike mechanical waves, *whose speed varies according to the medium in which they propagate, electromagnetic waves travel at a constant speed that is the speed of light.*

XVI. A DISTURBING HOMECOMING

ODYSSEUS NARRATES most of the *Odyssey* in the past tense because the epic begins in medias res—that is, in the middle of the story. Prior events are then described in the past tense as the plot proceeds in the present.

When readers first meet Odysseus, he is sitting on a beach, staring at the sea in tears. Following the destruction of his ship, he has washed up on the shore of the island home of Calypso, a sea nymph like Circe who falls in love with him at first sight. She nurses him back to health and for the next seven years tends to his every need, sleeping with him nightly. Eventually, however, Odysseus tires of their union and begins longing for his wife, Penelope, and their home on Ithaca.

Taking pity on him, Athena persuades Zeus to send Hermes to tell Calypso that she must let Odysseus go. "I loved him, I took care of him, I even told him I would make him immortal and ageless," the unhappy Calypso complains. Thus we learn that Odysseus has had the opportunity to transcend his humanity but has chosen not to do so. The implication is clear: Odysseus is a human, and he recognizes his place in the world as such. Indeed, his experiences prior to landing on Calypso's island speak primarily to what is and what is not human.

Calypso then speaks with Odysseus. "The two forms, human and divine, came to the cave / And he sat down in the chair that moments before / Hermes had vacated, and the nymph set out for him / Food and drink such as mortal men eat. / She sat opposite godlike Odysseus / And her maids served her ambrosia and nectar." (Ambrosia and nectar are the food and drink of the gods.) The contrast couldn't be clearer. As "godlike" as Odysseus may be by virtue of being a goddess's consort, he is still human.

With Calypso's help, Odysseus builds a raft and finds his way back to human civilization. On Ithaca, however, he discovers that, believing he is dead, disrespectful suitors have come to court his wife, Penelope. With the help of his son, Telemachus; his father, Laertes; a few loyal servants; and Athena, Odysseus slays all of the suitors and reestablishes his rightful place as king of Ithaca, husband to Penelope, father to Telemachus, and son to Laertes.

When Odysseus finally returns *home to Ithaca after twenty years of war and wandering, he must still reestablish his place within human society.*

XVII. THE RETURN OF THE MEDICIS

IN CALLING FOR REFORM of the church, Savonarola often criticized the pope directly. His remarks so angered Rome that in 1497, he was excommunicated. Soon afterward, a Franciscan friar challenged Savonarola to defend his social and political prophecies in a trial by fire. (That is, Savonarola would walk through fire; and if he emerged unscathed, his prophecies would be deemed true.) One of Savonarola's close associates accepted this challenge on his behalf, and a large crowd gathered to witness the event. When it was called off at the last minute, a dissatisfied mob stormed Savonarola's residence, and the Signoria ordered his arrest. Savonarola was hanged and his corpse burned to prevent followers from gathering relics and proclaiming his martyrdom.

Following the death of Savonarola, the political elite attempted to reinstate the oligarchy that had governed Florence before the rise of the Medicis. The *popolo*, however, finally enjoying genuine political participation as members of the Great Council, put up such strong resistance that the elite had to give up this plan and try something else. They soon focused on the position of *gonfaloniere*, the chief executive officer of the Signoria. In 1502, they successfully installed Piero Soderini, one of their own, as *gonfaloniere* for life. But Soderini surprised everyone by governing as a populist and limiting elite ambitions.

During ten years as *gonfaloniere*, Soderini encouraged political experimentation, especially with regard to the military. Following the advice of Niccolò Machiavelli, he disbanded Florence's mercenary army and established a permanent citizen's militia. The militia didn't last long, however. In 1512, an army composed of troops from the Papal States, the Holy Roman Empire, and Spain invaded Florence and returned the Medicis to power. Immediately, a new *balìa* was established, which eliminated the Great Council and Machiavelli's militia as well.

Yet the political elite was disappointed once again, because the Medicis had no intention of sharing power. Furthermore, once Giovanni became Pope Leo X in 1513,

he and his younger brother, Giuliano, shifted their attention to Rome and placed lesser relations in charge of Florence. These men, in turn, delegated important responsibilities to their clients, who came from smaller Tuscan cities ostensibly subject to Florence. The effrontery of this arrangement—Florentines being ruled by their own subjects—galled the political elite to no end.

Pope Leo X with two of his cardinals.

Unable to wrest control of Florence from the *resurgent* popolo *after Savonoarola's death, the political elite chose to back a return of the Medicis—a decision they later regretted.*

XVII. HEDGE FUNDS

IN CONTEMPORARY PARLANCE, the term *hedge fund* seems to carry with it an aura of mystery and complexity. Yet stripped down to its essentials, a hedge fund is basically a mutual fund that doesn't offer shares to the general public and thus isn't regulated by the SEC. In fact, one could argue that the only meaningful difference between hedge funds and other mutual funds is that hedge funds are exclusive to the very rich.

Like other mutual funds, hedge funds are companies formed for the purpose of joint investing. Also like other mutual funds, hedge funds hire outside managers to handle the actual work of investing for them. A slight difference is that while hedge fund managers live and work domestically, the hedge funds themselves are usually domiciled in tax havens such as the Cayman Islands. Another slight difference is that while hedge funds issue and redeem shares at NAV, they only do so at specified times, such as the end of each month. Many hedge funds also enforce minimum holding periods of one or two years. Such restrictions ostensibly allow hedge fund managers to invest in illiquid securities without having to worry about selling them off quickly should more investors than expected produce shares for redemption.

The first hedge funds were set up to go both long and short, hence their name. The idea was that such hedging would reduce the investors' overall market risk while generating profit in both up and down years. Today, however, many hedge funds employ strategies that involve no hedging at all—strategies that are no different from those employed by low-cost public mutual funds.

It seems that the only people who consistently make money from hedge funds are the people running them. Most hedge funds charge investors both a management fee (typically 2 percent of the assets under management) and a performance fee (often 20 percent of the profits generated). Let's say that a $5 billion hedge fund produces an 8 percent return in a given year (about what the S&P 500 returns in a typical year). In that case, the hedge fund managers would split a management fee of $100 million and a "performance fee" of $80 million—even though their fund's performance was no better than that of the Vanguard S&P 500 Index Fund. Furthermore, once the $180 million in fees is paid, the shareholders' return in investment shrinks to just 4.4 percent.

Hedge funds are mutual funds that don't offer shares *to the public and thus aren't subject to SEC regulation.*

XVII. THE MODERN PRIMITIVE

Claude McKay in 1934.

BORN INTO A FARMING FAMILY in Jamaica, Claude McKay (1889–1948) immigrated to the United States in 1912 to attend the Tuskegee Institute. He was so appalled, however, by the segregation he encountered in Alabama that he soon transferred to Kansas State Agricultural College, where he studied agronomy for a year before realizing that he didn't want to be an agronomist. In 1914, he moved to New York City, where he wrote poetry and soon became a founding member of the Harlem Renaissance.

Unlike James Weldon Johnson, W. E. B. Du Bois, and other movement elders, McKay had a much more nuanced view of race. The characters he created weren't simply symbols of racial uplift but multidimensional human beings. Jake Brown, the protagonist of McKay's 1928 novel *Home to Harlem*, is a working-class everyman who spends his days chasing women, eating, and drinking booze. Yet his lifestyle, though picaresque, is rooted in the same basic needs that all people have for sustenance and acceptance. On the other hand, the novel's one intellectual character, a black nationalist named Ray, finds himself sadly alienated from the life that Jake leads (and McKay celebrates) because his vision is limited and he can see Harlem only as an enormous "pig-pen" filled with sex, drugs, and violence.

After reading *Home to Harlem*, Du Bois famously remarked that he felt he needed to take a bath, and other black critics attacked McKay for portraying blacks as overfed and oversexed. McKay countered that he presented life in Harlem as he saw it, without sandpaper or varnish. To the younger, more radical members of the Harlem Renaissance, what whites thought about blacks mattered little, and the gaining of white acceptance was not a concern. As Langston Hughes liked to point out, pride can only emerge from within; outsiders can't bestow it. This is the sensibility one finds in *Home to Harlem*.

More generally, McKay's novel exemplifies the modern primitivism found in much European and expatriate art of the period. (McKay himself lived as an expatriate from 1922 until 1934.) Primitivism, or the belief that one should live simply in a natural environment, gained a great deal of popularity after World War I because many intellectuals blamed the war on the excesses of civilization and believed that the thing to do was go primitive. Jake Brown personifies this argument as he relies on rural virtues to sustain him in the unnatural world of urban America.

McKay's *Home to Harlem* exemplifies *modern primitivism as it contrasts the alienation of postwar intellectuals with the life-affirming exuberance of its working-class hero.*

XVII. THE ELECTROMAGNETIC SPECTRUM

WAVES ARE TYPICALLY described in terms of wavelength, frequency, and speed. The wavelength (λ) of a mechanical wave is the distance between successive wave crests. In electromagnetic waves, wavelength is the distance between successive magnetic or electric field maxima (maximum values). The frequency (f) of a wave refers to the number of crests (or maxima) produced per unit time. The wave's speed, or velocity (v) is thus λf.

As discussed previously, all electromagnetic (EM) waves traveling in a vacuum move at a constant rate of speed equal to the speed of light. If wave speed is indeed a constant, then an EM wave's wavelength and frequency must be inversely proportional. In other words, as one goes up, the other goes down, and vice versa. Therefore, high-frequency EM waves must have short wavelengths, and low-frequency EM waves must have long wavelengths. The electromagnetic spectrum is the range of all possible combinations.

Electromagnetic waves with wavelengths of one meter or greater are called radio waves. These waves were the first EM waves manipulated as such by humans because their low frequencies make them easy for simple AC circuits to generate. All you need is a coil of wire with an AC current running through it. The changing direction of the current causes the magnetic field produced by the coil to reverse direction with the frequency (measured in hertz) of the current. The changing magnetic field creates a changing electric field, and so on as the pattern radiates out from the coil at the speed of light.

Electromagnetic waves with wavelengths between one meter and one millimeter are called microwaves. It wasn't until the 1920s that physicists developed electrical devices capable of oscillating fast enough (that is, with sufficiently high frequency) to generate microwaves. An interesting feature of microwaves is that when they are absorbed by water, their energy is converted into the random motion of water molecules, which is a form of heat. Microwave ovens work because water in the food absorbs the energy of the microwaves and converts that energy into heat, which cooks the food.

The rest of the electromagnetic spectrum includes (from longer wavelengths to shorter) infrared light, visible light, ultraviolet light, X-rays, and gamma rays. A rather small slice of the spectrum, visible light ranges in wavelength from 380 to 750 nanometers (10^{-9} meters), with long-wavelength red light at one end of this range and short-wavelength blue light at the other.

Electromagnetic waves are classified by *their wavelength, which is inversely proportional to their frequency.*

XVII. PIUS AENEAS

LIKE THE *Odyssey*, Virgil's *Aeneid* begins in medias res with Aeneas sailing toward Italy from Troy. A storm blows Aeneas's fleet off course, however, and the Trojan refugees land instead at Carthage, a Phoenician city on the North African coast. Aeneas's mother Venus (the Latin name for Aphrodite) and Juno (Hera) then conspire

Dido and Aeneas in a fifth-century CE illuminated manuscript of the *Aeneid*.

to make the queen of Carthage, Dido, fall in love with Aeneas, whose wife has died in the massacre at Troy.

As the patron deity of Carthage, Juno is bothered by the prophecy that descendants of Troy will destroy her city. Uniting Dido and Aeneas, however, would make the Trojans citizens and allies of Carthage. Aphrodite, meanwhile, merely wants her son Aeneas to survive so that he can reach Italy and found the colony of Alba Longa, from which Romulus and Remus (descendants of Aeneas) will eventually depart to found Rome.

As Aeneas recounts for Dido the story of Troy's defeat, the queen indeed falls in love with him. (This passage intentionally mimics similar passages in the *Odyssey* during which Odysseus narrates his own adventures.) Dido and Aeneas soon become lovers, and the Trojan refugees also become accustomed to the easy life in Carthage. When a sudden thunderstorm interrupts a hunting expedition, Juno takes the opportunity to perform an informal wedding ceremony. This marks the height of Dido and Aeneas's happiness together.

As in the *Iliad* and the *Odyssey*, however, the decrees of fate cannot be ignored, and it falls to Jupiter (Zeus) to implement them. He sends Mercury (Hermes) to move Aeneas along; and despite his heartache, Aeneas obeys. Dido, however, kills herself rather than endure the humiliation of Aeneas's rejection. This episode not only explains the historical enmity between Carthage and Rome but also demonstrates Aeneas's commitment to duty over his own personal happiness.

Although modeled closely on Homer, the *Aeneid* remains a distinctly Roman epic whose values reflect those of early imperial Rome, especially the value of *pietas* (piety). Virgil often refers to the title character *pius Aeneas*—an apt epithet because *pius* means not simply "devout" but also "proper," in the sense of doing things right. To be *pius* is to do one's duty, regardless of the difficulty or personal cost. Aeneas sacrifices the happy life he would have enjoyed with Dido but is rewarded as the progenitor of Rome with an eternal glory similar to the *kleos* bestowed on the Greek heroes of the Homeric epics.

Virgil uses the character of Aeneas to *embody the value of* pietas, *which has important civic meanings beyond its religious implications.*

XVIII. THE COLLAPSE OF THE REPUBLIC

EVENTS TURNED AGAINST the Medicis when Pope Clement VII (a cousin to Giovanni and Giuliano) tried to deceive Holy Roman Emperor Charles V and was caught in his duplicity. As a result, Charles invaded Italy in 1527, sacked Rome, and made Clement VII his prisoner. Meanwhile, the Florentine elite seized on this opportunity to cast out the Medici clients nominally in charge of the city.

Although the elite initiated this revolt, its true beneficiaries were the *popolo*. Just as in 1497, the elite found that they couldn't overcome the *popolo*'s numerical strength and so had to submit ultimately to the popular will. At the insistence of the *popolo*, the Great Council was restored, and Savonarola's moral reforms were reinstituted.

Soon, however, Clement made a deal with Charles V: In exchange for denying Henry VIII of England a divorce from Catherine of Aragon (Charles's aunt), the pope was released from prison and loaned enough imperial troops to reclaim Florence. When the Great Council refused to negotiate, the city was besieged in October 1529.

Defiance stoked by republican rhetoric was high; and the *popolo* were particularly zealous, believing that resistance to Medici tyranny was the will of God. Throughout the yearlong siege, they remained determined in the face of deprivations at home and setbacks on the battlefield. But what many saw as courage, the frightened elite saw as militancy and intransigence, and the elite turned out to be right. The *popolo* were no match for the forces arrayed against them; and in August 1530, the republic surrendered.

In the end, the siege was a catastrophe. More than a third of the Florentine population died—from either starvation, disease, or combat—and the city was transformed into a Medici duchy that lasted another two hundred years. These events marked the end of a remarkable period of political contention, during which humanism and republicanism jointly inspired the Florentine Renaissance. Recognizing this, the new Medici duke, Cosimo I, chose not to bury Florence's republican past but to celebrate it as a stage in the city's natural evolution. In proper humanist fashion, he cultivated the perception that, just as the Florentine republic had been heir to the ancient Roman republic, so was the Medici duchy now heir to the Florentine republic. As a sign of continuity, he retained the republican architecture of the city's municipal buildings but redesigned their interiors to express the splendor and glory of the new order.

A 1545 portrait of Duke Cosimo I.

Although Florentines briefly ousted the Medicis in 1527, *their city was soon besieged by troops of the Holy Roman Empire, forced to capitulate, and transformed into a Medici duchy.*

XVIII. BUBBLES AND CRASHES

BUBBLES AND CRASHES are probably inevitable features of markets. Why this is so has been studied extensively by behavioral economists. So far, these academics have produced extensive new vocabularies, but not yet any persuasive explanations.

Part of the problem is that bubbles are difficult to detect while they are happening. From the inside, a bubble seems like nothing more than the market functioning well. After all, traders buy an asset because they expect it to appreciate. Why should they be surprised when it does? Furthermore, if an asset has recently appreciated and seems to be trending upward, what rational investor wouldn't buy into it?

One tip-off that a bubble may be under way is that the investment theories driving the market upward are unusually complex, circular, and self-reinforcing. For example, during the Internet bubble of the 1990s, arcane new metrics such as "clicks per hour" were used to make money-losing start-ups seem attractive to investors. The business practices that take hold during bubbles can also be unsavory. During the notorious South Sea Bubble of 1720, South Sea Company directors lent insiders money at preferential rates so that they could buy more stock and run up the share price. As a result, the price of South Sea stock rose from £128 ½ in January to nearly £1,000 in August.

Bubbles typically climax in a speculative frenzy known as a blow-off top. With this peak, buyers burn out and stop buying so aggressively, while traders long in the stock begin selling to lock in their gains. Soon, short-sellers hurt in the stock's run-up reappear to recoup their losses. Finally, the selling reaches a crescendo when people who bought on the way down, looking for bargains, realize that there are none to be had. Thus, the self-reinforcing thinking that characterized the growth of bubbles works even more efficiently once the crash begins.

Because preventing bubbles and crashes is probably impossible, economists have focused on limiting the damage done. The most common prescription is to lower both interest rates and lending standards once the crash begins in order to promote liquidity and save traders from going bankrupt (as many did following the crash of 1987). Government regulations are also usually tightened after a crash to prevent its recurrence, but such regulatory changes do little to stop new bubbles from forming in entirely different types of assets.

Bubbles and crashes are inevitable features of markets, *often characterized by self-reinforcing thinking that first drives the market up and then brings it down.*

XVIII. WILLIAM FAULKNER

AFTER SERVING IN THE Canadian Royal Air Force during World War I and then working in a New York City bookshop, the Mississippi-bred William Faulkner (1897–1962) drifted down to New Orleans in early 1925, intending to sail for Europe. Instead, he fell in with a literary crowd that included Sherwood Anderson. Like Hemingway before him, Faulkner benefited greatly from his brief, fortuitous acquaintanceship with Anderson, who persuaded Faulkner to shift from writing poetry to writing fiction and later persuaded his own publisher, Boni and Liveright, to bring out Faulkner's first novel, *Soldier's Pay* (1926).

Like the novels of other Lost Generation writers, *Soldier's Pay* is colored by a pervading sense of world-weariness. Although Faulkner never saw combat himself, his protagonist, pilot Donald Mahon, is a wounded veteran in the mode of Jake Barnes. Shot down in a dogfight, Mahon suffers a debilitating head injury that results in a loss of memory and gradually in blindness.

Faulkner's great innovation was his approach to memory. On the one hand, he sees the past as always shaping the present. Yet, like Eliot, he manipulates the past using fragmentation, disorientation, and multiple perspectives to create new meanings out of old resources. Viewing modern society as harmfully material, he praises the "eternal verities" of "love and honor and pity and pride and compassion and sacrifice" and lauds the human capacity for endurance. Like many writers of the Lost Generation, Faulkner takes comfort in the belief that, even in lands rent by apocalyptic war, tales of renewal and hope will prevail.

Thus, the writers, artists, and intellectuals of the Jazz Age reacted in two very different ways to the same calamitous war. One the one hand, the Lost Generation produced deeply cynical works of art while leading famously hedonistic lifestyles. On the other hand, the members of the Harlem Renaissance refused to succumb to the blue devils of modern life and instead worked to establish a culture that was distinctively life affirming. These differences were certainly significant, and yet black and white artists nevertheless began working together during the Jazz Age, borrowing techniques from one another as they moved back and forth across the color line. This cultural melding can be heard most clearly in the music of jazz, which embodied the delicate balance between order and disorder that Western civilization faced as it rose from the ashes of war.

Like the rest of the Lost Generation, *William Faulkner saw modern society as a wasteland; yet, like the writers of the Harlem Renaissance, he maintained hope in the "eternal verities."*

XVIII. THE REPRODUCTION OF SOUND

SOUND IS A mechanical wave that travels through the air. Its peaks and troughs correspond to variations in air pressure. Humans are able to hear sound because these pressure variations cause our eardrums to vibrate. Small bones attached to nerve endings in the inner ear convert the vibrations into electrical signals, which are then sent to the brain.

Microphones work in the same way. A thin membrane built into the microphone vibrates in response to the pressure variations in the sound wave. Attached to this membrane is a small magnet surrounded by a fixed coil of wire. As the membrane and magnet vibrate together, the motion of the magnet creates a changing magnetic field that induces a current in the coil of wire. But this current isn't steady. In fact, the pattern of its variation matches the pattern of the magnet's vibration. Thus, the induced current functions as an electrical version of the sound.

This electrical signal, once captured, can be either transmitted or stored. In order to be stored on a compact disc or in a computer's hard drive, it first must be digitized, or encoded as 1s and 0s, which are the only words in the digital language.

Hard drives store information by creating patterns of magnetic domains. The incoming electrical signal powers a small electromagnet built into the disk drive's write head, creating a variable magnetic field that realigns the magnetic domains on the disk itself. The disk drive's read head works on the principle of giant magnetoresistance, according to which the magnetic field of the domain closest to the read head changes the resistance of the head. A very small current running through the read head detects this change, creating an electrical signal that can be amplified and processed by the computer.

Electrical signals can be converted back into mechanical sound waves simply by reversing the recording process. The current that runs into a loudspeaker passes through a coil of wire surrounding a magnet, which is connected to a membrane. The magnetic field created by the current exerts a magnetic force on the magnet, causing it to vibrate. The magnet's vibrations cause the membrane (often a paper cone) to vibrate in response, producing the sound that we hear.

The principles of electromagnetism allow *us to convert mechanical sound waves into electrical signals and then convert those signals back to sound again.*

XVIII. AENEAS IN THE UNDERWORLD

BOOK VI of the *Aeneid* tells the story of Aeneas's journey to the Underworld so that he may speak with the spirit of his dead father, Anchises. The narrative is modeled closely on Odysseus's journey to the edge of the world in Book XI of the *Odyssey*, but Virgil's treatment is different in several important ways. For example, rather than standing on the edge of the living world as Odysseus does, Aeneas walks through Hades itself, making the experience far more visceral. (Dante used this section of the *Aeneid* as a template for his own *Inferno*.)

Aeneas finds his way to the Underworld by consulting the Sybil, a priestess of Apollo who has been to the Underworld herself and thus knows how to get there. Even more importantly, she knows how to return to the world of the living. On his journey, Aeneas meets a former companion who, like Elpenor, is unable to cross the river Styx on the border of the Underworld. Thus, as Odysseus did, Aeneas learns that souls cannot enter the Underworld until they have received proper burial.

Also like Odysseus, Aeneas sees the ghosts of many famous men and women and speaks with some of the heroes of the Trojan War. (In Aeneas's case, of course, these are Trojan rather than Achaean heroes.) Aeneas even encounters Dido—who, wandering in sadness, refuses to acknowledge him. Virgil's depiction of the Underworld is far more detailed than Homer's, presumably because the mythological "map" of Hades became much more fleshed out during the seven centuries that separated the lifetimes of the two poets.

Ultimately, Aeneas makes his way to Elysium (Fields of the Blessed), a location in the Underworld reminiscent of the Judeo-Christian Heaven. There, he finds his father watching a stream of spirits rising from the depths of the Underworld and floating up toward the living world. These spirits, Anchises explains, are the souls of their descendants. He begins naming each one, eventually pointing out Augustus Caesar, the Roman emperor who commissioned the *Aeneid*.

This knowledge of the glory of his future descendants is the only reward Aeneas receives for his suffering. Once he establishes the Italian colony of Alba Longa, he becomes embroiled in a series of battles and finally dies in one of them, generations before the founding of Rome.

Aeneas's journey to the Underworld borrows heavily from *the* Odyssey *but differs in several instructive ways, including its propagandistic mention of Augustus Caesar.*

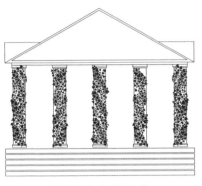

SYLLABUS

III

I. EARLY REFORM MOVEMENTS

FOLLOWING THE COLLAPSE of the Western Roman Empire, cities largely disappeared from Europe. Beginning about 1100, however, spurred on by rising commerce, they made a comeback. As a result, during the High Middle Ages (1000–1300), literacy rates jumped. Prior to this period, the few people who could read and write were mostly clerics (who could do so in Latin). As urbanization promoted commercial literacy, however, lay elites became increasingly interested in a variety of texts. Large portions of the New Testament were translated into the vernacular, and these popularized the idea of emulating Jesus, especially in his preaching and his poverty.

This new religiosity posed a problem for the Catholic Church, whose services contained little preaching and instead emphasized the celebration of the Eucharist (communion). Even more uncomfortably, the opulent lifestyles of bishops, abbots, and other prelates stood in stark contrast with the poverty of Christ. At the time, most church prelates were noblemen whose families had purchased their offices for them. Few were inclined toward pastoral ministry, and most simply collected revenue from their dioceses and monasteries while living elsewhere. Parish priests were also poorly trained; and many clerics, both great and small, had concubines, wives, or mistresses.

Catholic propaganda showing Waldensians worshiping Satan.

Soon, lay preachers (joined by some priests) began publicly relating what they had read in the Bible and criticizing the church for its wealth and its overemphasis on ritual. Eventually, reform movements emerged.

Two of the earliest groups of reformers, the Franciscans and the Dominicans, gained papal approval, but others were deemed heretical. The Waldensians, for example, were condemned as heretics in 1181 because they refused to recognize the authority of local bishops. The Cathars were similarly condemned because they rejected marriage and other sacraments. Nevertheless, by the end of the twelfth century, both groups had amassed huge followings in southern France and northern Italy, forcing the Catholic Church to step up its opposition. Through violent crusades and stern inquisitorial prosecutions, the church ultimately managed to suppress these movements, but the underlying problems remained, and reformers such as the fourteenth-century Lollards and fifteenth-century Hussites continued to pressure the church.

As literacy spread among the laity, *the Bible became more widely read, inspiring a new religiosity that cast the behavior of the Catholic Church in an unfavorable light.*

I. SEX AND GENDER

FEMINISM IS THE THEORY of the equality of the sexes—politically, economically, and socially. Like any theory, it rests on certain premises, among the most important of which is the distinction that feminists make between sex and gender. In everyday conversation, the terms *sex* and *gender* are used interchangeably, but to feminist scholars they have different, specific meanings.

Sex refers to the biological differences that exist between men and women. These include not only the presence or absence of a vagina or penis but also such secondary characteristics as breast size and voice intonation. When discussing sex characteristics, feminists use the terms *male* and *female*.

Gender, on the other hand, refers to those qualities attributed by society to men and women as a result of their biology (that is, their sex). Aspects of gender include the ways that people present themselves (their clothing and personal appearance), as well as the social roles that they occupy. For instance, the stereotypes that women are passive and prefer pink to blue are social expectations, not biological facts. Thus, according to feminist theory, they relate to gender and not to sex. When discussing gender, feminists use the descriptive terms *masculine* and *feminine*.

Feminist scholars who study the ways that gender expectations shift over time have discovered that social norms vary not only from one historical period to the next but also from one culture to another. More importantly, their work has shown that these expectations are essentially arbitrary, with no basis in biology. Rather, they arise from the prevailing patriarchy, which feminists define as a system of rule in which men are exclusively the leaders and decision makers.

A second foundational premise of feminism is that patriarchy has historically been responsible for the subordination of women, at least in an institutional sense. (There have been no female US presidents, for example.) Patriarchy has also generated the pervasive cultural beliefs that women are weak and irrational in comparison with men. Feminist research has shown, however, that as women are allowed greater access to male-dominated areas of society (such as the workplace), their performance and achievements undercut the long-standing patriarchal claim that women are biologically inferior to men. Although feminist conceptions of sex and gender do sometimes shift, what remains constant is the idea that gender expectations aren't reflective of biological predispositions but are rather the cultural products of patriarchal institutions.

A foundational premise of feminist theory is the distinction between *sex, which describes one's biology, and* gender, *which refers to the social expectations that arise from sexual difference.*

I. THE BOLSHEVIKS

IN 1917, two revolutions took place in Russia. In March (or February by the old-style Russian calendar), a coalition of antitsarist groups overthrew the repressive regime of Nicholas II and established a provisional government led first by Prince Georgy Lvov and then by socialist Alexander Kerensky. In November (October by the old-style calendar), the Kerensky government was itself overthrown by Vladimir Lenin's Communist party, which seized power in the name of the soviets (workers' councils).

For obscure reasons relating to infighting at the 1903 congress of the Russian Social Democratic Labor party, Lenin's followers were known as Bolsheviks—from the Russian adverb *bolshe*, meaning "more." The designation was meant to imply that Lenin's faction represented the majority of Russian socialists (which it didn't).

From the start, the United States government didn't care for the Bolsheviks. It wasn't that the new regime was totalitarian. That didn't become clear until after Lenin's death in 1924 and not really until Joseph Stalin began consolidating power in 1928. More importantly, the relationship got off to a very poor start. In March 1918, just as US troops were arriving in France to join the Allied side in World War I, the Bolsheviks signed the Treaty of Brest-Litovsk with the Central Powers, taking Russia out of the war. (Previously, Russia had been fighting with the Allies against Austria-Hungary, Germany, the Ottoman Empire, and Bulgaria.)

A 1919 Bolshevik poster.

The ideological divide between American capitalism and Russian communism also encouraged suspicion and distrust. The Bolsheviks wanted to replace capitalism with an international communist state, and in March 1919 they established the Comintern (Communist International) to work "by all available means, including armed force, for the overthrow of the international bourgeoisie."

Thus, when civil war broke out in Russia, the United States joined several other Western nations in sending troops to support the anti-Bolshevik Whites in their fight against the Bolshevik Reds. The multinational force fared poorly, however, and was withdrawn in 1920. After finishing off the White Army in 1921, the victorious Reds established the Union of Soviet Socialist Republics (USSR) in late 1922.

Although the US government supported Russian famine relief during the early 1920s and American businessmen established commercial relations with the Soviet government during the period of Lenin's New Economic Policy (1921–29), the United States didn't recognize the Soviet Union formally until 1933.

The US government felt *such immediate antagonism toward the new Bolshevik regime that it sent American troops to fight against the Reds during the Russian Civil War.*

I. WHAT IS GAME THEORY?

GAME THEORY IS a systematic way of thinking about the possibilities for conflict and cooperation in everyday life. It analyzes situations, referred to as "games," in which two or more "players" make interdependent decisions. Put succinctly, game theory is the science of strategy.

Beginning in childhood, we all learn to play games. Some of these games are simple, such as tic-tac-toe and rock-paper-scissors; others, such as chess, are more complex. No matter how simple or complex the game is, however, even novice players quickly realize that there are "right" ways to play. The goal of game theory is to determine the "right," or rational, ways to play any game.

An important insight of game theory is that simple parlor games can function well as metaphors for strategic interaction in the real world. Think, for instance, of the ways in which people talk about geopolitics. They often speak of world leaders as "engaged in a chess game" or "moving their pieces around the board." Similarly, people in conflict are often described as having strong or weak "hands," as though they were playing a card game. These analogies are actually quite meaningful, and game theory can be used just as well to evaluate diplomacy as to analyze the game of bridge.

Although game players are typically individuals, they can also be groups of people—such as corporations, political parties, nations, or international organizations. The starting point for game theory is the assumption that all players are rational. In game theory, the word *rational* has a specific meaning. A rational player is one who recognizes all the possible outcomes of the game and is able to rank them from most to least preferable. This ranking must be internally consistent. For example, if a player prefers pie to cake, and cake to ice cream, then—to be rational—he must also prefer pie to ice cream. In addition, players are assumed to be aware that the other players are rational, too. Finally, a rational player, in calculating his moves, will take into account the fact that the other players in the game are anticipating and reacting to the choices that he makes.

Game theory is the formal study of conflict and cooperation, *in which "games" are used to model and understand real-world situations involving multiple interdependent "players."*

I. THE ATMOSPHERE

BECAUSE METEOROLOGY IS fundamentally the study of the atmosphere, it's best to begin a course on meteorology with a description of the atmosphere itself, especially its composition and thermal structure. Three gases make up nearly all of the (dry) atmosphere by volume. These gases are nitrogen (78.08 percent), oxygen (20.95 percent), and argon (0.93 percent). Neon, helium, methane, krypton, and hydrogen are also present but only in trace quantities.

The earth's atmosphere as seen from space.

The concentrations of these gases remain fairly constant, but other atmospheric components vary. The amount of water vapor in the atmosphere, for example, can range from 0 to 4 percent. The amounts of carbon dioxide, ozone, and airborne dust also fluctuate, often impacting weather and climate.

Structurally, the atmosphere has four layers. Closest to the earth's surface is the troposphere, where most weather patterns occur. As one moves up through the troposphere, the temperature of the atmosphere decreases. The measurement that meteorologists use to express this decrease is called the lapse rate. Within the troposphere, the lapse rate averages 6.5°C/km. That is, the temperature falls on average 6.5°C with each increase of 1 km in altitude.

At a certain altitude above the earth's surface, usually around 7 km at the poles and 17 km at the equator, the atmospheric temperature stops decreasing. This transition point is called the tropopause, and it marks the boundary between the troposphere and the stratosphere. The stratosphere contains nearly all of the atmosphere's ozone, which is a form of molecular oxygen that contains three oxygen atoms (O_3) instead of the usual two (O_2). Ozone plays an important role in protecting life on earth because it absorbs dangerous ultraviolet (UV) radiation emitted by the sun. Because UV radiation is a form of energy, its absorption raises the temperature of the atmosphere. So, in the stratosphere, temperature increases with altitude.

Another transition point, the stratopause, occurs at an average of 50 km above the earth's surface. Above the stratopause is the mesosphere, where the temperature trend reverses again. In the mesosphere, temperature decreases with altitude until the mesopause is reached. Above the mesopause, at an altitude of about 80 km, the thermosphere begins. Temperature in the thermosphere is difficult to measure because the atmosphere there is sparse, but it generally increases with altitude.

The four layers of the atmosphere *are defined thermally, depending on whether the atmospheric temperature increases or decreases with altitude.*

II. CHRISTIAN HUMANISM

"ERASMUS LAID THE EGG THAT LUTHER HATCHED" is an old adage that quaintly sums up the relationship between Christian humanism and the early Protestant Reformation. By promoting Bible study among the laity and criticizing church abuses, Christian humanists created an atmosphere highly conducive to religious change.

Christian humanism—so named because of its emphasis on the humanities—developed as an outgrowth of the Renaissance learning that swept Italy during the fourteenth century and later spread to northern Europe. Inspired by the rediscovery of ancient Greek and Roman texts, the Christian humanists were moral activists who believed that well-educated men trained in the classics made the best leaders. In their view, Catholic leadership was inadequate, if not immoral. Of particular concern were the church's opulence, its inattention to pastoral ministry, and its shady financial dealings. A notorious example was the sale of indulgences, which were supposed to remit purchasers from purgatorial punishment based on sins committed on earth.

Following Johannes Gutenberg's invention of the moveable-type printing press about 1450, Christian humanists began publishing new editions of the Bible. At the time, the position of the church was that laypeople needn't concern themselves with church matters. Humanists, however, believed that reading the Bible promoted the sort of moral edification that could, in time, reform the church.

Among the leading Christian humanists were Desiderius Erasmus of the Netherlands and Thomas More of England. In his 1511 book *The Praise of Folly*, Erasmus denounced monasticism, superstition, and the immorality of church prelates. He certainly had cause: Pope Julius II (1503–13) actually led papal troops into battle, while Innocent VIII (1484–92) was known as the father of Rome because he sired so many children.

A 1523 portrait of Erasmus by Hans Holbein the Younger.

Martin Luther and other German reformers drank deeply from these currents. Yet once the Reformation began, the Christian humanist movement fragmented. Although some humanists joined the Reformation, many more sided with the Catholic Church because they wanted reform, not revolution. Denouncing the Protestants as schismatics, Erasmus picked apart Lutheran theology, while in England Thomas More persecuted Protestants as heretics. Thus, Christian humanism ultimately became subsumed into the bitter struggle it had helped to create.

Christian humanists were *moral activists who held church leaders up to the standards of ancient Greece and Rome and found those leaders lacking.*

II. THE HISTORICAL STATUS OF WOMEN

UNTIL THE LATE NINETEENTH CENTURY (and even later in many parts of the world), women lacked nearly all of the legal and political rights they now take for granted. For example, British and American women were subject to a principle known as coverture. Originating in English common law, coverture held that a woman was legally "covered" by her father or husband to the extent that she had no legal rights of her own. As a result, women couldn't retain their earnings, own property in their own name, or sue in court on their own behalf; nor could they vote. Essentially, they were property themselves, belonging initially to their families and later to their husbands.

Mary Wollstonecraft

Mary Wollstonecraft (1759–97) was born into this state of affairs; and because her father was abusive, she became particularly aware of the degradations that women suffered due to their dependent position in society. Because her father was also profligate, she worked from an early age to support herself and her siblings. In 1788, determined to become a writer, she moved to London, where she fell in with a circle of political radicals that included Thomas Paine, author of the pamphlet *Common Sense*.

Strongly influenced by Paine's ideas about "the rights of man," Wollstonecraft applied Paine's thinking to her own situation in *A Vindication of the Rights of Woman* (1792)—which, most scholars agree, laid the ideological groundwork for the majority of the women's activism that followed. In her book, Wollstonecraft argued that the inferior position women occupied in society resulted from societal constraints that limited women's opportunity to grow. The inferiority was not, Wollstonecraft made clear, related to any biological differences between the sexes. Although Wollstonecraft didn't distinguish between sex and gender in the way that modern feminists do, her writings nonetheless suggest that she recognized a difference between female biology and feminine social roles.

Several generations later, British philosopher John Stuart Mill (1806–73) likewise made an important contribution to the theoretical underpinnings of what later became feminist theory. Mill was a utilitarian, which meant that he believed the moral worth of an action depended on the good that it did for all people in general (an idea usually stated as "the greatest good for the greatest number"). In *The Subjection of Women* (1869), Mill called for the granting of full citizenship rights to women because doing so would benefit all of society.

Mary Wollstonecraft and John Stuart Mill *wrote early, compelling treatises on the status of women that laid the ideological groundwork for the women's activism that followed.*

II. THE NAZI-SOVIET NONAGGRESSION PACT

UNDER THE NEW ECONOMIC POLICY, the Soviet state controlled all of the nation's large economic enterprises—factories, mines, railroads, and so on. Only small businesses (those employing fewer than twenty people) were permitted to operate privately. Later, under Stalin's Five-Year Plans, the first of which was adopted in 1928 for the years 1929–33, the Soviet state moved toward even greater economic control. The First Five-Year Plan, for example, forcibly collectivized the peasantry and compelled the rapid development of new heavy industry. According to Stalin, the Soviet Union was "fifty or a hundred years behind the advanced countries. We must make good this distance in ten years. Either we do it, or they will crush us."

Meanwhile, soon after becoming president in March 1933, Franklin Roosevelt realized that the US policy of nonrecognition no longer made sense. It wasn't restraining Soviet Communism, but it was making it difficult for the United States to obtain Soviet cooperation with regard to a number of increasingly ominous international issues, such as the rise of militarism in Germany and Japan. For this reason, FDR invited Soviet foreign minister Maxim Litvinov to Washington, and on November 17 the two nations agreed to establish formal diplomatic relations.

As World War II approached, Stalin considered his options. Although his dislike for the Germans was great, his distrust for the British and the French was even greater. Specifically, he feared that if war came, Britain and France would assume defensive positions and let his nation face the German onslaught on its own. Thus, he began hinting to the Germans in April 1939 that he might consider negotiating an agreement to provide for Soviet neutrality in the event of war. Under the cover of trade talks, the two sides secretly negotiated the Nazi–Soviet Nonaggression Pact, announced to a stunned world in late August. Nine days later, Germany invaded Poland.

Stalin (in uniform) looks on as the Nazi–Soviet Pact is signed.

Fundamentally, the Nazi–Soviet pact was a delaying tactic for both sides. Although Stalin's Five-Year Plans were making headway, the USSR wasn't ready for war and wouldn't be until 1942. Meanwhile, Adolf Hitler wanted to avoid fighting in the east until Germany was victorious in the west. Originally, the Führer intended to wait until the fall of Britain before invading the USSR; but when the British held out longer than expected, Hitler invaded the Soviet Union in June 1941 anyway, anticipating that a swift German victory would demoralize the British into surrendering.

Stalin agreed to the Nazi–Soviet Pact *because he needed more time to prepare for war and also because he distrusted the British and French even more than he did the Germans.*

II. THE ORIGIN OF GAME THEORY

ALTHOUGH MANY PEOPLE, from generals to philosophers, had pondered for millennia the problems of strategic thinking, it wasn't until the mid-twentieth century that a formal science dedicated to the subject appeared. The scientist who initiated game theory, formulated its basic questions, and in some cases answered them was a polymath named John von Neumann. Born in Budapest, Hungary, in 1903, von Neumann was a child prodigy who published his first mathematical paper at the age of eighteen and completed both his undergraduate degree in chemistry and his doctorate in mathematics in just five years. For the next four years, von Neumann taught at universities in Germany. Then, in 1930, he traveled to the United States to become a visiting lecturer at Princeton, eventually accepting a permanent position there. In 1933, he joined the faculty of Princeton's newly founded Institute for Advanced Study, where he remained until his death in 1957. Among von Neumann's many eminent colleagues at the Institute for Advanced Study was the physicist Albert Einstein.

Von Neumann's interest in mathematics was driven primarily by practical problems—what mathematicians call empirical applications. During World War II, for example, he joined the Manhattan Project and provided several crucial calculations necessary to the successful design of the atomic bomb. After the war, he helped lead the way in the development of computers.

It was this practical bent that initially motivated von Neumann to take up the study of games. While other mathematicians had previously studied some aspects of parlor games, von Neumann was the first to show (in 1928) that, in a particular type of game (one with two players with directly opposed interests), there is always a rational way to play.

Von Neumann was also the first scientist to assert—boldly, for the time—that the same mathematical tools used to analyze parlor games could be applied to the analysis of less trivial interactions among people and nations. In *The Theory of Games and Economic Behavior* (1944), von Neumann and his coauthor, economist Oskar Morgenstern, proposed that a suitably developed theory of games should serve as the basis for most economic analysis. Half a century later, their vision has largely come true. Game theory is now a foundational tool not only in economics but also in other social sciences, in computer science, and in evolutionary biology.

Recognizing that interactions in parlor games *resembled interactions in the real world, John von Neumann used this insight to develop the science of game theory.*

II. THE SEASONS

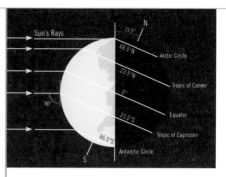

This diagram shows the winter solstice in the Northern Hemisphere.

ON AVERAGE, the earth is ninety-three million miles from the sun, but this distance varies according to the time of year. In January, when the earth reaches the point in its orbit closest to the sun (perihelion), the distance is about ninety-one million miles. In July, when the earth reaches its farthest point from the sun (aphelion), the distance is about ninety-five million miles.

The earth's distance from the sun, of course, doesn't cause the seasons—or else the entire planet would experience summer in January and winter in July. Instead, the seasons derive from the earth's 23.5° tilt. During the summer months in the Northern Hemisphere, the earth is oriented so that the North Pole points toward the sun. Because of this orientation, only at points north of the equator do the sun's rays strike the earth's surface at angles approaching perpendicularity. This is important, because when the sun's rays strike the earth's surface at lower angles, their energy in diffused.

Imagine holding a flashlight perpendicular to the ground. The circle illuminated by its beam is bright. Now imagine tilting the flashlight a little. The illuminated oval isn't nearly as bright, because the same amount of energy is now lighting (or heating) a larger area. The sun's rays behave in much the same way. The more perpendicular they are, the more energy they convey per unit area.

The winter solstice, the shortest day of the year in the Northern Hemisphere, occurs on December 21 or December 22, depending on the year. On this day, with the North Pole pointing away from the sun, locations north of the Arctic Circle (which begins at latitude 66.5°N) experience twenty-four hours of darkness. Meanwhile, the sun's rays are perpendicular to the earth at 23.5°S, a line of latitude known as the Tropic of Capricorn. The summer solstice, the longest day of the year in the Northern Hemisphere, occurs on June 21 or June 22. On this day, the North Pole points toward the sun, so the sun's rays are perpendicular to the earth at latitude 23.5°N (the Tropic of Cancer) and darkness covers locations south of the Antarctic Circle (which begins at latitude 66.5°S).

Equidistant between the solstices are the vernal (spring) and autumnal (fall) equinoxes. On these days, the sun's rays are perpendicular at the equator, and all locations on the earth experience twelve hours of both daylight and darkness.

The seasons are caused by the tilt of the earth. *They change because, as the earth orbits the sun, the sun's rays strike the earth at different angles in different hemispheres.*

III. GERMAN POLITICS

DURING THE LATE MIDDLE AGES (1300–1500), the Catholic Church ably resisted all attempts at reform, both from within and from without. So why did Martin Luther succeed where many others had failed? The answer lies in the politics of sixteenth-century Europe—particularly the politics of Germany, where independent-minded princes aligned themselves with religious reformers in order to bolster their autonomy within the politically fragmented Holy Roman Empire.

Emperor Charles V

An unwieldy creation of medieval politics and war, the Holy Roman Empire incorporated hundreds of duchies, city-states, and principalities in central Europe. All were nominally controlled by the Hapsburg dynasty in the person of Emperor Charles V, who reigned from 1519 until his death in 1556. As a practical matter, however, the German states functioned as independent realms, much to Charles's chagrin. He was determined to impose his will on them, but their princes were just as determined to resist.

Meanwhile, the German princes cast a covetous eye over the vast landholdings of the Catholic Church, which owned about 30 percent of all German real estate. As a consequence, many princes found ample reason to support the Reformation: Lutheranism gave them not only a moral rationale for resisting the authority of the Catholic emperor but also an excuse for seizing church-owned land.

Once the Reformation began, various popes urged Charles V and Francis I, then king of France, to join forces and crush the heretics. Unfortunately for the church, the ongoing dynastic rivalry between the Hapsburgs and the Valois trumped the papal call for solidarity. Emperor Charles V was also King Charles I of Spain, which made him a threat to France; and the two dynasties were currently competing for control of the rich commercial cities of northern Italy. In all, the Valois and Hapsburg dynasties fought five wars against each other between 1521 and 1559; and on several occasions, the Catholic king of France made the expedient choice to ally himself with German Protestant princes against the Hapsburg emperor.

Further distracting Charles V was the encroachment of the Ottoman Turks on his southeastern flank. Because the Turks were Muslims, they were considered even more loathsome than the Protestants, and Ottoman advances into Hungary and Austria during the 1520s became a major imperial preoccupation. In fact, Charles V made several important concessions to Lutheran princes in exchange for their support against the Turks.

A dynastic rivalry, *the desire for greater political autonomy, and the Turkish threat all made it difficult for Europe's two great Catholic powers to rid their lands of heresy.*

III. THE FIRST WAVE

THE HISTORY OF WOMEN'S ACTIVISM in the United States is most often described using the wave model. So far, according to this model, there have been three waves: the women's suffrage movement, the women's liberation movement of the 1960s and 1970s, and the Third Wave of the mid-1980s and 1990s. The first wave began with the Seneca Falls Convention held on July 19–20, 1848. Organized by Elizabeth Cady Stanton (1815–1902) and Lucretia Mott (1793–1880) among others, Seneca Falls was the first formal gathering in the United States at which suffrage for women was discussed publicly and candidly. In a petition to the New York State legislature supporting enactment of the recently passed Married Women's Property Act, a few women had complained that they were victims of taxation without representation; but they had gone no farther because to nearly all women at that time, female disenfranchisement seemed routine and inescapable.

Elizabeth Cady Stanton in 1856.

At Seneca Falls, on the second day of the convention, the delegates debated a statement of purpose prepared by the organizers. Modeled closely on the Declaration of Independence, it was called the Declaration of Sentiments, and it contained twelve resolutions. The ninth of these declared, "*Resolved*, That it is the duty of the women of this country to secure to themselves their sacred right to the elective franchise." Urging caution, Mott had asked on the eve of the convention that this resolution be omitted, lest it distract from the declaration's other objectives, especially the ending of coverture. "Lizzie," she said, "thee will make us ridiculous. We must go slowly." But Stanton insisted that the suffrage resolution remain, and Mott acquiesced.

The delegates immediately embraced the Declaration of Sentiments and all of its resolutions except one, the ninth. Some argued, as Mott had, that endorsing such a radical idea would invite public ridicule and undermine all that the convention might otherwise achieve. In fact, the suffrage resolution would likely have gone down had not Frederick Douglass, the well-respected abolitionist, intervened to place his considerable weight behind Stanton's proposal. According to Douglass, the right to vote was crucial, because it alone could provide the political leverage that women would need to achieve their other goals. Although the suffrage resolution passed by just a narrow margin, in later years it came to be seen as the convention's greatest and most remarkable achievement.

The first wave of women's activism *began in July 1848 at the Seneca Falls Convention, where delegates approved a controversial resolution calling for women's suffrage.*

III. A MARRIAGE OF CONVENIENCE

IN MARCH 1941, Roosevelt persuaded Congress to pass the Lend-Lease Act, which authorized the release of military aid to countries fighting Germany and Japan. The underlying purpose of Lend-Lease was to keep Britain and China afloat until FDR could bring isolationist America around. When the Soviets entered the war in June 1941, Roosevelt welcomed them as allies and sent them Lend-Lease aid as well.

After Pearl Harbor and US entry into the war, efforts were made to improve US–Soviet relations. Propaganda campaigns portrayed Russians as reliable, hardworking peasants watched over by their benevolent Uncle Joe (Stalin). Even so, neither the Americans nor the Russians could set aside the United States' long-standing animosity toward Bolshevism, and the marriage of convenience remained uneasy at best.

A continuing point of contention was the opening of a second front in Europe. In May 1942, Stalin sent Foreign Minister Vyacheslav M. Molotov to Washington to urge Roosevelt to take some action to relieve German pressure on the Soviet front. The president responded by promising Molotov an invasion of German-occupied France before the end of the year.

British prime minister Winston Churchill disagreed. He believed that with US troops mobilizing, the only way to lose the war was to invade France prematurely. At first, he went along with Roosevelt's invasion plan, not wanting to contradict an important ally, but the prime minister's reservations were so deep that he finally made the difficult trip to Washington in June to voice his objections personally.

Churchill reviews Soviet troops during his 1942 trip to Moscow.

After a great deal of back-and-forthing, Churchill finally persuaded Roosevelt to accept Churchill's own plan for a late-1942 invasion of North Africa. Of course, this change in strategy deeply upset Stalin, whose Red Army continued to bear the worst by far of the fighting against Hitler. Fearing that Stalin might now doubt his Western partners sufficiently to negotiate a separate peace, Churchill traveled to Moscow in August 1942 to placate "this sullen, sinister Bolshevik state I had once tried so hard to strangle at its birth." But there was little he could say to reassure Stalin. As Churchill later noted, "Stalin observed that from our long talk it seemed that all we were going to do was…pay our way by bombing Germany." Both men knew that this bombing wouldn't do much to restrain the Nazi offensive on the eastern front.

The German invasion of the Soviet Union *forced a marriage of convenience on the Americans, British, and Soviets that remained uneasy at best.*

III. UTILITY FUNCTIONS

IN MOST PARLOR GAMES, the interests of the players are diametrically opposed. If one wins, the other loses. For game theory to be broadly applicable, however, it must take into account situations in which the outcomes are not so stark. In economics, for example, one of the fundamental concepts is that of gain through trade. In other words, each trading partner benefits from the exchange, and thus both "win."

To capture these richer possibilities, game theory uses utility functions. Recall that a rational player, by definition, is able to rank possible outcomes from most to least preferable. Utility functions encode these rankings by assigning them numerical values. (By convention, higher values are assigned to more preferred outcomes.) The utility function of an eating game involving the player described earlier who prefers pie to cake and cake to ice cream might assign a utility of 2 to pie, 1 to cake, and 0 to ice cream. In analyzing this (or any) game, it's assumed that rational players will seek to attain outcomes with the highest possible utility.

Our analysis, however, can be richer still. What if our hypothetical player likes cake nearly as much as he likes pie. Learning this, we can modify his utility scale using the following thought experiment: Suppose he is offered the opportunity to toss a fair coin. If it comes up heads, he will receive pie; if not, he gets ice cream. We can calculate the *expected utility* of this gamble using the mathematics of probability. The result is $(1/2 \times 2) + (1/2 \times 0)$, or 1, because the two outcomes (2 for pie and 0 for ice cream) are equally likely. Now we ask the player whether he would prefer to gamble or to accept cake as a certain outcome. If he chooses cake, then we know that the utility assigned to cake indeed needs to be higher than 1 (the calculated utility of the gamble).

The player's utility scale can be further refined by altering the probabilities involved in the gamble. If the chances of receiving pie are increased to three in four (and thus the chance of receiving ice cream is reduced to one in four), the expected utility of the gamble becomes $(3/4 \times 2) + (1/4 \times 0)$, or $1 1/2$. If the player still prefers cake to the gamble, then the utility assigned to the cake should be higher even than $1 1/2$.

Utility functions express the game objectives *of rational players by assigning numerical values to the possible outcomes.*

III. THE EARTH'S ENERGY BUDGET

TEMPERATURE MEASURES HEAT ENERGY, which can be can be transferred in three ways: radiation, conduction, and convection. Radiation is the transfer of heat by energy waves. Conduction is the transfer of heat by contact. Convection is the transfer of heat by the circulation that occurs in fluids of uneven temperature owing to variations in density and the action of gravity.

Consider a bowl of water placed in a microwave oven. The energy waves generated by the oven heat the water by radiation. Now think of water in a pot on a hot stove. In this case, heat is transferred from stove to pot by contact with the burner—that is, by conduction. Gradually, the water at the bottom of the pot becomes hot (also by conduction), creating an imbalance in temperature. This imbalance causes the water to begin circulating, transferring heat from bottom to top by convection. (Once the water becomes hot enough, you can see this circulation in the form of rising steam bubbles.)

All matter emits heat in the form of radiation. The wavelength of this radiation depends on the temperature of the emitting body. Hot bodies, such as the sun, emit high-energy short-wave (SW) radiation. Cooler bodies, such as the earth, emit low-energy long-wave (LW) radiation.

During the course of a typical day, the earth's surface temperature follows a cyclical pattern. The lowest temperature usually occurs just before sunrise. This is because at night the earth radiates heat (primarily in the form of LW radiation) without receiving any energy from the sun. At dawn, however, the earth begins to absorb solar SW radiation. Although it continues to emit LW radiation, the energy being gained surpasses the energy being lost, causing the surface temperature to rise. The daily maximum is usually reached during the late afternoon.

The difference between the energy being emitted and that being absorbed is called the earth's energy budget. Its two most important factors are the LW radiation being emitted by the earth and the solar SW radiation being absorbed by it. However, other factors also need to be taken into account—such as the solar radiation being reflected back into space by clouds in the atmosphere or ice and snow on the surface and the LW radiation being absorbed and radiated back to the earth by water vapor in the atmosphere. This is why the surface temperature remains higher on cloudy nights than on clear ones.

The energy budget of the earth *is made up of the heat it absorbs (primarily from SW radiation) and the heat it emits (mostly in the form of LW radiation).*

IV. MARTIN LUTHER

ALTHOUGH CONDITIONS WERE RIPE for a split in the Catholic Church, it nevertheless took the forceful actions of an enigmatic German to inaugurate the Reformation. Martin Luther (1483–1546) was an Augustinian monk, a theologian at the University of Wittenberg, and a spiritually anxious man. In his mind, the long-standing criticisms of church practice that had been rattling around Europe for centuries came to a crisis and spawned a new theological direction.

Luther was born in Saxony, where he displayed such intellectual precocity that his father, the part-owner of a mine, resolved to send him to university so that he could

A 1525 portrait of Martin Luther by Lucas Cranach the Elder.

become a lawyer. After his graduation from the University of Erfurt, Luther enrolled in law school. But once, while returning from a visit home, he found himself caught in a violent thunderstorm, and he called out to St. Anne, the patron saint of miners, to protect him. As Luther later told the story, he promised to become a monk if St. Anne saved him, and she did. Much to his father's displeasure, Luther kept his promise, entering the Augustinian order in 1505. He earned a doctorate in theology from the University of Wittenberg seven years later and subsequently began teaching there.

The early sixteenth century was a period when the church placed a great deal of emphasis on the devil and punishment—two subjects that greatly agitated Luther, who was extremely scared of Hell, his own sinfulness, and God's righteous anger. Although extraordinarily devout and scrupulous in his behavior, Luther was consumed by anxiety over his sinful condition and his fear of divine retribution. Between 1515 and 1517, he immersed himself in the writings of St. Paul and St. Augustine, concluding that salvation derives not from a combination of faith and good works (as the church taught) but from faith in Christ alone. This principle, which came to be known as justification by faith, comforted Luther greatly.

Because Luther didn't believe that good works (such as taking communion or becoming a priest) had any bearing on salvation, he considered the thriving church trade in indulgences simply a fraud on the laity. In his *Ninety-five Theses*, composed in October 1517, he objected to their sale, arguing that popes had no authority to free souls from purgatory. Although Luther's intention was merely to start a scholarly debate on the subject, his theses (originally written in Latin) were soon translated into German and distributed widely to an eager audience.

Luther's doctrine of justification by faith *held that salvation depends on faith alone and not on a combination of faith and good works, as the Catholic Church taught.*

IV. RACE AND SUFFRAGE

LIKE MOST AMERICAN SOCIAL MOVEMENTS of the pre–Civil War era, the campaign
for women's suffrage had its roots in the fight to abolish slavery. Stanton and Mott,
for example, first met and became friends as they sailed with their husbands to
London for the June 1840 World Anti-Slavery Convention. Stanton's husband,
Henry, was a member of the American delegation, as were Lucretia and James Mott.
However, when Lucretia Mott presented her credentials to the convention, they were
rejected simply because she was a woman.

Such second-class treatment was familiar to Mott, of course, because she had
witnessed it often in the company of black friends from the abolitionist movement.
Yet the experience caused her to reflect even more deeply on the analogy that married
women were to their husbands as slaves were to their masters. Such thinking was
common among the Seneca Falls delegates, most of whom were also abolitionists,
and it found its way into the Declaration of Sentiments in a section decrying the
injustice that a married woman must "promise obedience to her husband, he
becoming, to all intents and purposes, her master."

Sojourner Truth in 1851.

In the years after Seneca Falls, the movements for
women's rights and African American rights moved closer
together. In May 1851, at a women's rights convention
in Akron, Ohio, former slave Sojourner Truth delivered
her stirring "Ain't I a Woman?" speech. This brief but
profound homily deepened the ties between those fighting
race oppression and those focused on gender oppression
while at the same time compelling the members of Truth's
audience to consider the differences between women who
were enslaved and those who were not.

In 1866, Stanton, Douglass, and Susan B. Anthony
(1820–1906) founded the Equal Rights Association
(ERA) to unite formally the causes of sexual and racial
equality. Three years later, however, a dispute over the Fifteenth Amendment
(which guaranteed black men the right to vote) brought about a schism within
the organization. Transcripts of ERA meetings show that Stanton frequently argued
against passage of the Fifteenth Amendment because it didn't enfranchise women.
Along with Anthony, she complained that the ERA was neglecting women's issues
in order to win suffrage for yet another class of *men*. Finally, Stanton and Anthony
became so dissatisfied that they left and founded their own organization.

Parallel experiences *and a commonality of interest drew the movements for racial and
sexual equality together, but a dispute over the Fifteenth Amendment split them apart.*

IV. THE BIG THREE AT TEHRAN

STALIN WAS FORCED to accept disappointment yet again in January 1943, when Roosevelt and Churchill postponed once more the invasion of France. Meeting in Casablanca after two months of successful North African operations, the British and Americans reached this conclusion because it gave them more time to finish off the Germans in Tunisia. But British economic interests in the Mediterranean were also a factor, and they influenced the subsequent decision to invade Sicily. Already dubious of his allies' loyalty, Stalin became even more suspicious when he saw Churchill apparently pursuing imperial self-interest at the expense of countless Russian lives.

Stalin, Roosevelt, and Churchill in Tehran.

The first face-to-face meeting of the Big Three took place in November 1943 in Tehran. To FDR, the Tehran Conference represented an eagerly awaited opportunity to test his formidable personal charm against the gruff Soviet leader. "After all," longtime aide Harry Hopkins told Lord Moran, the prime minister's personal physician, the president "has spent his life managing men, and Stalin at bottom could not be so very different from other people."

Although Roosevelt had never met Stalin before, he was briefed by ambassador to Moscow W. Averell Harriman, who once described Stalin as "the most inscrutable and contradictory character I have ever known." According to Harriman, Stalin was "better informed than Roosevelt, more realistic than Churchill, [and] in some ways the most effective of the war leaders. At the same time he was, of course, a murderous tyrant."

The highly sensitive issues discussed at Tehran included the status of a defeated Germany and the postwar borders of Poland, but the focus of the four-day conference was the new cross-Channel invasion plan code-named Overlord. With just a little prodding from Stalin, Roosevelt committed the United States to a launch date of May 1, 1944, and Churchill had no choice but to agree.

Nevertheless, Roosevelt came away from Tehran frustrated. "I couldn't get any personal connection with Stalin," the president complained. "He was correct, stiff, solemn, not smiling, nothing human to get a hold of." The Soviet leader, however, was pleased. In discussing the future of Poland with Roosevelt during a remarkably frank private session, he had learned that the president already understood, as Stalin explained, that "whoever occupies a territory also imposes his own social system. Everyone imposes his own system as far as his army can reach."

At Tehran, *during the first face-to-face meeting of the Big Three, Roosevelt and Churchill promised Stalin that a cross-Channel invasion would finally take place in 1944.*

IV. SIMULTANEOUS-MOVE GAMES

YOU AND YOUR FRIEND are shopping for dinner. Your friend goes to the supermarket, where he will buy either meat or fish. You go to the bakery, where you will buy either a chocolate cake or a lemon tart.

In game theory, this is called a simultaneous-move game, because both players must make their choices without knowing what the other player has done. Even if the moves (i.e., the purchases) don't take place at exactly the same time, as in rock-paper-scissors, they are nevertheless simultaneous in the sense that neither player can alter his choice based on what the other player has done.

Simultaneous-move games are easily expressed in table format. In the table below, your friend's choices are shown in the rows, and your choices appear in the columns. The possible outcomes fill the table's cells.

	CHOCOLATE CAKE	LEMON TART
MEAT	Meat with chocolate cake	Meat with lemon tart
FISH	Fish with chocolate cake	Fish with lemon tart

In order to analyze this game, however, we need some more information—specifically, the utility functions for each player. Suppose, above all, you're trying to eat less red meat. Also, all other things being equal, you prefer chocolate cake to lemon tart. Therefore, your highest utility would be assigned to the combination of fish with chocolate cake. Your friend, meanwhile, likes nothing so much as lemon tart and—again, all other things being equal—prefers meat to fish. Therefore, his highest utility would be assigned to the combination of meat with lemon tart.

These preferences can be encoded as utilities in the game table as follows. In each cell, we write a pair of utilities, where the first is the utility assigned to that outcome by the row player (your friend) and the second is the utility assigned to that outcome by the column player (you). Remember that higher utility values represent more preferable outcomes.

	CHOCOLATE CAKE	LEMON TART
MEAT	2, 2	4, 1
FISH	1, 4	3, 3

Simultaneous-move games, *in which players make choices without knowledge of one another's actions, are conveniently organized into tables.*

IV. SURFACE TEMPERATURE

DIFFERENCES IN SURFACE TEMPERATURE are primarily dependent on latitude. At latitudes closer to the equator, near-perpendicular sun angles and longer day lengths result in higher surface temperatures. Latitudes being equal, however, there are five additional factors that control surface temperature: heat absorption rates, ocean currents, geographic position, altitude, and albedo.

Land heats and cools much more quickly than does water. Therefore, compared with an ocean location at the same latitude, a land location will have a larger daily and annual temperature range.

The effect of albedo, or reflectivity, in Antarctica.

Ocean currents affect surface temperature by moving warm water from the equator to the poles and cold water from the poles to the equator. Warm-water currents tend to have a greater warming effect in the winter than in the summer, whereas cold-water currents tend to have a greater cooling effect in the summer than in the winter.

Geographic position takes into account a location's position in relation to the prevailing winds. For example, because the prevailing winds in North America are westerlies (blowing from the west), San Francisco lies on the windward side of the continent. Therefore, its winds come off the ocean, meaning that they are cooler in the summer and warmer in the winter than winds at the same latitude on the lee side of the continent—which first have to travel across three thousand miles of landmass, being heated during the summer and cooled during the winter. Locations on the windward side of mountain ranges experience a similar effect, having smaller temperature ranges and greater precipitation than locations on the lee side of the range.

Altitude affects temperature because, as previously discussed, the temperature in the troposphere decreases by 6.5°C for each kilometer rise in altitude. Therefore, when comparing locations at the same latitude, the location at the higher altitude will have the lower average temperature.

Albedo, or reflectivity, also controls surface temperature by affecting the amounts of SW and LW radiation absorbed by the earth. Thick low clouds will prevent solar radiation from reaching the surface by reflecting it back into space. Snow and ice on the surface similarly prevent absorption by reflection. Thin high clouds, however, warm the surface because they let SW radiation pass through them while absorbing and reemitting the earth's LW radiation back down to the surface.

Latitude notwithstanding, *the five factors that control surface temperature are heat absorption rates, ocean currents, geographic position, altitude, and albedo.*

V. THE EDICT OF WORMS

BETWEEN 1517 AND 1521, as Luther debated the sale of indulgences and the centrality of faith with other Catholic theologians, he came increasingly to question the authority of the Catholic Church and ultimately rejected many of its basic doctrines. A key moment occurred in 1519, when Luther declared during a debate in Leipzig that popes were fallible and that only the Bible was a legitimate source of religious authority. No longer merely critics, Luther and his followers were becoming revolutionaries, and what had been an accumulation of complaints about the prevailing regime was now being transformed into a theological system capable of standing on its own.

When Pope Leo X learned what Luther was saying, he demanded that the German monk recant. Luther refused, and so the pope excommunicated him in January 1521. A few months later, Charles V held a diet in the city of Worms attended by representatives of the hundreds of small states and principalities that made up the Holy Roman Empire. (Diets were formal deliberative assemblies at which local delegates and representatives of the emperor discussed matters of mutual concern.) At the direction of Charles V, the Diet of Worms issued an edict condemning Luther and declaring him an outlaw.

After the emperor, the seven most important people in the Holy Roman Empire were the electors who chose the new emperor when the old one died. One of these, the elector Frederick III of Saxony, took an interest in Luther and, following the Edict of Worms, had the monk whisked away to a secret castle location (the Wartburg in Eisenach). Although Luther remained sequestered there for just ten months (May 1521–March 1522), the Saxon electors continued to protect him for the rest of his life.

Soon, however, Luther's politics took a distinctly conservative turn. In 1521, some of his university colleagues, wanting to eradicate immediately all nonscriptural practices, incited the people of Wittenberg to destroy the religious imagery in their churches. Later, in 1524–25, hundreds of thousands of peasants across the empire revolted against the nobility, calling for social equality and basing their demands on a similar reading of the New Testament. These developments shocked Luther, who concluded that the nobility (Protestant and Catholic alike) had a duty to crush the rebellion, impose social order, and manage religious observance.

The 1521 Edict of Worms, *which declared Luther an outlaw, completed his transformation from critic to revolutionary.*

V. THE NINETEENTH AMENDMENT

IN MAY 1869, a few days after the ERA adopted a resolution supporting the Fifteenth Amendment, Stanton and Anthony founded the National Woman Suffrage Association (NWSA) to focus exclusively on gaining the right to vote for women. Six months later, Lucy Stone (1818–93)—along with her husband, Henry Brown Blackwell, and Julia Ward Howe— founded the American Woman Suffrage Association (AWSA), a more conservative organization that drew its membership from the other side of the ERA split.

An NWP protester outside the White House in January 1917.

Central to both groups was an awareness that sexual inequality resulted from a patriarchal system that denied women the vote because it perceived them as emotional rather than rational. Ideologically, NWSA and AWSA responded to this logic in much the same way, arguing that granting women the vote was a sine qua non for any democracy. But otherwise their approaches to women's suffrage were quite different. Being more radical, Stanton and Anthony wouldn't allow men to join NWSA, while the more idealistic Stone included men to foster a partnership between the sexes. More practically, Stanton and Anthony worked toward a federal constitutional amendment, while Stone pursued a state-by-state strategy.

When it became obvious that two women's suffrage organizations was one too many, NWSA and AWSA began merger talks. Eventually, in May 1890, they combined to form the National American Woman Suffrage Association (NAWSA), the premier first-wave women's rights organization with two million members.

Anthony became NAWSA's first president and remained in office for ten years. She finally resigned in 1900 in favor of her handpicked successor, Carrie Chapman Catt, who led NAWSA from 1900 to 1904 and again from 1915 to 1920. Under Catt's influence, NAWSA pursued the state-by-state strategy that Stone had preferred. Alice Paul, however, had a different view. Like Stanton and Anthony before her, she sought a constitutional amendment that would enfranchise all women at once. Her primary target was Pres. Woodrow Wilson; and in January 1917, she unleashed on Wilson her hundred-thousand-member organization, the National Woman's Party (NWP), which picketed the White House on a daily basis.

Catt considered Paul's approach unwisely combative and, after the US entry into World War I, highly unpatriotic. Nevertheless, NWP militancy complemented NAWSA's numerical strength, and together the two organizations achieved victory, gaining ratification of the Nineteenth Amendment in August 1920.

In 1890, NWSA and AWSA merged to form the two-million-strong NAWSA, yet it took NWP militancy as well to force passage of the Nineteenth Amendment.

V. YALTA

THE BIG THREE MET for the second and final time in February 1945 at Yalta on the Black Sea. Four issues dominated the conference: the creation of an organization to succeed the disbanded League of Nations, the future of Eastern Europe (especially Poland), the status of Germany, and Soviet entry into the Pacific war. With regard to each of these matters, Stalin knew both his own mind and his strength. Roosevelt, however, was in nearly the opposite position. He was dying, and his physical condition made it difficult for him to resist Stalin's demands.

With respect to the new United Nations, Stalin wanted veto power for permanent members of the Security Council and separate General Assembly seats for Belorussia (White Russia) and Ukraine. With respect to Poland, he wanted recognition for the Communist government he had set up in Lublin over the government-in-exile that had been operating in London since September 1939. From a defeated Germany, he wanted ten billion dollars' worth of industrial equipment as war reparations. Finally, in exchange for a secret commitment to declare war on Japan within "two or three months" of Germany's surrender, he wanted leave to annex the Kurile Islands while taking back all of the territory lost to Japan during the Russo-Japanese War of 1904–5.

Churchill and Roosevelt at Yalta.

Roosevelt and Churchill conceded nearly all of these demands because, short of declaring war on the Soviets, there was little they could do. Even had Roosevelt been in fine health, Stalin held the best cards, and he knew it. The Red Army's four years of hard fighting had placed the Soviets in a commanding military position, and Stalin intended to transform this advantage into lasting political gains. His troops already occupied Romania, Bulgaria, Hungary, and Poland, and advance units of the Red Army were currently within sixty-five miles of Berlin. The British and Americans, by comparison, had yet to cross the Rhine.

To save face, American and British officials filled the texts of the various Yalta agreements with an abundance of empty words. When Adm. William D. Leahy saw the Declaration on Liberated Europe for the first time, he exclaimed, "Mr. President, this is so elastic that the Russians can stretch it all the way from Yalta to Washington without ever technically breaking it." "I know, Bill, I know it," the president replied. "But it's the best I can do for Poland at this time."

Although some historians have *attributed Roosevelt's concessions at Yalta to his failing health, there was little he or Churchill could have done because Stalin's position was commanding.*

V. DOMINANT STRATEGIES

So HOW SHOULD YOU and your friend play the dinner game described in the previous lecture? One can often gain insight into the strategic structure of simultaneous-move games by thinking about what you would do if you knew the other player's move.

	CHOCOLATE CAKE	LEMON TART
MEAT	2, 2	4, 1
FISH	1, 4	3, 3

Suppose you know that your friend has purchased steak. What dessert would you then buy? Remember that rational players always seek outcomes with the highest possible utility. Therefore, as shown in the game table above, you would choose chocolate cake (to which you have assigned a utility of 2) over lemon tart (to which you have assigned a utility of 1). In game theory, this is called a best response. That is, your best response to your friend's choice of meat is to buy chocolate cake.

Now suppose your friend buys fish. What is your best response then? Again, your best response is to buy chocolate cake (because 4 > 3). Notice that your best response in both cases is to buy chocolate cake. In game theory, this is called a dominant strategy. By definition, a dominant strategy is always a best response, no matter what the other player does. In other words, whatever your friend does in this game, you should always buy chocolate cake.

Next, let's analyze your friend's decision. Suppose that he knows you have purchased chocolate cake. What entrée should he then choose? Because the utility he has assigned to meat (2) is greater than the utility he has assigned to fish (1), his best response to your choice of chocolate cake is to choose meat. If he knows that you have chosen lemon tart, his best response is still meat (because 4 > 3). Therefore, he also has a dominant strategy: meat.

Because both players have dominant strategies, the predicted outcome of this game is that you and your friend will be having meat with chocolate cake for dinner. This outcome, of course, depends on the assumptions that the utility values in the game table are accurate and that both players are rational.

A dominant strategy *is a choice that is always a best response for you, no matter what the other player does.*

V. HUMIDITY

WATER OCCURS NATURALLY on the earth in all three states of matter: as a solid, as a liquid, and as a gas. Changing from one state to another involves either the release or absorption of a form of energy called latent heat. When water vapor condenses to form droplets or droplets solidify to form ice crystals, latent heat is released, warming the air and causing it to rise. Rising air is important in meteorology, because it can fuel the large vertical clouds that become major storms.

Meteorologists quantify the amount of water vapor in a parcel of air using two measures: dew point and relative humidity. Warm air can hold more water vapor than cold air because, as temperature increases, the air molecules spread out, creating more space for water molecules. Likewise, as air cools, the space between air molecules shrinks, and excess water molecules are squeezed out through condensation. The dew point is the temperature at which this condensation begins, and it varies according to the amount of water vapor initially in the air. Relative humidity, expressed as a percentage, is the ratio of water vapor in the air to the amount the air can hold at saturation.

Importantly, humidity affects the density of air. Dry air contains mostly nitrogen molecules (N_2), with an atomic weight of 28. Water molecules (H_2O) have an atomic weight of 18. Thus, as humidity increases, water molecules displace nitrogen molecules, and the air becomes less dense. Temperature also affects the density of air. The spreading out of air molecules that results from an increase in temperature makes the air less dense as well. So, when a parcel of air close to the surface is warmed or moistened, it becomes less dense than the colder or drier air aloft, and it rises, creating instability. (In contrast, a stable air parcel is one that has warmer or moister air above it. Therefore, it's denser than the air above it and lacks the buoyancy to rise.)

As unstable air rises, it cools—because, in the troposphere, temperature decreases with altitude. Eventually, the dew point is reached, and—as long as sufficient moisture is present—clouds form. This phenomenon is known as convective lifting.

The amount of water vapor in a parcel of air affects its density. Moistening (or warming) an air parcel relative to the air aloft decreases its density and causes it to rise, creating instability.

VI. THE ANABAPTISTS

BELIEF IN THE BIBLE as the sole religious authority for Christians was a founding principle of the Protestant Reformation. Not even the ex cathedra utterances of the pope could rival the primacy of the biblical text. On this point, all Protestants agreed. Yet, with regard to what the text actually meant, there was much disagreement.

A cluster of Protestant groups emerged, known collectively as the Anabaptists. These groups tended to interpret the Bible more literally than other Protestants. (The name *Anabaptist* refers to the their practice of rebaptizing adults, the prefix *ana-* meaning "again.") Anabaptists believed that sacraments such as baptism required as a prerequisite a mature profession of faith. Because only adults could make such a profession, infant baptisms were considered meaningless, and adult converts to Anabaptism had to be baptized again.

The first Anabaptist groups emerged in Switzerland and Germany during the 1520s. They agreed with Luther on many points but felt that he hadn't gone far enough in rejecting the church and following the dictates of scripture. Numerous differences existed within the Anabaptist movement, but nearly all denominations embraced pacifism, the principle that local churches should be autonomous, and the separation of church and state. In general, the Anabaptists wanted to break free not only of church tradition but also of social convention. As a result, and because their ideas represented a starkly divergent approach to Christian practice, they formed the core of what historians have called the Radical Reformation.

Not surprisingly, other Christians regarded the Anabaptists with alarm and contempt. Although most Anabaptists simply wanted to be left alone, Catholic and Protestant authorities considered them too dangerous to be tolerated. The wisdom of this opinion was apparently confirmed in 1533, when millenarian Anabaptists came to power in Münster. Proclaiming the imminent return of Christ, they abolished private property, instituted polygamy, and declared Münster the New Jerusalem. A year later, provincial armies conquered the city and massacred many Anabaptists. Some were burned at the stake; others, in a measure of cruel irony, were drowned.

During the 1540s, Anabaptism made a comeback in the Netherlands and Germany under Dutch priest Menno Simons (1496–1561). Doubting the teachings of the church on the Eucharist and infant baptism, Menno went into hiding in January 1536, seeking a new spiritual direction. He emerged a year later, was rebaptized, and became the leader of a group of peaceful Anabaptists who gradually evolved into the Mennonites.

The Anabaptists were radicals *who wanted to break free not only of church tradition but also of social convention. As a result, they were severely persecuted.*

VI. THE SECOND WAVE

WITH THE RATIFICATION of the Nineteenth Amendment, the first wave of women's activism crested, and the movement entered a period of dormancy. NAWSA ceased to exist; and although Catt founded the new League of Women Voters, political actvity dropped off significantly following the achievement of a long-sought goal.

Most scholars attribute the beginnings of the second wave to the rise of the civil rights movement—which enlisted many young women, white and black, in the cause of racial equality. Working to achieve equal rights for African Americans sensitized these women to discrimination of all kinds, and they gradually came to see that the white-male-dominated patriarchy that subjugated blacks also subjugated women.

Betty Friedan in 1960.

A key step in this reawakening was the publication in 1963 of Betty Friedan's *The Feminine Mystique*, one of the defining texts of the second wave. In her landmark, best-selling study of women's social roles, Friedan challenged the prevailing expectation that all American women should find satisfaction and fulfillment in housewifery. Revealing and reconsidering this and other sexual stereotypes, *The Feminine Mystique* encouraged women to think more critically about their roles in society and planted the idea that they could lead happy, successful lives without being dependent on husbands or consumed with child rearing.

When Martin Luther King, Jr., and other leaders of the civil rights movement began pushing in mid-1963 for new legislation to end the most public forms of racial discrimination, a few feminists lobbied Congress for an amendment that would outlaw discrimination on the basis of gender as well. (Although the first known use of the word *feminist* occurred in 1895, the term didn't come into widespread use until after the publication of Friedan's book.)

Ironically, such an amendment was finally offered on the floor of the House by Howard Smith of Virginia, an ardent segregationist who had tried but failed to keep the civil rights bill bottled up in the Rules Committee, which he chaired. Smith proposed adding sex to Title VII—which banned discrimination by employers on the basis of race, religion, or national origin—hoping that the issue would splinter the coalition supporting the bill, and indeed some liberals initially opposed Smith's amendment because they feared he was right. In the end, however, the amendment passed, Smith's parliamentary gambit failed, and the Civil Rights Act of 1964 made sex discrimination illegal.

Feminist activism reemerged *during the civil rights era, when women began to see that the white-male patriarchy that oppressed blacks subjugated women as well.*

VI. THE DIVISION OF GERMANY

ONCE AMERICAN AND BRITISH FORCES crossed the Rhine in March 1945, Dwight D. Eisenhower, the supreme Allied commander, pursued three main goals: capturing the Ruhr Valley, Germany's industrial heartland; preventing a Nazi withdrawal to the Bavarian Alps; and avoiding an unintentional clash with Soviet troops heading west. To this latter end, Eisenhower sent a cable to Stalin on March 28 informing him of the western Allies' plans and requesting similar information concerning Red Army intentions. The cable angered Churchill because its political subtext was clear: Eisenhower was ceding Berlin to the Soviets. But the British had scant leverage, and Eisenhower had other concerns, including the Ruhr and his moral duty to end the war as soon and with as few casualties as possible.

Shortly before dawn on April 16, the Soviets began their main assault on the German capital. "For the last time, the deadly Jewish-Bolshevik enemy has started a mass attack," Hitler declared. "He is trying to reduce Germany to rubble and to exterminate our people." The final phase of the battle, which began on April 26, featured savage street fighting, with SS units roaming the city and summarily executing any soldiers found to have abandoned their posts. On April 30, Hitler killed himself in his bunker beneath the Chancellery.

On May 2, the day that Berlin surrendered, Adm. Karl Dönitz, Hitler's successor as German head of state, offered to conclude a separate peace with the western Allies so that the German army could continue fighting the Soviets, presumably with Anglo-American support. Now that Hitler was dead, Dönitz reasoned, an anticommunist alliance made obvious sense. But the new US president, Harry Truman, refused Dönitz's offer, insisting that the Germans surrender simultaneously on all fronts.

The surrender finally came on May 7, after which Germany was divided into four occupation zones along boundaries previously determined by a joint commission. The initial plan discussed at Tehran had been for three zones, but at Yalta the Soviets had agreed to a French zone carved out of the British and American sectors. During the closing weeks of the war, some American units had pushed a few hundred miles beyond these agreed-upon boundaries, but in July the Americans pulled back at the same time the Soviets allowed the western Allies into Berlin. (Although Hitler's capital lay entirely within the Soviet zone, because of its importance it was also jointly occupied.)

Following the surrender of Germany in May 1945, *the country was divided into four occupation zones controlled by the US, Britain, France, and the Soviet Union, respectively.*

German generals sign the surrender documents on May 7.

VI. THE PRISONER'S DILEMMA

WITH REGARD TO OUR DINNER GAME, game theory clearly predicts that you and your friend will be eating meat with chocolate cake (an outcome with a utility of 2 for both players). However, there is a perverse aspect to this outcome, because both your and your friend would prefer to eat fish with lemon tart (an outcome with a utility of 3 for both players). A game of this type, in which both players follow dominant strategies to yield a less-than-optimum result, is called a prisoner's dilemma.

The classic story goes like this: Two prisoners are suspected of robbing a bank. The district attorney is sure that he can convict both on lesser weapons charges but isn't sure he can win robbery convictions. So he separates the prisoners and offers them each the same deal. In exchange for their testimony, the district attorney will have their sentences reduced—by half, if the other prisoner also takes the deal; or to time served, if the other prisoner remains silent.

Suppose that a robbery conviction carries a 36-month sentence, while a weapons conviction carries only a 6-month sentence. We can now create a utility function for each player, in which the utilities represent the number of months of freedom each will have over the next 36 months. For instance, a 6-month sentence would mean 30 months of freedom. (We can't simply use the number of months in the sentence, because by convention higher utilities denote more preferable outcomes.) The game can thus be summarized in the table below.

	CONFESSES	REMAINS SILENT
CONFESSES	18, 18	36, 0
REMAINS SILENT	0, 36	30, 30

As you can see, the dominant strategy for both players is to confess. If both indeed confess, then each will enjoy 18 months of freedom. However, if both players remain silent, then each will enjoy 30 months of freedom—a preferable outcome.

Variations on the prisoner's dilemma arise in many different real-world contexts. Consider, for example, the fishing industry. Individual fishermen want to catch as many fish as possible because the more fish they catch, the more money they make. Yet overfishing can decimate fish populations. Thus, if fishermen follow their dominant strategy (to catch as many fish as possible), they risk putting themselves out of business.

A prisoner's dilemma *is a simultaneous-move game in which both players follow dominant strategies but the predicted outcome is not the outcome that both would prefer.*

VI. CLOUDS AND PRECIPITATION

CLOUDS ARE FORMED not only by convective lifting but also by orographic lifting, frontal wedging, and convergence. Orographic lifting takes place near mountains or highlands. As winds blow air toward a mountain, the air is forced up the mountainside. As it rises, it cools to dew point, and clouds may form. Frontal wedging occurs when a mass of cold air encounters a mass of warm air. Rather than mixing, the denser cold air acts as a wedge, forcing up the lighter warm air and leading to the same cooling process.

Cumulus clouds over Colorado.

Convergence refers to the lifting that occurs when air flows into a region from multiple directions. For example, the daytime heating of the Florida peninsula causes the air over it to rise, generating sea breezes from both the Gulf of Mexico and the Atlantic Ocean to fill the void. These breezes collide over the peninsula, greatly increasing the air pressure and generating a fast-rising wind. Again, the air cools and forms clouds—which is why Florida experiences many late-afternoon rainstorms.

Clouds are classified according to form and height. Cirrus clouds are thin, white, and composed primarily of ice crystals. They often appear feathery or wispy. Cumulus clouds are puffy and white and look like flat-bottomed cotton balls. Stratus clouds are gray and layered—usually covering the sky like a sheet, with few visible breaks. Prefixes are added to these form to indicate cloud height. Clouds at altitudes below two kilometers use no prefix, clouds at altitudes between two and six kilometers use the prefix *alto-*, and clouds at altitudes above six kilometers use the prefix *cirro-*.

Once clouds form, precipitation becomes possible. The two primary processes by which cloud droplets become large enough to fall out of the sky are collision coalescence and the Bergeron process. In collision coalescence, wind and gravity move the droplets around in a cloud, causing them to collide with one another. Sometimes, they stick together, increasing droplet size until finally they become too large to be supported by the wind. In the Bergeron process, the droplets evaporate and then deposit on nearby ice crystals, making the ice crystals grow until they fall as precipitation. Depending on several factors, especially the temperature of the air through which the precipitation falls, it may reach the ground as snow or rain or in some other form.

As air cools to its dew point, *clouds may form. The water droplets in these clouds increase in size, either by the Bergeron process or collision coalescence, until they become too large to be held aloft by wind.*

VII. THE PEACE OF AUGSBURG

AT FIRST, Luther was primarily concerned with the gap that existed between Christian principles and Catholic practice. After the Edict of Worms was issued in 1521, however, his theology, which had been largely unformed, began to evolve in distinct directions. His thinking was premised on two basic convictions: that the Bible was the sole source of religious authority and that Christians were saved by faith alone. Thus, while the corruption issue spawned Luther's protest, it was the later conflict over doctrine that led to the permanent Catholic–Protestant split.

One area of dispute was priestly celibacy, which Luther opposed because he believed it had no scriptural basis. In one of Paul's letters to Timothy, the saint wrote that the bishop should "be the husband of one wife." (Taking Paul's advice, Luther

Katherine von Bora

married former nun Katherine von Bora in 1525.) Another hallmark of early Lutheran theology was the doctrine of predestination, which held that God foreordains who will be saved.

During the 1530s and 1540s, a number of influential Catholics and Protestants sought to reconcile reform views with Catholic teachings. Among these were Cardinal Lorenzo Campeggio; the ecumenically minded Erasmus; and Philip Melanchthon, another Christian humanist who was close to Luther. On two occasions, their efforts came remarkably close to fruition: The first came in 1530, when the Diet of Augsburg considered, but ultimately rejected, a document written mostly by Melanchton that stressed points of mutual agreement. A similar document served as the basis for the 1541 Regensburg Colloquy, but the compromises tentatively reached proved acceptable to neither side.

These negotiations over religious doctrine took place, of course, within the context of political conflict between the German princes and the Holy Roman emperor. In 1531, a group of Lutheran princes formed a military alliance known as the Schmalkaldic League. Although moderates on both sides kept hard-liners at bay during the 1530s and early 1540s, the hard-liners' advocacy of a military solution to the problem of religious division eventually brought on the Schmalkaldic Wars of 1546–47 and 1552–53. With neither side able to dominate the other, a peace was finally arranged at Augsburg in 1555. The treaty was despised by both sides yet ultimately beneficial. According to its terms, each German prince would henceforth be free to decide whether his realm would be Catholic or Lutheran.

The Peace of Augsburg, *which ended the Schmalkaldic Wars, made permanent the religious split between Protestants and Catholics.*

VII. LIBERAL AND RADICAL FEMINISM

TO ENSURE THAT THE MOMENTUM created by passage of the Civil Rights Act wouldn't be lost, Friedan and twenty-seven other men and women came together in June 1966 to form the National Organization for Women (NOW). Serving as NOW's president from its founding until 1970, Friedan helped revive organized feminism around such issues as an end to sexism in employment, abortion rights, and stronger penalties for rape.

A 1970 women's liberation march in Washington, DC.

As NAWSA dominated the first wave of women's activism, so did NOW dominate the second. Like NAWSA, NOW worked within the political system to achieve its goals. Some feminists, however, believed that NOW's emphasis on legislative change was too narrow because it sought to emend, rather than eliminate, the patriarchy that lay at the root of women's oppression. Soon, two poles of feminist thought emerged: liberal feminism and radical feminism.

Unlike liberal feminists, most of whom belonged to NOW, radical feminists were a much more heterogeneous group—skeptical of traditional activism and willing, as Alice Paul had been, to take their grievances into the streets. While NOW's brand of feminism emphasized personal fulfillment on an individual basis, radical feminists formed cadres to combat "male chauvinism" and topple the "male power structure." According to the radicals, women could never be free within the current system. Liberation would come only through revolution.

A defining issue was the sexual partners a woman chose. Despite liberal feminism's emphasis on independence of thought as a key element of feminist consciousness, Friedan was careful to disassociate NOW from lesbianism. Thus, many lesbians who otherwise supported NOW's goals came to feel alienated by the organization's implicit homophobia and started women's groups of their own.

Many radical feminists, on the other hand, embraced lesbianism as part of a more general rethinking of sexuality and human relationships. They believed that people were sexually fluid and that being a lesbian was a political choice, not a biological predisposition. They also thought that women who relied on men for sexual pleasure would never be free of the patriarchy that oppressed them. Therefore, many radical feminists practiced lesbianism for ideological reasons, even though their desire wasn't necessarily limited to other women. They didn't hate men; rather, they believed that, because of patriarchal oppression, women could never be free within the context of a traditional heterosexual relationship.

Liberal feminists, *represented by NOW, chose to work within the political system. Radical feminists, on the other hand, believed that the answer wasn't change but revolution.*

VII. THE MANHATTAN PROJECT

WHEN PRESIDENT ROOSEVELT DIED on April 12, 1945, Vice President Truman received a terrible shock—not so much that FDR was dead, as the president's health had deteriorated badly. Rather, Truman was shocked to learn what FDR had been up to in New Mexico.

Henry L. Stimson arrives at the White House for a 1945 meeting.

As vice president, the former Missouri senator had been considered too low-level to be briefed on the Manhattan Project, the code name given the US effort to develop an atomic bomb. In fact, Truman wasn't fully briefed until April 25, when Secretary of War Henry L. Stimson told him that "within four months we shall in all probability have completed the most terrible weapon ever known in human history." Disturbed by this prospect, Stimson predicted that the world "in its present state of moral advancement compared with its technical development" would come to be at the mercy of such a weapon. "In other words," he said, "modern civilization might be completely destroyed."

The idea of the Manhattan Project originated in an August 1939 letter that Hungarian émigré Leo Szilard persuaded his friend Albert Einstein to write, informing President Roosevelt of some troubling developments in nuclear physics. Szilard, the first physicist to conceive of a nuclear chain reaction, had been monitoring recent German research on neutron bombardment, including experiments by Otto Hahn and Fritz Strassman in December 1938 that confirmed Szilard's hypothesis. In early 1939, a secret German War Office report stated that "the newest developments in nuclear physics...will probably make it possible to produce an explosive many orders of magnitude more powerful than the conventional ones...That country which first makes use of it has an unsurpassable advantage over the others."

The subsequent US atomic effort was supervised by Maj. Gen. Leslie R. Groves of the Army Corps of Engineers, with physicist J. Robert Oppenheimer directing the scientific work. The first major step was taken in December 1942, when Italian émigré Enrico Fermi, working in a laboratory beneath the University of Chicago football stadium, created the first controlled nuclear chain reaction. Meanwhile, in Oak Ridge, Tennessee, and Hanford, Washington, other scientists worked on refining uranium and plutonium into nuclear fuels. But the most famous Manhattan Project site was Los Alamos, New Mexico, where the design and testing of the bombs took place on the grounds of a private school for boys that Oppenheimer had visited during the 1920s.

The existence of the Manhattan Project *was such a closely held secret that even Vice President Truman wasn't informed until after Roosevelt's death.*

VII. PLAYING AGAINST RATIONAL PLAYERS

CONSIDER THE PROBLEM faced by a hypothetical movie studio, Upstart Productions, trying to break into the lucrative family-film market. It knows that the biggest player in the market, Behemoth Films, will be releasing a new animated feature next summer. There are two possible release dates: Memorial Day and July 4. In general, Upstart knows that its film will gross less if its release date coincides with that of the Behemoth feature; however, there are other factors to take into account as well, such as moving up the production schedule to meet an earlier release date. The following table outlines the payoffs to the two studios in millions of dollars. Behemoth is the row player, and Upstart is the column player.

	MEMORIAL DAY	JULY 4
MEMORIAL DAY	60, 10	100, 20
JULY 4	80, 40	110, 30

Suppose Upstart expects a Memorial Day release from Behemoth. Then, Upstart's best response would be to release on July 4 (because 20 > 10). Now suppose that Upstarts expects a release date of July 4 from Behemoth. In that case, its best response would be to release on Memorial Day (because 40 > 30). Therefore, Upstart's best response depends on what it expects Behemoth to do. In other words, it has no dominant strategy.

So when should Upstart release its film? If you're an Upstart executive and you understand game theory, then you'll assume that your counterpart at Behemoth is rational, and you'll put yourself in his position. According to the game table, Behemoth has a dominant strategy. No matter what Upstart does, Behemoth makes more money with a July 4 release (because 100 > 60 and 110 > 80). Therefore, Upstart should expect Behemoth to release on July 4, and it should release on Memorial Day.

This game illustrates the crucial role that the assumption of rationality plays in game theory analysis. If other players are rational, then one can often determine their moves by evaluating the game from their point of view. This idea is central to sound strategic thinking.

The assumption of rationality, *which lies at the heart of game theory, allows players without dominant strategies to analyze the situations of other players and often predict their moves.*

VII. WIND

AIR PRESSURE IS A MEASURE of the weight of the air directly above a specific location. At sea level, air pressure averages 14.7 pounds per square inch (or 1013.25 millibars when measured with a barometer). As altitude increases, air pressure decreases, because there is less air above higher locations and the density of that air is less as well.

Pressure differentials are created by unequal heating of the earth's surface and also by changes in humidity. Given constant humidity, cold air is always denser than warm air and thus generates higher pressure. Similarly, given constant temperature, dry air is always denser than moist air, and so generates higher pressure as well.

A pressure difference between two locations creates a pressure gradient force (PGF), which produces wind. The direction of the PGF is always straight from the high-pressure center to the low-pressure center. On weather maps, isobars indicate lines of equal pressure. Typically, these are drawn at regular intervals, such as 10 millibars. The closer together these lines are, the greater the PGF, and the faster the resulting wind.

Curiously, once air has been set in motion by a PGF, it appears to deflect from its straight-line path. This is a result of the Coriolis force (CF), which is generated by the earth's rotation. The wind actually does move in a straight line when viewed from a stationary point in space; but to an observer on the rotating earth, it appears to be deflected because the earthbound observer is rotating, too. Imagine throwing a football to a person on a merry-go-round. From your point of view, the path of the ball will appear to be straight; but from the point of view of the merry-go-round rider, the pass will seem to curve away.

In the upper atmosphere, the CF often acts in opposition to the PGF, resulting in winds that blow along isobars—that is, perpendicular to both forces. At the surface, however, the friction generated by the flow of air over irregular ground slows down the wind and reduces the CF, which is proportional to wind speed. This reduction in CF shifts the wind in the direction of the PGF, causing it to cross isobars at an angle of 30° to 45°, depending on the amount of friction. In the Northern Hemisphere, the result is that wind bends to the right. In the Southern Hemisphere, it bends to the left.

Differences in air pressure create pressure gradient forces that generate wind. The Coriolis force, mitigated by friction, acts against the PGF to deflect wind from its straight-line path.

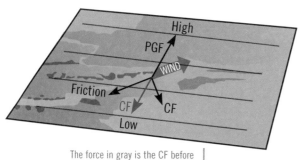

The force in gray is the CF before friction is taken into account.

VIII. JOHN CALVIN AND REFORMED PROTESTANTISM

REFORMED PROTESTANTISM ORIGINATED with a pair of Zurich pastors, Ulrich Zwingli (1484–1531) and Heinrich Bullinger (1504–75), who shared Luther's zeal for reform but not all of his theological ideas. They rejected, for example, Luther's view of the Eucharist. Whereas Luther believed that Jesus Christ was spiritually present in the sacrament, Zwingli and Bullinger regarded the taking of communion as a purely symbolic act. (Catholics, for their part, believed in transubstantiation, or the view that Christ is physically present in the Eucharist.) Primarily because of this disagreement, the followers of Zwingli and Bullinger declined to join forces with the Lutherans and instead formed their own movement.

Zwingli, in particular, developed a large following in the cities of southern Germany, but his evangelical career ended abruptly in 1531, when he died while serving as a chaplain in a Swiss army. Bullinger succeeded him, but their partisans soon became absorbed into the following of the French humanist John Calvin (1509–64), who settled in Geneva in 1534. A legal scholar, Calvin had been forced to flee France after converting to Reformed Protestantism. In Geneva, he helped organize a new Reformed community; and in 1536, he published *The Institutes of the Christian Religion*, a comprehensive manual of Reformed Protestant theology that became enormously influential.

John Calvin in a portrait from his lifetime.

Calvin accepted Luther's positions on the primacy of scripture and justification by faith, but he also stressed the inscrutability of God and the total depravity of humankind. By the former, he meant that God and His purposes were so utterly beyond human understanding that people shouldn't judge or complain about them. By the latter, he meant that humans were incapable of doing good in and of themselves—that is, without divine assistance. As a result, in Calvin's view, salvation depended entirely on divine grace, and God's attention was only on the elect (those predestined for salvation).

Catholics didn't believe in predestination, and for Luther it was much less central, but Calvin placed the doctrine at the heart of Reformed Protestantism. He believed that Christ died on the cross to save the elect, and the discipline he imposed on his followers was intended to manifest the godly character of the elect.

Because of his emphasis on discipline, Calvin had a rough relationship with the Geneva city government, and he was banished in 1538. He returned in 1541, however, after which Geneva became a refuge for religious exiles from England, France, and the Low Countries.

At the center of Reformed Protestantism *(also known as Calvinism) lay the doctrine of predestination and the idea that God concerned himself only with the elect.*

VIII. SOCIALIST FEMINISM

DURING THE SECOND WAVE, some feminists moved beyond a singular focus on patriarchy and came to believe that capitalism was equally responsible for women's oppression. These socialist feminists were a mixture of feminists who moved closer to socialism and socialists who moved closer to feminism. Yet as the group developed, its members became increasingly dissatisfied with male socialist colleagues who refused to acknowledge the parallels between capitalism's treatment of the working class and patriarchy's treatment of women. Thus, the socialist feminists became more closely associated with feminism than with socialism.

Whether socialist feminism of the second wave belonged to the liberal camp or to the radical camp is difficult to say—which is why most scholars treat it as a separate category. All socialist feminists agreed that patriarchy and capitalism were inseparable, yet different people had different ideas about what should follow from this principle. Some socialist feminists thought that working within the system was sufficient; others believed that nothing short of a proletarian revolution would do.

Most importantly, socialist feminism introduced a new way of understanding women's oppression, encouraging feminist thinkers of all inclinations to explore the ways in which economic conditions facilitate the exploitation of women. Before socialist feminism, a typical feminist's argument in favor of abortion rights would have been limited to the assertion of a woman's right to choose what happens to her body. With the advent of socialist feminism, however, that same argument could by supported with an analysis of the ways in which a pregnant women's choices are contingent on her economic reality. Why, for example, should wealthy women have access to safe abortions and not poor women as well? In general, socialist feminist critiques improved feminist arguments by adding a new perspective that provided greater sophistication and depth.

The activist phase of socialist feminism reached its peak during the second wave—notably with the work of the Freedom Socialist party, founded in 1966 by Gloria Martin and Clara Fraser. Its theoretical influence, however, continues to be felt. Many leading contemporary feminists—including Angela Davis, the former Black Panther and current academic, and novelist Dorothy Allison—consider themselves socialist feminists because their work explores the relationship between class oppression and gender-based injustice. Employing similar methods to analyze the roles that women play in the international economy is Cynthia Enloe, an important figure in the field of women's studies.

Socialist feminism, *which emerged during the second wave, introduced a new mode of analysis that allowed feminists to examine the ways in which class and gender interact in women's lives.*

VIII. KNOWLEDGE OF THE BOMB

AS PART OF HIS APRIL 25 BOMB BRIEFING, Truman learned that the British knew all about the Manhattan Project, but the Soviets hadn't yet been informed. During the summer of 1944, physicist Niels Bohr had urged Churchill and Roosevelt in separate meetings to tell Stalin what was going on, because Soviet cooperation would be essential to the development of postwar atomic controls. Had Roosevelt and Churchill heeded Bohr's advice, the nuclear arms race might have been ameliorated. Instead, they chose to keep Stalin in the dark, thereby undermining their many other efforts to win the Soviet leader's trust.

Although Truman adopted Roosevelt's policy, the question of whether or not to inform the Soviets continued to be discussed by the Interim Committee, established in May 1945 to advise the president on atomic policy. The members of this top-secret group, which included scientists as well as government officials, talked often about the "demonstration" that dropping a bomb would make. In this regard, they considered the Soviets nearly as important an audience as the Japanese.

The Japanese cities targeted for atomic attack, Hiroshima and Nagasaki, were intentionally spared other bombing so that the immense destructive power of the new weapons could be demonstrated against pristine urban landscapes. Also, top US officials—most notably James F. Byrnes, whom Truman appointed secretary of state on July 3—influenced the language of the surrender terms offered Japan so that—perhaps intentionally, perhaps not—the Japanese felt obliged to continue fighting, thus justifying the use of the bombs.

Even a cursory examination of Interim Committee minutes shows that the group had much wider goals than merely the defeat of Japan. As one member, Nobel laureate Arthur Compton, observed, "If the bomb were not used in the present war, the world would have no adequate warning as to what was to be expected if war should break out again." Thus, the higher cause of world peace required an initial cautionary slaughter.

J. Robert Oppenheimer in 1944.

During one committee meeting, Oppenheimer suggested that "if we were to offer to exchange information [with the Soviets] before the bomb was actually used, our moral position would be greatly strengthened." But this idea was quickly dismissed. Byrnes and others wanted to operate from a position of demonstrated strength, and they responded that flaunting the bomb would be the best way to ensure its usefulness as an incentive to postwar cooperation.

Despite other efforts to gain Stalin's trust, *FDR and Churchill decided to withhold knowledge of the Manhattan Project from the Soviets, and Truman continued this policy.*

VIII. THE NASH EQUILIBRIUM

ON THE LONG-RUNNING TV GAME SHOW *The Newlywed Game*, recently married couples were separated and asked questions designed to test their knowledge of each other. When the bride's answers matched those of the groom, the couple scored 10 points. The following game table captures the payoffs for the question *Is the groom's favorite color red or blue?*, with the bride as the row player and the groom as the column player.

	RED	BLUE
RED	10, 10	0, 0
BLUE	0, 0	10, 10

Each player's strategy depends on what he or she expects the other player to do, so neither player has a dominant strategy. Therefore, the methods of analysis we've used so far don't help us with this game. We need to expand our toolkit.

Suppose both bride and groom expect the other to say "red." Then each will say "red" in an attempt to match the other and thus win points for the couple. If both indeed say "red," then both will be happy, and neither will regret the choice of saying "red" because it turned out to be a best response for both. Such a situation, in which each player plays a best response, is called an equilibrium (or Nash equilibrium). In 1950, John Nash proved mathematically that an equilibrium always exists whenever the number of choices each player has is finite.

An equilibrium, however, needn't be unique. In the game table above, for example, you can see that a second equilibrium occurs when both bride and groom say "blue." In this case as well, the choice is a best response for both, and neither player has any regrets.

Think back to the other games we've analyzed. We can now see that, in the dinner game, the meat-with-chocolate-cake outcome represents an equilibrium. Given that your friend chose to serve meat, you don't regret your choice of chocolate cake; and given your choice of chocolate cake, your friend is content with his choice of meat. Similarly, in the movie game, the combination of Behemoth's July 4 release and Upstart's Memorial Day release is another equilibrium.

A Nash equilibrium *describes a situation in which players make choices that turn out to be best responses for each.*

VIII. WIND PATTERNS

LOCAL WINDS—including sea, valley, and mountain breezes—typically result from unequal heating of the earth's surface. For example, colder, denser air often "falls" down from mountains, while warmer, lighter air rises up from valleys. Global winds, on the other hand, are initiated by the large temperature differences that exist between the equator and the poles.

If the earth didn't rotate, the planet would function as two enormous convection cells—one per hemisphere. Warm air would rise at the equator, cooling as it rose. It would then travel north or south in the upper atmosphere, moving as on a conveyor belt and finally sinking at the poles. However, because the earth does rotate, the Coriolis force deflects the moving air, forming three convection cells per hemisphere.

The first cell operates between latitudes 0° and 30°. The rising air at the equator creates a band of low pressure that initiates winds blowing from latitude 30°. These winds don't blow straight, however, because of the Coriolis effect. In the Northern Hemisphere, the CF deflects them to the right so that they become northeasterlies (that is, winds blowing from the northeast). In the Southern Hemisphere, they become southeasterlies. In both cases, they are known as trade winds.

Air that has risen at the equator, cooled, and moved north or south through the upper atmosphere sinks at latitude 30°—producing a band of high pressure, suppressing cloud formation, and creating most of the earth's deserts. When this sinking air reaches the ground, it diverges, some heading back to the equator (forming the trade winds) and some blowing toward latitude 60°.

In the Northern Hemisphere, the portion of sinking air that blows away from the equator produces the prevailing westerlies that cover most of the United States. At latitude 60°N, the warm southwesterly winds that form part of these westerlies run into the cold, dense polar front and are forced to rise quickly, often producing heavy precipitation. Finally, at the North Pole, air sinking down from the upper atmosphere heads south, forming the polar easterlies.

Although the winds in the upper atmosphere generally blow from the equator toward the poles, some are bent by the CF to form undulating ribbons of high-speed westerlies called jet streams. The subtropical jet stream is located near latitude 30°, and the polar jet stream is located near latitude 60°.

Local winds result from unequal surface heating, *while global winds are generated by the large temperature differences that exist between the equator and the poles.*

IX. THE ENGLISH REFORMATION

Henry VIII of England

THE PROTESTANT REFORMATION took a unique course in England, where kings had exercised some authority over religious officials since the High Middle Ages. Initially, the Tudors, who ruled England from 1485 until 1603, were no different. Yet, because of unusual political and religious circumstances, the English Crown soon came to exercise complete jurisdiction over the English church.

Luther's views first began to gain currency in England among the erudite clerics who taught at Cambridge. One of their number, William Tyndale, translated the New Testament into English in 1525. At first, King Henry VIII (reigned 1509–47) condemned Protestantism and ordered its partisans prosecuted. However, the king's religious conservatism quickly gave way to political expediency when he discovered that his first wife, Catherine of Aragon, could not bear him a male heir.

Henry asked the pope for an annulment, but there was a problem. The queen was aunt to the Holy Roman emperor, whose troops currently occupied Rome. As a virtual prisoner of Charles V, the pope was in no position to grant an annulment. So Henry broke with the Roman church and between 1529 and 1533 pushed through Parliament a series of acts giving him complete control over the new Church of England. In May 1533, Archbishop of Canterbury Thomas Cranmer voided the king's marriage to Catherine so that he could marry Anne Boleyn. Between 1536 and 1539, Henry dissolved the English monasteries and sold their property for the benefit of the royal treasury. Otherwise, especially in its theology, the Henrician church differed little from its Roman predecessor.

During the reigns of Edward VI (1547–53) and Mary I (1553–58), England moved back and forth between Protestantism and Catholicism. Young Edward was a Reformed Protestant whose government made the *Book of Common Prayer*, compiled by Cranmer, the basis of English worship. With Edward's death, Mary (Catherine's daughter) rolled back these Protestant gains and returned England to Catholicism. (She was known as Bloody Mary because she ordered so many Protestants executed.)

The steely Elizabeth I (reigned 1558–1603) finally brought religious order to England by adopting a broad middle way. She reintroduced the *Book of Common Prayer*, for example, but had its language modified to make Church of England services more palatable to Catholic audiences. In general, the Elizabethan church followed many Catholic practices but leaned heavily on Protestant doctrine.

Initiated by Henry VIII for political reasons, *the English Reformation oscillated between Protestantism and Catholicism until Elizabeth imposed a middle way.*

IX. THE THIRD WAVE

SOME SCHOLARS DATE the beginning of the Third Wave to the mid-1980s. Others don't believe it began until the early 1990s. In either case, most associate its emergence with a rise in the diversity of feminist leadership and a resurgence of feminist consciousness among young women, many of whom began adopting the label *feminist*. (During the late 1970s and early 1980s, many women of color specifically rejected feminism because they believed it had become preoccupied with bourgeois issues affecting mostly white women.)

The two traits that have come to define Third Wave feminism are its embrace of critiques offered by women who previously felt excluded from the women's movement and its emphasis on the experiences of individual women (as opposed to the use of universal categories, such as *female*, which tend to mask important differences).

Third Wavers such as Chicana author Gloria Anzaldua were among the first feminists to show through critical analysis the ways in which historical accounts of earlier feminist movements minimize or deny altogether the roles played by women of color (such as Sojourner Truth). The work of these writers thus makes clear what can happen when some women attempt to speak on behalf of all women.

More generally, Third Wave feminists have called attention to the use by second-wave feminists of universal categories that tended to obscure the unique experiences of female minorities—including women of color, transnational women, lesbians, and working-class women. To address this problem, Third Wavers devised a lexicon, still in use today, that emphasizes the particularities of each person's experiences.

Because one of the most important principles of Third Wave feminism is cultural and ideological inclusivity, many Third Wavers have resisted the temptation to acknowledge that the movement has a canon. Nevertheless, most Third Wave feminists would agree that *To Be Real: Telling the Truth and Changing the Face of Feminism* (1995), a collection of essays by and about younger feminists, remains a pivotal text. Edited by Rebecca Walker, daughter of feminist scholar and novelist Alice Walker, *To Be Real* explores how young feminists of the mid-1990s defined themselves against traditional stereotypes and also against the feminism of their parents' generation.

Third Wave activism has ranged broadly from the training of young women as political activists to the promotion of women's and African American studies departments to the spread of feminist ideas through the popular culture (notably by feminist punk rockers such as the Butchies, Bitch and Animal, and Ani DiFranco).

Third Wave feminism *is defined by its inclusivity, especially its embrace of critiques of historical feminism and its respect for an individual's particularity.*

IX. POTSDAM

Truman and Secretary of State Byrnes en route to Potsdam.

IN JULY 1945, Truman traveled to the Berlin suburb of Potsdam to meet with Churchill and Stalin. Most of the items on the agenda involved the German occupation, but two other subjects preoccupied Truman: planning for the invasion of Japan, anticipated to cost hundreds of thousands of American lives; and the Manhattan Project, which might save those lives by obviating the need for an invasion.

As the conference began, Stalin was remarkably forthcoming. On the first day, July 17, he reaffirmed his promise to enter the Pacific war, even specifying a date (August 15); and he informed his allies that he had been receiving peace overtures from the Japanese. (American intelligence knew of these, having broken the Japanese code, but Stalin didn't know that they knew.)

Truman was initially elated by the firm August 15 date. "Fini Japs when that comes about," he wrote in his private diary. The very next day, however, his attitude changed. "Believe Japs will fold up before Russia comes in," he wrote. "I am sure they will when Manhattan appears over their homeland. I shall inform Stalin about it at an opportune time." The crucial intervening event was a brief cable he received on the morning of July 18 informing him the first atomic test had been even more successful than anticipated. Now the US could end the Pacific war quickly and without Soviet involvement.

As it happened, Truman didn't tell Stalin about the bomb until nearly a week later; and even then, he did so only informally. "I casually mentioned to Stalin that we had a new weapon of unusual destructive force," Truman wrote in his presidential memoir. "The Russian premier showed no special interest. All he said was that he was glad to hear it and hoped we would make 'good use of it against the Japanese.'"

Stalin, of course, already knew about the bomb from Soviet spies within the Manhattan Project, and a secret Soviet atomic program was already under way. Perhaps Bohr's recommendation of candor might have changed the course of Soviet behavior, perhaps not. But what can be said is that Anglo-American secrecy unquestionably exacerbated Soviet mistrust. By welcoming at Potsdam imminent Soviet entry into the Pacific war, while at the same time maneuvering to preempt that entry, Truman and Churchill confirmed Stalin's deepest fear: that the bomb was meant for Moscow next.

The attempt to *withhold knowledge of the Manhattan Project confirmed Stalin's worst fear: that the atomic bomb was meant to be used against the USSR as well as Japan.*

IX. MULTIPLE EQUILIBRIA

SOCIAL INTERACTIONS OFTEN CONTAIN ASPECTS of both conflict and cooperation. In *A Discourse on Inequality* (1755), French philosopher Jean-Jacques Rousseau described the following simultaneous-move "game," which he used as a metaphor for cooperation: A band of prehistoric tribesmen arranges to hunt a stag. Capturing such a large animal requires the coordinated action of the entire group. If the group is successful, there will be plenty of meat for the tribe. However, each member of the group has another "move": He can change his mind and decide to hunt rabbits instead. While a single hunter can capture a rabbit on his own, the payoff in meat is much less. In the meantime, the stag hunt will fail because the others wait for the rabbit hunter, who never appears.

The payoff structure of this game is reflected in the table below, where Hunter A is the row player and Hunter B is the column player.

	STAG	RABBIT
STAG	10, 10	0, 3
RABBIT	3, 0	3, 3

If Hunter A expects Hunter B to show up for the stag hunt, then his best response is to show up as well. If, on the other hand, he expects Hunter B to defect and hunt rabbits, then Hunter A's best response is also to hunt rabbits. (Because the game is symmetric, this analysis is also true for Hunter B.) Notice that there are two equilibria: one in which both players hunt stag and another in which both players hunt rabbit.

Like *The Newlywed Game*, the stag hunt requires coordination. But now it doesn't just matter *whether* the hunters coordinate; it also matters *how* they do so. If they coordinate to hunt stag, both will be better off than if each hunts rabbit. However, choosing to hunt stag is riskier. In game terms, each hunter can assure himself a payoff of 3 by hunting rabbit, whereas hunting stag may produce a payoff of 10, but it also may produce a payoff of 0.

The defining characteristic of this type of multiple-equilibria coordination game is that the outcome is determined by the player who exerts the least amount of effort. Hunting rabbit is, in a sense, easier than hunting stag. So, if either hunter chooses to hunt rabbit, the best outcome the other can expect for is the lesser (3,3) equilibrium.

In coordination games, *there are sometimes multiple equilibria. Which of these occurs often depends on the players' expectations.*

IX. AIR MASSES

AN AIR MASS IS DEFINED as a large body of air with generally uniform temperature and humidity at a given altitude. Because air masses can be a thousand kilometers wide and cross twenty degrees of latitude, their temperatures are somewhat variable. In general, however, the temperature of an air mass changes much more rapidly with altitude than with latitude.

For an air mass to form, the air needs to remain stationary over a fairly uniform source region for several days. During this time, the air takes on the qualities of the topography beneath it. For example, during the summer months in the Northern Hemisphere, air hovering over the northern Pacific Ocean will become cool and moist, whereas air hovering over the southwestern United States will become warm and dry.

Air masses are classified using two-letter codes that indicate their temperature and moisture content. The first letter designates moisture. From wetter to drier, the two categories are: m (maritime) and c (continental). To indicate an air mass's temperature, uppercase letters are used. From coldest to warmest, the three categories are: A (arctic), P (polar), and T (tropical). Thus, a cA would be an extremely cold, dry air mass that would have formed over land at the highest latitudes.

Many different air masses affect the weather on the North American continent. For example, cA and cP air masses that form in Canada carry cold, dry air as far south as Texas. Meanwhile, mP and mT air masses forming over the Pacific Ocean carry moist air eastward across the continent. In the Southwest, cT air masses form, subsequently moving north and east, while mP and mT air forming over the Atlantic can sometimes be pushed westward during coastal storms.

Once air masses start moving, however, their characteristics begin to change. As polar air moves south, for example, it warms. Similarly, as maritime air passes over land, it "dries" (as it causes precipitation and mixes with drier continental air). One result of this sort of localized modification is lake-effect snow, which occurs when a cold dry air mass passes over a large lake, such as one of the Great Lakes. The relatively warm water of the lake heats and moistens the air mass, causing it to rise and cool. Towering cumulus clouds are formed; and, if the topography on the lee side of the lake is sufficiently steep, snow falls heavily.

Air masses are large bodies *of air that take on the characteristics of the topography over which they form.*

X. THE COUNTER-REFORMATION

ALTHOUGH FACTIONS WITHIN the Catholic Church had been urging reform for decades, Luther's break with the church greatly amplified these calls for change. By the 1530s, even the most conservative Catholics realized that, unless ecclesiastical abuses were curbed and the church's integrity restored, Catholicism might not survive. Finally brought to crisis, the Catholic Church responded with a systematic housecleaning that came to be known as the Counter-Reformation.

The Counter-Reformation had its roots in late-fifteenth-century Spain, which Ferdinand II of Aragon and Isabella I of Castile (Catherine of Aragon's parents) ruled as joint monarchs. Both were devout Catholics determined to reinvigorate the church, and they did so by placing their royal power behind Cardinal Francisco Jiménez de Cisneros, Spain's leading ecclesiastic. Cisneros's program included better training for the clergy, the awarding of high church office based on ability rather than wealth, and improved pastoral care. Cisneros believed that the church had a duty to protect the faithful from heresy, so he persuaded Ferdinand and Isabella to create the Spanish Inquisition, whose vast power made Spain a bulwark of the Counter-Reformation.

At the turn of the sixteenth century, a spate of new religious orders began to appear—including the Oratory of Divine Love (1497); the Theatines (1524); the Capuchins (1528); the Ursulines (1535); and, most importantly, the Jesuits. The organization to which the Jesuits belonged, the Society of Jesus, was founded in 1540 by Spanish nobleman Ignatius Loyola. It attracted so many recruits that it quickly became the dominant order of the Counter-Reformation. Jesuits were especially active in religious education, overseas missionary work, and the returning of Protestants to the Catholic fold.

Jesuit missionaries at the court of a Muslim prince.

Also propelling the Counter-Reformation was a revitalized papacy. Paul III (1534–49) was the first of a new breed of Catholic churchmen who corrected abuses and punished heresy. Beyond appointing reformers, Paul III overhauled the College of Cardinals and revived the Roman Inquisition.

The third pillar of the Counter-Reformation was the Council of Trent, called by Paul III in 1545. Meeting off and on until 1563, the council rejected Protestantism, reaffirmed Catholic doctrine, and enacted sweeping policy changes to deal with various abuses. The Council of Trent also produced new policies relating to papal primacy, the pastoral duties of priests, and the training of clerics.

During the Counter-Reformation, *a reenergized Catholic Church responded to the challenge of the Protestant Reformation by revitalizing its own religious life.*

X. INTERSECTIONALITY

AMONG THE MOST IMPORTANT intellectual concepts associated with Third Wave feminism is the theory of intersectionality. The word *intersectionality* was coined by law professor Kimberle Crenshaw during the early 1980s when she was still an undergraduate. "In the Africana studies program at Cornell, the gender aspect of race was woefully underdeveloped," she recalled in an interview. The idea of intersectionality, she continued, "grew out of trying to conceptualize the way the law responded to issues where both race and gender discrimination were involved. [It] simply came from the idea that if you're standing in the path of multiple forms of exclusion, you are likely to get hit by both. These women are injured, but when the race ambulance and the gender ambulance arrive at the scene, they see these women of color lying in the intersection and they say, 'Well, we can't figure out if this was just race or just sex discrimination. And unless they can show us which one it was, we can't help them.'"

The concept of intersectionality didn't become widespread, however, until the 1990s, when sociologist Patricia Hill Collins began using the term—especially in her groundbreaking book *Black Feminist Thought* (1990)—to describe the manifold ways in which black women experience oppression and how these ways differ from the experiences of white women. In adopting the rubric of intersectionality—and with it, a focus on class and ethnicity as well as race and gender—Collins was able to expand from black women to all women her theory that patterns of social oppression are interlinked. In Collins's view, analyses that highlight these "intersecting oppressions" are critical to the creation of a feminist theory that takes seriously the contributions of black women and the unique ways that other marginalized groups experience patriarchal oppression.

In current feminist theory, intersectionality refers more generally to the complex ways in which individuals assume particular identities that may contradict the identities ascribed to them by society. For example, a light-skinned woman of mixed race who identifies herself as black may be identified by others, especially passersby, as white. Feminist scholars now typically refer to identities either as ascribed or assumed in order to emphasize the disconnect that can sometimes exist between how people identify themselves and how society identifies (or categorizes) them.

Intersectionality describes the ways *in people who are multiply identified—in terms of race, class, gender, and so on—can sometimes experience intersecting forms of oppression.*

X. CONTAINMENT

AFTER THE US BOMBED Hiroshima and Nagasaki in August 1945, Soviet–American cooperation broke down completely. Meanwhile, the Soviets rearranged the map of Eastern Europe. Poland was allowed to remain nominally independent, but the USSR annexed the Baltic states of Latvia, Lithuania, and Estonia. To the south, Hungary, Czechoslovakia, Romania, Bulgaria, and Albania all became Soviet satellites. "An iron curtain has descended across the continent," Churchill declared in March 1946.

Just two weeks earlier, on February 22, George F. Kennan, the chargé d'affaires at the US embassy in Moscow, had sent a fifty-three-hundred-word cable to Secretary of State Byrnes on the same topic. A career foreign service officer, Kennan had become a Russia expert after being posted to Tallinn, Riga, and other "listening posts" early in his career while the US and USSR lacked formal relations. Kennan's memorandum, now famous as the Long Telegram, outlined the strategy of containment that soon became the basis of postwar US foreign policy.

George F. Kennan in 1951.

After returning to Washington in April 1946, Kennan published his reasoning in a landmark July 1947 *Foreign Affairs* article that he signed only as X. "The main element of any United States policy toward the Soviet Union," Kennan wrote, "must be that of a long-term, patient but firm and vigilant containment of Russian expansive tendencies." To this end, he called for "adroit and vigilant application of counterforce at a series of constantly shifting geographical and political points, corresponding to the shifts and maneuvers of Soviet policy."

In Kennan's view, the postwar USSR had two goals: establishing a security corridor around its homeland and exporting Communism to other countries. The first reflected traditional Russian imperialism and couldn't be resisted short of war. The second, however, could be contained because Marxist-Leninist evangelism mattered much less to Russians than secure borders. Although efforts to recover Eastern Europe would likely fail, firmness with regard to political expansion should be effective.

Kennan discussed four regions of vital interest to the US: Western Europe, the Western Hemisphere, Japan, and the Middle East. Describing each as an unlikely target for Soviet invasion, he predicted that the USSR would almost certainly limit its efforts to political subversion, which could be countered by propping up unstable pro-Western regimes. As long as the US kept applying sufficient counterpressure, Kennan emphasized, there would be no need to militarize the Cold War.

In advocating containment, *Kennan distinguished between the USSR's military presence in Eastern Europe (to secure its borders) and its political adventurism elsewhere.*

X. EQUILIBRIUM CONVERGENCE

LET'S SAY you're walking down a narrow sidewalk, and you approach a person walking in the opposite direction. To avoid a collision, you and the other person adjust your paths. If both of you step to your right, or both of your step to your left, then you will miss each other. (These strategies are thus equilibria.) However, if one of you steps to his right and the other steps to his left, then you will collide. This game has the same structure as *The Newlywed Game*, as shown in the table below.

	LEFT	RIGHT
LEFT	10, 10	0, 0
RIGHT	0, 0	10, 10

Let's say, furthermore, that you play this game repeatedly as you walk down the sidewalk; and rather than trying to outthink each person you pass, you follow a simple rule of thumb, such as always stepping to your right. If the majority of the people you pass have also decided to follow a "step to your right" rule, then you will tend to avoid collisions. However, people walking behind you who have adopted a "step to your left" rule will fare much less well.

Suppose that, from time to time, each person evaluates how well his strategy is working. People following the "step to your left" rule will soon realize that they would be better off with "step to your right," and they will change. Meanwhile, people already following "step to your right" will see that they are doing well and stick with what they've got. Thus, over time, everyone will adopt the same strategy— either (right, right) or (left, left), depending on whether the majority begins with a "right" or "left" rule.

In *Evolution and the Theory of Games* (1982), biologist John Maynard Smith applied a variation of this idea to the study of species evolution. According to Smith, the behavioral "rule" that each animal in a population follows is determined by its genetic makeup. The payoffs in this game correspond to fitness levels. Members of the population who follow rules that yield higher fitness levels tend to have more offspring, who inherit their genetic makeup and thus their behavioral rules. Just as in the walking game, animal behavior will, over time, tend to converge on an equilibrium, even though the individuals involved cannot be said to be thinking strategically.

Even when players fail *(irrationally) to contemplate what the other players will do, adaptive dynamics may still produce an equilibrium.*

X. FRONTS

WHEN AIR MASSES of differing temperature come into contact with each other, the line along which they meet is called a front. The name given to the front identifies the type of air that is moving into a location. Thus, a cold front is the leading edge of a cold air mass that is pushing a relatively warm air mass out of the way. Cold fronts tend to move quickly and push warmer, less dense air rapidly upward. This forceful frontal wedging often results in the development of cumulonimbus clouds and heavy precipitation. (Cumulonimbus clouds are thunderheads, and the prefix *nimbo-* means "rain-producing.")

Frontal wedging occurs with warm fronts as well. But the less dense warm air can't force the cold air up, so the warm air rises instead, using the cold air as a ramp. Therefore, warm fronts are much less likely to produce severe weather. Instead, the gentler lifting associated with them produces cirrus, cirrostratus, altostratus, nimbostratus, and cumulonimbus clouds. The nimbostratus clouds can lead to moderate precipitation, while the cumulonimbus clouds can produce much more intense precipitation.

When warm and cold air flow in opposite directions along a front (rather than one air mass moving into the other), the front is said to be stationary. Occluded fronts occur when fast-moving cold fronts catch up to slow-moving warm fronts traveling in the same direction. This traps the warm air between two cold air masses, one behind the cold front and the other ahead of the warm front. As a result, the warm air is squeezed upward. The frontal wedging that takes place sometimes follows the cold-front model and sometimes the warm-front model.

The edges of the cold, dense air masses that cover both poles (beginning near latitude 60°) are known as polar fronts. Usually, these are stationary, with the cold air on the polar side and the warm air on the midlatitude side moving in opposite directions. However, polar fronts are also the starting points for midlatitude cyclones, which are storm systems centered on areas of low pressure around which winds rotate (counterclockwise in the Northern Hemisphere and clockwise in the Southern Hemisphere). Cyclones begin with a change in pressure aloft, usually caused by a disturbance in the polar jet stream. This permits air to rise, creating a low-pressure center at the surface. The resulting PGF initiates the flow of wind toward the center, and the CF bends the wind around it.

Fronts are boundaries *between large air masses of differing temperature.*

XI. WITCHCRAFT IN THE AGE OF REFORMATION

THE TENSION AND ANXIETY produced by the religious disorder of the Reformation manifested itself in several different ways. One was the noticeable jump that took place in the number of witchcraft prosecutions. Between 1500 and 1700, as many as one hundred thousand people were put on trial for witchcraft, and about thirty thousand of these were subsequently executed. Four out of five victims were women, reflecting the misogyny of the age. Often, their sentences were grisly. One common method for putting witches to death was to burn them alive at the stake.

Before Enlightenment thinking ridiculed its practice, magic was routinely called upon in Europe to repair misfortune and confer power. Throughout the premodern era, magicians offered healing potions, love potions, prognostications, and many other forms of aid. During the Late Middle Ages, however, the relationship between magic and evil underwent a transformation. Repeated outbreaks of plague, heresy, and

The frontispiece to Matthew Hopkins's 1647 manual on the hunting of witches.

ecclesiastical scandal caused the devil to loom rather large in the popular imagination. A number of books written by fifteenth-century inquisitors, especially the *Malleus Maleficarum* (1486), promoted the idea that Satan regularly made pacts with humans to carry out his evil designs. Typically, according to the mythology that developed, he approached single women and, after engaging them in sexual relations, bestowed upon them the power to harm others.

Most witchcraft prosecutions were triggered by simple misfortunes, such as a destructive hailstorm or the death of a child. Remembering old grudges, the victims would accuse neighbors of diabolical magic, and a trial would sometimes result. Because prosecutors were required to produce a confession to win a conviction, they often utilized torture to loosen the tongue of the accused. In some cases, the infliction of pain led to the naming of so many coconspirators that the public began to feel trapped within a diabolical web. Especially if the underlying misfortunes persisted, this feeling could produce a panic, during which dozens of people might be executed.

Not surprisingly, the height of the witchcraft prosecutions (1580–1650) coincided with the most intense period of Reformation warfare. Afterward, the number of prosecutions dropped off rapidly—in part because religious tensions eased and in part because of new judicial safeguards, including greater restrictions on torture and centralized oversight of the rural venues where most of the abuses had occurred.

One way in which *the tension and anxiety of the Reformation manifested itself in society was a sharp rise in the number of witchcraft prosecutions.*

XI. WOMANISM

AFTER REVISITING the first and second waves and reevaluating them in terms of intersectionality, many Third Wavers, especially the black women among them, found the term *feminism* wanting. To these women, *feminism* had the inescapable connotation of bourgeois privilege, because feminist movements of the past had been primarily white, primarily middle class, and largely indifferent to race- and class-based oppression. Third Wavers of color wanted a new word that would describe their own unique experiences as women.

More suitable than *feminist*, these women thought, was the term *womanist*, coined by Alice Walker in her 1983 book *In Search of Our Mother's Gardens*. Walker invented the term to describe the black woman's experience of multiply determined, intersectional prejudice, but other nonwhite women adopted the label as well.

In *In Search of Our Mother's Gardens*, Walker offered this literal definition:

> **womanist** 1. *From* womanish. *(Opp. of "girlish," i.e., frivolous, irresponsible, not serious.) A black feminist or feminist of color. From the black folk expression of mothers to female children, "You acting womanish," i.e., like a woman. Usually referring to outrageous, audacious, courageous, or willful behavior. Wanting to know more and in greater depth than is considered "good" for one...*
>
> *2. A woman who loves other women, sexually and/or nonsexually. Appreciates and prefers women's culture. Committed to survival and wholeness of entire people, male and female.*

Importantly, Walker located the etymology of *womanist* directly in black folk culture. Although the usage was new, the word itself had deep, nourishing roots. Walker's use of adjectives such as *outrageous, audacious,* and *courageous* implied that black women, having endured slavery, were neither passive nor weak. She valorized women's sexuality and their love for one another, accepting both friendships and same-sex attraction as part of a fluid understanding of sexuality that resists demarcation.

Concluding her definition, Walker famously wrote that "womanist is to feminist as purple is to lavender." While critics have offered many different interpretations of this analogy, what Walker generally seems to be emphasizing is the vibrancy of womanism compared with the lackluster quality of feminism.

Because Walker's term also has strong spiritual connotations, womanism has become the basis of a new school of theology that emphasizes God's relationship to the oppressed. Its proponents are primarily women theologians of color, most notably Jacquelyn Grant.

Many Third Wave women *of color adopted the label* womanist, *invented by Alice Walker, to distinguish their intersectional experiences from the experiences of white feminists.*

XI. THE TRUMAN DOCTRINE

BELIEVING KENNAN'S ASSESSMENT of the situation to be correct, Truman realized that there was little he could do to liberate territory already under Soviet control. With the defeat of Germany and the decline of Britain and France, the Soviets were now the dominant military power in Europe; and in Eastern Europe at least, they could do as they pleased. But Soviet expansionism was another matter—especially when it came to nonaligned nations on the borders of the new Soviet empire, which were increasingly feeling the pressure to genuflect.

In Greece, for example, where a civil war was under way, the Communist-led insurgency was gaining ground against the pro-Western government. Meanwhile, across the Aegean, a weak Turkish government was buckling under pressure from the Soviets to share control of the Dardanelles, which would give the Soviet Black Sea fleet access to the Mediterranean. In a bygone day, British aid would have stabilized both governments; but in February 1947, the British government informed the US State Department that it could no longer afford to help either Greece or Turkey.

Having already spoken with the Greek president, Truman concluded that only substantial American aid could keep Greece and Turkey out of the Soviet sphere. Seeking bipartisan support, he instructed Undersecretary of State Dean Acheson to meet with the congressional leadership. During this meeting, Acheson articulated what later came to be known as the domino theory. He claimed that if Greece and Turkey were allowed to fall, other countries would follow them—Iran to the south and India to the east—like a line of falling dominoes. Impressed by Acheson's argument, the Republicans who controlled Congress agreed to appropriate four hundred million dollars in economic and military aid for Greece and Turkey on the condition that the president personally explain the severity of the crisis in a nationally broadcast speech before a joint session of Congress.

Truman agreed; and in making this speech on March 12, he enunciated what came to be known as the Truman Doctrine: the commitment of the United States to aid, economically and/or militarily, any nation threatened by Communism. "At

the present moment in world history, nearly every nation must choose between alternative ways of life. " Truman explained. "The choice is too often not a free one…I believe that it must be the policy of the United States to support free peoples who are resisting attempted subjugation by armed minorities or by outside pressures."

Truman gives his March 1947 speech.

The Truman Doctrine *made it the policy of the United States to aid all nations threatened by Communism.*

XI. UNPREDICTABILITY

A FAMOUS SCENE in the film *The Princess Bride* features a battle of wits between the Sicilian and the Pirate. Between them are two goblets of wine. The Pirate tells the Sicilian that he will secretly poison the wine in one of the goblets. The Sicilian must then choose a goblet from which to drink, while the Pirate simultaneously drinks from the other. Of course, the person who drinks from the poisoned goblet loses.

We can express this game in the usual simultaneous-move table, where the Pirate is the row player and the Sicilian is the column player. Notice that this is a zero-sum game, meaning that one player's gain is exactly offset by the other player's loss.

	GOBLET A	GOBLET B
POISON A	1, -1	-1, 1
POISON B	-1, 1	1, -1

Let's analyze the Pirate's position first. If he expects the Sicilian to drink from Goblet A, his best response is to poison Goblet A (because 1 > -1). If he expects the Sicilian to drink from Goblet B, his best response is to poison Goblet B. Turning next to the Sicilian's position, we can see that if he expects the poison to be in Goblet A, he should drink from Goblet B. If he expects the poison to be in Goblet B, he should drink from Goblet A.

At first glance, this game seems to have no equilibrium. No matter what the outcome, one of the players will surely have regrets. What this means strategically is that if the Sicilian expects the Pirate to poison Goblet A, he should drink from Goblet B. The Pirate, however, should anticipate this and poison Goblet B. But the Sicilian should anticipate this and drink from Goblet A—and so on in an infinite regression.

But how can there be no equilibrium? Didn't Nash prove that there has to be an equilibrium in a game like this? The answer lies in the idea of unpredictability. When analysis of a game leads one into endless logical cycles, the best strategy for playing the game is to play it unpredictably. In other words, players must choose randomly from among their options or else risk being exploited by the other player. Only by choosing randomly can a player have no regrets.

Strategic analysis of some games leads one into endless logical loops. When this occurs, *the best way to play the game is to be unpredictable and make one's choices randomly.*

XI. HURRICANES

A hurricane as seen from space.

HURRICANES ARE POWERFUL tropical cyclones that produce high winds, heavy rains, and huge storm surges. (Storm surge is the wall of water carried onto shore by a hurricane's winds.) Hurricanes begin over the ocean at latitudes between 5° and 20°. The warm water found at these latitudes supplies the heat and moisture that hurricanes need to form (initially as loosely organized thunderstorms) and grow. Above 20°, the water isn't warm enough; and below 5°, there isn't enough CF to start the cyclone spinning.

As the moist air within a newly formed cyclone rises, it cools, and the water vapor condenses. This condensation releases large amounts of latent heat, which keep the air within the storm warmer (and thus more buoyant) than the air surrounding it. So, within the storm, air continues to rise and cool, and the resulting condensation continues to release latent heat. Eventually, this process creates towering cumulonimbus clouds as tall as twenty kilometers.

Meanwhile, all of this rising air creates an area of extremely low pressure at the center of the cyclone, increasing the PGF and speeding up the surface winds that bring the storm its fuel (more warm, moist ocean air). As this air flows toward the center of the low, the CF bends it, generating the cyclonic flow.

As more and more air accumulates at the top of the storm, the pressure there builds until divergence begins. At this point, upper-level winds blow out from the center of the storm, reducing the pressure so that surface air can continue to rise— a necessity for continued storm growth. The storm remains a tropical depression, however, until its maximum sustained surface wind speed reaches 37 mph (61 km/h), at which point it becomes a tropical storm and receives a name. When its wind speed reaches 74 mph (119 km/h), the storm becomes a hurricane.

Hurricanes are measured using the Saffir-Simpson scale, which takes into account such factors as air pressure, wind speed, and storm surge. The scale ranges from one to five, with a category five hurricane being the most destructive. To be classified as a category five, a hurricane would have to exhibit a barometric pressure below 920 millibars, winds greater than 155 mph (250 km/h), and a storm surge greater than 18 feet (5.4 m). Hurricane Katrina, by comparison, was only a category four hurricane when it made landfall.

Hurricanes are powerful tropical cyclones, *fueled by a continuous flow of rising air that has been heated and moistened by warm ocean water.*

XII. THE FRENCH WARS OF RELIGION

ALTHOUGH THE PEACE OF AUGSBURG resolved the conflict between Catholics and Lutherans in Germany, it was by no means a comprehensive solution to the problems of the Reformation. The peace made no provision for other Protestant denominations (such as Calvinism); nor did it apply to non-German lands. In France, for example, Catholics still hoped to eradicate their Protestant opposition.

The violence in France began with the weakening of the monarchy. In 1559, Henry II died from a wound suffered in a jousting accident (a lance splintered and pierced his eye). Henry's sickly fifteen-year-old son, Francis II, ascended to the throne but died a year later. Next came Francis's nine-year-old brother, Charles IX, whose fourteen-year reign (1560–74) was dominated by his mother, Catherine de' Medici. When Charles died, his younger brother, Henry III, succeeded him. Although Henry was too old to be dominated by Catherine, he nevertheless suffered from psychoses and participated rather too openly in homosexual orgies.

With the Valois line obviously in decline, powerful noble factions took matters into their own hands. One faction, led by the duke of Guise, was militantly Catholic; the other, led by the Bourbon family of Navarre, was just as adamantly Calvinist.

The French Wars of Religion began in 1562, when the duke of Guise ordered soldiers in the town of Vassy to fire on unarmed Huguenots (French Calvinists). Intermittent but bloody fighting continued in France for the next thirty-six years. The most horrifying episode came in August 1572, when an unusually large number of Huguenot nobles were gathered in Paris for an important political wedding. On St. Bartholomew's Day, Catholics aligned with the Guises massacred three thousand of these Huguenots in a plot approved by Catherine de' Medici, acting on behalf of Charles IX.

A Huguenot service in Lyons ca. 1565.

The conflict's final phase, the War of the Three Henrys, featured shifting alliances among Henry III, Henry of Navarre, and Henry of Guise. When assassinations felled Guise and then the king in 1589, Navarre (who was Henry III's cousin) became Henry IV, founder of the Bourbon dynasty. Supported by Spain and still in control of Paris, Guise's Catholic League carried on the fight; but in 1593, Henry IV undercut his opposition by converting to Catholicism. Five years later, he subdued the Catholic League and issued the Edict of Nantes, which granted some religious freedoms to the Huguenots.

The French Wars of Religion *were fought between the Catholic Guises and the Protestant Bourbons while a string of ineffective monarchs occupied the French throne.*

XII. FEMINISM IN THE ACADEMY

THE ACADEMIC FIELD OF WOMEN'S STUDIES emerged during the early 1970s in response to the growing influence and activism of second-wave feminists on college and university campuses. These women, both students and faculty, along with male allies, were becoming increasingly concerned that existing academic disciplines, all of which were dominated by men, either ignored or distorted the experiences and perspectives of women. Initially, they organized forums and conferences during which women's views could be aired; soon, they began offering courses as well. (In this way, the development of courses in women's studies paralleled the slightly earlier development of courses in black studies, which members of the civil rights movement had been demanding.)

An important step was taken in 1977, when the National Women's Studies Association (NWSA) was founded. Later, as women's studies departments proliferated, the discipline became institutionalized. At first, women's studies courses focused on the history of women's activism and feminist theory; but as the field grew and became more interdisciplinary, it expanded to cover women's activities and experiences more generally. Throughout its development, however, the field of women's studies has remained closely aligned to the goal of achieving equality for women in society. This underlying commitment to social change is what makes the discipline of women's studies essentially feminist.

Since the late 1970s, the number of women's studies departments has grown exponentially, especially in recent years with Third Wave agitation for expanded course and degree offerings. The related disciplines upon which women's studies majors now draw range from biology to sociology and philosophy to comparative literature. Not surprisingly, given the intersectional worldview of modern feminism, the students and faculty who populate women's studies departments tend to resist standard academic categories in favor of combinations—such as feminist literary theory, feminist science studies, feminist political theory, and so on.

At times, this willingness to move beyond established boundaries has taken women's studies in unexpected directions. For example, one of the most important intellectual developments of recent years, queer theory, owes much of its existence to the growth medium that women's studies departments provided. Queer theorists study the ways in which categories of gender and sexuality are understood by people and contested in society. Like Third Wave feminists, queer theorists believe that identities aren't fixed but floating; therefore, people can't be categorized by them.

A creation of the second wave, *the field of women's studies encourages students to work in other disciplines while remaining committed to the study of gender and the pursuit of sexual equality.*

XII. DISARRAY IN POSTWAR EUROPE

IN JANUARY 1947, two months before the Truman Doctrine speech, the US, British, French, and Soviet foreign ministers gathered in Moscow to discuss the future of Germany. At Yalta and again at Potsdam, it had been agreed that Germany would be reunified under a central, freely elected government. But the French remained nervous that a reunified Germany might pose a future threat; and the Soviets, to no one's surprise, were also proving quarrelsome.

Disputes arose at the Moscow conference over war reparations, the level of industry that should be permitted in a reunited Germany, whether the great coal and steel industries of the Ruhr (the traditional bases of German economic and military strength) should be placed under international control, and how centralized the new German government should be. In the end, no agreement was reached; and the new US secretary of state, George C. Marshall, left Moscow convinced that the Soviets wanted a deadlock because political stalemate only aggravated the growing economic disarray in occupied Germany and in Western Europe more generally.

Indeed, the economic and political situation in Western Europe was becoming dire. Nearly six years of pervasive Allied bombing had turned most of the large cities into seas of rubble while destroying much of Europe's economic infrastructure. Meanwhile, the businesses and factories that did survive lacked many of the industrial supplies they needed to be productive. Unemployment was severe, and even people who had jobs were demoralized by the constant shortages. Food, in particular, was so scarce that millions were on the verge of starvation.

The effect that this economic turmoil was having on the political situation in Europe could be seen by everyone, not just the Soviets. The British withdrawal from Greece and Turkey was one direct result; and in France and Italy, where shortages were particularly acute, Communist movements were gaining electoral ground. In Germany as well, the US occupation authorities warned, widespread poverty was undermining governmental authority.

Upon his return from Moscow, Marshall (who had been army chief of staff during the war) decided that something more would have to be done if the United States was indeed to contain the Soviet Union within its current borders. He began by instructing Kennan, who had recently been appointed the State Department's new director of policy planning, to investigate the economic situation in Europe and determine what assistance the US might be able to provide.

Marshall in 1947 after returning from Moscow.

The devastation of *nearly six years of war left Western Europe in economic disarray, providing fertile ground for the growth of Communist movements there.*

XII. HOW TO BE UNPREDICTABLE

BEING UNPREDICTABLE means more than simply varying one's choices. Mathematically, it means playing the game in such a way that all of one's opponent's choices have the same expected payoff.

	GOBLET A	GOBLET B
POISON A	1, -1	-1, 1
POISON B	-1, 1	1, -1

Consider again the battle of the wits. The optimal strategy for both players is to randomize their choices, giving equal weight to both goblets. Given this arrangement, each of the four outcomes will occur with a probability of $1/4$, and the expected utility (average payoff) for each player will be $1/4$ x -1 + $1/4$ x 1 + $1/4$ x -1 + $1/2$ x 1, or 0.

To understand why these strategies are optimal, think about what happens when a player favors one of his choices. Suppose the Pirate is more likely to poison Goblet A; in fact, the probability of this is $2/3$, meaning that the probability of his poisoning Goblet B is $1/3$. If the Sicilian chooses Goblet B, his expected utility is $2/3$ x 1 + $1/3$ x -$1/3$, or $1/3$. If the Sicilian chooses Goblet A, his expected utility is $2/3$ x -1 + $1/3$ x 1, or -$1/3$. So, by choosing Goblet B, the Sicilian can obtain a better average payoff than he could have gotten if no tendency existed (because $1/3 > 0$). Furthermore, because this is a zero-sum game, an average payoff of $1/3$ for the Sicilian means an average payoff of -$1/3$ for the Pirate.

In this game, any deviation from equal probability results in a clear best response for the other player, which he can use to his advantage. Therefore, in games where randomization is important, the frequency of your choices should vary so that all of your opponent's choices have the same expected payoff.

Awareness of this principle can make you a much better poker player. Consider the practice of bluffing. Players who bluff too much or too little are easily beaten because their play is predictable. If a player's tendency is to bluff, you should always call his raises. If his tendency is not to bluff, you should always fold when he raises. You won't win every hand; but, as the above calculations demonstrate, you will gain an important advantage.

In mathematical terms, *being optimally unpredictable means ensuring that all of your opponent's choices have the same expected payoff.*

XII. THUNDERSTORMS

THE LIFE CYCLE OF A THUNDERSTORM has three distinct stages. During the first stage (the cumulus stage), updrafts of warm, moist air form huge cumulus clouds. During the second stage (the mature cumulonimbus stage), precipitation begins to fall—often heavily and usually accompanied by strong winds, thunder, and lightning.

Whatever form the precipitation takes, whether it's rain or hail, it drags down some of the air in the cloud, creating downdrafts that exit at the cloud's base, generating gusty winds. The downdrafts also cause cool, dry, upper-level air to be drawn into the cloud. This phenomenon, known as entrainment, further cools the cloud by causing the evaporation of water droplets and/or ice crystals. (This evaporation has a cooling effect because the water absorbs energy from the air around it in order to make the phase change.)

Downdrafts and entrainment increasingly dominate the storm until the third stage (the dissipation stage) is reached. At this point, the downdrafts become so strong that they cut off the updrafts entirely. Without updrafts, the storm loses its fuel—the rising warm, moist air—and it dies.

Thunderstorms can form in several different ways, but the most common way involves the intense heating of land by the sun. The land, in turn, heats warm, moist air near the surface, causing it to rise rapidly, leading to the formation of cumulonimbus clouds.

The presence of one thunderstorm can sometimes lead to the creation of more thunderstorms along a gust front. Gust fronts form when the cold, dry air

A developing thunderstorm in the Yucatán.

carried by the downdrafts spreads out along the ground—wedging itself under warm, moist air and creating new updrafts. These updrafts create new cumulus clouds, which can develop into thunderstorms. Thunderstorms can also form along a cold front in the same manner.

Supercells are extremely powerful thunderstorms that form in association with inversions aloft. Normally in the troposphere, temperature decreases with altitude; but in an inversion, the air is layered so that temperature increases with altitude. Cold air beneath warmer air is highly stable, because the cold air resists rising. Therefore, the inversion acts as a cap—blocking the rise of warm, moist surface air, which lacks the buoyancy to break through the inversion. However, if a small break develops in the inversion, then the blocked surface air will rush through that break with tremendous force, creating towering cumulonimbus clouds capable of producing tornadoes.

Thunderstorms begin with updrafts *that produce large cumulonimbus clouds. The resulting precipitation initiates downdrafts, which cut off the updrafts and dissipate the storm.*

XIII. THE DUTCH REVOLT

SOON AFTER CIVIL WAR erupted in France, a second theater of conflict opened in the Low Countries (present-day Belgium, Luxembourg, and the Netherlands), which were then possessions of the Spanish Hapsburg king. During the early sixteenth century, the seventeen provinces of the Low Countries had enjoyed salutary neglect from the Hapsburgs, but the Reformation ate away at their stability. The fighting that consumed the Low Countries during the second half of the sixteenth century began, as in France, as a religious conflict. However, because the Catholic side was strongly royalist, a political dimension was added to the struggle, and the Calvinists soon turned the war into a national revolt against Hapsburg authority.

During the 1540s and 1550s, Calvinism had found a receptive home in the Netherlands, at first in the southern cities and later in the northern provinces. When its partisans began pushing for religious reformation during the late 1550s, the Spanish king Philip II moved to impose tighter controls. The resulting tensions came to a head in 1566, when Calvinists in Flanders and Holland rioted, destroying Catholic images. Philip responded by sending the duke of Alba to oversee a

Fernando Álvarez de Toledo, the third duke of Alba.

retributive tribunal with unlimited authority. The Spanish called Alba's court the Council of Troubles, but the Dutch knew it as the Council of Blood, because it ordered the execution or imprisonment of thousands of Calvinists.

At first, Alba's council wasn't resisted, because the Calvinist nobility lacked arms and believed, wrongly, that aristocratic privilege would protect them. However, the nobility eventually joined with Dutch urban elites under William of Orange's leadership to challenge Alba's authority, claiming that it violated traditional Dutch autonomy.

A major shift occurred in 1572, when pirates in league with the rebels gained control of the northern coast of Holland. By 1579, the Low Countries were split in two. Affirming their loyalty to Spain, the ten southern provinces joined together in the Union of Arras, while the seven northern provinces declared their independence in the Union of Utrecht. Although the Spanish were the stronger side, the Dutch military proved quite agile and benefited from its local knowledge, often flooding regions in order to thwart promising enemy operations. By 1609, the Spanish became so overextended that they agreed to a truce, effectively recognizing Dutch independence. (Formal recognition came in 1648 with the Treaty of Münster.)

When religious warfare spread *to the Low Countries during the late sixteenth century, it took on a political character and became the Dutch Revolt.*

XIII. TRANSNATIONAL FEMINISM

ANOTHER INFLUENTIAL FIELD that emerged during the 1990s from the petri dish of women's studies departments was the field of global feminism, which sought to identify similarities in the experiences of oppressed women worldwide. Before the development of global feminism, most US women's studies departments focused exclusively on women living in the United States. So, to the extent that global feminism broadened the worldview of American feminists, it was welcomed.

However, global feminism soon came under strong criticism because of its focus on similarities rather than differences. The distinction is important because concentrating on similarities—what some have called global sisterhood—can obscure the experiential differences that Third Wave feminism has found so meaningful. Although feminist theory does hold that all women are oppressed by patriarchy, the ways in which they are oppressed vary considerably from one place and culture to another according to a wide range of intersectional criteria. Treating women the world over as though they are all interchangeable, fundamentally identical "sisters" incorrectly implies that all women share the same experiences.

Sensitivity to difference also informed a second critique of global feminism relating to data collection. Unless researchers paid close attention to cultural differences, it was argued, they ran the risk of unconsciously prejudicing the information they collected and thereby distorting any subsequent interpretation. For example, behavior that might appear to a "liberated" American researcher as acquiescent could actually represent, within another cultural context, resistance.

As a result of these critiques, global feminism morphed into transnational feminism, which focuses on the differences that exist among oppressed women while at the same time creating an ideological framework within which relations among women of different countries and cultures can become more beneficial and productive.

The use of the label *transnational* acknowledges the field's close relationship to postcolonial theory, whose advocates originally popularized the term. Postcolonial theorists explore the history of European colonization and its contemporary effects, especially the ways in which colonialism, power, and resistance are interrelated. Transnational feminists similarly study the intersectionality of nationhood and statehood with race, class, and gender.

Transnational feminists *study the intersectionality of nationhood and statehood with race, class, and gender to understand the relationship between women's oppression and the particularities of their culture.*

XIII. THE MARSHALL PLAN

The first shipment of Caribbean sugar is delivered under the Marshall Plan.

ON JUNE 5, 1947, in a speech to the graduating class at Harvard University, Secretary of State Marshall outlined the foreign policy problems that the United States was facing in Europe. "Europe's requirements are so much greater than her present ability to pay that she must have substantial additional help or face economic, social, and political deterioration of a very grave character," Marshall said, Then he proposed a bold, creative solution: He wanted the European nations to devise a joint recovery plan based on the principles of self-help, resource sharing, and German reintegration; and he wanted the United States to fund it.

Marshall's offer was quickly taken up by the British and French foreign ministers, who issued a joint communiqué inviting twenty-two nations and representatives from occupied Germany to a conference in Paris that would begin the work of drawing up a cooperative plan. Sixteen of the invitees took part, the exceptions being the Soviet Union and five of its client states. Stalin opposed the plan for several reasons—including its vision of an integrated European market, where free movement of goods and services presumably meant free movement of people as well—but Western leaders saw his antagonism simply as another effort to block postwar stabilization. Thus, it added to growing international tension.

The European plan, presented in September, became the basis of the European Recovery Program (ERP) proposed to Congress in December 1947. The price tag on the bill was a steep seventeen billion dollars; and although few Americas expected their country to pull back from international engagement as it had after World War I, seventeen billion dollars was still a lot of money. Opponents of the bill argued that the US economy couldn't afford it, while those in favor pointed out that the plan would create new export markets for US goods and that, if it weren't passed soon, there might not be any European democracies left.

Ultimately, events abroad settled the matter. After a Soviet-backed coup d'état ousted the democratically elected government of Czechoslovakia in February 1948, opposition to the bill disappeared, and it passed in April. During the next four years, the US government spent $13.3 billion, or between 5 and 10 percent of its annual budget, on ERP aid, making the Marshall Plan the most expensive foreign policy initiative in US history (calculated in constant dollars). Along with the Truman Doctrine, it signaled America's embrace of its new role as a global leader.

The goal of the Marshall Plan *was to promote European economic recovery and thus halt the political destabilization that economic hardship was causing.*

XIII. RANDOMIZATION

AT FIRST GLANCE, the principle of optimal randomization seems paradoxical. After all, the assumption of rationality states that players seek to maximize their own payoffs. Yet the goal of randomization is to manipulate the other player's payoffs so that all of them have the same expected utility.

The resolution of this paradox is found in the nature of the zero-sum game, in which one player's loss is necessarily the other players gain and vice versa. If Player A has a known tendency, then Player B can, by choosing wisely, receive an expected payoff that is greater than 0. In such cases, Player B's expected payoff is necessarily less than 0. Therefore, for Player B to maximize his own payoff, he needs to minimize Player A's payoff (by limiting it to 0).

In 2001, economists Mark Walker and John Wooders tested the advice game theory gives on randomization by analyzing ten men's Grand Slam tennis finals, beginning with the 1974 Rosewall-Smith Wimbledon final. Walker and Wooders observed that the best professional players, on their first service at least, almost always serve the ball as far as possible to one side of the service court or the other. Game theory suggests that, if players in a particular match are playing optimally, they will win the same proportion of points whether they aim for the right side of the service court or the left (because if they tended to win more points serving to one side of the service court, they would serve more often to that side until an equilibrium was reached).

For each of the ten matches they studied, Walker and Wooders found the predicted pattern: Whether serving to the left or the right, the server won the same percentage of points—about 65 percent across all the matches. However, even though the probability of the server winning the point remained fairly constant from match to match, the means by which he won those points (serving more to the left or more to the right) varied greatly. For example, in the 1974 Wimbledon final, when serving to the "ad" court, Ken Rosewall served to the left and to the right exactly the same number of times (thirty-seven). Yet when serving to the "deuce" court, he served to the left seventy out of seventy-five times. Therefore, randomization doesn't necessarily entail equal probabilities, just equal expected payoffs.

The principle of optimal randomization *has practical benefits in that it can help game players formulate winning strategies.*

XIII. TORNADOES

AT ANY GIVEN MOMENT, there are about two thousand thunderstorms worldwide. Of these, more than a few are capable of producing tornadoes, but fewer than 1 percent actually do.

Tornadoes are short but violent windstorms that form in association with severe thunderstorms when wind shear occurs between the air on the ground and the air directly above the ground. The term *wind shear* refers to a radical change in wind speed and direction over a very short distance. This disparity sets the sheared air in motion, creating a tube of rotating air in much the same way that rolling clay between one's palms creates a cylindrical coil. This tube of air then rolls along the ground until it reaches an area of land that has been heated intensely by the sun, generating a strong updraft (the cumulus stage of a thunderstorm). When the rolling tube encounters this updraft, the strength of the updraft pushes the tube upright.

The air within the tube now begins to spiral rapidly upward, creating at the base of the tube an area of extremely low pressure. This low pressure greatly increases the PGF, which greatly increases the surface wind speed, causing more air to rush in and strengthening the now-rotating updraft. At this point, if the conditions are right and a cumulonimbus cloud has formed, a thin fingerlike cloud will drop down from the rotating portion of the thunderstorm base. When condensation occurs and this rotating finger becomes visible, it's called a funnel cloud. Once it touches the ground, it becomes a tornado.

The thunderstorms most likely to spawn tornadoes are supercells. These form regularly during the spring months over the central United States, a region known as Tornado Alley because the contrasting air masses that cause wind shear frequently collide there.

A tornado in Cordell, Oklahoma.

Tornado intensity is commonly described using the Fujita scale (F-scale), which measures damage done. The lowest intensity on the F-scale is F0, which corresponds to light damage and wind speeds below 72 mph (116 km/h). An F3 tornado, on the other hand, would cause severe damage, ripping off some roofs and knocking down some walls. Its wind speeds would range from 158 to 206 mph (254–332 km/h). The highest intensity on the F-scale is F5, which corresponds to catastrophic damage, such as houses being lifted off their foundations and car-sized debris flying through the air. Wind speeds for an F5 tornado would exceed 260 mph (419 km/h).

Tornadoes begin as rolling tubes of air, *created by horizontal wind shear, that updrafts push upright to form dangerous rotating thunderstorms.*

XIV. ENGLAND'S GLORIOUS REVOLUTION

WHEN THE STUART KING James VI of Scotland became James I of England upon Elizabeth I's death in 1603, his government faced both political challenges abroad and financial difficulties at home. Parliament pressed James for a greater role in policy making, but the king had a rather exalted view of the prerogatives of monarchy, and he ruled with an aloofness that alienated nobles and commoners alike.

Charles I of England

When James died in 1625, he was succeeded by his son Charles I, who had even greater contempt for Parliament. Charles was also a high church Anglican, which meant that he emphasized the Church of England's Catholic-style liturgy at the expense of its Protestant-style doctrine. Charles's Catholic sympathies scandalized the Puritans in Parliament, so named because they wanted to purify the Anglican Church of all Catholic vestiges.

After 1629, Charles ruled England as an absolute monarch, refusing to call Parliament and resorting to means other than taxation to raise revenue. In 1640, however, when Charles imposed the *Book of Common Prayer* on Calvinist Scotland, the Scots revolted, and Charles had to convene Parliament in order to raise funds for an army. Relations disintegrated from there; and in 1642, civil war broke out, with Oliver Cromwell emerging as the leader of the parliamentary (Puritan) side. Cromwell's New Model Army routed the royalists at Naseby and took Charles prisoner in 1645. When Cromwell finally consolidated his control over the country, he put the king on trial for treason and had him beheaded in 1649.

For the next decade, Cromwell ruled England ruthlessly, smashing all political opposition—and there was a lot of it. The experience was so negative that, following Cromwell's death in 1658, pressure built for a restoration of the Stuart monarchy. In 1660, Charles I's son returned from France to become King Charles II.

Like his father, however, Charles II was a Catholic-sympathizing absolutist with no love for Parliament, and Parliament had no love for him. His son James II, who ascended to the throne in 1685, was even more overtly Catholic. In 1687, James had his son (and presumptive heir) baptized Catholic—an event that set in motion the Glorious Revolution of 1688, during which Parliament bloodlessly deposed James II and invited the Calvinist stadtholder of the Netherlands, William of Orange, and his wife, Mary Stuart, to become the new constitutional monarchs of a decidedly Anglican England.

The Glorious Revolution of 1688 *established a stable constitutional monarchy in England and affirmed the permanency of the Anglican Church.*

XIV. FEMINIST DISABILITY STUDIES

ANOTHER SUBSET OF FEMINIST THEORY that emerged during the 1990s was feminist disability studies. For many years, feminist scholars had examined the relationship between gender expectations and irregular body types, but it wasn't until the late 1990s and early 2000s that feminist interest in nonstandard physicality joined with the broader discipline of disability studies to create a new and distinct field of feminist inquiry. A key milestone was the publication of Rosemarie Garland-Thomson's essay "Integrating Disability, Transforming Feminist Theory," which appeared in the Fall 2002 issue of the *NWSA Journal* (the flagship publication of the National Women Studies Association).

According to Garland-Thomson, feminist disability theory "introduces the ability/disability system as a category of analysis…and fosters complex understandings of the cultural history of the body." In other words, the field of feminist disability studies explores not merely the experiences of disabled people but more generally the ways in which some physical attributes come to be privileged while other are designated as abnormal. Although feminist disability studies doesn't exclude male disabilities, it differs from disability studies in that it makes use of a distinctly feminist mode of analysis.

In determining what constitutes a disability, feminist disability theorists interpret *disability* broadly to include any bodily trait that society considers out of the ordinary. Some of these may be disabilities in the traditional sense—particularly misshapen, missing, or malfunctioning limbs. But others include changes made to the body intentionally in order to challenge social standards of acceptability—covering one's body with tattoos, for instance. By exposing the arbitrariness of these classifications, feminist disability studies challenges people to reconsider what is and isn't "natural."

Feminist disability theorists specifically dispute the idea that malformed or malfunctioning bodies are undesirable, asexual anomalies. Using historical examples—Helen Keller, for one—they have shown that such disabilities haven't always been considered obstacles to the living of fully functional, contented lives.

In accordance with so much other Third Wave feminism, the underlying premise of feminist disability studies is that none of the bodily attributes considered abnormal are inherently so. Rather, such classifications are, like gender expectations, the product of social norms that change from time to time and place to place. Thus, it is society—and not the individual marked by society as "disabled"—that has a problem and requires change.

What makes feminist disability studies *feminist isn't that it concerns disabled women only but that it probes the identity category of disabled using a feminist mode of analysis.*

XIV. THE BERLIN AIRLIFT

AS THE SOVIET PREFERENCE for a disintegrated, unstable Germany became clear, the Americans and British moved to shore up their sectors. Already in January 1947, notwithstanding Soviet objections, they had merged their occupation zones, creating a single political unit known as Bizonia. In March 1948, the French agreed to add their sector—creating Trizonia, the territory that would later become West Germany.

In mid-June, the US and British authorities took an even more significant step in the creation of an independent state in western Germany. They abruptly introduced a new currency: the Deutsche mark. Although seemingly mundane, currency reform was, in fact, crucial to the economic recovery of western Germany because the Nazi Reichsmark, the only currency then in circulation, was worthless. As a result, prior to June 1948, nearly all transactions in postwar Germany took place on the black market using a barter system. With the introduction of a new sound currency, however, shopkeepers began accepting cash again, and merchandise that had previously been sold only illegally returned to fill empty store shelves.

The new currency appeared in West Berlin on June 23. The next day, the Soviets cut off all road, rail, and water access to the city—halting the shipments of food, fuel, and other vital supplies that kept West Berlin alive. The western Allies protested, asserting that their occupation rights included the right of access; but the Soviets disagreed. Thus, the Americans and British were left with only one option short of capitulation—a massive airlift, which they began on June 26. (The French joined the airlift in November after an airfield was constructed in their sector.)

At first, the task seemed hopeless. West Berlin needed a minimum of forty-five hundred tons of supplies per day for its 2.5 million people, and the C-47 cargo planes that were initially available could carry only three tons per flight. But Truman quickly sent over a hundred large-capacity C-54s to make up the difference and more. On April 16–17, 1949, as "an Easter present for the people of Berlin," some four hundred Allied aircraft made nearly fourteen hundred flights, or one per minute, delivering thirteen thousand tons of cargo. By May 12, when the Soviets finally lifted their blockade, West Berlin had become not the initial

A C-54 prepares to land in Berlin during the airlift.

battlefield of World War III but an international symbol of US resolve to counter Soviet aggression without resorting to direct conflict.

When the Soviets *cut off road, rail, and water access to West Berlin, the Americans and British responded with a massive airlift of critical supplies.*

XIV. SEQUENTIAL-MOVE GAMES

THE FOUNDATION OF ALL OUR ANALYSES thus far has been the concept of a best response. We have defined an equilibrium as an arrangement in which each player plays his best response to what the other players are doing. In simultaneous-move games, this requires each player to anticipate what the others will do. When moves are sequential, however, the second player to move already knows what the first player has done.

To understand how such a sequential-move game works, let's reconsider the film-release game. However, now let's suppose that Behemoth (the row player) moves first. Our previous best-response analysis tells us (and Behemoth) how Upstart will respond. If Behemoth chooses a Memorial Day release, Upstart will respond with a July 4 release. If Behemoth announces a July 4 release, Upstart will respond with a Memorial Day release. What, then, should Behemoth do?

	MEMORIAL DAY	JULY 4
MEMORIAL DAY	60, 10	100, 20
JULY 4	80, 40	110, 30

Suppose that Behemoth announces a Memorial Day release. At this point, the original game becomes truncated, because the possibility of a July 4 Behemoth release has been eliminated. The game table now looks like this:

	MEMORIAL DAY	JULY 4
MEMORIAL DAY	60, 10	100, 20

Upstart's best response is clearly to release on July 4. Therefore, Behemoth will earn a profit of 100 million dollars.

The same logic applies equally well to a July 4 Behemoth release: If Behemoth decides to release on July 4, Upstart will release on Memorial Day (its best response), and Behemoth will earn 80 million dollars. Therefore, because 100 > 80, Behemoth should release its film on Memorial Day.

When analyzing sequential-move games, *it's important to take into account how the second player will react to the first player's move.*

XIV. WEATHER FORECASTING

IN ORDER TO MAKE accurate weather forecasts, meteorologists need to start with accurate data, which they obtain from many different types of instruments installed at over ten thousand land-based observatories around the world. In addition, there are thousands of ships and data buoys at sea monitoring ocean conditions and reporting them back at hourly intervals. Automated Surface Observing Systems (ASOS) operate at nearly nine hundred US airports, providing information on temperature, dew point, wind speed and direction, precipitation, relative humidity, and other factors.

Around the world, approximately eight hundred radiosondes are sent aloft twice a day in weather balloons. These small transmitters broadcast conditions in the upper atmosphere—especially pressure, temperature, and humidity. Satellites provide further information on cloud cover, while thousands of ground-based radar stations give us real-time images of precipitation falling in many regions around the world.

The release of a weather balloon.

Once meteorologists gather all this data, they use it to draw weather maps that represent current conditions visually, making them easier to understand. The National Weather Service prepares weather maps for both the surface and the upper atmosphere several times a day. These charts are among the most important tools used by forecasters when making short-term predictions about the weather. (In meteorology, short-term predictions are those that look twenty-four hours or less into the future.)

During the last quarter century, increases in computer power have enabled meteorologists to create and utilize complex mathematical models of the atmosphere. These models are made up of equations that attempt to describe the behavior of the atmosphere under varying conditions. Computers solve these equations using millions of global data points, producing reports known as prognostics (or simply progs).

Meteorologists use these progs in combination with maps of existing weather to forecast conditions up to ten days in the future. Forecasting, however, remains something of an art, because the maps have to be interpreted and the output of the computer models has to be adjusted to reflect local conditions. Over time, as meteorologists compare model predictions with actual results, they become familiar with the model's limitations and learn to compensate for them. For instance, a meteorologist may notice that when the chance of rain is 30 percent or greater, the temperature projected by the prog is usually one degree too high. In these cases, the forecaster will adjust the prog by subtracting a degree.

Instruments all over the world *continuously collect millions of data points that are fed into computer models and made into maps, which forecasters use to predict the weather.*

XV. THE THIRTY YEARS' WAR

THE PRECARIOUS CALM imposed on Germany by the Peace of Augsburg finally fell apart during the early seventeenth century. The religious composition of the Holy Roman Empire had changed a lot since 1555, with Calvinism—a faith not provided for in the Peace of Augsburg—gaining large followings in the Rhineland, Bohemia, and the Palatinate. Meanwhile, Jesuits pressed the Counter-Reformation.

Just as these religious shifts were becoming militarized, a political struggle broke out between the Holy Roman emperor, who wanted much greater control, and understandably resistant princes. The incident that ultimately triggered the Thirty Years' War occurred in Bohemia, where the Hapsburg heir Ferdinand was elected king in 1617. Ferdinand's devotion to Catholicism and absolutist ways soon outraged the largely Calvinist Bohemian nobility, who showed their displeasure in May 1618 by throwing two royal officials out of a castle window in Prague (the Defenestration of Prague). A full-scale revolt followed, with the Bohemians choosing as their new king Frederick V, elector of the Palatinate. In November 1620, the Hapsburgs won a great victory at White Mountain, crushing the Bohemian rebellion and taking control of the Palatinate as well.

A 1618 woodcut of the Defenestration of Prague.

Even though the Hapsburg victory was complete, the war in Bohemia presented an opportunity for other nations to settle old scores and gain new territories. The Danish king Christian IV joined the fight against the renascent Hapsburgs, but his armies proved no match for the forces of Bohemian general Albrecht von Wallenstein, the supreme commander of the armies of the restored King Ferdinand (now also Holy Roman Emperor Ferdinand II). At the nadir of the Protestants' fortunes, the Swedish king Gustavus Adolphus invaded Germany. Turning back the Hapsburgs, the Swedes won a major victory at Breitenfeld in 1631.

The final phase of the Thirty Years' War, which had nothing to do with religion, began in 1635, when Catholic France and the Calvinist Netherlands formed a military alliance designed simply to weaken the Hapsburgs further. This phase ended in 1648 with the Peace of Westphalia, which marked a significant turning point in European history. The peace concluded more than a century of religious warfare in Europe and left the continent a patchwork of various religious allegiances. Southern Europe remained generally Catholic, and northern Europe remained generally Protestant, but the Hapsburgs entered into a long period of decline, while France emerged as the new continental power.

The Thirty Years' War *brought an end to the religious wars of the Reformation and made permanent the fragmentation of western Christendom into territorial churches.*

XV. INTERSEX STUDIES

SINCE THE MID-1990S, when the field of intersex studies emerged, feminists have approached the topic with both curiosity and fervor. In the feminist lexicon, *intersex* refers to people born with male and female sex characteristics, as well as to those whose secondary sex characteristics are inconsistent with their genital configuration. (The majority of people who identify themselves in this way prefer the term *intersex* to the medical diagnosis *hermaphrodite*.)

In her influential 1998 book *Lessons from the Intersexed*, Suzanne Kessler wrote about the surgical operations performed on intersex people in order to create new genital configurations or secondary sex characteristics that can be easily identified as male or female. As Kessler pointed out, no medical reason impels these operations. Rather, parents are typically told that their intersex children require the surgeries in order to avoid lifetimes of ridicule and rejection. As a result, most of these parents agree to cosmetic surgeries that reconfigure their children's genitalia during the first few weeks of life.

The number of children who undergo these operations—even the number of children born with an intersex diagnosis—is difficult to determine because of the secrecy that surrounds the topic (a by-product of parental embarrassment). No statistics are kept—but even if they were, researchers in the field still haven't agreed on a consensus definition of intersex. Some consider an enlarged clitoris, or micropenis, an intersex trait; others use different criteria. As a result, estimates of the intersex birth rate range from one in every five hundred people to one in every two thousand.

Like scholars of feminist disability studies, those who practice intersex studies are interested in both how social norms are determined and how these norms affect people whom society deems aberrant. Although some of these scholars have produced astute work on the relationship between sex and gender, many have been criticized recently by intersex activists for being drawn to the field by intellectual curiosity rather than by a genuine concern for the well-being of intersex people. Not coincidentally, this criticism has taken place during a significant upsurge in intersex activism led by the Intersex Society of North America (ISNA). Pursuing its mission to reverse the shame and secrecy that surrounds intersex operations, ISNA has brought together a coalition of scholars, medical professionals, and intersex adults to put an end to these surgeries, or at least delay them until the intersex person is old enough to provide informed consent.

Scholars of intersex studies *examine the ways in which sexual categories—and not merely gender expectations—are socially and medically constructed.*

XV. NATO AND THE WARSAW PACT

ACCORDING TO KENNAN'S THEORY of containment, to which Truman and Marshall subscribed, militarization of the Cold War was both unwise and unnecessary. The Soviets weren't likely to deploy armed force beyond their Eastern European security corridor, and economic and political counterpressure should be enough to meet all other forms of expansionism. If the United States took part in the creation of military alliances, Kennan believed, they would only provoke the Soviet Union to do the same.

Although America's European allies understood this reasoning, they were still nervous. After World War II, they had quickly demobilized, but the Soviet Union still retained both a massive army and an extensive military infrastructure. Seeking safety in numbers, Britain, France, and the Benelux countries (Belgium, the

Netherlands, and Luxembourg) signed in March 1948 the Treaty of Brussels—which provided for, among other things, their mutual defense. But this alliance had no hope of standing up to the Soviet Goliath without the help of the United States.

The blockade of Berlin, which began just three month later, underlined this point, and so negotiations began with Washington concerning a formal, permanent military alliance between the United States and its European allies. The result was the North

Truman displays the North Atlantic Treaty.

Atlantic Treaty, signed in April 1949, which established the North Atlantic Treaty Organization (NATO). In addition to the US and the five Treaty of Brussels states, the founding members of NATO included Canada, Italy, Denmark, Norway, Iceland, and Portugal. The last three nations, all proposed by the United States, were initially resisted by the other European members on the grounds that they were too geographically, politically, and culturally disparate. The same reasoning was later applied to Greece and Turkey, although both were offered membership in 1952.

The addition of West Germany was difficult for other reasons. While NATO couldn't possibly field enough conventional forces to resist a Soviet invasion without German manpower, the idea of a military alliance with the chief belligerent of World War II was distasteful to some countries, and all knew that the Soviets would react negatively. In fact, five days after West Germany's formal admission to NATO on May 9, 1955, the Soviets responded with the creation of a rival military alliance— the Warsaw Treaty Organization, or Warsaw Pact—composed of the USSR and its client states in Eastern Europe (East Germany, Poland, Hungary, Czechoslovakia, Romania, Bulgaria, and Albania).

NATO was founded *at the request of America's European allies to act as a bulwark against Soviet expansionism. The USSR responded by establishing the Warsaw Pact.*

XV. THE VALUE OF COMMITMENT

LET'S NOW COMPARE the simultaneous- and sequential-move versions of the film-release game. Our analysis of the simultaneous-move version predicted a July 4 release for Behemoth and a Memorial Day release for Upstart. However, our analysis of the sequential-move version predicted exactly the opposite. Furthermore, if we look at the payoffs, we see that Behemoth can expect to earn more from the sequential-move game than from the simultaneous-move game (100 million dollars compared with 80 million dollars), while Upstart can expect to earn less (20 million dollars compared with 40 million dollars).

This may seem surprising at first. Shouldn't Upstart benefit in the sequential-move game from already knowing Behemoth's play? If so, why does Upstart earn less money than in the simultaneous-move game? The answer is that, in sequential-move games, the real benefit comes from having the ability to commit.

Our analysis of the simultaneous-move game showed that Behemoth's best response is always a July 4 release. Therefore, releasing on July 4 is a dominant strategy for Behemoth, leaving Upstart with no reason to expect a Memorial Day release. In the sequential-move game, however, Behemoth's decision to release on Memorial Day is a fait accompli. Once Behemoth makes this play, Upstart can no longer anticipate a July 4 release and must instead respond to the Memorial Day choice. Therefore, Behemoth's ability to commit influences the way Upstart plays the game. In other words, Behemoth makes itself better off by truncating Upstart's choices.

Although Upstart maintains more freedom of action in the sequential-move game, Behemoth takes advantage by anticipating the effect this freedom will have on Upstart decision making. Recognizing that Upstart wants to avoid releasing its film on the same day that Behemoth releases, Behemoth sees that it can earn more money releasing on Memorial Day and thus forcing Upstart into a July 4 release.

This example illustrates the general principle that having the ability to commit is always a good thing. Commitment (meaning the reduction of one's strategic flexibility) can only increase a player's payoff. The proof is that the first player in a sequential-move game can always choose to play the game as though it were a simultaneous-move game (by delaying his move). If the first player chooses to play sequentially, it must be because he expects a better payoff. Therefore, having the option to commit can only be an advantage.

In sequential-move games, *the true benefit comes not from freedom of action but from having the ability to commit.*

XV. CLIMATE

CLIMATE DESCRIBES THE OVERALL weather conditions that occur in a particular area, or globally, over a long period of time. The most important climatic variables are temperature and precipitation. The world's climate is constantly changing, sometimes because of natural factors and sometimes because of human activity. By studying how climate changes over time, we can better predict future climates and perhaps prevent unwelcome changes, or at least prepare for them.

The global climate during the twentieth century can easily be reconstructed from the detailed weather records that were kept. Before the twentieth century, however, very little weather data was collected or recorded, so scientists attempting to reconstruct past climates must make do with other, less direct records—such as polar ice, ocean sediments, tree rings, and plant and animal fossils. For example, scientists analyze the bubbles of air trapped in polar ice cores to determine the composition of the atmosphere at various times in the past. (The deeper the core, the older the ice.) Because carbon dioxide and methane are known to affect temperature, studying how the atmospheric concentration of these gases has changed over time can help us understand how the earth's temperature has changed.

The analysis of ocean sediments can also help scientists reconstruct global temperatures during the distant past. This sediment contains a great deal of calcium carbonate ($CaCO_3$) created by ancient sea organisms for use in their shells. In order to create this calcium carbonate, the organisms had to extract oxygen from the seawater. Most of the oxygen extracted was oxygen-16, but some was the less common isotope oxygen-18. (Isotopes are atoms of the same element with different numbers of neutrons and thus different atomic weights.)

Because oxygen-18 atoms are heavier than oxygen-16 atoms, they don't evaporate as easily when temperatures are cool. Therefore, the ratio of O-18 to O-16 in seawater will be higher when the earth's temperature is cool. Consequently, more O-18 will be ingested by sea organisms to make calcium carbonate. Analyzing the decomposed shells found in different layers of sediment (the deeper, the older) allows scientists to create a time line of climate change.

Although tree rings only date back a few thousand years, they are excellent indicators of drought. In general, the smaller the width of the tree ring, the drier the year in which it was formed. Tree rings are not very accurate indicators of temperature, however.

Meteorologists study climate, *the overall weather conditions that occur during a particular period of time, in order to predict future climates and prevent unwelcome changes.*

XVI. ABSOLUTISM

THE PROTESTANT REFORMATION and Catholic Counter-Reformation contributed in significant ways to the growth of monarchical power in seventeenth-century Europe. In France, in the Netherlands, and in England, fractious nobles had instigated highly destructive civil wars. Widespread awareness of this fact gave monarchs the public support they needed to limit aristocratic power.

Political theorists such as Thomas Hobbes of England provided the ideological basis for absolutism, arguing that absolute royal authority was preferable to the anarchy that would otherwise prevail. Other theorists, notably Jacques-Bénigne Bossuet of France, revived the notion that kings ruled by divine right and thus needn't look to aristocrats for their legitimacy.

During the seventeenth century, absolutist states emerged in France, Austria, Prussia, and Russia. (England and the Netherlands were two notable exceptions.) In these nations, neither political parties nor representative institutions diluted royal sovereignty. Nevertheless, one shouldn't conflate seventeenth-century absolutism with twentieth-century totalitarianism. While absolutists ruled without opposition, their power was still limited in fundamental ways by the laws of the realm. Totalitarian dictators, on the other hand, sought to control all aspects of society and used law merely as a tool of the state.

Echoing the Peace of Augsburg, the Peace of Westphalia affirmed the right of rulers to determine the religious affiliation of their realms. Using this leverage, most monarchs quickly gained control over important clerical appointments—demanding from those prelates they elevated internal stability and political loyalty. In return, the nationalized churches enjoyed a monopoly on religious observance that either outlawed or marginalized other denominations.

Absolutist governments were typically staffed by commoners, rather than by aristocrats, to keep power out of the hands of the nobility. Likewise, professional armies were created so that kings wouldn't have to rely on troops raised by nobles and thus loyal to them.

Ultimately, most nobles became willing participants in the absolutist regimes. Few were willing to confront their newly empowered monarchs, and many more were enticed by the privileges and shared spoils the kings offered. As a result, absolutism dominated European politics until the French Revolution.

Absolutism flourished in Europe *during the seventeenth and eighteenth centuries because of the close collaboration that existed between states and their territorial churches.*

The absolutist king Louis XIV of France.

XVI. MEN'S STUDIES

ACCORDING TO TRADITIONAL interpretations of the Bible, God created woman from man (specifically, from Adam's rib). Within the academy, however, men's studies came forth from women's studies, emerging as an independent field of analysis during the late 1980s. Unlike the field of women's studies, which seeks to secure equal rights for women, men's studies has no political agenda of its own. Rather, its goal is to situate the experiences of men within a theoretical framework that is fundamentally feminist, especially in its interpretation of gender as a social construct. Scholars active in men's studies explore, for example, the ways in which male privilege manifests in various societies and how gender expectations adversely affect young boys (as they do young girls).

An important early work in the field of men's studies was *Men's Lives* (1989), a collection of essays on various aspects of masculinity edited by Michael S. Kimmel and Michael A. Messner. Among the topics addressed in *Men's Lives* are stereotypes that depict men either as aggressive or unemotional. Using feminist methods of analysis, scholars of men's studies have shown that these stereotypes don't reflect biological predispositions to violence or disengagement but rather are stand-ins for gender expectations that can prevent men from becoming sympathetic and loving partners and fathers.

Other topics of interest to practitioners of men's studies include the violent rituals that college fraternities use to haze pledges and the slurs—for example, *fag* and *sissy*—that men direct at other men who show emotion. Nevertheless, scholars of men's studies don't focus exclusively on the ways in which gender expectations cause men to suffer. They also explore the ways in which patriarchal society privileges men. (In men's studies, the term *male privilege* refers to the benefits, resources, and opportunities that society grants men merely because they are male.)

Like other subsets of feminist inquiry, men's studies also investigates the intersectionality of gender with other factors, including race and nationhood. In the United States, for example, the great disparity in incarceration rates between white men and black men demonstrates that a man's race has a direct bearing on the male privilege that he receives.

Men's studies shouldn't be confused with the conservative, antifeminist "men's rights" movement, which seeks to resurrect traditional gender roles. To the contrary, men's studies seeks to illuminate the ways in which men and boys suffer from gender expectations, with the ultimate goal of redefining men's nurturing side as their "natural" state.

The field of men's studies, *which developed out of women's studies, uses a feminist theoretical framework to analyze men's experiences, masculine stereotypes, and also male privilege.*

XVI. THE HISS CASE

ON AUGUST 3, 1948, just over a month into the Berlin airlift, *Time* magazine senior editor Whittaker Chambers was called to testify before the House Un-American Activities Committee (HUAC). Sitting in a nearly empty hearing room, the untidy, rather uneasy Chambers told the congressmen that he had once been part of a secret Communist cell in Washington, DC. According to Chambers, another member of the cell had been Alger Hiss, a former State Department official who had accompanied FDR to Yalta and later presided over the creation of the United Nations. On August 5, a poised and elegant Hiss appeared before the committee. Compared with the edgy

Whittaker Chambers testifies before HUAC on August 25, 1948.

Chambers, Hiss was cool and relaxed, and he denied everything. Clearly, one of them was lying. On the surface, it seemed to be Chambers, so the committee backed off Hiss. But then one of its members, freshman Republican Richard M. Nixon, questioned Chambers again privately and decided that he was telling the truth.

Another hearing was held on August 25. By this time, the public's interest had been piqued, and the hearing was televised live (a congressional first). Under intense questioning, especially from Nixon, Hiss lost his cool, and some parts of his story began to unravel. Even so, the uncorroborated case against him would likely have gone away had he not tried to save face by suing Chambers for slander. To defend himself, Chambers produced State Department documents from 1937 and 1938 written in Hiss's hand and typed on his personal typewriter. If genuine, as they appeared to be, these documents were proof that Hiss had committed espionage.

Although the statute of limitations on espionage had run out, Hiss could still be charged with perjury, and he was on December 15. His first trial ended in a hung jury, but his second resulted in a conviction and a sentence of five years, of which Hiss served forty-four months.

Whether Hiss was guilty or not—and the issue is still debated—what made his case so important was its psychological impact. Between 1941 and 1945, Americans had been told repeatedly that the Russians were their friends; now, they were being told, and could see for themselves, that this wasn't so. Understandably, people felt anxious, and the Hiss case became a prominent focus for their anxiety. If such an important man as Hiss had been a Soviet spy, what did that imply about what had been done and who could be trusted?

The Hiss case became a focus for American anxiety *about the secret role that Communists might be playing in the nation's public life.*

XVI. COMMITMENT TACTICS

WE HAVE SEEN that the timing of moves—whether they are simultaneous or sequential—can have a dramatic effect on a game's predicted outcome. In the real world, however, there is an additional wrinkle. Unlike parlor games, whose rules typically specify the timing of moves, real-world situations rarely have so fixed a structure. In fact, strategizing the timing of moves is often an important part of the game itself.

In analyzing the sequential-move version of the film-release game, we made two key assumptions: First, that Behemoth's move was *visible* to Upstart. In other words, Upstart would know Behemoth's move before making its own, and Behemoth could rely on this knowledge. Second, we assumed that Behemoth's move was *irrevocable*. In other words, Upstart could rely on Behemoth's inability to change the selected release date.

It follows that, in order to avail himself of the benefits of commitment, a player needs to take actions that are both visible and irrevocable. Using the film-release model, Behemoth would have to announce its decision to release on Memorial Day in such a way that Upstart learned of the decision and also believed that Behemoth wouldn't subsequently postpone until July 4. A simple press release wouldn't suffice, because another could easily be issued later. Behemoth would have to make changing its mind much more costly in order to persuade Upstart of its credibility.

One way to do so would be for Behemoth to sign a contract with a chain of movie theaters guaranteeing a Memorial Day release. If such a contract included steep penalties for Behemoth's failure to deliver, Upstart would likely be convinced that the Memorial Day release was, for the purposes of our analysis, irrevocable.

A second approach might be for Behemoth to put its reputation at risk. As the leading studio in the family-film market, Behemoth no doubt cherishes its excellent reputation among parents and kids. If it were to undertake a large advertising campaign trumpeting a Memorial Day release, it would incur high expectations among its clientele. A subsequent postponement would no doubt result in a costly backlash, decreasing both ticket sales and the value of the film's merchandising licenses. The high probability of such a consequence would likely be enough to persuade Upstart that Behemoth was indeed irrevocably committed to a Memorial Day release.

In real-world situations, *in order to obtain the benefits of commitment, one must take actions that are both visible to the other players and also believably irrevocable.*

XVI. CLIMATE CHANGE

DURING THE EARTH'S EARLY HISTORY, when the sun was much weaker than it is today, the planet's atmosphere contained vast amounts of carbon dioxide. This carbon dioxide acted as a blanket, trapping the LW radiation being emitted by the earth and redirecting it back toward the surface. Over the next several billion years, however, as the sun strengthened, much of the carbon dioxide in the atmosphere became incorporated into the planet's rocks and oceans, substantially reducing this blanketing effect and preventing the earth from overheating.

During the past several million years, the amount of carbon dioxide in the atmosphere has followed a predictable cycle, falling to about 0.0001 percent of the total amount of gas in the (dry) atmosphere during ice ages and rising to as much as 0.00028 percent during interglacial periods. Recently, however, the amount of carbon dioxide in the atmosphere has risen to a level not seen in many millions of years. Even more dramatic is the rate at which this level is increasing. Whereas it used to take a hundred thousand years for the concentration of carbon dioxide in the atmosphere to double, that same doubling will now take place in just one century if current trends continue.

The increased presence of carbon dioxide in the atmosphere is a direct result of the consumption of fossil fuels and, to a lesser degree, deforestation. When fossil fuels such as oil, coal, and natural gas are burned, the carbon dioxide trapped within them (as a result of photosynthesis) is released. Locked inside minerals, the carbon dioxide has no effect on climate; but floating in the air, it warms the planet as it did during the earth's infancy.

Since 1900, when fossil fuel use began to expand exponentially, the overall temperature of the earth has risen by nearly two degrees Fahrenheit. By 2100, given all the carbon dioxide that continues to pour into the atmosphere, the planet's temperatures may rise another ten degrees.

Some of this change can be attributed to feedbacks in the climate system. For example, as the earth's temperature warms, polar ice and snow begin to melt, changing the surface albedo. Currently, bright white snow and ice reflect sunlight away from the earth's surface, preventing the absorption of SW radiation. As the snow and ice melt, however, exposing darker soil underneath, much more of the sun's energy will be absorbed by the earth, further warming the planet.

During the last century, *expanding fossil fuel consumption has released large amounts of carbon dioxide into the atmosphere, possibly accelerating climate change well beyond its normal cycle.*

XVII. THE RISE OF SCIENCE

DURING THE MIDDLE AGES, the closest any European university came to teaching science was instruction in an area of Christian theology known as natural philosophy. The origins of this discipline can be traced back to St. Thomas Aquinas (1225–74), who fused Aristotelian thought with Catholic theology to create an understanding of the natural world as fixed and unchanging (because God had made it that way). Challenges to this doctrine, known as essentialism, were considered heretical.

The Renaissance spirit of inquiry, however, led some intellectuals to consider other explanations. The first important conflict arose in the field of astronomy. The sun, acording to Catholic doctrine, revolved around the earth (an astronomical model known as geocentrism). But Polish astronomer Nicolaus Copernicus (1473–1543) recognized that geocentrism couldn't explain the empirical data he was collecting. Instead, Copernicus quietly proposed an alternative theory, heliocentrism (the idea that the earth revolves around the sun). Fearing repercussions, however, he withheld his findings and published them only posthumously.

The brilliant but contentious Florentine polymath Galileo Galilei (1564–1642) had no such qualms. Galileo rejected the Catholic view that a scientific theory need only be consistent with church doctrine to be correct and instead argued that theories should be accepted as true only if they are supported by experimental or observational data. Unwilling to suppress the evidence he had gathered for heliocentrism, Galileo was put on trial before the Roman Inquisition in 1633. Found guilty, he was forced to recant and placed under house arrest for the remainder of his life.

While Galileo certainly suffered a personal defeat, the Scientific Revolution continued apace. In England, Francis Bacon (1561–1626) championed the empirical method of gathering data to develop and prove general hypotheses. Medieval

Francis Bacon

scholars, following Aquinas, had used church-approved axioms and logical reasoning to arrive at deduced interpretations of nature. Bacon argued that this method was backward. Instead, scholars should used inductive reasoning to move from facts to general laws that describe the ways in which natural phenomena occur and the causes from which they proceed.

Somewhat later in France, René Descartes (1596–1650) established a firm philosophical basis for the autonomy of science—arguing that, while revelation ruled the spiritual world, rationality governed the natural.

The Reformation transformed European intellectual life *by challenging the church's hold on scholarship and making possible the emergence of scientific thinking.*

XVII. QUEER THEORY

WHEN QUEER THEORY FIRST EMERGED out of women's studies during the late 1980s and early 1990s, its purpose was to investigate and explain the ways in which society normalizes certain sexual identities and behaviors while labeling others as deviant. The early queer theorists sought to deconstruct and destabilize these categories, paying particular attention to the concepts "normal" and "natural."

Although queer theory has been used most often to examine the ways in which society stigmatizes same-sex desire and relationships, the discipline itself doesn't confine its analyses to the study of homosexuality. Rather, the *queer* in queer theory has a double meaning, referring both to the derogatory slang term for gays and to the quality of being odd. Thus, queer theory encompasses not merely homosexual behaviors but all sexual practices and identities that deviate from social norms.

Most scholars trace the origins of queer theory back to two influential feminist texts: Eve Kosofsky Sedgwick's *Epistemology of the Closet* (1990) and Judith Butler's *Gender Trouble: Feminism and the Subversion of Identity* (1990). In both, the authors draw on the work of French philosopher Michel Foucault to illustrate the ways in which social institutions make distinctions among different sexualities, categorizing some as acceptable and others as unacceptable.

The critique of sexuality launched by queer theory follows directly from the basic feminist critique of gender. Specifically, queer theorists have taken the idea that gender expectations are arbitrary and used it to show that sexual categories are no more natural. In fact, according to queer theory, sexual categories are produced by the same social and institutional powers (called disciplinary powers by Foucault) that regulate gender expectations. Although the roots of queer theory are thus firmly grounded in feminism, the discipline stands apart because its rejection of a stable difference between male and female undermines by implication, some would argue, the legitimacy of feminist theory.

Queer theory acknowledges that many human beings identify themselves as women, but it nevertheless seeks to uproot the naturalness of this category. Consequently, feminists who take queer theory seriously have been forced to grapple with the idea that the category of woman, upon which all of feminism depends, may actually be a product of the same hidden disciplinary powers that determine what is heterosexual and what is homosexual, what is masculine and what is feminine, and what is normal and what is aberrant.

Queer theory applies feminist ideas *about gender to its own critique of sexual categories.*

XVII. MCCARTHYISM

McCarthy (center) with aides in 1954.

NIXON, A CALIFORNIAN, BECAME SO FAMOUS during the Hiss case that in 1950 he was able to secure a Senate nomination after just three years in the House. His opponent in that campaign was Helen Gahagan Douglas, a Democratic congresswoman whom Nixon dubbed the Pink Lady in order to call attention to her alleged "softness" on Communism—a condition from which, according to Nixon, the entire Truman administration suffered. One of Nixon's most effective tactics that year was the distribution of "pink sheets" comparing Douglas's liberal voting record with the published platform of the American Communist party. (It was during this campaign that Democrats began calling Nixon Tricky Dick.)

Once elected to the Senate, Nixon joined the Permanent Investigations Subcommittee chaired by Sen. Joseph R. McCarthy of Wisconsin, who was also making a name for himself as an aggressive anticommunist. On the night of February 9, 1950, less than three weeks after Hiss's perjury conviction, McCarthy, then an obscure Republican elected largely on the basis of a self-inflated war record, had delivered a Lincoln Day speech to the Republican Women's Club of Wheeling, West Virginia. Eager for a way to rouse the lackluster crowd he was addressing that evening, McCarthy held up a sheet of paper (no one has ever determined what was written on it) and declared, "I have here in my hand a list of 205—a list of names that were made known to the Secretary of State as being members of the Communist party and who nevertheless are still working and shaping policy in the State Department."

Much to McCarthy's surprise, this unsupported but incendiary charge ended his obscurity overnight and launched a wave of anticommunist hysteria that dominated domestic politics for the next decade. The period was later named for McCarthy because it was characterized by the frequent use of misrepresentation and innuendo in which he specialized.

It didn't matter that McCarthy never produced any list of names—the number of which kept changing, as though he couldn't keep his accusations straight. It didn't matter that during four years of investigations he never documented a single case of disloyalty. The fears of Communist infiltration that the Hiss case had aroused, combined with the August 1949 explosion of a Soviet atomic bomb and the victory of Mao's Communists in China month later, ensured McCarthy a wide and compliant audience.

The charges that McCarthy made *about Communist infiltration of the State Department began a destructive crusade that manipulated domestic fears for political gain.*

XVII. PERFECT AND INCOMPLETE INFORMATION

SO FAR, we've analyzed games in which the players have perfect information—that is, each knows all of the relevant information at the time he makes his move. Rarely, however, do people in the real world have perfect information. More commonly, they have only some of the relevant information.

Here is a stylized example of such a situation: Suppose Bob has a used car that Alice wants to buy. Both Bob and Alice know the car is worth 50 percent more to Alice than to Bob. However, only Bob can assign a dollar value to the car because only he, and not Alice, drives and maintains it. All Alice knows is that the value of the car to Bob is less than $10,000. Alice is going to make a take-it-or-leave-it offer. What should this offer be?

A first guess might be $5,000, or the average of the possible values of the car to Bob. But consider how Bob will react to such an offer. He will only accept the offer if the car's value to him is $5,000 or less. If Bob accepts the offer, then Alice will know that the value of the car to her is somewhere between $0 and $7,500 (because the car is worth 50 percent more to Alice than to Bob). In other words, the expected value of the car to Alice, if Bob accepts the offer, is $3,750 (the average of the $0–7,500 range), or $1,250 less than Alice has offered to pay for it!

The same logic holds for any other offer Alice might make. No matter what her offer is, if Bob agrees to it, then it's a bad deal for Alice. The key is that Bob will accept only those offers that at least match the value of the car to him. Given the parameters of this game, the only offer that Alice can make whose average outcome isn't a loss for her is $0. In other words, she should walk away from the negotiation.

Notice the effect that incomplete information has in this game. Because Alice values the car significantly more than Bob does, they should be able to make a mutually satisfactory deal. But they never reach such a deal, because Alice has almost no idea of the car's dollar value. Economists in the field of mechanism design study problems like this and work out ways to mitigate the effects of incomplete information.

A player with perfect information *possesses all relevant information at the time of his move. One can often make up for a lack of information by considering how an opponent will react.*

XVII. OZONE DEPLETION

OZONE IS A NATURALLY OCCURRING form of molecular oxygen with three atoms (O_3) instead of the usual two (O_2). Most of the ozone in the atmosphere is concentrated in the stratosphere at an altitude of about twenty kilometers. Ozone is important to life on earth because it absorbs harmful ultraviolet (UV) radiation that can damage the DNA of living things and cause deadly cancers. In fact, without the ozone layer, most life on earth would not be able to survive.

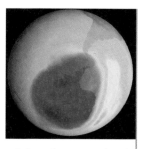

An image from a space-based spectrometer of the thinning in the ozone layer over Antarctica.

Ozone forms when UV radiation (or sometimes lightning) splits an O_2 molecule into single oxygen atoms. Sometimes these highly reactive atoms collide with one another to re-form O_2, but sometime they collide with O_2 molecules to form ozone.

The opposite reaction takes place when an ozone molecule absorbs enough UV radiation to split apart again into a single oxygen atom and an O_2 molecule. As a by-product of this reaction, heat is released. Thus, the ozone–oxygen cycle both produces and dissipates ozone while converting UV radiation into heat that warms the upper atmosphere. (This is why the temperature in the stratosphere rises with altitude.)

Chlorofluorocarbons (CFCs) are a class of chemical compounds used in many industries. At atmospheric temperatures, CFCs are gaseous, and they collect in the stratosphere, where they interrupt the normal functioning of the ozone–oxygen cycle. This happens because sunlight causes a chemical reaction in which the chlorine is separated from the rest of the CFC molecule, generating a stream of chlorine atoms (Cl) that react with ozone to form diatomic oxygen (O_2) and chlorine monoxide (ClO). The chlorine monoxide then reacts with a free oxygen atom to release the chlorine atom and form more diatomic oxygen. These paired reactions deplete the ozone layer, because they use up two free oxygen atoms without creating any new ozone. Meanwhile, the chlorine atom goes on to convert more ozone.

Since 1987, more than two hundred countries have signed the Montreal Protocol, an international treaty designed to protect the ozone layer by phasing out CFCs. The thinning of the ozone layer that has already occurred remains significant, especially over the South Pole; but the level of ozone-depleting gases has already dropped, and computer models predict that the percentage of ozone in the atmosphere will return to 1980 levels by 2050. Until then, extra protection from the sun's UV rays is warranted—especially for people in areas close to the South Pole, such as Australia.

The ozone layer, *which protects life on earth from dangerous UV radiation, has been depleted by chemical reactions caused by the release of CFCs into the atmosphere.*

XVIII. REFORMATION IN THE WIDER WORLD

DURING THE SIXTEENTH CENTURY, riding the wave of European colonialism, the Protestant and Catholic Reformations flowed out into the wider world. Because Protestant denominations had fewer clergy to spare, only a small number established communities overseas (the Plymouth and Massachusetts Bay Colonies being notable exceptions). The Catholic Church, however, embraced missionary work and carried the evangelism of the Counter-Reformation to Africa, Asia, and the Americas.

The Spanish and Portuguese explorers who sailed across the Atlantic during the late fifteenth century were motivated in part by a strong desire to bring Christianity into new lands. Later, once the Counter-Reformation got under way, Franciscans, Dominicans, and Jesuits began accompanying these voyagers in ever-increasing numbers, often remaining behind to convert the indigenous populations.

Wary of Europeans, most natives greeted Christianity with suspicion. But once missionaries began incorporating elements of local religious cultures into Christian practices, inroads were made. Jesuits, in particular, often fashioned images of saints to resemble local holy figures. Such syncretistic strategies acclimated natives, paving the way for conversion. In the late sixteenth century, Catholic authorities backed away from these "idolatrous" practices. By then, of course, the work was largely done.

The Jesuits were also active in Asia, where in 1549 Francis Xavier introduced Christianity to Japan. The missionary work was slow but steady; and by the end of the sixteenth century, as many as three hundred thousand Japanese had converted to Christianity. During the 1580s, however, a new feudal lord, Hideyoshi Toyotomi, came to power. Strongly xenophobic, he expelled all of the foreign missionaries from Japan. Later shoguns executed all converts, thus eliminating Christianity from Japan until the nineteenth century.

Meanwhile, in China, the Jesuits achieved lesser but more enduring success. The pioneer there was Matteo Ricci (1552–1610), who dressed as a Confucian scholar to promote Christianity as a return to classic Confucianism (as opposed to the prevailing neo-Confucianism, which incorporated many Buddhist concepts). Because of their advanced learning and technical skills, Ricci and his fellow Jesuits were quite popular at court but not so successful in their evangelizing. At the time, China's population exceeded one hundred million people, but most were ethnocentric with little interest in a foreign religion. By the mid-eighteenth century, only two hundred thousand Chinese had converted.

Matteo Ricci as painted by a Chinese convert.

More so than Protestants, *Catholics rode the wave of European expansion to bring Christianity to the wider world.*

XVIII. TRANSFEMINISM

AN OFFSHOOT OF FEMINISM and queer theory, transfeminism focuses on the experiences of transgendered people, or people whose gender identities deviate in some way from the norm. Some transgendered people have genitalia associated with one sex but live as members of the opposite sex. Other transgendered people intend to change or have changed their sexual characteristics through hormone treatments and/or sex-reassignment operations. Still others have lived as more than one sex. What all of these people have in common is a rejection of the sexual and/or gender identity given to them at birth. Thus, like the term *queer*, the designation *trans* refers to any individual who defies normative gender roles and expectations.

In the novels *Stone Butch Blues* (1993) and *Drag King Dreams* (2006) as well as in a collection of essays titled *TransLiberation: Beyond Pink or Blue* (1999), transfeminist author Leslie Feinberg has mixed personal testimony with theoretical sophistication to highlight the difficulties that transgendered individuals face in their everyday lives. Examples of this include finding doctors who won't gawk at their bodies and hoping that employers will accept forthcoming sex-change surgeries.

Politically, transfeminists seek to expand the category of woman to include all such people. This stance has brought them into conflict with more conservative feminists who believe that including transgendered women in the category of woman would allow men to co-opt it.

Their dispute has a long and complicated history. It dates back to the second wave, when most feminists held that transgendered women weren't women but merely men trying to pass themselves off as women. Since then, both Third Wave feminism and queer theory have established that this sort of thinking ignores the basic feminist distinction between sex and gender. In other words, even if the genitalia of a transgendered person is male, she can still have a feminine gender because gender isn't biologically based but socially constructed. Nevertheless, some feminists continue to believe that only those individuals with female genitalia who have lived as women from birth can properly be called women.

While this debate at one time produced some interesting theories concerning the relationship between sexual identity and cultural categories, it has lately receded as scholars of intersex studies have demonstrated that genitalia doesn't always determine experience. For the most part, a fair number of contemporary feminists now accept into the category of woman all individuals who identify themselves as such.

Transfeminism utilizes feminist principles *to expand the category of woman to include all individuals who identify as women regardless of their given sex at birth.*

XVIII. NSC-68

IN PART because of lessons learned during World War II and in part because of the developing Soviet threat, Congress passed the National Security Act of 1947, which reorganized the government's military and foreign policy establishments. The new law streamlined the armed forces by consolidating the War and Navy Departments into a single Department of Defense. It also created the Central Intelligence Agency (CIA) as a successor to the wartime Office of Strategic Services and the National Security Council (NSC) as a focus for national security planning within the executive branch. The statutory members of the NSC included the president, vice president, secretary of state, secretary of defense, director of central intelligence, and several other sub-cabinet officials.

In January 1950, Truman requested that the NSC conduct a comprehensive review of US national security strategy in light of such recent developments as the Soviet bomb and the Communist takeover of China. The result was a fifty-eight-page memorandum designated NSC-68 and delivered on April 7. Authored by the State Department's policy planning staff under the direction of Paul Nitze (who had recently replaced Kennan), this highly influential document laid out in detail the national security strategy that the US would follow for the next twenty years.

Nitze's group began with two premises: first, that the defeat of Germany and Japan and the decline of Britain and France had left the US and the USSR as the only two world powers; second, that the USSR was "animated by a new fanatic faith, antithetical to our own," and sought to "impose its absolute authority over the rest of the world." After considering various possibilities, NSC-68 concluded that the only way to meet the new Soviet threat was with a massive military buildup.

Others, led by Kennan, disagreed. Not even the new Soviet bomb had shaken Kennan's conviction that the threat was primarily political; and he criticized Nitze's assertion that the Soviets were bent on world domination through use of force. The buildup that Nitze was advocating, Kennan warned, would produce not security but a destabilizing arms race.

A B-52 over Korea in 1952.

Kennan appeared to be winning the argument until June 25, when Communist North Korea invaded US-backed South Korea, leading to more Republican charges that Truman was soft on Communism. In response, during the next three years, the Truman administration tripled defense spending as a percentage of gross domestic product, increasing it from 5 percent in 1950 to 14 percent in 1953.

NSC-68, which called for a military *rather than a political response to the Soviet threat, determined US foreign policy for the next twenty years.*

XVIII. THE LESSONS OF GAME THEORY

ALTHOUGH DERIVED FROM the study of specific games, the most important lessons of game theory are general. Economists commonly use simple games (such as Alice and Bob's used-car bargaining game) to model more complex real-world activity. By investigating these simple games, they can gain useful insight into real-world situations.

The used-car bargaining game is, of course, much more restricted than an actual used-car negotiation. However, in analyzing this game, even within its simplified parameters, we found that Alice has an important problem: Her lack of information means that she can never make an offer against which Bob can't press his informational advantage. Economists refer to this process of doing business with people one should avoid as adverse selection.

Adverse selection is particularly relevant in the field of insurance. Sellers of insurance calculate premiums based on the average risk among the insured group. A company selling life insurance, for example, will calculate its premiums based on the life expectancy of the population. Because smokers have a shorter-than-average life expectancy, buying a policy whose premiums are based on average life expectancy is a good deal for them. On the other hand, nonsmokers, who have a longer-than-average life expectancy, may choose not to buy such a policy, because they would be paying a higher rate than their relatively low risk warrants. Recognizing the high number of smokers among its policyholders, the insurance company might want to raise its rates, but this will only drive away more nonsmokers, hence the adverse selection.

The important point is that, although the Alice and Bob bargaining game can't be said to encompass all the haggling that takes place during a real used-car negotiation, our analysis clearly revealed the problem of adverse selection. Thus, we can now see, as a benefit of game theory, that to be successful in real-world bargaining, we need to understand and mitigate the problem of adverse selection.

Game theory, which is as much a way of thinking as it is a set of facts, teaches us how to combine various assumptions—about the motivations of people, the timing of their decisions, and the information they possess—into a unified whole from which general principles can be drawn. These principles are then widely applied in economics, in the social sciences, and even in such fields as computer science and evolutionary biology. Looked at another way, game theory is a practical tool for understanding how people make decisions.

The most important lessons of game theory *are the general principles that can be applied to everyday decision making without the need for detailed game analysis.*

XVIII. RAINBOWS

THE INTERACTION OF SUNLIGHT with the atmosphere produces many fabulous optical phenomena. These include halos, coronas, sun dogs, and mirages, but the best known are rainbows. Although sunlight appears white, it's actually composed of many different colors in a continuous spectrum, each color corresponding to a different wavelength. Like all light, it can be reflected and refracted.

Refraction is the bending that takes place when light passes from one medium (such as air) into another medium (such as water). This bending is caused by the different speeds at which light travels through unequally dense media. A common demonstration of refraction is the placement of a straw in a glass of water. The water, which has a different refractive index than the surrounding air, bends the light illuminating the straw so that the straw appears broken or misaligned in the glass.

Reflection occurs at the boundary between two media when a light ray, instead of entering the new medium, changes direction and returns to the original medium. The angle at which the light ray strikes the new medium, measured from a line drawn perpendicular to the new medium (the normal), is called the angle of incidence. The angle at which it returns to the original

This diagram illustrates how refraction and reflection create rainbows.

medium, also measure from the normal, is called the angle of reflection. According to the law of reflection, the angle of incidence and the angle of reflection are always equal. A smooth surface, such as a mirror, will reflect all of the different colors of light in the same direction.

Rainbows are the combined product of the reflection and refraction that takes place when sunlight passes into a raindrop. The change in medium (from air to water) separates the sun's white light into different colors (because different wavelengths of light undergo different amounts of refraction). Although these colors form a continuous spectrum, they are grouped by convention into just seven shades: red, orange, yellow, green, blue, indigo, and violet.

After being refracted, these different colors of light travel through the raindrop and are reflected off its rear surface (rather than passing through into the air on the other side). This reflected light is then refracted again as it leaves the raindrop, producing a rainbow.

When sunlight enters a raindrop, *it is refracted, reflected, and then refracted again, ultimately producing a rainbow.*

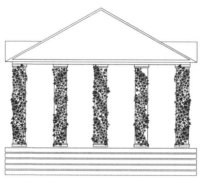

SYLLABUS

IV

I. THE IMPERIAL FORM OF GOVERNMENT

AROUND 221 BCE, after unifying several disparate states, Qin Shi Huangdi established an imperial form of government in China that lasted for nearly two thousand years. It featured a complex, centralized bureaucracy administered by highly educated men. At the top sat the emperor, who derived his legitimacy by claiming the Mandate of Heaven (a principle similar to the European divine right of kings). Although not

Officials of the Qing government.

affiliated with a particular religion, the Chinese emperor ostensibly represented the will of the gods on earth, and thus was considered divinely inspired, though not a god himself.

The Mandate of Heaven notwithstanding, power changed hands often in China over the centuries as the fortunes of ruling families rose and fell. Historians commonly interpret these fluctuations using a paradigm called the dynastic cycle. Typically, dynasties were founded by strong, charismatic military leaders who wrested control of the empire from weak rulers and then passed that control on to their heirs, usually from father to son. Initially, new dynasties tended to rule vigorously, and the empire flourished; but as time passed, dynasties grew weak, ineffective, and corrupt. Ultimately, they were overthrown by new strongmen, who began their own dynasties.

The Qing dynasty came to power in 1644 in just this manner. Not ethnically Chinese, the Qing were Manchu tribesmen who arrived as invaders from the north. Like the Mongols and other "barbarian" conquerors before them, however, the Qing gradually became sinicized and were for the most part assimilated into Chinese society.

Part of this assimilation involved the adoption of Confucianism, the ideology that informed all of China's social and political institutions. Developed in the sixth century BCE by Kong Fuzi (Confucius), Confucianism established precepts for morality and just rule. Yet by the late Qing period, imperial rule in China was hardly just. Much of the civil service had been taken over by career bureaucrats motivated only by self-interest. (Many were eunuchs who had castrated themselves to show their loyalty to the emperor in the hope of winning lifetime appointments.) Even less attuned to the needs of the people was the Empress Dowager, Cixi, who assumed control of the court as regent following the death of her husband (Emperor Xianfeng) in 1861. Once a court concubine, she had clawed her way to the top through guile and murder; and once there, she spent nearly all of her time plotting political intrigues.

The imperial form of government *established by Qin Shi Huangdi served China well for nearly two thousand years, but it was ill suited to the modern world.*

I. THE ORIGIN OF WESTERN PHILOSOPHY

THE GREEK WORD *PHILOSOPHIA* means "love of wisdom." Because one can hardly be wise and yet remain ignorant of the truth, it follows that a person who is wise must possess the truth. Therefore, a philosopher, or lover of wisdom, must be one who seeks the truth.

Such a goal is surely admirable, but how can philosophers—or any other human beings, for that matter—distinguish between truth (what really is the case) and falsehood (what merely *seems* to be the case)? What we need is a method.

In the earliest Greek texts, the epic poems *Iliad* and *Odyssey*, the eighth-century BCE poet Homer appeals to the Muses to communicate the truth to him. Homer expects the Muses to know the truth because their omniscient father, Zeus, chief of the Olympian gods, would have communicated it to them. Homer's knowledge of the truth therefore relies on the method of *revelation*.

With revelation, there is not much room for argument: Either Homer believes the Muses or he doesn't. However, for those of us without a direct connection to the divine, the choice is more complex. We have to decide not only whether the Muses have actually communicated to Homer but also whether Homer has accurately reported what they have said. If we choose to believe in the truth of what Homer has written, then we are said to have *faith* in his work. So now we have two methods for obtaining the truth: revelation and faith.

A medieval depiction of Thales of Miletus.

Early in the sixth century BCE, a Greek named Thales lived in Miletus, a city on the coast of Asia Minor. What made Thales special—and the reason he is considered the father of Western philosophy—is that he developed a third method for accessing the truth: *critical reason*. Thales believed that human beings could discover the truth on their own, using only the evidence of their senses and their capacity to think. We don't know much about Thales because none of his writing survives, but later sources tell us that he predicted eclipses and taught that all things were made of water. This idea may seem silly at first, but it was based on Thales's profound insight that despite the fact that objects in the world—cats and rocks, for example—appear to be very different, they are actually composed of a universal underlying material. Our theory of elements is based on this same idea.

The intellectual activity known as philosophy *began early in the sixth century BCE, when Thales of Miletus developed the method of critical reason for distinguishing truth from falsity.*

I. THE BEGINNINGS OF THE RENAISSANCE

BEFORE THE RENAISSANCE BEGAN, the primary artistic style in Europe was the Byzantine (named for the Byzantine Empire, whose capital was Constantinople). Byzantine artists painted in a flat style that was not nearly as lifelike as the art of ancient Greece and Rome had been. Artists working in the Byzantine style made use of two dimensions only—that is, their paintings lacked perspective—and instead of placing their figures in naturalistic settings, they surrounded them with gold backgrounds that only emphasized their flatness. The artistic period known as the

Giotto, *Scenes from the Life of Christ: Last Supper* (1304–6)

Renaissance began when the Florentine painter Giotto di Bondone (ca. 1267–1337), dissatisfied with the static nature of Byzantine art, decided to depict the world more realistically.

According to sixteenth-century biographer Giorgio Vasari, Giotto "became so good an imitator of nature that he banished completely that rude Greek [i.e., Byzantine] manner and revived the modern and good art of painting, introducing the portraying well from nature of living people, which had not been used for more than two hundred years."

The cycle of religious frescoes that Giotto created for the Scrovegni Chapel in Padua is perhaps his most famous work. In terms of narrative complexity and spatial organization, it wouldn't be surpassed until Michelangelo decorated the Sistine Chapel two centuries later. More than three dozen scenes in three registers (levels) make up the Scrovegni frescoes, one of which depicts the Last Supper.

Because the Last Supper is such a common subject in Renaissance art, it serves as an ideal baseline for assessing the ways in which different artists addressed the same compositional challenges. For example, Giotto's departure from the Byzantine style can immediately be seen in the way he uses light and shadow to make the figures of the apostles appear volumetric—that is, three-dimensional. His faithfulness to nature can also be seen in the hairstyles and facial expressions of the apostles, who are presented as specific individuals rather than as generic types. Giotto's sensitivity even extends to the apostles' robes, which are rendered with convincing drapery folds. Yet for all of Giotto's achievement, several generations would pass before other artists became fully conversant with his methods and goals.

The artistic period known as the Italian Renaissance *can be traced to Giotto's departure from the prevailing Byzantine style and his inclusion of naturalistic detail in his work.*

I. ESSENTIALISM

BEFORE THE 1859 PUBLICATION of Charles Darwin's *On the Origin of Species*, the general scientific consensus was that species are fixed. In other words, groups of related organisms—such as horses, tomatoes, or humans—don't change over time. This idea can be traced all the way back to the fourth century BCE, when the Greek philosopher Plato developed his metaphysical theory of forms (also known as the theory of types). According to Plato, all objects have a perfect representative form (*eidos*), which is eternal, immutable, and exists outside the physical world in which we live. In the separate world of forms, one finds the universal dog, the universal cat, the universal table, and so forth. These universals define the essential nature of physical objects—the dogs, cats, and tables we see every day. The variations that we see among physical objects, such as differences in size and color, are, in Plato's scheme, insignificant. Their form is what matters.

Later, Plato's student Aristotle applied the same sort of universalism to the biological groupings we now call species. Aristotle considered species to be perfect and thus not transmutable. Furthermore, he arranged the known species into a scale, beginning with lesser organisms and ascending ultimately to divine perfection. He called this progression a *scala naturae*, which is usually translated as "chain of being."

From these ancient theories developed the Western tradition of essentialism. Also called typological thinking, essentialism is the view that specific entities are defined by fixed sets of properties that don't change over time and space. Like Plato and Aristotle, essentialists believed that, while there are many different horses in the natural world (some short, some tall; some with thick manes, some with thin manes), there exists only one universal

A medieval Arabic edition of Aristotle's biological work *De historia animalium*.

category "horse"—which serves as a single, representative blueprint for all the different horses and which doesn't change.

Christian essentialists of the Middle Ages, in addition to adopting the idea that species are fixed, also embraced Aristotle's hierarchical *scala naturae*. Not surprisingly, they placed humans near the top of the list—above all other earthly creatures but below heavenly beings such as angels. This typological conception of the natural order of things, reinforced by the biblical narrative of creation found in the book of Genesis, permeated Western culture until the nineteenth century.

Essentialist thought developed from *Plato's theory of forms, which held that objects in the world have an essential nature (or form) that is fixed and immutable.*

I. DEFINING ISRAEL

EVEN THOUGH JEWS represent less than 1 percent of the world's population, the Jewish tradition has been of inestimable significance in the development of Western, and indeed human, civilization. The Jews' greatest contribution is thought to have been

A Jew (or related Semite) of the late fourth century BCE.

their invention of monotheism—the exclusive worship of a single, sovereign God—but this is by no means the only aspect of the tradition of interest to the student of religion.

Who are the Jews, and where did they come from? Any investigation of this question requires that some terms be clarified at the outset. Members of the Jewish community have historically referred to themselves collectively as Israel, a nation with a special relationship to the God of their forefathers; yet the use of the name has changed dramatically over time. Originally, Israel was a tribal confederacy that emerged sometime around the thirteenth century BCE in the northern part of the territory today known both as Israel and as Palestine. Israel was also the name given to the kingdom that arose a few centuries later with its political and cultic center at Jerusalem. Even later, Israel was the name of the northern state that broke away from the control of the dynasty at Jerusalem. (At the time of this division, the southern remnant of the original kingdom took the name Judah, from which we get the appellation *Jew*.) Even more confusingly, Israel is today the name of the Jewish state governing the area once occupied by the ancient Israelite kingdom.

Yet to assert that modern Jews are simply the descendants of the ancient Israelites would be a vast oversimplification, as would the suggestion that the Jewish religion is based solely, or even primarily, on the Hebrew Bible, which dates back to the time of the Israelites and is also known as the Old Testament. Nevertheless, it is generally true that Jews consider themselves to be the heirs of the religious legacy of ancient Israel—especially the covenant between God and Abraham, the Israelite patriarch from whom Jews conventionally trace their ancestry. Likewise, the Hebrew Bible has always been the principal document through which Jews have come to understand their relationship with their God and the origins of their community. Although Jews of the postbiblical period have developed and adopted many important religious practices and institutions totally unrelated to the religion of ancient Israel, the Hebrew Bible remains the ultimate lens through which Jews view their unique heritage, history, and destiny.

Who the Jews are *and what Judaism is can be understood properly only through the story of where the Jews came from.*

II. WESTERN ENCROACHMENT

THE CHINESE HAD LONG CONSIDERED themselves to be at the center of the civilized world. Even when conquered, they were confident that the invaders would eventually adopt Chinese ways and become Chinese themselves. China was also the focus of a complex tributary system that required all kingdoms desiring trade to recognize China's superiority. The Westerners who began arriving during the mid-seventeenth century were treated in much the same way.

The first Westerners to establish a permanent presence in China were the British, who set up a base in the port of Canton (Guangzhou) in 1759. Soon, a good deal of English money (mostly silver coin) began pouring into China to pay for exports of tea, silk, and porcelain. By 1793, the balance of trade had become so unfavorable to the British that a diplomatic mission was sent to the court of the emperor Qianlong to plead for more equitable relations, especially an expansion of Chinese imports. Qianlong refused, declaring that "China possesses all things" and needed nothing from the outside world.

As the Industrial Revolution transformed the nations of the West, China remained tied to a centuries-old worldview that thwarted change. Consequently, the economic and technological disparities between China and Great Britain continued to grow until even the Qing emperors were forced to take notice. Meanwhile, the British discovered a commodity for which they could manufacture enormous demand in China: opium. Once the British introduced opium (cultivated in British India) to the vast Chinese market of several hundred million people, the balance of trade began to shift, and silver began flowing out of the country as quickly as it had previously flowed in.

In 1839, the Qing government sent Lin Zexu to Canton to put a stop to the opium trade. Imprisoning some 350 British traders, Lin held them until they agreed to surrender their opium stocks, which Lin promptly destroyed. The British government responded with a declaration of war. Not surprisingly, China's antiquated fleet proved no match for the Royal Navy, which dominated the trade routes and brought Britain victory in the First Opium War (1839–42). As part of the Treaty of Nanjing (Nanking), China was forced to give up legal jurisdiction over British citizens; control of its own import tariffs; and the island of Hong Kong, which became a British colony.

An eighteenth-century view of the Western settlement at Guangzhou.

Although commerce with the West *initially benefited China, the introduction of opium to the Chinese market quickly reversed the money flow.*

II. PLATO'S DIALOGUES

PLATO (CA. 428–347 BCE) WAS BORN in Athens. Apart from a few years spent traveling, he lived there his entire life. About 385 BCE, he founded an influential school called the Academy, which survived as a place of learning until the sixth century CE. Other than this scanty information, very little is known with certainty about Plato beyond his writings.

Those writings consist of about thirty dialogues ranging in length from just a few pages to a few hundred pages. Some of the dialogues are written, like plays, in direct discourse: A character's name is followed by a colon and then by a speech. Others are presented as narrative descriptions of conversations that the narrator has overheard.

Fragments of a third-century CE manuscript of Plato's *Republic.*

Plato himself never appears as a character in the dialogues, which is puzzling. Certainly, he wasn't trying to hide his identity. Everyone knew that he was the author of the dialogues. Yet he chose instead to focus on a character named Socrates, who appears in all but one of the dialogues. Because Plato knew the historical Socrates (in fact, he was Plato's teacher), readers of the dialogues might reasonably expect the words of this character to be those of the historical Socrates. Yet scholars reject this conclusion. No one believes that the dialogues are transcripts of actual conversations; and though some believe that a few of the dialogues closely mirror the views of the historical Socrates, all scholars believe that the dialogues, in general, represent Plato's views and that he put his own words into the mouths of his characters.

Most of Plato's dialogues have what is known as a "dramatic date"—that is, a more or less specific date on which the action in the dialogue takes place. For example, Plato's *Apology*, which purports to be the defense speech given by Socrates at his trial for impiety, has a dramatic date of 399 BCE (the date of the historical trial). Of course the dramatic date of a dialogue has no relation to its date of composition—that is, the date when Plato actually wrote the dialogue. We don't know very much about dates of composition, but most scholars do agree that during the half century Plato spent writing philosophy, he gradually moved away from the influence of his friend and teacher Socrates. For example, the *Laws*, which Plato wrote at the end of his lifetime, is the only dialogue in which the character Socrates doesn't appear.

In order to express his philosophical views, *Plato composed dialogues in which the main character was often his teacher Socrates.*

II. THE COMPETITION FOR THE BAPTISTERY DOORS

THE BLACK DEATH that swept across Europe during the 1340s hit Florence so hard that decades passed before the city-state recovered. It wasn't until the end of the century, for example, that civic leaders began discussing long-postponed improvements to the city's cathedral, Santa Maria del Fiore. Among the first projects they undertook was the replacement of the old wooden doors to the baptistery. Because the new doors would be made of expensive bronze, the wool merchants' guild, which was underwriting the cost, decided to hold a design competition. In 1401, artists from all over Italy were invited to submit test panels depicting the biblical sacrifice of Isaac. The two finalists, Filippo Brunelleschi (1377–1446) and Lorenzo Ghiberti (ca. 1378–1455), were both young men in their early twenties, and—incredibly—their test panels survive.

The baptistery door panels designed by Brunelleschi (left) and Ghiberti.

From these panels, one can infer the rules of the competition. For instance, both panels include the same seven figures set within a quatrefoil frame: Abraham, Isaac, an angel, two shepherds, an ass, and a ram. A specific moment in the narrative must also have been prescribed: the moment when the angel interrupts the sacrifice. Other similarities more likely reflect prevailing taste—such as the naturalism of the rocky ledges, animals, and windblown drapery, as well as the treatment of the nude Isaac, which in both panels evidences an intense interest in the sculpture of classical antiquity.

Notwithstanding these similarities, the differences between the two panels are striking, reflecting an important divergence in early Renaissance style. While Brunelleschi chose to arrange his figures statically on three horizontal levels, modeling each separately and then pegging it to a neutral ground, Ghiberti fills his frame with both figures and landscape, organizing the composition not horizontally but along the diagonal running from the upper left (where the ram is perched) to the lower right.

In the end, Ghiberti won the competition, not only because of the merit of his design but also because his test panel used considerably less material than Brunelleschi's, suggesting to the wool merchants judging the competition that his doors would be less expensive to produce. Ghiberti eventually created two sets of doors for the baptistery, the second set of which an impressed Michelangelo called "the gates of paradise." Brunelleschi, though he lost the competition, also achieved great fame as one of Italy's most important fifteenth-century architects.

The baptistery doors competition *sponsored by the wool merchants is often cited as the start of the Renaissance because it began a trend toward secular patronage of the arts.*

II. EVOLUTION BEFORE DARWIN

ALTHOUGH IT WAS *ON THE ORIGIN OF SPECIES* that finally overturned essentialism, Darwin was by no means the first to articulate the idea that organisms change over time and that their current form is the result of natural processes. As early as the sixth century BCE, the Greek philosopher Thales of Miletus suggested that living things originated from simple elements, and Thales's student Anaximander later promulgated the idea that humans had evolved from fishlike creatures. Once essentialism became Christian doctrine, however, evolutionary models lost favor.

As late as the eighteenth century, essentialism was little challenged. But with the Enlightenment came a growing interest in scientific discourse and analytical thinking that gradually separated philosophy from theology. In particular, a new generation of European thinkers began challenging the political status quo—pointing out, among other things, the lack of class mobility within European society.

The rigid social structure that prevailed in Europe was, in a way, just another form of essentialism. Like species, social classes were thought to be fixed, immutable categories. Commoners were by their essential nature commoners, just as aristocrats were by their essential nature aristocrats—and these natures didn't change from one generation to the next. Encouraged by Enlightenment thought, however, commoners began to contemplate the possibility of a world in which their class status could evolve; and when the French Revolution proved that such a world was possible, other essentialist doctrines also began to fall.

There was, for instance, new empirical data to support an evolving world. During the early nineteenth century, geologists such as Charles Lyell showed that the earth was much older than previously thought. Furthermore, the fossils then being uncovered contained vast evidence of biological change that couldn't be easily explained. In response, a new scientific movement arose, primarily in France, called environmentalism, whose advocates believed that species indeed change over time as they adapt to changing environments.

The most famous of the environmentalists was Jean-Baptiste Pierre Antoine de Monet, chevalier de Lamarck (1744–1829), who believed in the "transmutation" of species through the inheritance of acquired traits. Lamarck thought, for example, that giraffes originally had short necks. During periods of drought, however, they had to stretch their necks in order to reach hard-to-get food. This stretching lengthened their necks, and the elongation (an acquired characteristic) was then passed down to the giraffes' offspring. Although Lamarck's ideas were widely discussed, they were not taken seriously outside the French environmentalist camp.

The idea that species change over time *predates Darwin's work by more than two millennia.*

II. THE COVENANT WITH ABRAHAM

JUDAISM IS MOST OFTEN ASSOCIATED WITH the principle of radical monotheism: the belief that there is a single transcendent God who created and governs the universe. Yet there is another concept associated with Judaism that predates monotheism and is arguably even more fundamental: the idea of covenant, which is the belief that the deity known by the unpronounceable name YHWH entered into an abiding, eternal compact with the people of Israel, according to which their continuing faith in Him would result in their ultimate redemption.

As it has come to be understood, the covenant between God and Israel appears to presuppose monotheism, but this was not always so. The narratives in the book of Genesis that describe the origins of the covenant—composed well before the creation narrative that now opens the Bible—say nothing one way or the other about the existence of other gods. Nor do they assert that YHWH is the universal creator.

Rather, what they directly claim is a preferential relationship and abiding bond between YHWH and Abraham, the forefather of Israel.

Chapters 12 through 25 of the book of Genesis tell the story of Abraham in a series of vignettes that begin with God's summoning of the patriarch: "Go now from your country and your family and your father's house to the land that I will show you; I will make of you a mighty nation, and bless you, so that you [i.e., your name]

A detail from an Italian Renaissance painting showing Abraham.

should become a blessing." Abraham leaves his home in Ur of the Chaldees, a locality in Mesopotamia (modern-day Iraq), and travels to the Promised Land. Along the way, he learns various details of the covenant, including the stipulation that he and all the men of his household should be circumcised.

Although some aspects of the Abraham story recall the culture of the second millennium BCE (as far as that culture can be reconstructed from the archaeological record), few scholars consider Abraham to have been an actual historical person. Rather, most view him as a symbolic ancestor whose actions provide etiologies for various aspects of Israelite religious and cultural practice. For example, the scholarly consensus is that Israelites of a later period adopted circumcision in order to distinguish themselves from the Canaanites, another tribal nation occupying the Promised Land—suggesting that circumcision may not have been instituted during the putative lifetime of Abraham himself.

The founding principle of the Jewish religion *is the covenant between YHWH and the people of Israel and not necessarily the claim that He is the only God who truly exists.*

III. THE SELF-STRENGTHENING MOVEMENT

CHINA'S DEFEAT in the Second Opium War (1856–60) humiliated the Qing, most of whom now realized that their country would have to modernize or perish. First, however, there needed to be moral renewal. Governmental corruption was endemic, and the new Empress Dowager (who came to power in 1861) was a despot. Thus, leading Qing officials initially set about restoring the country's core Confucian values.

Empress Cixi

As a rationale for keeping themselves in power while these changes were attempted, the Qing court declared (with Cixi's blessing) a "restoration," or period of dynastic renaissance. Named for Cixi's five-year-old son, on whose behalf she ruled as regent, the Tongzhi Restoration lasted until 1875, when Tongzhi died at the age of eighteen.

In order to modernize, the Qing had to import new technology from the West, but they were nonetheless deeply concerned about the threat Western values posed to Chinese society. Therefore, the Tongzhi Restoration's emphasis on native Confucian values was also intended to inoculate the Chinese people against the insidious Christian and democratic ideologies of the West.

There were a few successes. The reformers Zeng Guofan and Li Hongzhang rose to prominence by successfully marrying Eastern philosophy to Western technology. Zeng, a Confucian scholar-official turned general, and his protégé Li employed Western advisers to help them train armies and build arsenals capable of producing modern weaponry. Both became national heroes and leading advocates of the Self-Strengthening Movement, which sought to use Western technology for Chinese ends. "Western technology, Chinese values" was a popular slogan, yet it was difficult to import Western science without being influenced by the worldview that produced it.

The Self-Strengthening Movement was planned and implemented in three stages over fifty years. The first stage focused on national defense. During the second stage, the government attempted to partner with private enterprise to modernize the nation's infrastructure. The third stage emphasized the mass production of export goods. But the program was basically a failure. Although the Qing wanted to modernize, they didn't commit to the program wholeheartedly because they were too fearful of Westernization. Also, corruption remained rampant. Perhaps the most flagrant example of late Qing misconduct was the grand marble pleasure boat built for the Empress Dowager using funds intended for the modernization of the Chinese navy.

The Qing developed *the Self-Strengthening Movement to modernize China while at the same time protecting Chinese society from Western values.*

III. THE HISTORICAL SOCRATES

WHY WOULD PLATO WRITE DIALOGUES instead of expressing his views directly in treatises? Perhaps it was because the historical Socrates (469–399 BCE) engaged Athenians in face-to-face dialogues similar to those that Plato depicts. Although this course focuses on the philosophies of Plato and Aristotle, their ideas can't be explored without first discussing Socrates, who lived in Athens at the height of the Classical age and became one of the most notorious philosophers in Western history.

During the fifth century BCE, Athens was the richest and most powerful city-state in the Mediterranean world. Art, drama, history, medicine, technology, science, philosophy, music—all flourished there. During his lifetime, Socrates witnessed the construction of the Parthenon and the development of democracy. His contemporaries included Sophocles, Euripides, Aristophanes, Thucydides, Pericles, and Hippocrates.

There isn't much we know with certainty about Socrates, in part because he never wrote anything down. In fact, we have only three contemporary sources for information about him: the comic playwright Aristophanes; the historian Xenophon; and, of course, Plato. In 423 BCE, Aristophanes wrote a play, *The Clouds*, in which a character named Socrates founds a school called the "wisdom factory" and talks about the heavens while suspended in a basket. It's difficult to know, however, the extent to which the words and actions of this comic character match those of the historical Socrates. (Imagine trying to learn about a contemporary US president just from his portrayal on *Saturday Night Live*.) The Socrates described by Xenophon, on the other hand, is rather dry and philosophically unsophisticated, while Plato's Socrates is a much more interesting and memorable character. Are any of these characterizations accurate? We can't know for sure.

Nevertheless, most scholars agree that the following is true: Socrates spent his entire life in Athens. He came from a common family and had a wife and children. He served the city bravely in battle on several occasions. He was poor yet became friendly with some of the most powerful aristocrats of his day. He had no known employment, typically went barefoot, and was conventionally unattractive, with eyes that bugged out and a snub nose. One of the many puzzles about Socrates is how such a poor, unattractive man, who never held public office, could become such an influential and significant person in a city that so admired beauty, wealth, and success.

Socrates was a notorious character *in fifth-century BCE Athens and later became one of the most important figures in Western philosophy.*

A fresco of Socrates at an ancient site in Turkey.

III. THE LURE OF ANTIQUITY

SOON AFTER LOSING THE BAPTISTERY DOORS competition, Brunelleschi journeyed to Rome in the company of his young sculptor friend Donatello (ca. 1386–1466). Both men probably sought career opportunities, but the more important consequence of their visit was the artistic knowledge they gained wandering among the ruins of the ancient empire. The trip afforded Brunelleschi, whose interests were already inclining toward architecture, the opportunity to study and measure the many historic structures still standing in Rome. Donatello, for his part, studied the sculptural fragments being excavated from various sites around the city. Both Brunelleschi and Donatello would likely have produced numerous sketches and carefully measured drawings of all that they saw, but no such documents survive.

Meanwhile, in Florence, interest in antiquity was also growing, fed by the prosperity of the rising merchant class. Newly wealthy bankers and traders had created a market not only for the ancient texts then being translated by humanist scholars but also for antique art. Thus, it took very little time for Brunelleschi and Donatello to realize, upon their return to Florence, that the appropriation of antique style could significantly enhance the stature and market value of their work.

The vogue for antiquity was so extreme that pagan forms began appearing even in distinctly Christian contexts. An early manifestation of this trend can be seen in the sculptural program created for the Florentine church of Orsanmichele. Originally a grain storage facility, the building was converted into a chapel for the city's powerful craft and trade guilds late in the fourteenth century. Upon completion of the work in 1404, the guild commissioned statues of their patron saints to adorn the building's fourteen exterior niches.

The four saints that Nanni di Banco (ca. 1380–1421), a contemporary of Donatello, created for the stonemasons' guild are especially notable because, rather than presenting the men as Christian martyrs, Nanni depicts them as togaed figures from the classical past. Also, like many Greek and Roman statues, the figures stand in *contrapposto*, a pose in which the body responds naturalistically to the placement of its weight upon a single leg. Even the faces of the saints evoke classical portraiture, and the savvy Florentine viewer would have recognized that one saint bears a strong resemblance to ancient busts of Greek philosophers, while the others borrow heavily from Roman imperial sculpture.

Nanni di Banco,
Quattro Santi Coronati
(1408–13)

Visits to Rome *gave Brunelleschi and Donatello the chance to study ancient remains firsthand, thus forming the basis of a Renaissance style informed by antiquity.*

III. DARWIN'S EDUCATION

CHARLES ROBERT DARWIN (1809–82) was the fifth of six children born to Robert Waring Darwin, a wealthy physician in the English town of Shrewsbury, and Susannah Wedgwood Darwin, daughter of pottery baron Josiah Wedgwood. By most accounts, Charles was a shy, reserved boy with a slightly mischievous streak. When he was eight years old, his often-ill mother died; and the following year, he became a boarding student at the local Anglican grammar school. As was typical

Robert Waring Darwin

at the time, the school's curriculum emphasized rote memorization of Greek and Latin, which Darwin found stifling. As a result, he performed poorly, angering his father. "You care for nothing but shooting, dogs, and rat-catching," Robert Darwin scolded his son in a letter, "and you will be a disgrace to yourself and your family."

Yet the young Darwin was still expected to become a doctor like his father and grandfather. So, for two years beginning in the fall of 1825, he studied medicine at the University of Edinburgh. Unfortunately, he found the sight of blood so nauseating that he again performed poorly and withdrew. Next, his father sent him to Christ's College, Cambridge University, with the expectation that he would become an Anglican minister. During his years at Cambridge, however, Darwin developed an avid interest in natural history. He joined the Plinian Society, an organization of student-naturalists, and through his own research provided evidence for homology (the likeness in structure between parts of different organisms, attributable to common ancestry). Darwin even spent the summer of 1829 assisting the Rev. F. W. Hope with his entomological field work in North Wales.

Darwin's interest in beetles subsequently led him into an important relationship with the Rev. John Stevens Henslow, a professor of botany at Cambridge, who became Darwin's mentor. Henslow recognized Darwin's gifts and advised him to defer taking the Holy Orders so that he could continue to focus on natural history. In 1831, the year of Darwin's graduation, the Royal Navy asked Henslow to serve as a naturalist aboard the HMS *Beagle*, which was being dispatched to map the coastline of South America. When Henslow's wife refused to let him join the multiyear expedition, he recommended his brother-in-law, who also had to decline. Finally, Henslow recommended Darwin. At first, Robert Darwin objected, not wanting his son to delay the start of his clerical career; but he was ultimately persuaded by Darwin's uncle to let the young man go.

After failing in his medical studies *at Edinburgh, Darwin entered Christ's College, Cambridge, expecting to become a clergyman, but his interest in natural history blossomed instead.*

III. THE SACRIFICE OF ISAAC

FROM THE OUTSET, GOD'S PROMISE to Abraham hinges on the question of progeny. Repeatedly, God tells Abraham that he will become a mighty nation with descendants as numerous as the stars in heaven or the sands upon the seashore. Yet these promises stand in stark contrast with the undeniable fact that Abraham's wife, Sarah, is barren. In Genesis 16, Abraham attempts to realize the divine promise of offspring by bedding his wife's servant, the Egyptian slave Hagar. The result of their union is a son, Ishmael, but this solution to the paradox of the promise is all too human, and Ishmael and Hagar are eventually cast out of Abraham's camp. (Saved from oblivion by God, Ishmael grows up to become the father of a desert people identified by later interpreters as the Arabs.) Not until Genesis 21 is the covenant fulfilled when a son, Isaac, is miraculously born to Abraham and Sarah.

Yet, just when the covenantal promise is finally realized, the Lord commands Abraham to offer Isaac up as a holocaust (a sacrificial offering completely consumed by fire). Faithful to the last, Abraham submits, after which the narrative unfolds in the verses of Genesis 22 with a torturous rhythm as Abraham takes up the knife and the tinderbox while the boy Isaac is made to carry the firewood for his own immolation. When the place that God has chosen for the sacrifice—"a mountain in the land of Moriah"—is reached at last, Abraham prepares to carry out the deed, but at the last moment the Lord intervenes. The ordeal was only a test, Abraham learns, to determine whether he genuinely fears God. Now that Abraham has shown that he does fear God, even to the point of sacrificing his only son, God permits him to sacrifice a ram instead.

A depiction of the sacrifice of Isaac from the 1493 Nuremberg Chronicle.

Over the centuries, exegetes from different religious communities have offered interpretations of this difficult story. For Jews, it celebrates Abraham's astounding faith in God and confirms that Isaac and his progeny, the nation Israel, are the true heirs of the biblical covenant. Christians and Muslims have interpreted the story in similar ways, except that in their views the true heirs of the covenant are their own respective communities. Christians, for example, see Isaac, the willing sacrifice, as a prefiguration of Jesus, whereas Muslims believe that the faithful son almost sacrificed was *not* Isaac but rather their own forefather, Ishmael.

God tests Abraham *by commanding him to sacrifice his only son, even though Isaac represents the fulfillment at long last of the covenantal promise.*

IV. THE TAIPING AND BOXER REBELLIONS

FROM THE QING POINT OF VIEW, there was no Western ideology more insidious than Christianity. Although the religion never really took root in China, it did provide a useful tool with which to attack the government. In the 1840s, a failed scholar named Hong Xiuquan began preaching an unorthodox version of Christianity to the peasants of southern China. Hong explained that he was the younger brother of Jesus and that Christ had appeared to him in a vision, asking him to save mankind.

Whether or not Hong's Christianity appealed to the peasantry is difficult to gauge, but his xenophobic call for the overthrow of the corrupt Manchu regime certainly won him many followers. These converts began arming themselves, and in 1851 Hong declared the establishment of the Heavenly Kingdom of Great Peace (*Taiping tianguo*) with himself as absolute ruler. Motivated by their hatred of the Qing, Hong's followers moved from region to region, targeting Qing institutions and generally wreaking havoc. By the time the Qing suppressed them in 1864, more than twenty million people were dead.

Fighting in Beijing during the Boxer Rebellion.

Another threat to the Qing emerged in 1898—when, in response to the failure of the Self-Strengthening Movement, activists in Shandong began organizing a secret society dedicated to turning back foreign incursions. Steeped in shamanism, the members of the Society of Righteous and Harmonious Fists (more commonly known as Boxers) were ardent practitioners of the martial arts, especially kung fu (*gong fu*).

Spurred on by poor economic conditions and a series of floods and droughts that seemed to be bad omens, the Boxers challenged the Qing's mandate to rule, blaming the government and the Western interlopers (especially Christian missionaries) for the nation's ills. In Beijing, the Boxers led a series of uprisings, to which the government initially responded with force. As the Boxers increasingly targeted missionaries, however, the Qing did less and less to stop them. By 1899, an alliance had formed between the Qing and the Boxers, and the rallying cry of the Boxers changed from "Overthrow the Qing, destroy the foreigners!" to "Support the Qing, destroy the foreigners!" In June 1900, the Empress Dowager declared war on the Western powers and ordered their legations in Beijing attacked. The British, French, and US embassies, among others, held out for fifty-five days until a coalition of foreign armies arrived to free the diplomats and crush the rebellion.

In addition to the encroachment of Westerners, the Qing also had to worry about internal dissent, which further enervated the government.

IV. SOCRATES'S TROUBLE WITH THE ATHENIANS

THE MOST IMPORTANT THING we know about Socrates is that he was tried and executed for impiety in 399 BCE. In four dialogues—the *Euthyphro*, *Apology*, *Crito*, and *Phaedo*—Plato depicts Socrates in the context of his famous trial. The *Euthyphro* takes place on the steps of the courthouse where Socrates has gone to answer the indictment against him. We learn that, at the instigation of a young man named Meletus, Socrates has been charged with corrupting the youth of Athens and not believing in its gods. Socrates's defense is presented in the *Apology*, whose title in the original Greek (*apologia*) means "defense." (Certainly, Socrates isn't "sorry" for what he has said and done.) By the dramatic date of the *Crito*, Socrates has been

Jacques-Louis David, *The Death of Socrates* (1787)

convicted, and he sits in prison, where his friend Crito attempts to persuade him to escape. Refusing, Socrates argues that to escape would be to *do* an injustice, while by remaining in prison he only *suffers* an injustice. Therefore, he will accept the death penalty the court has imposed. The *Phaedo* takes place on Socrates's last day in prison. At the end of this dialogue, Socrates drinks the poison (hemlock) he has been given by the court and dies.

The most famous of these four dialogues is the *Apology*, which begins with a discussion of the difference between persuasion and truth. According to Socrates, his accusers (whose words are not part of the dialogue) have spoken *persuasively* but hardly *truthfully*. This is a distinction that Plato believed to be extremely important. When speakers are persuasive, they get listeners to believe what they are saying, whether or not their words are true. When an advertisement is persuasive, it gets people to buy products, whether or not those products are needed. The key point is that persuasion can make us believe things that, in fact, are false. One might reasonably conclude that the best reason to believe something is because it is true; nevertheless, persuasion can clearly succeed in getting people to believe things that are not.

This thought was just as troubling to ancient Athenians as it is to us. In a democracy such as that established in Athens, where citizens were regularly called upon to discuss and decide the best course of action for the city, a clever speaker could dangerously sway public opinion to a position that was persuasive but not true.

In the *Apology*, *one of four dialogues that concern Socrates's trial and execution, Plato develops a central distinction between persuasion and truth.*

IV. BRUNELLESCHI'S DOME

THE CONSTRUCTION OF FLORENCE'S cathedral church Santa Maria del Fiore (more commonly known as the Duomo) began in 1296, when the first stone was laid. After the death of architect Arnolfo di Cambio in 1302, however, work on the project ground to a halt and remained stuck until 1331, when the prosperous wool merchants' guild took over the church's patronage. Three years later, Giotto

A view of the Duomo showing the dome engineered by Brunelleschi.

was hired to oversee renewed construction, and gradually the huge bulk of the cathedral rose above the city. By 1418, only the dome remained to be completed.

At this point, however, the project became stuck again. The hope had been that, by the time the rest of the cathedral was finished, advances in architecture would have revealed a construction solution for the dome. But the architects involved with the project still couldn't figure out the engineering, so the wool merchants decided to hold another competition. The chief problems to be overcome were the dome's size (it would have to span 140 feet); its corresponding weight, which would have to rest on relatively thin walls; and its great height above the ground, which precluded the use of conventional scaffolding. The seriousness of these problems can be gauged by the creativity of some of the proposed solutions, one of which was to fill the choir with a mixture of dirt and gold coins. The dirt would raise the level of the ground level and thus permit scaffolding, while the coins would incentivize the public to remove the dirt when the dome was complete.

The puzzle was eventually solved by Brunelleschi, who found his answer in the vast domed space of the Pantheon in Rome, as well as in ancient brickwork techniques. First, rather than constructing a hemisphere, Brunelleschi opted for an octagonal dome divided into segments by supporting ribs. This reduced the structure's lateral thrust by channeling its weight downward rather than outward. Next, he decided to build two shells, one interior and one exterior, separated by a passageway. The hollow space between the shells greatly reduced the dome's bulk and also facilitated maintenance. Finally, Brunelleschi developed a bricklaying method, based on ancient techniques, that enabled workers to create concentric, self-supporting rings without the need for ground-based scaffolding. Instead, the bricklayers used scaffolding that attached to holes in the dome's face and could be moved up as the construction progressed.

Using ideas adapted from antiquity, *Brunelleschi was able to engineer the long-sought solution to the puzzle of Florence's massive cathedral dome.*

IV. THE VOYAGE OF THE BEAGLE

CHARLES DARWIN'S VOYAGE aboard the *Beagle* began in December 1831 and ended in October 1836. During those five years, while circumnavigating the globe, Darwin made comparative observations of geological, paleontological, and biogeographical patterns across several continents. What he

An 1841 watercolor of HMS *Beagle*.

saw gradually forced him to reconsider the prevailing view that species are fixed.

Early on, while visiting the Cape Verde Islands off the coast of western Africa, Darwin discovered a horizontal band of white shells nearly fifty feet above sea level. Having read Charles Lyell's *Principles of Geology*, Darwin recognized that this band supported Lyell's theory of uniformitarianism, which held that the earth's current shape is the result of slow geological forces acting uniformly over a long period of time. Later, after Darwin experienced an earthquake near Santiago, Chile, he noticed that the quake had lifted up swaths of marine rock. Even in the high Andes, he found evidence of extinct marine life. Taken together, these discoveries persuaded Darwin that Lyell's theory was correct and that the age of the earth must be many, many times greater than the figure of six thousand years commonly extrapolated from the Bible.

Among the fossils Darwin found were many of extinct organisms he couldn't identify. As with the living plants and animals he was also studying, Darwin compared these fossils with one another, paying particularly close attention to slight variations he sometimes found among individuals of the same species. Because there seemed to be a correlation between variation and geographic location, he wondered whether, as Lamarck had suggested, the variations were the result of environmental factors.

In September 1835, the HMS *Beagle* reached the Galapagos Islands, a tiny archipelago off the coast of Ecuador. During the ship's monthlong stay there, Darwin recorded the most important empirical evidence for what would later become his groundbreaking theory of evolution. Observing the islands' birds—in particular, several different species of ground finch—Darwin began to formulate the idea of descent with modification. "Seeing this gradation and diversity of structure in one small, intimately related group of birds," he later wrote, "one might really fancy that from an original paucity of birds in this archipelago, one species had been taken and modified for different ends." The theory of descent from a common ancestor was becoming to take shape in Darwin's mind.

Darwin's theory of evolution *emerged from the observations he made while aboard the* Beagle—*interpreted through the prism of Lyell's theory of uniformitarianism.*

IV. JACOB AND THE TWELVE TRIBES

TENSION AND UNCERTAINTY REGARDING OFFSPRING also trouble Isaac until his wife, Rebecca, finally gives birth to twins in Genesis 25. Even before they are born, however, Isaac's two sons contend with one another in Rebecca's womb: "Two nations are in your womb, and two peoples will come forth from within you; one shall dominate the other, and the older will serve the younger." Esau is the firstborn son, with Jacob emerging immediately thereafter, grasping Esau by the heel. Chapters 25 through 27 of Genesis chronicle the rivalry between them, which culminates in the wily Jacob stealing the blessing that rightfully belongs to Esau and cheating his older brother out of his birthright.

Fearing retribution, Jacob flees for his life. His subsequent wanderings through the northern reaches of the Promised Land, followed by a sojourn in Mesopotamia, constitute a miniature epic within the Genesis cycle, encompassing chapters 27 through 36. During Jacob's stay in Mesopotamia, he takes two wives, Rachel and Leah, both of whom belong to the house of his uncle Laban. These wives, along with the concubines Bilhah and Zilpah, bear Jacob twelve sons, who become the ancestors of the Twelve Tribes of Israel.

The nation of Israel takes its name from a famous scene found in Genesis 32. After Jacob wrestles with a semidivine being at the ford of the river Jabbok, God bestows upon Jacob a new name: Israel (meaning "he who contends with God"). This story establishes Jacob as the eponymous ancestor of the twelve Israelite tribes, who likely developed the story in order to promote a political alliance based on their mutual descent. Over time, the alliance deepened, and the tribes united as a single nation, called Israel for their common mythic ancestor.

Of his twelve sons, Jacob's favorite is the youngest, Joseph. As related in Genesis, the story of Joseph evokes the themes of chosenness and providence that resonate throughout the Abraham narrative and the rest of the Hebrew Bible. Joseph is sold into slavery by his jealous brothers, only to be saved by God and brought into Egypt, where he rises to a position of prominence at the pharaoh's court. Ironically, when famine strikes the Promised Land, Joseph uses his influence to save his brothers and their families. The salvation of Jacob's children at Joseph's hands demonstrates God's continuing fidelity to the people of Israel and foreshadows an even greater deliverance to come.

Jacob, from an eighteenth-century Russian icon.

The story of Jacob *and his sons provided the twelve ancient Israelite tribes with an origin tale that affirmed their common heritage.*

V. THE 1911 REVOLUTION

THE BOXER PROTOCOL that the Qing negotiated with the Western powers following the Boxer Rebellion required China to pay $333 million in reparations. This heavy economic burden, along with the debacle of the rebellion itself, stoked the flames of revolution in China. The death of the Empress Dowager in 1908 created even more instability; and with the child emperor Puyi on the throne, the Qing limped along as various factions competed for control.

Sun Yat-sen

Among the most prominent reformers was Dr. Sun Yat-sen, who left his medical practice to become a revolutionary. During sixteen years in exile, Sun organized revolutionary cells among expatriate Chinese, and his United League found enthusiastic support among students, the intelligentsia, and the urban elite.

When an October 1911 insurrection in Wuchang set off a wave of provincial rebellions, the Qing government looked to Gen. Yuan Shikai to restore order. Once a close political ally of the Empress Dowager, Yuan had been forced to give up command of the powerful North China Army after Cixi's death. Now, rehabilitated, he emerged as a strongman in the north and a champion of the flagging Qing government.

Meanwhile, the coalition of southern insurrectionists known as the Revolutionary Alliance asked Sun, who had returned from exile in December 1911, to become the president of a new Chinese republic. Although Sun accepted, he recognized that the military forces of the southerners were no match for Yuan's army, and so he wrote to Yuan, offering him the presidency if Yuan would accept the republic. The turning point came when forty-four of Yuan's senior officers petitioned him to support the republic. Fearing a mutiny, Yuan agreed. On February 14, two days after the abdication of Puyi, Yuan became president of the new Republic of China.

Yet Sun's influence continued to grow. In August 1912, he formed the Nationalist party (Guomindang) and organized it around his Three Principles of the People: nationalism, democracy, and the people's livelihood. Later that year, after the right to vote was granted to forty million propertied men (about a tenth of the total population), a parliament was elected. Yet even as the institutions of a modern representative state were being introduced, Yuan proved increasingly unwilling to share power or tolerate an active opposition. During 1913, he began assassinating parliamentary leaders; and when this tactic didn't produce the dictatorial power he desired, he dissolved the parliament and abolished all local and provincial assemblies.

The 1911 Revolution *finally toppled the Qing regime; but its replacement, though republican in name, was dictatorial in nature.*

V. SOCRATIC WISDOM

IN THE COURSE OF THE *APOLOGY*, the character Socrates claims that, unlike his accusers, he will speak the truth, whether or not the truth is persuasive. By his own account, he is seventy years old, has lived in Athens his entire life, and has become a notorious figure there. If he is convicted, he explains, the reason will be not the charges against him but his reputation. Therefore, he sets about explaining to the court why his popular reputation is inaccurate.

According to Socrates, Athenians see him as possessing wisdom of some sort. Some, perhaps influenced by the character Socrates in Aristophanes's *The Clouds*, believe that he has studied "natural philosophy" (that is, the study of nature and the universe, similar to what we call science). Others consider him a Sophist, or one of a group of people paid to teach young men virtue. Socrates, however, denies that he is either of these things. He claims to know nothing of natural philosophy and, more importantly, to know nothing of how to make people virtuous—although he wishes that he did.

If this is true, then why does Socrates have the reputation of being wise? His explanation is that, some time ago, a friend of his traveled to Delphi to inquire of the oracle there whether any person was wiser than Socrates. The oracle's reply was that no one was wiser—an answer that perplexed Socrates, who didn't believe he knew anything special, so how could he be the wisest person? In order to understand the oracle's pronouncement, he approached several people in Athens with well-known reputations for wisdom. He asked each questions about virtue—his premise being that wisdom was knowledge of the truth about virtue. What he found was that while many of these people *thought* they knew the truth about virtue, they actually did not. In other words, they didn't know something and yet thought that they did.

Socrates, of course, claims to know nothing of virtue, either. But, unlike these other people, neither does he claim to have such knowledge. Socrates is different in that when he doesn't know something, neither does he think he knows it. Only in this sense, he concludes, can he be said to be wiser than other people. Because of its forceful statement in the *Apology*, this idea of wisdom as the awareness of one's own ignorance is now commonly known as Socratic wisdom.

In the **Apology**, *Socrates explains that he differs from most people in that he is aware of his own ignorance. When he doesn't know something, neither does he think he knows it.*

V. A RECIPE FOR LINEAR PERSPECTIVE

LINEAR PERSPECTIVE is the means by which artists make the three dimensions of the real world appear accurately on a two-dimensional painted surface. Ancient Roman artists were fluent in this technique, but not since the fall of Rome—Giotto's efforts to render architectural spaces notwithstanding—had an Italian artist been able to master, much less teach, the skills involved.

This situation began to change sometime during the second decade of the fifteenth century, when Brunelleschi, inspired by his architectural investigations in Rome and subsequent conversations with Donatello, started experimenting with linear perspective. Testing his system by painting the Santa Maria del Fiore baptistery and Florence's nearby government hall, Brunelleschi found that he could repeatedly

Masaccio,
The Trinity (1427–28)

create highly accurate images. In the one-point system that he developed, all of the lines in the composition recede to a single point, called the vanishing point. Soon, Brunelleschi began teaching the system to others.

One of the first artists to make use of Brunelleschi's system was Masaccio (1401–28). Around 1425, the Lenzi family of Florence commissioned the twenty-four-year-old Masaccio to design a fresco for the church of Santa Maria Novella. Using linear perspective, Masaccio created the illusion of a barrel vault set into the wall of the church (a far less expensive alternative to the construction of an actual vault).

The vanishing point in Masaccio's Santa Maria Novella fresco, known as *The Trinity*, is located in the center of the composition at the level of the kneeling patrons. Viewers at this level are made to believe that they are looking into an actual three-dimensional space while at the same time looking up at the figures of the Holy Trinity situated within it. The sacred portion of the space is defined by the two Ionic columns. Lower down in the picture plane, closer to the viewer and thus within the secular sphere, are the portraits of the kneeling donors. Lower still and closest to the viewer is the altar table, which seemingly projects out of the painting and into the church itself. Beneath this table is a skeleton in an antique sarcophagus, a pointed reminder of human mortality.

The first published account of Brunelleschi's system appeared during the 1430s in *On Painting*, a treatise by Leon Battista Alberti, which described the technique in mathematical detail. Interestingly, Alberti dedicated his book not only to Brunelleschi but also to four other Florentine artists, including Donatello and Masaccio.

Based on experiments *conducted in the piazza of the Florentine cathedral, Brunelleschi developed a system for creating linear perspective that he passed on to Masaccio.*

V. NATURAL SELECTION

WHEN THE *BEAGLE* RETURNED to England in 1836, Darwin brought back with him an enormous collection of notes and samples, which he soon set about turning into manuscripts suitable for publication. Fortunately, even after five years as an unpaid naturalist, he could still count on his family's wealth for support, and his marriage to first cousin Emma Wedgwood three years later ensured his financial security for life.

Darwin's first major work, published in 1839, was a scientific-chronicle-cum-travel-memoir titled *Journal and Remarks* (also known as *The Voyage of the Beagle*). It brought Darwin fame and inspired many amateur naturalists—including Alfred Russel Wallace, a civil engineer with a passion for collecting insects. Although Wallace (1823–1913) was far from financially stable, he gave up his engineering practice and in 1848 traveled to the Amazon, where he conducted fieldwork for the next four years. (Naturalist-explorers of the time supported themselves by collecting rare specimens and shipping them back to an agent, who sold them on the naturalist's behalf.)

Unlike Darwin, Wallace left England believing strongly in species change, and he made it a goal of his fieldwork to find supporting evidence. Meanwhile, Darwin continued to putter away at a manuscript, begun a decade earlier, in which he intended to present his "secret" theory of descent with modification.

Alfred Russel Wallace

An important commonality between Darwin and Wallace was that both men had read and been influenced by the work of political economist Thomas Malthus. In *An Essay on the Principle of Population* (1798), Malthus had demonstrated statistically that population tends to increase exponentially (1, 2, 4, 8,…), while growth in food supply follows a linear progression (1, 2, 3, 4,…). Therefore, Malthus concluded, unless a population's growth is checked by restraint or by nature, it will inevitably be checked by starvation.

What both Darwin and Wallace took from Malthus was the idea that population growth is ultimately checked by the competition for survival among individual members of a species vying for the same scarce resources. Given such a situation, Darwin and Wallace independently realized that some traits would give individuals an advantage because they promote survival. Individuals possessing these traits would live longer and produce more offspring, thereby increasing the prevalence of advantageous traits in succeeding generations. This is the essence of natural selection.

The theory of natural selection, *developed independently by Darwin and Wallace, holds that competition for survival promotes the proliferation of advantageous traits.*

V. THE EXODUS

ALTHOUGH JOSEPH ARRANGED for the Israelites to be welcomed into Egypt, their status deteriorated over multiple generations, and the ultimate outcome of their descent into Egypt was captivity and exploitation. As related in the book of Exodus, the Israelites became subject to the Egyptians and were forced to provide slave labor for the pharaoh's ostentatious building projects—developments that once again called into question the validity of God's promises to Abraham.

But then a liberator emerges—Moses, who leads the people of Israel out of bondage. His story, especially his dramatic confrontations with the Egyptian pharaoh and the miracles subsequently wrought by God on Israel's behalf, is one of the best-known episodes in the Hebrew Bible. During the modern holiday of Passover, which commemorates Israel's deliverance from bondage in Egypt, Jews recall the bitterness of their oppression and express gratitude for the wonders worked by God to save them.

A fresco thought to be of Moses in an ancient synagogue in present-day Syria.

The Exodus, however, is followed *not* by an immediate return to the Promised Land but by a period of waiting during which Moses receives the Ten Commandments and the rest of the Torah from God atop Mount Sinai. Meanwhile, despite all that God has done for them, the Israelites grow disobedient and rebellious, and so are made to wander in the desert for forty years before God permits them to enter the Promised Land—at which point they begin challenging the Canaanites and Philistines for control.

The Torah—comprising the books of Genesis, Exodus, Leviticus, Numbers, and Deuteronomy—presents the early history of Israel, from the Israelites' emergence as a people to the moment when their nationhood is realized in a practical sense with their conquest of the Promised Land. The historicity of the events described in the Torah is, of course, questionable. However, if one were to date those putative events, reasonable approximations might be sometime around the turn of the second millennium BCE for the age of the Patriarchs (Abraham, Isaac, and Jacob) and perhaps sometime around 1500 BCE for the Exodus. Israelite history from the time of the Exodus through the conquest of the Promised Land, as chronicled in the books of Joshua and Judges, is also obscure; but what we do know is that by 1000 BCE, the Israelites had emerged as a single kingdom called the United Monarchy, the historicity of which can be disputed only with great difficulty.

Forty years after *God delivers the people of Israel from Egypt, they come at last to the Promised Land, where they become a nation in the conventional political sense.*

VI. THE MAY FOURTH MOVEMENT

THE START OF WORLD WAR I in August 1914 pulled European attention away from Asia—giving China's longtime rival, Japan, a new opportunity to further its expansionist designs. On January 18, 1915, the Japanese presented Yuan's government with a list of twenty-one demands that would have seriously undermined Chinese autonomy. For example, in a bid to obtain control over ports and natural resources in northeastern China, the Japanese demanded that all German leases and privileges be turned over to them. (Both Japan and China were nominally

Yuan Shikai

aligned with the Allies.) Even more egregious were the demands that Japan be allowed to deploy its own police force in China and that Japanese industrialists be granted ownership interests in Chinese companies.

Recognizing that these and other stipulations would have rendered China virtually a protectorate of Japan, Yuan appealed to the West for help. But the European powers, preoccupied with war and less than fond of Yuan's regime, chose not to intervene. Because Japan didn't want to force a war, Yuan was able to negotiate a preservation of Chinese sovereignty, but his humiliated government still had to give up control of Shandong Province, southern Manchuria, and eastern Inner Mongolia. A year later, after attempting to declare himself emperor, Yuan died, leaving the provinces on the periphery of Beijing in the hands of local warlords.

While China played only a small role in World War I, Japan formally entered the war on the Allies' side and was rewarded at Versailles with the German holdings it had sought as part of the Twenty-one Demands. The Chinese people responded with outrage. On May 4, 1919, some three thousand students gathered in Beijing's Tiananmen Square to protest the action taken at Versailles. When the house of a government official came under attack, the police moved in to end the rally, and by nightfall the students were dispersed, but not before workers had joined the students in calling for a general strike. Meanwhile, many merchants closed their doors to support a boycott of Japanese goods.

The events of May 4 triggered an outpouring of Chinese nationalism and anti-Japanese sentiment that came to be known as the May Fourth Movement. This movement catalyzed students and other intellectuals to become much more politically involved and to act on what they had only been thinking about. Even more importantly, it suggested the potential strength of an alliance between the intelligentsia and the proletariat.

The ratification at Versailles *of one of Japan's notorious Twenty-one Demands led to spontaneous protests in Beijing that formed the basis of the May Fourth Movement.*

VI. VIRTUE

OFTEN IN THE PLATONIC DIALOGUES, the character Socrates insists that he has no knowledge of what virtue is. (Among scholars, this is known as the Socratic disavowal of knowledge.) Yet the dialogues make it plain that Socrates considers virtue—whatever it is—to be the most important thing for humans to emulate. Therefore, we need to explore more closely the ancient Greek concept of virtue.

The English word *virtue* is a translation of the Greek word *aretē*, which also means "excellence." Thus, something virtuous in the ancient Greek sense is, one might say, an excellent example of its type. A virtuous (or excellent) horse, for instance, would be one that is strong, fast, and beautiful. A virtuous knife would be one that cuts well. Human virtue, it follows, entails being an excellent human being. In classical Athens this would have been understood to mean being courageous, just, wise, and temperate.

To an Athenian, courage meant being able to endure frightening or difficult situations, such as a battle or a serious illness. Justice meant fairness toward others. Wisdom meant having knowledge, in particular knowledge of the right thing to do. Temperance meant having control of one's desires—including, paradigmatically, those for food, drink, and sex. Virtuous actions included not only what we would consider morally correct actions, such as the returning of a lost purse, but also conduct such as eating an appropriate amount of dessert. It may seem odd to us to think of eating an entire cheesecake as immoral, but doing so would certainly have contradicted the Athenian concept of virtue. The ancient Greeks believed that overindulgence was not something an excellent person would do, because it showed a lack of control over one's desires.

Above all, according to Socrates, a person should do the right thing. In the *Crito*, he secures his friend's agreement on this point:

SOCRATES: *So one must never do wrong.*
CRITO: *Definitely not.*
SOCRATES: *Nor should one who has been wronged do wrong in return, as most people say, because one must not do wrong in any way.*
CRITO: *It seems not.*

Socrates thus believes that one should never act contrary to virtue, yet he denies knowing what virtue is, which seems paradoxical. His explanation is that, until he finds what virtue is, he can only reflect on his life and think about whether he has led it in the best way.

Virtue, in the sense of excellence, *was a central concept for the ancient Greeks. Striving to be virtuous, according to Socrates, was the most important thing a human could do.*

VI. THE PROBLEMS OF OPTICAL CORRECTION

ALTHOUGH BRUNELLESCHI'S SYSTEM of one-point perspective worked well for the creation of architectural spaces, it offered little help when it came to rendering the much more irregular contours of the human form. For sculptors working in the unforgiving medium of stone, the challenge was even more formidable. By the middle of the fifteenth century, Renaissance painters had developed a perspectival method, known as foreshortening, to depict human figures and other objects much more realistically. But sculptors continued to struggle with what was essentially a trial-and-error process.

Donatello, for instance, was commissioned early in the fifteenth century to carve a colossal marble statue of David for the Florentine cathedral, one of several Old Testament portraits that were intended to decorate the base of Brunelleschi's new dome. In addition to manipulating the figure's proportions so that they would appear lifelike from the viewpoint of a spectator in the piazza below, Donatello knew that he would have to exaggerate certain features of the statue, such as the curls of the hair and the size of the hands, in order to make them visible from such a great distance.

Archival records indicate that he completed the commission, and it was hoisted into place, only to be removed later without explanation. Other records indicate that Donatello then began experimenting with weather-resistant alternatives to marble. Apparently, he was looking for a malleable medium that would allow him to make corrections as he worked, suggesting that there had been problems with the perspective of the statue of David. Finally, Donatello settled on clay, creating a colossal terra-cotta (baked clay) statue of the prophet Joshua. This statue, too, was hoisted into place, only to be removed after suffering considerable damage from the elements.

Although Donatello's statue of Joshua didn't last, the principles that he developed for the accurate sculptural representation of human form (known as optical correction) did survive. An examination of his later work reveals numerous manipulations, not obvious in situ but very noticeable in the context of a museum installation. For example, in his figure of St. John the Evangelist, created for the facade of the Florentine cathedral, the purposeful distortions include a grotesquely elongated torso, atrophied legs, and unnaturally large hands. All of these features look odd when viewed today in the cathedral museum; however, when the statue is viewed from below, as originally intended, the figure takes on completely natural proportions.

Just as linear perspective revolutionized painting, *Donatello's experiments with optical correction transformed sculpture.*

VI. ON THE ORIGIN OF SPECIES

IN EARLY 1858, when Darwin's book on descent with modification was about half done, he received a letter from Wallace, who was exploring the Malay Archipelago (present-day Malaysia and Indonesia). After reading Wallace's letter, which described a manuscript on natural selection that Wallace was writing, Darwin confided in Charles Lyell and botanist Joseph Dalton Hooker. Both men were privy to Darwin's "secret" work on natural selection, and they urged him to prepare a manuscript of his own immediately. On July 1, 1858, papers by both Darwin and Wallace were presented jointly to the Linnean Society in London.

One of the reasons Darwin had been working slowly and carefully was that he knew his theory would be controversial because it contradicted the biblical account of creation. Surprisingly, the Linnean Society presentation caused little stir, but not so the publication of *On the Origin of Species* a year later. The first edition of 1,250 copies sold out on the first day; and 3,000 copies of a second edition, published three months later, sold out nearly as fast.

THE ORIGIN OF SPECIES

BY MEANS OF NATURAL SELECTION,

PRESERVATION OF FAVOURED RACES IN THE STRUGGLE FOR LIFE.

By CHARLES DARWIN, M.A.,

LONDON:
JOHN MURRAY, ALBEMARLE STREET.

The first edition of *On the Origin of Species* (1859).

The book begins with an explanation of natural selection. First, Darwin discusses the variations found in domesticated plants and animals that are the result of intentional breeding. Then he shows how these artificially generated adaptations mirror a similar process at work among natural populations. Finally, he relates the process to Malthusian selection: "As more individuals are produced than can possibly survive, there must in every case be a struggle for existence."

In another section of the book, Darwin presents potential objections to his new theory, including the lack of transitional forms and the evolution of complex organs, along with detailed rebuttals. Darwin's basic point is that evolution takes place in minute, gradual steps. In making this point, he introduces the revolutionary concept of phylogeny: that all species are related to one another through common ancestors. This framework allowed Darwin to make sense of the confusing relationships that exist among different species.

By compiling detailed evidence from different biological disciplines—among them taxonomy, embryology, and anatomy—Darwin made a compelling and largely successful case for the variability and transmutability of species—in other words, for evolution. Yet he was much less successful in persuading the scientific community of natural selection's role as the primary mechanism underlying species change.

In making the case for species mutability, On the Origin of Species *presents a mechanism for change (natural selection) and a framework within which that change can be understood (phylogeny).*

VI. AN ALTERNATE VIEW OF ISRAELITE ORIGINS

THE EXACT CHRONOLOGY OF ISRAEL'S TRANSFORMATION from a loose tribal confederation into a united kingdom is notoriously difficult to extrapolate from the Bible, and the archaeological record offers little help. For example, no physical evidence exists to support the claim that a mass exodus from Egypt took place anytime during the second millennium BCE. However, the archaeological record does seem to show that the Israelites were present in the Promised Land about this time. An Egyptian inscription dating to ca. 1350 BCE refers to a nomadic people called the Hapiru (Hebrews), and the stele of Mer-ne-ptah, which dates to ca. 1230 BCE, mentions both the Israelites and the Canaanites.

Questioning the veracity of the biblical Exodus story, some scholars have argued that the Israelites didn't arrive in the Promised Land en masse but rather emerged as a nation there gradually, entering slowly in small groups over the course of several centuries. According to this view, which is supported by archaeological evidence, there were few initial differences between the Israelites and the Canaanites; as time went on, however, the Israelites developed practices such as circumcision that served to distinguish them from their ethnically and linguistically similar neighbors.

Researchers have speculated that some Israelites came from Mesopotamia, while others came from Egypt. This would explain the need for an origin myth that encompassed both Mesopotamia and Egypt. The biblical narrative, for example, includes both Abraham's journey from Ur of the Chaldees and the Exodus from Egypt, thus embracing the ancestral heritage of both groups.

In other words, the Israelite community probably did not emerge over the course of centuries during one long journey from Mesopotamia to the Promised Land to Egypt and back again to the Promised Land. Rather, each of these movements, westward from Mesopotamia and eastward from Egypt, is more likely to have taken place simultaneously during the gradual formation of the Israelite nation within the Promised Land itself. According to this view, the biblical story of the Israelites' descent in a single lineage from Abraham through Isaac and Jacob is first and foremost a powerful myth created by a group of allied nomadic peoples seeking an explanation for where they came from and what their common origin might have been.

Because no evidence exists *of a large Israelite invasion of the Promised Land, some scholars believe that Israel emerged gradually within the Promised Land.*

VII. THE EMERGENCE OF CHINESE COMMUNISM

IN 1918, inspired by the recent Russian Revolution, a group of Beijing University students led by librarian Li Dazhao began studying the writings of Karl Marx. Later, working with former dean Chen Duxiu, at this time the editor of the popular journal *New Youth* and a leading figure in the May Fourth Movement, Li and his circle began

Li Dazhao

publishing analyses of Marxist thought that encouraged others to begin reading Marx for themselves.

In April 1920, the recently formed Third Communist International (Comintern) sent a delegation to China. Its mission was to establish contact with Chinese Marxists, especially Li's group in Beijing and Chen's in Shanghai. The Russian agents were particularly tasked with opening a Comintern bureau in Shanghai; and when the Chinese proved receptive, a meeting was held in May, attended by representatives of many reform-minded groups—including communists, socialists, anarchists, and even members of

Sun's Guomindang. A Comintern bureau was indeed established at the meeting, with Chen as its general secretary. A year later, in July 1921, Li, Chen, and others formed the Chinese Communist Party (CCP), again with Chen as general secretary.

One of the first important issues to be resolved by the CCP was whether or not to ally itself with Sun and his Guomindang party. Although some Chinese Communists continued to admire Sun, the father of the republic, most considered him insufficiently revolutionary. Ultimately, a compromise was reached: It was decided that the CCP should support Sun while he led the democratic phase of the revolution, then supplant the Guomindang when it came time for the inevitable dictatorship of the proletariat.

Sun, meanwhile, focused his efforts on reunifying China—which, since Yuan's death, had fractured again into shards run by petty strongmen. Proclaiming a new government at Canton (Guangzhou), he began working to assemble the military power necessary to subdue the northern warlords. He asked the Western powers for help, but they refused. The Soviet Union, however, was much more forthcoming. At a meeting with Soviet diplomats in early 1923, Sun agreed to an alliance known as the First United Front. In exchange for Soviet aid, Sun accepted members of the CCP and agents of the Comintern into the membership of the Guomindang. The relationship was uneasy, however, and it began to come apart with the death of Sun in March 1925.

With the help of Russian agents *sent by the Comintern, early Chinese Marxists, notably Li Dazhao and Chen Duxiu, formed the Chinese Communist Party in July 1921.*

VII. THE RECOLLECTION THEORY

IN THE DIALOGUE *MENO*, Socrates and the title character attempt to discover what virtue is. Initially, Meno says that he thinks he knows. However, once Socrates begins questioning him, Meno becomes perplexed and admits that, actually, he can't say what virtue is. Because (as always) Socrates himself disavows knowledge of virtue, the two of them decide to investigate the matter together.

At this point, Meno asks Socrates how they can possibly search for something if neither of them knows "at all" what the thing is. For example, if I ask you to search for a crunk, and you have no idea what a "crunk" is, how can you search for it? This problem is known among philosophers as Meno's Paradox. In making his reply, Socrates begins by describing an ancient theory according to which the soul is immortal.

We have to pause here because, like virtue, the English concept of soul differs from the ancient Greek concept. For the ancient Greeks, having a soul meant simply being alive. That is, the possession of a soul was merely the difference between animate and inanimate objects. Both Plato and Aristotle would have agreed that a human being consists of both a body and a soul—the latter including (at least) one's mind and thoughts; one's emotions, likes, and dislikes; one's character traits; and so on. However, unlike the modern use of the word, the Greek concept of soul doesn't by itself imply that the soul is immaterial or immortal. The ancient Greeks would have found a debate over whether people have souls ridiculous. To deny the existence of the soul would be to deny that people are alive and that they have minds, thoughts, emotions, and so on.

A Roman copy of a bust of Plato.

Now back to the *Meno*. According to the theory that Socrates describes, the soul has an existence independent of the body to which it has been joined. The soul has thus had a previous existence, during which it has learned many things—including, perhaps, mathematics and what virtue is. Socrates suggests that what people commonly call "learning" is, in fact, "being reminded of" things their souls once knew but have forgotten. Therefore, it indeed makes sense for Socrates and Meno to search for what virtue is, because their souls once possessed this knowledge and now have only forgotten it. All scholars agree that this recollection theory is an invention of Plato's, perhaps inspired by his reflection on puzzles such as Meno's Paradox.

According to Plato's recollection theory, *learning is "being reminded of" knowledge that our souls acquired before being joined to our bodies but have since forgotten.*

VII. THE PATRONAGE OF THE MEDICIS

DURING THE LATE FOURTEENTH CENTURY, the Medicis of Florence enjoyed such fabulous success in banking and commerce that they accumulated a great deal of political power. Equally important to their growing influence, however, was their broad popularity, built upon charitable acts and generous patronage of the arts.

Cosimo de' Medici (1389–1464), often called Cosimo the Elder, is generally considered to be the founder of the Medici political dynasty. Although he never held political office in Florence, he effectively ruled the city-state from 1434 until his death. Living quite simply, he spent much of his wealth on literature and the arts, amassing the largest library in Europe (including many ancient Greek texts obtained from sources in Constantinople) and elevating Florence to the premier cultural center of the age, strongly identified with the new humanism.

Fra Angelico,
San Marco Altarpiece (1439–42)

Cosimo's most important architectural projects were a new family palace and adjacent church built by Brunelleschi and the renovation of the Dominican convent of San Marco a few blocks to the north. The construction aspects of the San Marco project, which included the enlargement of the church and the addition of dormitory space as well as a large new library, were allotted to Michelozzo, an occasional partner of Donatello and the architectural heir to Brunelleschi. The decoration of these spaces, however, was turned over to the friar painter Fra Angelico (ca. 1400–55), who adorned each dormitory cell with a devotional image appropriate to its inhabitant's status— whether novice, cleric, or layman. The deep level of Cosimo's involvement in the project is evidenced by the construction of a double cell specifically for his use when visiting the library.

Cosimo also commissioned from Fra Angelico a new altarpiece for the choir of the renovated church. The painting, completed in 1438, conforms to the genre of the "sacred conversation," depicting an enthroned Mary and Child attended by saints from different eras. (This type of painting is called a conversation because the saints appear to be conversing with each other or with the audience.) The prevailing trends in Renaissance art can be seen in Fra Angelico's use of linear perspective and classical architectural motifs, which are quite notable in this strictly Christian context.

The Medici family *practiced patronage on a great scale, helping to transform Florence into the artistic capital of Europe and the center of Renaissance style.*

VII. ADAPTATION BY NATURAL SELECTION

DARWIN AGREED WITH LAMARCK THAT SPECIES change over time; that living things move from simpler to more complex forms; and that, as organisms evolve, they become better suited to the environments in which they live. This last process is called adaptation. Darwin and Lamarck differed, however, in their understanding of how adaptation takes place. Lamarck believed that species acquire traits through direct response to environmental conditions—for example, the lengthening of a giraffe's neck in order to reach hard-to-get food. Darwin believed that for adaptation to take place, three conditions have to be met. First, there has to be ample variation in the population. In *On the Origin of Species*, Darwin described the great variation that exists among primroses: different colors, odors, flowering times, and so on. But his basic point was simple: Natural selection based on variation can't occur if no variants exist.

The second condition necessary for adaptation to take place is that the traits being selected for must be transmittable from one generation to the next. In other words, the traits must be heritable (capable of being inherited). Cutting off a mouse's tail, for example, will not result in adaptation. Such an occurrence creates a new short-tailed mouse but not subsequent generations of short-tailed mice.

Lastly, the traits being selected for must impact the species' overall reproductive success—that is, its ability to produce more viable offspring than individuals with other traits. This Malthusian principle, later known as differential fitness, was the main thrust of Darwin's (and Wallace's) argument concerning adaptation. Its simplicity inspired naturalist Thomas Henry Huxley to remark, "How stupid not to have thought it before!"

A *Vanity Fair* cartoon of Thomas Henry Huxley.

Adaptation by natural selection quickly became the hallmark of Darwin's theory of evolution, as converts (notably Huxley) adopted and championed the idea. In fact, it didn't take long for Darwin's views about common ancestry to gain widespread acceptance. Yet there was a sticking point: his insistence on gradualism. For Darwin, the idea that change took place continuously implied that individual variations were small—in fact, minuscule. Therefore, selection based on these small variations resulted in adaptations that were themselves small. In this way, adaptation proceeded slowly and gradually, with differential selection ultimately producing noticeable shifts in trait composition but only after many generations.

According to Darwin, *the three conditions necessary and sufficient for adaptation are variation, heritability, and differential fitness among individuals in a population.*

VII. THE UNITED MONARCHY

ACCORDING TO THE BOOKS OF JOSHUA AND JUDGES, when the Israelite tribes reached the Promised Land, they found themselves hard pressed to survive, especially given the resistance they faced from the Canaanites and Philistines who lived there. Specifically because of the trouble they had with the Philistines—a tough, seafaring people perhaps descended from the ancient Greeks who fought at Troy—the Israelites turned from their tribal chieftains (whom the Bible collectively refers to as the Judges) and began following a single king, Saul. Because of Saul's sins, however, as related in the books

King David plays the harp in an illuminated panel from ca. 1470.

of 1 and 2 Samuel, he lost divine favor, and the monarchy passed not to his son Jonathan but to the shepherd boy David.

During the period known as the United Monarchy, which began about 1000 BCE with the ascent of Saul and ended in 920 BCE with the death of Solomon, Israel's ten northern and two southern tribes were led, if not dominated, by the southern tribe of Judah. While the monotheistic idea and practices such as circumcision no doubt predate the United Monarchy, it is practically indisputable that certain central institutions of the Israelite religion were asserted during this time. The most obvious example is the temple built in Jerusalem during the reign of King Solomon. According to the biblical account in 2 Samuel, this sanctuary, known as the First Temple, was the only place sanctioned by God for His worship. Yet we know from both biblical and archaeological evidence that other Israelite places of worship existed in the Promised Land prior to the construction of the First Temple, most notably at Dan and Bethel in the north and Shilo in the south. The Ark of the Covenant, in fact, seems to have originated at Shilo, residing there until its relocation by the Judahites to the First Temple.

Other major developments, such as the creation of a Temple priesthood and the establishment of David's descendants as the divinely sanctioned kings of Israel, likewise seem to reflect the hegemony of the Judahites. By promoting a single capital city in Judah, sanctified by the presence of the only legitimate temple, the Judahite kings advanced their claim to represent all of Israel. The idea of monotheism fit especially well into this ideological program, because it served to unify the Israelites by differentiating them from the comparatively heterogeneous Canaanites and their panoply of separate gods.

The religious institutions *asserted by the Judahite kings of the United Monarchy served to promote their political program, which called for Israelite unity under Judahite rule.*

VIII. JAPANESE EXPANSIONISM

THE FIRST SINO-JAPANESE WAR (1894–95) was fought between China and Japan over control of Korea, then a Chinese tributary. The fighting ended badly for the Chinese, with Japan imposing "independence" on Korea. The war demonstrated that, while the Self-Strengthening Movement in China had failed miserably, a similar program undertaken by Japan had been hugely successful.

During the early twentieth century, the balance of power shifted even more dramatically toward the Japanese, whose ultimate goal was to control China's natural resources and dominate its markets. Japan was motivated in this expansionism by a deep sense of economic and military vulnerability. Its own territory lacked many of the natural resources necessary for the proper functioning of a modern industrial economy, and it feared being supplanted in the Pacific by Russia and the United States.

Japanese in Western dress meet with Qing officials during the First Sino-Japanese War.

Important voices in the upper echelons of Japanese society insisted upon autarky—that is, national economic self-sufficiency—and they believed that the quickest route to such independence passed through coal- and ore-rich Manchuria. As a result of its victory over Russia in the Russo-Japanese War of 1904–5, Japan obtained territory along the South Manchuria Railway and on the Liaodong Peninsula that Russia had previously leased from China. Possession of this land and the extraterritorial rights attached to it enabled Japan to deploy a military force in the heart of Manchuria.

This force, called the Kwantung Army, enjoyed considerable autonomy and acted more aggressively than the Tokyo bureaucracy would often have preferred. Such was the case on September 18, 1931, when Kwantung extremists covertly blew up a section of the South Manchuria Railway in order to blame the sabotage on the local Chinese military. Using the incident as a pretext, the Kwantung Army then invaded the provincial capital at Mukden (now Shenyang), assisted by Japanese forces stationed across the border in Korea. China appealed again to the West for help, and this time the League of Nations sent an investigative body, the Lytton Commission, which found that the sabotage had indeed been staged. Even so, League sanctions against Japan were largely ineffective, and in February 1932 Japan masterminded the creation of Manchukuo, a new nation-state in Manchuria and eastern Inner Mongolia ruled ostensibly by the former Qing emperor Puyi but actually by Japan.

Craving Manchuria's coal and mineral resources, *the Japanese established a foothold on the mainland and then used the Kwantung Army to wrest Manchuria from China.*

VIII. THE THEORY OF FORMS

IN THE PROCESS OF QUESTIONING various characters about their knowledge of virtue, Socrates often asks them, "What is virtue?" This is known among scholars of Plato as the *What is F?* question, because sometimes Socrates asks about virtue in general and sometimes about a particular virtue, such as courage. What Socrates seems to want in response isn't a dictionary definition, which would merely give us the meaning of the word *virtue* or the word *courage*. Instead, he seems to want to know what all instances of virtue have in common—that is, the underlying property that joins them all together.

For example, suppose Socrates asked, "What is water?" He would want to know what all instances of water have in common—that is, the thing that makes them water. A reasonable answer might be a description of water's molecular structure (H_2O). Without this essential property, water would not be water. Such an answer to the *What is F?* question describes the essence of the thing, without which it would cease to be the thing that it is. So, if a triangle no longer had three sides, taking on another side or losing one, it would cease to be a triangle.

An essential property in this sense is also a universal, which is a property that's instantiated in different individuals. (Instantiation is the representation of an abstraction in concrete instances.) For example, "human being" is the universal that the individuals Tom, Dick, and Sue instantiate. Part of the problem in dealing with universals is that while particular instances of a universal exist in the physical world, the universal itself can't be perceived by our five senses. You can see, smell, hear, touch, and taste (!) a particular dog, but you can't sense the universal "dog." Similarly you can see a beautiful object, but you can't see beauty itself. Plato's response to this problem is to hypothesize that universal essences, which he calls forms, exist in another universe. Although they can't be sensed, they are objects of thought and thus can be understood.

In the dialogue *Phaedo*, Plato connects his theory of forms to his theory of recollection. He argues that souls, before they are joined to bodies in the sensible universe, gain knowledge of forms in some nonsensible universe. At birth, we forget this knowledge; but if we practice philosophy, Plato suggests, it can be recovered.

According to Plato's theory, *forms are universal essences that exist as unchanging, eternal entities outside the sensible universe.*

VIII. THE OBSERVATION OF NATURE

AROUND 1470, interest in the natural world took another great leap forward. The culture at large seized upon the direct observation of nature and became fascinated with the details of life it produced. Such investigations significantly advanced scientific knowledge and also, artistically, led to radical changes in pictorial style.

A good example is the *Baptism of Christ* altarpiece produced by the Florentine studio of Andrea del Verrocchio during the early 1470s. The painting is somewhat of a pastiche, featuring the work of several artists—including those of the young Sandro Botticelli (1445–1510) and the even younger Leonardo da Vinci (1452–1519), who were both training with Verrocchio at the time. As the master of the workshop (and in keeping with standard practice), Verrocchio painted the most important elements, including the figures of Christ and St. John the Baptist. Leonardo painted the kneeling angel on the left and much of the landscape, while Botticelli is believed to have contributed the second angel.

Verrocchio, *Baptism of Christ* (1472–75)

The standing figures painted by Verrocchio manifest a noticeably heightened level of anatomical detail. This can be seen in the bulging muscles of Christ's right arm and legs and even more so in the distinctions Verrocchio makes in the Baptist's left forearm among the musculature, the connective tendons, and the emphatically defined veins. In the Baptist's neck and chest as well, Verrocchio delineates not only the Adam's apple but also the carotid artery and the pectoral muscles. Such careful representations of anatomical form indicate that Verrocchio must have spent a considerable amount of time observing the human body. The next generation of artists, most notably Leonardo, would take this approach even farther, dissecting cadavers in order to understand more completely how the human body is put together.

Leonardo's lifelong interest in nature perhaps began with his contributions to the *Baptism of Christ*. The rocky ledge that he painted in the foreground and his rendering of the cattails and other water vegetation at the feet of John the Baptist are so precise that they could be scientific illustrations. Equally detailed and interesting is the landscape that he painted behind the kneeling angels, which would later appear (somewhat reworked) as the background in the *Mona Lisa*.

During the last quarter of the fifteenth century, *Renaissance artists began paying even closer attention to the natural world, observing its details much as a scientist would.*

VIII. COMMON DESCENT

Darwin in 1855.

BEFORE DARWIN, the prevailing Western explanation for species origin was a religious doctrine known as special creation. This is the idea that living things didn't evolve but were created in their current form over the course of six days six thousand years ago as described in the Bible. According to the doctrine of special creation, species are fixed, divinely designed entities that have remained essentially unchanged since their creation. Furthermore, the relationships among species, as defined by the *scala naturae*, are similarly fixed. Not evolutionary in origin, they are instead based entirely on the Creator's divine plan.

Even Lamarckian environmentalists, who rejected essentialism, believed that evolution was following some sort of progressive plan. Lamarck himself saw the *scala naturae* as a ladder that species climb as they evolve, moving incrementally in a linear progression from "lower" to "higher" forms of life. Darwin, on the other hand, threw out the two-thousand-year-old concept of the *scala naturae*, insisting that evolution takes place in multiple dimensions and that it follows no prefigured plan.

Importantly, as Darwin looked forward in time, he also looked backward. His clever insight was the realization that if species branch out as time progresses, then they should also consolidate as one moves backward in time. Observing what happens as one moves backward in time would thus reveal the ways in which different species are related. For example, the point at which two species consolidate into one (the metaphoric joining of their branches) would reveal their common ancestor. With enough information, a researcher could theoretically construct an enormous phylogenetic "tree" showing every species and its relation to every other species. Ultimately at the root of this tree would be a single common ancestor. As Darwin himself observed in *On the Origin of Species*, "All of the organic beings which have ever lived on this earth have descended from some one primordial form, into which life was first breathed."

The idea that species with extremely different characteristics can, and indeed do, share a common ancestor revolutionized the field of biology. Called common descent, this principle gave anatomists, taxonomists, and embryologists not only a new rationale to study the commonalities that exist among different living things but also a framework within which to place their discoveries.

Darwin's belief that all species are related *via common descent conflicted strongly with the prevailing views of essentialists and environmentalists regarding species divergence.*

VIII. THE KINGDOMS OF ISRAEL AND JUDAH

BECAUSE A STRONGLY PRO-JUDAHITE PERSPECTIVE suffuses much of the Pentateuch (the Five Books of Moses that make up the Torah), many scholars believe that the texts from which the Pentateuch was later assembled date to the period of the United Monarchy. This was perhaps the time when different traditions were combined to support the claim that the Israelite people were all descended from the patriarch Abraham and thus, at root, a single nation chosen by God for a great destiny.

The United Monarchy, however, was extremely short-lived, enduring for less than a century. Upon Solomon's death in 920 BCE, the northern tribes seceded and created their own independent monarchy, as described in 1 Kings 12. This northern state took the name Israel, while the remnant of the original kingdom based at Jerusalem adopted the name Judah. Not surprisingly, the kings of Judah retained the major institutions of the United Monarchy, including the Temple and its priesthood; meanwhile, the kings of Israel revived ancient traditions indigenous to the northern tribes that had been suppressed under Judahite rule. Most conspicuously, they rebuilt the ancient shrines at Dan and Bethel.

According to the account in 1 Kings, Jeroboam, the first ruler of the northern kingdom, placed a golden calf in each of the rebuilt shrines. Although many historians believe this account to be accurate, the golden calves should *not* be thought of as idols and thus violations of monotheism, as the author of 1 Kings claimed that they were. Rather, they were more likely markers for the place within the shrine where the divine would be manifest. In this way, they served a purpose analogous to that of the Ark of the Covenant, which the Judahites had placed within the Holy of Holies, the innermost sanctum of the Jerusalem Temple.

For two hundred years, the two kingdoms coexisted, more or less in a state of détente, until the Assyrian Empire overran the northern kingdom about 720 BCE. In fact, the Assyrians annihilated the ten "lost" tribes, either killing their members or permanently dispersing them. Accounts preserved in the Hebrew Bible—such as that of the prophet Isaiah, who apparently witnessed the destruction firsthand—attributed the calamity to the sins of the northern tribes, especially their illegitimate forms of worship. However, it should be noted that the books of the Bible that describe this period display the same Judahite bias that colors the Pentateuch.

Following the death of Solomon, *the United Monarchy collapsed, and two new kingdoms were formed, Israel in the north and Judah in the south.*

IX. THE LONG MARCH

AT THE TIME OF SUN'S DEATH IN 1925, the Nationalists controlled most of southern China, while a patchwork of warlords, some receiving aid from the Japanese, ruled in the north. Because the Soviets were eager to strengthen China as a buffer against expansionist Japan, the USSR aided the Guomindang in launching the Northern Expedition of 1926–28. Led by Sun protégé Chiang Kai-shek, this campaign subdued the warlords and reunified China. Meanwhile, Chiang emerged as the strongest military leader in the country. In fact, by early 1927, he felt secure enough to show his true political mind. Although Sun had considered the Communists useful allies in the fight against Japanese imperialism, Chiang was deeply anticommunist; and in April 1927, he interrupted the Northern Expedition to turn his army against the CCP.

A month earlier, under the leadership of Zhou Enlai, Communist labor unions in Shanghai had thrown out the local warlord—a turn of events that greatly worried the many Western powers with commercial interests in Shanghai. Using the warships that they kept on the Yangtze River to "protect" their interests, these Western powers attacked the Chinese Communists, who expected Chiang's army to provide relief. Instead, their erstwhile ally used the incident as a pretext for purging them from the Guomindang. Beginning April 12, Chiang's forces either killed or imprisoned every prominent Communist they could find, not only in Shanghai but across the country. CCP founder Li Dazhao, for example, was executed in Beijing on April 28.

Driven from the cities by Chiang's White Terror campaign, those Communists who survived fled to remote Jiangxi Province in southeastern China, where Mao

Guomindang executioners at work in 1927.

Zedong assumed a leadership role from 1931. In Jiangxi, the Communists attempted to form their own army and accumulate supplies so that they could take the fight back to the cities; but Chiang's pursuit was relentless, and it eventually put them to flight again. The lengthy, arduous trek that followed came to be known as the Long March. It began on October 16, 1934, and ended on October 20, 1935, at Yenan in Shaanxi Province. During the intervening year, the marchers feinted and doubled back across inhospitable mountain terrain so often that, in the end, they covered some six thousand miles, or about seventeen miles a day. Of the hundred thousand people who began the march, fewer than eight thousand survived.

Chiang's campaign *to eradicate his erstwhile Communist allies began in April 1927 in Shanghai and continued through the Long March of 1934–35.*

IX. PLATO'S CONCEPT OF THE SOUL

WE HAVE ALREADY SEEN THAT, for ancient Greeks, the distinction between things with souls and things without souls is primarily the distinction between animate and inanimate objects. Plato, however, has much more to say about the nature and structure of the human soul than this.

Plato is what philosophers call a dualist, which means that he believes in the existence of two fundamentally different kinds of substance. The first of these is material substance. Being material, as the French philosopher René Descartes once explained, means taking up space. Material substances are thus physical objects. Often, you can see them, as you can see a table or a doughnut. But sometimes you can only feel them, as you can only feel (but not see) the wind. Sometimes, you can't perceive them at all—at least not without the aid of an instrument. Your unaided senses can't perceive germs, for example, yet germs are certainly material substances because they take up space.

The second kind of substance in which a dualist believes is immaterial substance, which exists independently and is not physical. Within the Judeo-Christian-Islamic tradition, one generally conceives of the soul in this way. Similarly, Plato doesn't think of the soul as a physical part of the body akin to the heart, liver, or brain. With a powerful enough microscope, a person can see a germ; but no microscope, no matter how powerful, can reveal the soul, or any other immaterial substance, because it takes up no space.

In the *Phaedo*, Plato explains that a human being's soul is immaterial and immortal and that, upon death, it leaves the body. Plato also, in places, appears to endorse reincarnation, or the idea that one's immaterial soul is subsequently joined to another material body—sometimes another human body but perhaps, depending upon how one has lived his life, an animal body. We shall see later that this tenuous connection between the body and the soul in Plato's account—the suggestion that the same soul can be placed in any body—troubled Aristotle, who believed that body and soul were much more intimately related.

As a dualist, *Plato conceived of the soul as an immaterial, immortal substance joined to a material, mortal body. Sometimes, he also claimed that the soul could be joined to other bodies through the process of reincarnation.*

IX. LEONARDO'S LAST SUPPER

DURING THE 1490S, Leonardo was commissioned to paint a scene of the Last Supper for the refectory (dining hall) of the Dominican convent of Santa Maria delle Grazie in Milan. The charge was in keeping with the long-standing tradition of decorating refectories with this subject, so that the monks could symbolically share their meals with Christ and his disciples. Certainly, Leonardo would have been familiar with the compositional challenges involved. Having spent his formative years in Florence, he would have been exposed to several Last Suppers by artists such as Andrea del Castagno, Domenico Ghirlandaio, and Perugino.

Limited to some degree by the biblical text, artists who took on the Last Supper were required to seat Jesus and the twelve apostles at a table. Giotto's not-so-satisfactory solution was to seat half of the apostles with their backs to the viewer. More typically, the figures were placed at the back and sides of the table so that their faces could be seen—with the exception of Judas, who was usually shown sitting alone at the front.

In Leonardo's *Last Supper*, Christ and the apostles occupy only the far side of the table, leaving the front entirely open for the imagined participation of the viewer. On the central axis of the painting—framed by the largest of the windows, which offers natural light in lieu of a halo—Leonardo placed the figure of Jesus, behind whose head rests the composition's vanishing point. Interestingly, rather than segregate Judas, the much more subtle Leonardo relied on characterization instead of placement to convey Judas's guilt.

Leonardo's work is also unusual in that it depicts simultaneously two distinct moments in the narrative: Christ celebrating the Eucharist (that is, blessing the wine and bread) and also his revelation of Judas's impending betrayal, to which the apostles react in various ways. To Jesus's right, grouped together, are the three main protagonists of the story—the young, sleepy John the Evangelist; the eldest apostle, Peter; and the traitor, Judas. The remaining nine apostles are likewise arranged in groups of three, connected by gesture as well as intensity of conversation. In this way, Leonardo avoids the monotony characteristic of previous Last Suppers; in fact, his solution was so successful that it quickly became, despite its rapidly deteriorating condition, one of the most copied images of Western art.

Leonardo da Vinci, *The Last Supper* (1498)

The perfection of linear perspective, *coupled with an increased awareness of the natural world, resulted in the dramatic artistic advances observable in Leonardo's* Last Supper.

IX. DARWIN'S OWN "OBJECTIONS"

BECAUSE DARWIN WAS by nature an extremely thorough person, he examined his theory of evolution from many different angles before allowing it to be published, and he made sure to address in *On the Origin of Species* all of the potential objections he could imagine. Using a characteristically deferential tone, he wrote, "That many and serious objections may be advanced against the theory of descent with modification through variation and natural selection, I do not deny."

The first "serious objection" to which he addressed himself was the lack of transitional forms. If evolution indeed takes place in a gradual, stepwise manner proceeding from a single common ancestor, then why are there such great differences among species, and what happened to all of the intermediate forms? Darwin's response was that, at any given point in time, variation in a species' morphology (the structural characteristics of its anatomy) is small because adaptation takes place slowly and in minuscule steps. Over very long periods of time, however, these minuscule steps accumulate into vast differences. Regarding transitional forms, Darwin countered that the problem wasn't a lack of existence but a lack of evidence. Knowledge of the fossil record was still incomplete, Darwin pointed out; and as it developed, evidence of transitional forms would certainly be discovered.

Another serious objection that Darwin identified and addressed concerned the evolution of complex organs. In 1802, British theologian William Paley published a highly influential book titled *Natural Theology*, in which he defended the existence of God based on the purposeful design of certain complex anatomical structures, such as the human eye. Using what is now called the watchmaker analogy, Paley argued that the inner workings of a watch were so complex that the watch's existence necessarily implied the existence of an intelligent watchmaker. Darwin's theory of evolution, of course, provided an alternative explanation.

As Darwin later wrote, "The old argument of design in nature, as given by Paley, which formerly seemed to me so conclusive, fails, now that the law of natural selection has been discovered. We can no longer argue that, for instance, the beautiful hinge of a bivalve shell must have been made by an intelligent being, like the hinge of a door by man. There seems to be no more design in the variability of organic beings and in the action of natural selection, than in the course the wind blows."

Wishing to respond even before he could be criticized, *Darwin identified likely objections to his theory and addressed them with detailed counterarguments.*

IX. THE BABYLONIAN EXILE

DURING THE SEVENTH CENTURY BCE, the Babylonians succeeded the Assyrians as the dominant imperial power in the Near East. In 586 BCE, they invaded and conquered the kingdom of Judah, destroying the First Temple at Jerusalem and forcing Judah's political and religious leadership—the heirs of David—to return with them to Babylon. This period of captivity, known as the Babylonian Exile, precipitated a major crisis of faith among the last of the Israelites, because it called into question the validity of the ancient promise God had made to Abraham that his descendants would become a mighty and numerous nation.

The book of Psalms vividly captures the terrible doubt and soul-searching that the exiled people of Judah underwent during their captivity in Babylon. Some of them, their faith shattered by the destruction of the Temple and their removal to Babylon, no doubt spurned the god of Abraham and assimilated into Babylonian cults. Many others, however, became more fervently monotheistic than ever, believing that YHWH would eventually redeem them. In fact, this expectation of redemption strongly informed the biblical books written during this period—which, in turn, had a profound effect on the formation of the Jewish (as opposed to Israelite) religion.

According to Psalm 137, some Babylonians taunted the Judahites who still clung to their ancient religion: "There our captors asked of us words of song, our

tormenters asked us for mirth—'Sing us one of the songs of Zion.' But how should we sing a song of the Lord in a foreign land?" The prophet Ezekiel must have been taunted about his people's lost kingdom and razed temple in just this way, because one day as he walked beside the river Chebar in Babylon he had a startling vision: a divine chariot bearing the presence of God aloft in the heavens. The most important aspect of this vision was the sense of continuity it communicated: God had not abandoned His people, but rather had chosen to follow them into exile, the chariot symbolizing not only divine might and majesty but also divine mobility. Despite the political catastrophes that had befallen the people of Israel, including the annihilation of the northern tribes and the exile of the southerners, the special relationship between God and Israel endured.

A ca. 1310 depiction of the prophet Ezekiel.

The Babylonian Exile challenged *the faith of the Israelites. Some abandoned the god who had seemingly abandoned them, though others continued to believe He would redeem them.*

X. THE RAPE OF NANKING

FOLLOWING THE MANCHURIAN INCIDENT of September 18, 1931, no one in China doubted the boldness of the Japanese or their willingness to use force with impunity. This realization provoked a great deal of anti-Japanese sentiment among the Chinese—so much so that on January 28, 1932, Shanghai's municipal council posted local Guomindang troops around the city's foreign enclave to protect the Japanese civilians living there.

Chinese prisoners in Manchuria in 1937.

Nevertheless, because the Japanese didn't trust the Chinese to protect them, Japanese marines were sent ashore to defend the Japanese legation. The two forces clashed; and the following day, Japanese naval aircraft bombed the city. The fighting continued until May, when an armistice was signed.

The truce, however, didn't bring peace. Japanese troops occupied more of Manchuria, extending their sphere of control southward; and on July 7, 1937, while conducting night maneuvers near the Marco Polo Bridge outside Beijing, they exchanged fire with local Chinese forces. This skirmish quickly escalated; and by the end of July, the Second Sino-Japanese War had begun. At Shanghai, where Chiang's troops outnumbered the Japanese by ten to one, the generalissimo went on the offensive. But his attacks were ineffective, and high Chinese casualties soon forced Chiang to withdraw inland.

The Japanese soon pursued Chiang up the Yangtze Valley to Nanking (Nanjing), the Nationalist capital, which fell on December 12. Even though the Guomindang troops abandoned the city without much of a fight, the Japanese army unleashed a torrent of violence on Nanking, raping and murdering its inhabitants and looting the city over a period of ten weeks. Some conservative Japanese estimates place the number of civilian dead at forty thousand, while the official Chinese figure is three hundred thousand. The actual total is probably somewhere in between. In addition, about twenty thousand women were raped, and a third of the city burned to the ground. Meanwhile, Chiang retreated to Chungking (Chongqing), where he set up a provisional capital for his government in flight.

Sadly, Japanese atrocities of this sort were commonplace in China. Soldiers routinely conducted bayonet practice on live Chinese POWs; and in the northeast, outside the city of Harbin, Japanese doctors assigned to Unit 731 of the Kwantung Army tested gruesome bacterial weapons on numerous Chinese civilians.

Following the Marco Polo Bridge Incident of July 1937, *Japan and China began a war whose first phase culminated with the Japanese Rape of Nanking.*

X. THE STRUCTURE OF THE SOUL

IN BOTH THE *REPUBLIC* AND THE *PHAEDRUS* (not to be confused with the *Phaedo*), Plato describes the soul as consisting of three parts: the rational, the spirited, and the appetitive. The rational part of the soul is the part that thinks—about abstract ideas, such as mathematics or the forms, as well as about practical matters, such as what to make for dinner. The spirited part embodies honor and competition. For example, when you feel wronged, it's the spirited part of your soul that gets angry and wants payback. Finally, in the appetitive part of the soul resides one's appetites, or desires—especially for food, drink, and sex.

In a virtuous or just person, the three parts of the soul exist in harmony, each fulfilling its role excellently. Reason leads, spirit assists, and appetite obeys. Spirit can be a particularly useful assistant to reason in those cases when your soul is conflicted. For instance, let's say you have a strong desire (based in the appetitive part of your soul) to eat a quart of ice cream. At the same time, the rational part of your souls tells you that eating a quart of ice cream will be bad for your health. In this case, your spirit can help, either by getting mad at your appetite ("Only losers eat that much ice cream!") or by supporting your reason with its competitiveness ("C'mon, don't eat the whole carton! You want to be healthy and look good!").

An important advantage of this theory is that it allows Plato to explain easily the nature of psychological conflict. Thus, when a person does what he knows he shouldn't, such as following his appetite rather than his reason, Plato calls this "weakness of will," or "incontinence." An incontinent person is one who knows that he shouldn't eat an entire quart of ice cream (and that he will be angry at himself if he does so); yet, if a carton of ice cream is placed in front of him, his desire for it will overcome his reason, and he will eat it. In a virtuous person, however, reason predominates. Such a person exists in a harmonious state and experiences no such conflict. His appetite is obedient and satisfies itself with what his reason says it ought to have. The virtuous person knows he should exercise *and wants* to exercise; he knows he shouldn't eat a quart of ice cream, nor does he *want* to eat it.

According to Plato, *the soul is divided into three parts: the rational, the spirited, and the appetitive. In a virtuous person, all three parts operate in harmony.*

X. THE CLASSICAL NUDE

DURING PAGAN ANTIQUITY, nudity in art was commonplace. Throughout the Middle Ages, however, nudity was carefully restricted in the church-dominated world of the visual arts. The secular patronage of the guilds and the Medicis notwithstanding, most artists in Florence continued to paint and sculpt religious subjects for religious purposes. As a result, they rarely had the opportunity to depict female nudes, except for the occasional Eve being expelled from Eden. By the late fifteenth century, however, the increased availability and popularity of classical texts made pagan stories fashionable, and artists began receiving commissions for works based on Greek and Roman myths. Among those closely associated with the classical revival was Botticelli.

Pagan subjects offered considerable freedom, but they also posed a challenge. Classical texts often left a great deal to the imagination; thus, creating a visual counterpart could be demanding. Fortunately, there were plenty of contemporary retellings, both dramatic and textual, upon which artists could draw. A particularly popular subject was the birth of Venus, which performers often reenacted on the streets of Florence as well as in private homes. In fact, Botticelli is believed to have

based his famous 1480s painting of this subject on a contemporary retelling performed in honor of the Medicis, in whose countryside villa the painting would hang.

According to ancient tradition, Venus, the Roman goddess of love and beauty, was born out of the sea, which is why Botticelli shows her standing on a huge scallop shell

Botticelli, *The Birth of Venus* (1482–86)

about to wash ashore in a shower of roses. The breeze at her back is provided by the figures on the left—Zephyr, the god of the west wind, and a female figure usually identified as Zephyr's future wife, Chloris. As Venus wafts toward land, she is awaited by an attendant, who has brought forth a robe covered in flowers with which to clothe her. The painting's theme is overall one of abundance and fertility, suggesting not only springtime and rebirth but also marriage, a subject of particular interest to the dynasty-conscious Medicis. Only within such a mythic context, however, could Botticelli have felt comfortable depicting the central figure as an attractive female nude. Without the classical context, the painting would surely have been considered lewd.

The increased availability and popularity of ancient texts, *especially those relating to mythology, allowed artists to experiment with female nudes in non-Christian contexts.*

X. THE PROBLEM OF HEREDITY

THE MOST SERIOUS OBJECTION to Darwin's theory of evolution involved heredity—that is, the transmission of traits from parents to offspring. Nowhere in *On the Origin of Species* did Darwin explain satisfactorily how selected traits pass from one generation to the next. This was particularly troubling because for adaptation to occur, traits needed to be inherited across generations.

That some sort of heredity must exist was obvious to anyone who had ever noticed a family resemblance, but no one could explain in 1859 its material basis. The laws of genetics hadn't been discovered yet. Thus Darwin offered merely the commonly held belief that the traits of offspring represented an average of the traits of the parents. Yet there was an obvious problem with this "blending" model, which Scottish engineer Fleming Jenkins pointed out in an 1867 review: If the impact of variant traits is halved with each succeeding generation, then the overall tendency will be for variation to be lost altogether.

In 1868, Darwin responded with a "provisional hypothesis" that he called pangenesis. According to this new theory of heredity, different parts of the body generate invisible "gemmules," which travel through the bloodstream and collect in the reproductive organs for transmission to the next generation. Thus, advantageous traits are passed on in their entirety through intact gemmules. The existence of gemmules also explained how a mouse with a mutilated tail has offspring with normal tails. (Before its mutilation, the tail produced gemmules that were stored in the

August Weismann

mouse's reproductive organs.) Nevertheless, even Darwin recognized that aspects of this theory, especially the lack of a material basis for the gemmules, were troubling.

In 1893, more than a decade after Darwin's death, German embryologist August Weismann proposed a new "germ plasm" theory based on the observation that, in multicellular organisms, "germ" cells (reproductive egg and sperm cells) are sequestered from "soma" cells, which make up the rest of the body. According to Weismann's theory, the soma cells play no role in heredity. Only the germ cells pass on traits, and they aren't affected by any traits the soma cells acquire during the organism's lifetime. Meanwhile, to prove that both Lamarck's theory of inheritance and Darwin's theory of pangenesis were incorrect, Weismann conducted an experiment in which he cut off the tails of approximately fifteen hundred mice. Across twenty generations, not a single tailless mouse appeared.

The most serious problem *with Darwin's theory of evolution was its inability to explain the material basis for heredity.*

X. FROM JUDAHITES TO JEWS

THE BABYLONIAN EMPIRE would prove to be short-lived. During the middle of the sixth century BCE, the Persian Empire rose to prominence, and Cyrus the Great quickly smashed Babylon's power. But the Persian emperor wasn't content simply to copy the policies of his Babylonian predecessor. To distinguish himself from previous claimants to imperial grandeur and to glorify himself as a true *shahanshah* (king of kings), Cyrus decided to restore the kingdoms and principalities vanquished by the Babylonians and reinstate their political and religious elites, thus creating a new form of empire. Following this policy, in 538 BCE, he permitted willing Judahites to return to their homeland under the leadership of a priestly elite. In 515 BCE, the restored priesthood dedicated a new sanctuary at Jerusalem, known as the Second Temple.

The Second Temple as depicted in a ca. 1475 text.

Although the Persian period is one of the most obscure in Israelite history, we do know that the early years of the restored polity were fraught with doubt and uncertainty. The new principality was certainly not the United Monarchy of old, nor even the kingdom of Judah restored to its former glory. The number of Judahite priests and nobles who returned from Babylon was relatively small, and they must have had quite a difficult time attempting to rebuild the Israelite nation. Even after the decline of the Persians, the new principality never became an independent state. Instead, it simply continued in subservience to the next regional power, always financially exploited and occasionally persecuted as well.

Because of these changed circumstances, during the Second Temple period (515 BCE–70 CE) we see a decisive shift in the identity of the Israelite community. Previously, Israel had been a confederation of nomadic tribes, then a monarchical state, and then *two* such states, until the eradication of the northern kingdom compelled Judah to carry on the Israelite legacy alone. After the Babylonian Exile, the community of Israel no longer enjoyed sovereignty over its own affairs. Thus, its people had to rely on other means to distinguish themselves within the cosmopolitan empires to which they subsequently belonged. In short, during the Persian period and especially during the Greek period that followed, being a member of the people of Israel meant less that one belonged to an Israelite political entity and more that one followed ancestral customs that marked one as ethnically and religiously Judahite, or *Jewish*.

During the Second Temple period, *Israelite identity became much more dependent on commonly held ancestral traditions, religious customs, and history.*

XI. WORLD WAR II IN CHINA

DURING THE MID-1930S, Chiang's troubles with the Japanese gave the Communists a respite, during which the survivors of the Long March became the hardened core of a new revolutionary vanguard. As its leader, Mao decided that the Communists

should fight both Chiang and the Japanese simultaneously. Because Chiang's policy was similar (taking on both Mao and the Japanese), Chinese resistance to the occupying Japanese army was sporadic and uncoordinated.

The first attempt to bring the Nationalists and the Communists together was made by the Soviet Union, which directed Mao in early 1936 to join with Chiang in resisting the Japanese. Chiang continued to reject such a partnership, however, until December 1936, when soldiers under the command of Guomindang

Chiang Kai-shek in 1942 or 1943.

general Zhang Xueliang kidnapped Chiang outside the city of Xian and coerced him into accepting the Communists as allies. Terms were subsequently negotiated, and the Second United Front was declared in April 1937. Although this nominal union lasted until the end of World War II, it never amounted to much and ended for all practical purposes in January 1941, when Guomindang forces ambushed and defeated the CCP's New Fourth Army.

The United States also had an interest in containing Japanese expansionism; and although some in the State Department were suspicious of Chiang, he was the obvious choice over Mao. Even before Pearl Harbor, the US government facilitated the recruitment of former military pilots to serve in Chiang's air force, and this unit—known as the First American Volunteer Group, or the Flying Tigers—provided much-needed support for Guomindang troops. After Pearl Harbor, the War Department sent Gen. Joseph W. "Vinegar Joe" Stilwell to China to serve as Chiang's chief of staff; improve his army's combat efficiency; and, most importantly, keep China in the war.

When Stilwell found Chiang uncooperative and reluctant to pursue the war aggressively, he courted Mao as well, sending a group of envoys to Yenan in July 1944. Known as the Dixie Mission because it was sent to the "rebels," this delegation didn't achieve much. The Communists were running an effective guerrilla campaign and rescuing downed American pilots. Expecting them to do more was asking a lot, and the Americans didn't have much to offer. The US commitment to Nationalist rule in postwar China was already clear, and the best Mao could hope for was American tolerance of a coalition government—which didn't seem to be worth much.

Although both the US and the USSR pressured their Chinese allies *to fight the Japanese aggressively, Chinese resistance was hampered by the enmity between Chiang and Mao.*

XI. THE KALLIPOLIS

IN THE *REPUBLIC*, widely considered his most important work, Plato connects his views about the soul and the forms to ideas about political philosophy. The centerpiece of the *Republic* is Plato's theory of the ideal state—which he calls the Kallipolis, from the Greek meaning "beautiful city" or "noble city."

Plato divides the residents of the Kallipolis into three classes, each of which corresponds to a different part of the soul. The lowest class, corresponding to the appetitive part of the soul, is made up of the city's workers—shipwrights, shoemakers, and farmers, as well as doctors, painters, and architects. The next highest class, corresponding to the spirited part of the soul, is the class of guards, whose members are elevated from the working class on the basis of their physical and mental prowess. The task of the guards is to protect the city from enemies within (as a police force) and without (as an army). The highest class of all, corresponding to the rational part of the soul, is chosen from among the best of the guardian class. These people, the rulers, are responsible for making the laws of the city and managing other decisions.

A basic principle of Plato's utopia is that each citizen should stick to his own task and not meddle in the tasks of others. A harmonious, just city—like a harmonious, just soul—is one in which rulers (the rational part) rule, guards (the spirited part) assist the rulers, and workers (the appetitive part) obey.

Perhaps the most memorable aspect of this scheme is Plato's concept of the philosopher-king. "Until philosophers rule as kings," Plato has the character Socrates say, "or those who are now called kings and leading men genuinely and adequately philosophize—that is, until political power and philosophy entirely coincide—...cities will have no rest from evils, nor, I think, will the human race."

According to Plato, only philosophers, who love wisdom, have knowledge of the forms, including those of justice and the good. Therefore, only philosopher-kings can make laws that are truly just and good. If members of the other two classes, who lack knowledge of the forms, attempted to rule the city, they would make decisions based not on reason but according to spirit or, even worse, appetite. Under such governance, the city would cease to be harmonious; and, like an incontinent individual, it would become conflicted and go wrong.

Plato's most important work, *the* Republic, *applies his theory of the tripartite soul to the political organization of an ideal city, which he calls the Kallipolis.*

XI. A MODERN MARCUS AURELIUS

ONE OF THE GREATEST TRIBUTES an ancient Roman could receive was to have an equestrian statue created in his honor. These monumental sculptures were typically made of bronze, a much more expensive medium than marble, so they were awarded sparingly. In fact, they were usually reserved for emperors.

Because bronze was so valuable—and so easily recast into munitions during times of war—few equestrian statues survived beyond Roman times. Yet Renaissance elites were well aware of them and their prestige from textual sources and also because one notable example did endure: the statue of Marcus Aurelius in Rome. This bronze survived the Middle Ages because for centuries it was misidentified as Constantine, the first Christian emperor of Rome, and thus preserved by medieval Christians.

As the program for the decoration of Florence's cathedral waned during the 1430s, sculptors sought new commissions. The prospect of working in bronze rather than in marble was especially appealing to older artists such as Donatello, who sought to ease the wear and tear on their hands. The advantage of sculpting in bronze was that the creative work was done in the highly malleable medium of wax. The sculptor created a full-sized wax model and left the rest of the work to bronze-casters, who used the lost-wax technique developed during antiquity to produce a hollow statue.

Although some technical advances were made, working in bronze remained sufficiently expensive that the opportunity to create a larger-than-life statue was considered the chance of a lifetime. Just such a chance lured Donatello from Florence to Padua in 1443. The project, which would decorate the front of Padua's Il Santo cathedral, was an equestrian statue of the Venetian mercenary Erasmo da Narni, popularly known as Gattamelata.

The completed monument is a sophisticated recapitulation of the Marcus Aurelius bronze, which Donatello undoubtedly studied while visiting Rome. In both statues, for example, the horse is posed with one leg raised; likewise, the rider sits

erect, gesturing with one hand while reining in his steed with the other. Features of Gattamelata's horse, notably the coiffures of its mane and tail, also borrow heavily from antiquity—yet Donatello modernizes the genre by adjusting the proportions of the rider to the mount, so that the perspective would appear more lifelike, and also by particularizing Gattamelata's face, so that the statue would seem less generic and more like a portrait.

Mid-fifteenth century prosperity, *along with a continuing interest in antiquity, led to the commissioning of monumental bronzes in the style of ancient Rome.*

Marcus Aurelius (ca. 161–80)

XI. MENDELIAN GENETICS

Gregor Mendel

BETWEEN 1856 AND 1863, Moravian monk Gregor Mendel conducted a detailed study of inheritance. His experiments involved the crossbreeding of purebred pea plants that varied in traits such as height (tall versus dwarf) and seed shape (round versus wrinkled). Each of the first generation (F_1) hybrids produced by Mendel exhibited the same trait—the dominant one. However, when Mendel crossed the apparently uniform F_1 hybrids, he found in the subsequent (F_2) generation a dominant-to-recessive ratio of 3:1—that is, for every three offspring with the dominant trait, there was a single offspring with the recessive trait.

Mendel also experimented with F_1 hybrids whose parents differed in two traits, When he crossed these dihybrids, he found in the F_2 generation a ratio of 9:3:3:1— meaning that for every nine offspring showing two dominant traits, there were six with one dominant and one recessive trait and one that showed both recessive traits.

The consistency of these ratios led Mendel to the insight that the factors underlying inheritance must retain their integrity over generations and be biparental. In other words, organisms possess two copies of each trait-producing factor: one originating from the maternal gamete (egg cell) and the other from the paternal gamete (sperm cell). When these gametes combine, the resulting organism inherits both copies, with the dominant trait prevailing if at least one copy of it is present. This model explained Mendel's results perfectly: Because the F_1 hybrids inherited one dominant and one recessive factor, they all showed the dominant trait. However, when the F_1 hybrids were crossed, each parent randomly passed on just one of these factors, thereby allowing for the reemergence of the recessive trait.

Because Mendel published his work in an obscure journal, it went unnoticed until 1900—when botanists Hugo de Vries and Carl Correns, working independently, uncovered Mendel's findings.

Although Mendelian genetics finally provided the material basis for heredity that Darwinian theory had been lacking, its rediscovery produced no consensus. Rather, a rift quickly developed between Mendelians, who believed that species divergence occurs through large abrupt trait jumps (such as from dwarf to tall), and biometricians, who believed that traits diverge in very minute steps. Speaking for the Mendelians, William Bateson argued that evolution is largely driven by large random mutations; while Karl Pearson and Walter Weldon, representing the biometricians, defended the gradual natural selection that Darwin had proposed.

Mendelian genetics explained *the mechanism by which traits are inherited—a mechanism that Darwinian theory had notably been lacking.*

XI. THE EMERGENCE OF JUDAISM

PERSIAN HEGEMONY over the Near East lasted about two hundred years. Then, during the late fourth century BCE, Alexander the Great conquered most of the known world, spreading Greek culture along with Greek political influence and creating the phenomenon known as Hellenism. Throughout the lands that Alexander conquered,

Greek language, customs, art, philosophy, and education mingled with and decisively shaped indigenous cultures from Africa to India. Following Alexander's sudden death in 323 BCE, his successors, the Diadochi, fought with one another for control of his empire. Finally, after years of inconclusive warfare, Alexander's domain was partitioned and several smaller empires established.

A mosaic of Alexander the Great.

In the former kingdom of Judah, now known as Judaea, the community of Israel continued to live semiautonomously, as it had under Persian rule. By this time, however, the community was distinguished even less by its political identity and more by its common cultural and religious heritage. Thus, by the Greek period, we speak not of Judahites but of Jews, indicating a people distinguished specifically by custom and belief rather than by political affiliation or place of residence. Although the word *Jew* derives from the Greek *Ioudaios*, meaning "Judahite," the term was (and is) used to identify not only the people of Israel living in Judaea but also those residing outside the Promised Land. Already during the Greek period, there were large Jewish communities in Babylon (where many Judahites had remained even after the restoration), in Egypt, and in Asia Minor.

More generally during the Second Temple period, scripturalism—the culture of preserving, studying, and celebrating the Torah—became increasingly central to Jewish identity. In fact, "Torahcentrism" began to rival even sacrificial worship at the Temple as the main distinguishing element in Jewish religiosity. This was especially true in the growing number of Jewish communities outside Judaea, which consolidated along ethnic and religious lines yet couldn't escape the pressures of Hellenism.

The spread of these Jewish communities throughout the Hellenized world during the period of the Second Temple began what has since come to be known as the Diaspora (from the Greek word meaning "scattering"). Within the communities of the Diaspora, the Torah was critical because it was portable and not, like the Temple itself, tied to Jerusalem. As a result, the Torah was increasingly studied, recited, and preached in communal centers known as synagogues.

Judaism emerged during the period of the Second Temple *out of ancestral Israelite traditions influenced by new geopolitical realities.*

XII. CIVIL WAR

FOLLOWING THE JAPANESE SURRENDER in August 1945, Chiang and Mao sat down under US auspices to negotiate the formation a coalition government. No one doubted that the US favored Chiang, but Mao wanted to buy time. Meanwhile, as fifty-three thousand US Marines took over Japanese positions in the north, US Navy ships and Army Air Corps planes ferried Guomindang troops up from the south to hold those positions. The Soviet Union provided similar aid to the CCP in Manchuria, which the Red Army had taken from the Japanese. More generally, the Guomindang took control of most Chinese cities, while the CCP expanded its influence in the countryside—except in the northeast, where Red Army troops continued to hold the major cities.

A tenuous truce prevailed until the Red Army began withdrawing in the spring of 1946. At this point, the contest for control of Manchuria's cities turned violent; and by November, the parties were no longer negotiating. Instead, a civil war began, and Chiang quickly went on the offensive, following the Japanese practice of targeting urban areas and major transportation routes. For the most part, the Nationalists ignored the large swaths of countryside where the CCP dominated. They did overrun Yenan in February 1947, but the CCP leadership had already cleared out.

Although the military forces of the Guomindang outnumbered the Communist People's Liberation Army (PLA) and also possessed more and better armaments, the brutality of the Nationalist regime and Chiang's oppressive taxation policies alienated much of the citizenry, which gradually threw its support behind Mao.

During the Huaihai campaign, fought during the winter of 1948–49, the PLA soundly defeated the Guomindang army, whose leadership proved highly unreliable. It was a turning point in the war. Afterward, the PLA picked off one Nationalist city after another, besieging them and starving them out. Not only Chiang's soldiers but also his generals began to defect in large numbers. On October 1, 1949, after the fall of Beijing, Mao announced the establishment of the People's Republic of China (PRC). Meanwhile, Chiang and the remaining Nationalists fled to the island of Taiwan, where they established a new Republic of China (ROC) government.

A 1949 poster celebrating the founding of the PRC.

Despite the Guomindang's military superiority *and US backing, the CCP won the Chinese civil war because Chiang's brutality alienated large segments of the citizenry.*

XII. THE WORKS OF ARISTOTLE

ARISTOTLE (384–322 BCE) was seventeen years old when he traveled to Athens from Macedonia in northern Greece to study at Plato's Academy. He remained there until Plato's death twenty years later. Then, after traveling to Asia Minor and some islands in the Aegean Sea, he returned to his Macedonian homeland, where he tutored the young Alexander the Great. In 334 BCE, Aristotle returned to Athens and founded his own school, the Lyceum. Following Alexander's death in 323 BCE, Aristotle left Athens because of anti-Macedonian feeling there and died the following year.

A Roman copy of a Greek bronze bust of Aristotle.

In all, the surviving works of Aristotle number about twenty-four hundred pages (or about twice the extent of Plato's dialogues). Many of Aristotle's works have been lost, however. We know this from sources that refer, for example, to dialogues that he composed, probably in a style similar to that used by Plato. The texts we do have consist of lecture notes, some more polished than others, which Aristotle probably revised at various points during his lifetime. These notes were compiled and circulated by Andronicus of Rhodes about 250 years after Aristotle's death.

They cover a broad range of subjects—including substance and existence, change, time, space, and astronomy. Aristotle's *Rhetoric* explains how to write persuasive speeches for different purposes. His *Poetics* is the first known treatise on literary theory. About a third of his extant work concerns biology. Among the most important of his surviving works are the *Metaphysics*—which discusses, among other things, what it is to be an independently existing thing; *On the Soul*—which concerns the nature of the soul in plants, animals, and human beings; and the *Nicomachean Ethics*, which describes the good life for a human being. Aristotle also invented logic, and most philosophers followed his general approach to the subject until the late nineteenth century.

Although many of these subjects were first discussed by Plato, it was Aristotle whose works came to dominate philosophical thought during the Christian Era. By the Middle Ages, Aristotle's philosophy had become so pervasive in the West that he was known simply as the Philosopher. In contemporary times, his status is not quite so great, yet he remains highly influential. The Neo-Aristotelians, for example, are a group of modern philosophers working on ethical issues who have taken as their starting point Aristotle's own works on ethics.

The most important of Plato's students was Aristotle, *whose wide-ranging works have had an unrivaled influence on the history of philosophy down to the present day.*

XII. MICHELANGELO'S DAVID

THE MEDICI DYNASTY in Florence reached its height during the reign of Lorenzo the Magnificent, who came to power as a twenty-year-old in 1469 and ruled the city until his death in 1492. Following Lorenzo's death, Florence endured a decade of political upheaval, which ended finally with the establishment of a new republican government.

To shore up its legitimacy, the fledgling city council began commissioning new civic monuments that functioned both as art and as political propaganda. News of these commissions brought Leonardo back from a two-decade sojourn in Milan and also recalled Michelangelo Buonarroti (1475–1564), who had left his native Florence for the relative peace of Rome in 1496. Although Michelangelo was still a young man when he returned to Florence in 1501, the splendid *Pietà* he had carved while in Rome made him the obvious choice for the first and most prized of the commissions: a statue of David to be carved out of a giant block of marble that had been sitting in the cathedral stone yard for nearly a century. The block had originally been allotted to Donatello for a colossal statue that was never realized

The heroic figure of David had long been associated with the city of Florence, communicating the triumph of courage over tyranny. The two Davids most recently produced in the city had been bronzes created by Donatello and Verrocchio under commissions from the Medicis. Both statues depicted David standing astride the head of a vanquished Goliath, but Michelangelo chose instead an earlier point in the narrative: the moment when David, looking into the distance, sees his enemy and contemplates what to do. Because of this innovative choice, Michelangelo's *David* possesses a psychological intensity that engages viewers directly as they stand before it.

Today, the statue resides in a Florentine museum; but in 1504, the year it was completed, it was installed in front of the Palazzo della Signoria (also called the Palazzo Vecchio). With the seat of the republican government at its back, the statue gazed pointedly to the south, vigilant against political threats, especially those coming from Rome.

The new republican government *in Florence employed the greatest artists of the early sixteenth century to decorate the civic center with ambitious propaganda, including Michelangelo's* David.

Michelangelo, *David* (1501–4)

XII. THE MENDELIAN–BIOMETRICIAN DEBATE

ALTHOUGH MENDELIAN GENETICS doesn't contradict Darwinian theory, some biologists initially thought that it did. Darwin had identified ample variation as one of three conditions necessary for adaptation by natural selection. Yet the existence of dominant and recessive traits seemed to imply that the dominant traits would eventually "take over," thus reducing genetic variation and bringing evolution to a halt.

The confusion resulted primarily from a misunderstanding of the concept of gene dominance. Most organisms are diploid, meaning that they possess two sets of genetic factors (known as alleles), one maternally derived and the other paternally derived. Identifying a trait as dominant means simply that when two competing alleles are present, that trait prevails. For example, if one parent passes on the allele for blue eyes and the other parent passes on the allele for brown eyes, the eye color of the resulting child will indicate which allele is dominant. This does not mean, however, that the recessive allele disappears. In fact, it is just as likely to be passed on as the dominant allele.

This confusion was resolved in 1908, when British mathematician G. H. Hardy and German physician Wilhelm Weinberg showed mathematically that both dominant and recessive alleles will remain in a population unless an evolutionary force (such as selection) acts on that population. This simple concept, now known as the Hardy-Weinberg equilibrium principle, reaffirmed the validity of Mendelian genetics and laid to rest all lingering support for the blending model of inheritance.

Meanwhile, the debate over evolutionary tempo between the Mendelians and the biometricians (also known as the Darwinists) continued to rage until British statistician R. A. Fisher finally put an end to it. Between 1918 and 1930, Fisher investigated quantitative traits, which result from multiple genes interacting with environmental factors (as opposed to so-called Mendelian traits, which result from single genes). Fisher's breakthrough was his use of a Mendelian statistical framework to explain the complex nature of quantitative traits, which were the focus of most biometric research.

What Fisher found was that the continuous variation observed by Darwin was, in fact, the product of multiple, discrete Mendelian factors acting in concert with environmental factors (such as temperature and nutrition). This discovery, along with Sewall Wright's work on inbreeding and J. B. S. Haldane's study of the mathematics of natural selection, created a new field, population genetics, the focus of which was the distribution and frequency of alleles over time and space.

Out of the Mendelian–biometrician debate *emerged the field of population genetics, which investigates the variation and behavior of genes in specific populations.*

XII. THE MACCABEAN REVOLT

DURING THE THIRD AND SECOND CENTURIES BCE, Hellenism continued to influence the Jewish communities living under Greek rule. The impact of Greek thought can be seen, for example, in the writings of the Jewish philosopher Philo of Alexandria, who interpreted the texts of the Hebrew Bible allegorically and sought to reconcile them with Greek ethics and metaphysics. Meanwhile, the Greek language became the lingua franca of educated people throughout the Mediterranean world and much of the Near East—among them the educated Jewish elites.

A detail of a Roman goblet showing Jewish religious objects.

Although the Torah and the Temple remained touchstones, cosmopolitan influences did lead to an attenuation of Jewish identity. Eventually, a culture war developed in second-century BCE Judaea between Hellenized liberals, some of whom sought to mask the marks of their circumcisions, and ethnocentric conservatives, who idealized Israel's religious heritage and objected to Hellenizing practices such as intermarriage. This infighting was soon interrupted, however, by the Maccabean Revolt.

Although our chief sources for this period, the deuterocanonical books 1 and 2 Maccabees and the writings of the Jewish historian Flavius Josephus, offer conflicting details on many points, it seems clear that the Jews found themselves caught in a geopolitical struggle between the Ptolemies (the Greek rulers of Egypt) and the Seleucids (the Greek rulers of Syria). When the Seleucid emperor Antiochus IV Epiphanes failed in an effort to conquer Ptolemaic territory, he turned his attention to the Jews, who had once been subjects of the Ptolemies.

For reasons that remain obscure, Antiochus chose to interfere in the internal affairs of the Jews in the most provocative way possible: Reportedly, he erected a statue of Zeus within the Second Temple—an unpardonable blasphemy against the God of Israel. He also oppressed the Jews by prohibiting their observance of the Torah, martyring gruesomely anyone who resisted.

The insurgency that arose in response to this oppression was led by a man named Judah, better known by his Aramaic epithet Maccabee (the hammer). Beginning in 167 BCE, Judah led a revolt against Antiochus; and after several years of struggle, the Maccabees succeeded in freeing the people of Israel from Seleucid domination. The Jewish holiday Hanukkah commemorates this victory and the subsequent miracle wrought by God when He made one day's worth of consecrated oil last the full eight days necessary for new oil to be pressed and consecrated.

Tensions that had developed in Judaea *between Hellenized Jews and religious traditionalists were only temporarily resolved by the Maccabean Revolt.*

XIII. THE GREAT LEAP FORWARD

AMONG THE GREATEST CHALLENGES facing the new People's Republic was a problem that had been dogging China since the Opium Wars: modernization. In the realm of agriculture, the CCP addressed this problem with radical land reform. Acting in the name of class struggle, the state confiscated the holdings of capitalist landlords and well-to-do farmers, redistributing the land to the peasantry. However, the peasants weren't allowed to farm the land as they pleased. Instead, as in the Soviet Union of the late 1920s, they were "collectivized," or grouped together into cooperatives to produce food for the state. Meanwhile, millions of their former landlords were put on trial and sentenced to death.

The task of modernizing Chinese industry was made particularly difficult by the government's lack of funds. Much of China's wealth had been spent on the long war with Japan, and Chiang had absconded with the rest. What the Communists were able to accomplish was done largely with Soviet aid. The USSR also sent ten thousand technical advisers to help China plan and construct factories, communications systems, power plants, and other large infrastructure projects. As a result, the First Five-Year Plan (1953–57) yielded a 9 percent increase in Chinese national income.

Nevertheless, as it became clear that Soviet-style industrialization wasn't well suited to China's predominantly agrarian economy, the CCP decided to shift its focus from industrial development in the cities to industrial development in the countryside. During the Great Leap Forward (1958–60), the state strengthened its authority over the rural population, extending collectivization and mobilizing large pools of rural labor for irrigation, flood control, and land reclamation projects. Manipulating the personality cult that had developed around Mao, the CCP was able to whip the peasants into a nationalist frenzy that made it possible to work them day and night with only short breaks for sleeping and eating.

In 1958, as part of the Great Leap Forward, the state rolled out a "backyard furnace" program that was supposed to boost Chinese steel production. The idea was that farmers could work these small-scale iron smelters in their spare time. The furnaces, however, were poorly constructed and proved to be inefficient as well as dangerous, producing very little usable steel. Moreover, the time required for overworked peasants to run them was time taken away from agriculture. Crops went unharvested, and the result was a massive famine that killed as many as thirty million people. Clearly, the infallible Mao had blundered.

During the formative years of the People's Republic, *radical political, economic, and social reforms were undertaken, culminating in the disastrous Great Leap Forward.*

XIII. THE MOST BASIC SUBSTANCE

THE QUESTION OF WHAT SORT OF SUBSTANCE is the most basic goes all the way back to the beginnings of Greek philosophy. For Plato the most basic, unchanging substances are the forms. When Aristotle takes up this question, however, he seems to turn Plato on his head.

Aristotle begins with the premise that the most basic substances are concrete individuals (meaning objects), such as the human being Socrates and the shirt I am wearing. When Aristotle says that these substances are the most basic, what he means is that they have to exist in order for other things to exist. For example, red can't exist in the world without something, such as my shirt, being red. Without objects, there can be no properties, so the objects must be more basic than the properties.

The same is true of other universals, such as "human being." Aristotle's view is that the existence of universals depends on the existence of concrete individuals. Without concrete individual human beings, there can be no universal "human being."

In both the *Physics* and the *Metaphysics*, however, Aristotle wonders whether concrete individuals might themselves be reduced into even more fundamental components. Consider a table. What is it essentially? One might answer in terms of its material constitution—wood, for instance. Aristotle would say that while a table may be *made* of wood, what it is to *be* a table is more than simply wood. The wood has to be arranged and shaped in a particular way for a particular purpose. Aristotle calls this idea of shape and arrangement a thing's "form" (not to be confused with Plato's theory of the forms).

In the *Physics*, Aristotle analyzes several concrete individuals with regard to their form and also what he calls their matter. The form of a house, for example, would be the design created by its architect; the matter would be the bricks, mortar, and other materials used in its construction. Aristotle then considers which aspect is more fundamentally the thing itself, the form or the matter? His answer is that, although both are important, the form is more fundamentally the thing, because only when the form is added does the matter become the thing. The matter, by contrast, is only *potentially* the thing.

Consider the example of the house again. A pile of bricks and mortar is *potentially* a house, but only when these materials are properly arranged does the house *actually* come into existence.

In exploring the question *of what substance is most basic, Aristotle turns Plato on his head. While Plato considers the universal most basic, Aristotle thinks it is the concrete individual.*

XIII. THE ART OF THE NEW REPUBLIC

IN ADDITION TO COMMISSIONING Michelangelo's *David*, the republican government in Florence decided to decorate the walls of its primary audience hall, the Sala dei Cinquecento, with two monumental paintings. The subjects would be historic battles—both victories for Florence over regional enemies who posed contemporary threats. Leonardo was commissioned in 1503 to paint the battle of Anghiari, a 1440 conflict in which the Florentines defeated the Milanese. Soon afterward, Michelangelo was chosen to paint the battle of Cascina, a 1364 victory over the Pisans.

Because of the incredible size of these paintings, the artists had to work out their ideas in hundreds of sketches, ultimately culminating in full-scale paper cartoons— that is, drawings that could be transferred to prepared plaster in order to facilitate the painting. Records show that at least the central portion of Leonardo's cartoon was transferred to a wall in the Sala dei Cinquecento and painting begun; Michelangelo's cartoon, on the other hand, never left the studio allotted to him. Both men departed Florence before completing their work: Leonardo to Milan in pursuit of an equestrian commission and Michelangelo to Rome to create a tomb for Pope Julius II.

In the meantime, many talented young artists were drawn to Florence by the opportunities available there. An ambitious twenty-one-year-old native of Urbino named Raphael Sanzio (1483–1520) came, perhaps seeking one of the battle-scene commissions. Instead, he had to settle for lesser (but profitable) commissions from

Raphael, *Madonna of the Goldfinch* (1505–6)

Florence's affluent merchant class, whose members wanted him to paint portraits and religious scenes for their homes.

An example is Raphael's *Madonna of the Goldfinch*, which shows the strong influence of Leonardo. In this small panel painting, the Madonna lifts her gaze up from her prayer book to glance at, and place her arm around, the baby John the Baptist, who is offering the Christ child a goldfinch (symbolizing his future martyrdom). Typically, these figures would have been situated in an architecturally rendered space (such as a court), representing heaven. But, influenced by Leonardo's emphasis on the natural world, Raphael sets his figures within an intimate, naturalistic landscape, complete with finely rendered plant life. Rather than the usual throne, Mary sits on a rock. In addition, by dressing her in contemporary clothing and deemphasizing the halos, Raphael makes the interaction between mother and son seem more intimate, befitting the painting's intended domestic setting.

Florence at the turn *of the sixteenth century became a magnet for artists in search of commissions, attracting Leonardo and Michelangelo as well as the young Raphael.*

XIII. POPULATION GENETICS

THE EARLY PIONEERS OF POPULATION GENETICS—Fisher, Wright, and Haldane—were especially interested in identifying the mechanisms that govern allele frequency within a given population. According to the theory of natural selection, advantageous alleles will, by definition, improve an organism's reproductive success. Therefore, natural selection promotes the spread of these alleles, because the organisms possessing them will produce more viable offspring. Eventually, all individuals in a population should possess the same advantageous alleles.

This principle was well understood, but biologists were still having trouble separating out the other evolutionary forces at work, so the early population geneticists began to construct simple models using single genes with only two alleles. According to the Hardy-Weinberg equilibrium principle, allele frequency should remain constant in a population over time unless that population is acted upon by one or more evolutionary forces. Characterizing these forces became the focus of much of the population geneticists' work.

Eventually, population geneticists identified four main evolutionary forces: mutation; migration; random genetic drift; and, of course, natural selection. In general, the first two produce new genetic variation on which natural selection operates. Mutation refers to the physical changes in DNA that take place randomly from time to time. Migration (also called gene flow) describes the variation introduced into a population when organisms from adjacent populations join it. Random genetic drift, meanwhile, expresses the statistical effect of chance on allele transmission.

During the 1920s and 1930s, Fisher, Wright, and Haldane used this framework to characterize the multitude of factors capable of causing populations to fall out of Hardy-Weinberg equilibrium. These factors included inbreeding (the nonrandom mating of close relatives), changes in mutation rates, migration from nearby populations, and the strength of selection on a particular allele. An allele producing keen eyesight, for example, would be strongly selected on and perpetuated in a population because it would improve reproductive success among possessing organisms compared with other individuals in the population.

Although all populations experience some degree of flux as individual alleles come and go, a population in Hardy-Weinberg equilibrium maintains the same general frequency of alleles over multiple generations. If this frequency changes over time, then some evolutionary force must be at work, which is why population geneticists define evolution as a change in allele frequency within a given population.

The early population geneticists *identified four main evolutionary forces: mutation, migration, genetic drift, and natural selection,*

XIII. THE HASMONEAN DYNASTY

FOR A CENTURY after the Maccabean Revolt, Israel became once more an autonomous state. Governed by Judah Maccabee's descendants (known as the Hasmoneans), the Jewish community in Judaea flourished and even expanded beyond the borders of the United Monarchy. However, neither the political successes of the Hasmoneans nor the wealth that flowed into the country could mask the social and religious tensions that roiled the Jewish nation, just as they had during the early second century BCE.

The ongoing conflict between Hellenizers and traditionalists led to the emergence of four distinct groups that functioned in part as religious sects and in part as political movements. All of them debated actively what it meant to be a Jew. These groups were the Sadducees, the Pharisees, the Essenes, and the Zealots.

Dominated by several aristocratic families, the Sadducees were the Temple elite—its priests, scribes, and other functionaries. They were also, ironically, the most radical Hellenizers. The Pharisees, by contrast, seem to have been middle-class populists who resented the Sadducee-dominated priestly establishment. The cornerstones of their creed were strict observance of the Torah—supplemented and considerably amplified by the Pharisees' own oral teachings—and a strident emphasis on ritual purity.

The Essenes were members of the priestly establishment who broke with the Sadducees, most likely because they disagreed with certain policies of the Temple administration. Forming their own sect, they abandoned Jerusalem and moved into the Judean wilderness, establishing a semimonastic community near the Dead Sea. Most of all, they were defined by their emphasis on communal living and their

A piece of a Dead Sea Scroll.

belief in an impending, violent apocalypse, following which the members of the sect would be redeemed by a messiah. (The teachings of the Essenes are known primarily through texts discovered near the Dead Sea and hence called the Dead Sea Scrolls.)

The fourth group, the Zealots, emerged only after the annexation of Hasmonean Judaea by the Romans in 64 BCE. In the view of Josephus, our primary source for this period, the Zealots were illegitimate deviants from true Judaism—distinguished most of all by their refusal to accept the sovereignty of the Romans, against whom they continually fomented violent rebellion. Josephus correctly points out the lack of any basis in Jewish tradition for such extremism, but he fails to mention his own bias as an assimilated Roman citizen.

Although politically and economically successful, *the Hasmonean dynasty couldn't resolve internal disputes over the true legacy of Israel and what it meant to be a Jew.*

XIV. THE SINO-SOVIET SPLIT

SINCE THE 1920S, THE SOVIET UNION had played an influential role in Chinese politics. It had encouraged the formation of the CCP, aided Sun and Chiang in the reunification of the country, supported Mao in the civil war, and provided the money and technical expertise necessary to implement the First Five-Year Plan. During the Great Leap Forward, however, relations between the PRC and the USSR began to deteriorate.

An important turning point came in February 1956, when Soviet premier Nikita Khrushchev made a famous speech to the Twentieth Congress of the Soviet Communist Party denouncing the late Joseph Stalin. Because the CCP was deeply Stalinist (especially in its monolithic control of the state), Mao hadn't been briefed in advance about the speech's contents. Thus he was taken by surprise and personally embarrassed. Khrushchev's new de-Stalinization policy also put the Soviet party at odds with the CCP.

In 1957, Khrushchev invited Mao to attend the fortieth anniversary celebration of the October Revolution in Moscow. (The trip was Mao's second and last outside China.) While in Moscow, he and Khrushchev signed a secret agreement pledging the Soviets to provide scientific and technical assistance to China, including nuclear weapons expertise. The next year, however, during a visit to China, Khrushchev publicly criticized the Great Leap Forward because it emphasized rural peasants at the expense of the urban proletariat that orthodox Marxists considered the only true revolutionary class. Khrushchev also saw the Great Leap Forward as reckless and misguided because China's rural communes lacked the technical know-how necessary for efficient industrial production.

During the next few years, a series of diplomatic squabbles and slights widened the rift. For example, in August 1958, the PLA shelled the Nationalist garrison on the island of Quemoy, precipitating an international crisis. Because Mao hadn't informed Khrushchev in advance, the infuriated Soviet leader refused to support China's action and later canceled the nuclear weapons deal, recalling all of its 1,390 scientific advisers. (Despite this loss of Soviet aid, China still managed to develop a nuclear weapon by 1964.)

The Chinese retaliated by stepping up their criticism of Khrushchev as a "revisionist." By the mid-1960s, the two former allies were engaging in border skirmishes that claimed hundreds of lives. Meanwhile, China grew increasingly isolated on the international scene, and Mao began to feel domestically vulnerable.

Strains began to appear *in the once close Sino-Soviet relationship following Khrushchev's denunciation of Stalin at the February 1956 Twentieth Party Congress.*

XIV. THE FOUR CAUSES

ACCORDING TO ARISTOTLE, in order to understand something, one needs to know why and how it is the way it is. As discussed previously, a thing comes into being when its form is added to its matter. This distinction between form and matter helps us understand what things are. But in order to understand a thing fully, Aristotle says, we have to identify what he calls the four "causes," or "explanations," of a thing. These four features explain why and how the thing is the way it is.

The first cause is the material cause, which is simply the thing's matter. Staying with the example of the house, this would be the bricks, mortar, the glass, and the other construction materials. Of course, what constitutes matter changes in relation to the compound in question. So, relative to the compound house, bricks are matter. Yet a brick is itself a compound, whose material cause is clay.

The second cause is the formal cause, which corresponds to the thing's form. In the case of a house, the formal cause is the building's specific architecture. Moreover, in Aristotle's view, the formal cause is the essence of the thing—that which makes it what it is.

The third cause, the efficient cause, is what bring the thing into existence. (The name of this cause doesn't refer to the English word *efficient*, meaning "productive without waste," but to the Latin word *efficio*, which means "to bring about.") Of the four causes, this is the one most similar to the everyday meaning of the English word *cause*. We wouldn't say that bricks or plans *caused* a house to be built. Rather, we would attribute that to the builder's construction work, which is the efficient cause of a house.

The fourth cause is the final cause, which is the end or goal of the thing. This is a simple enough idea when applied to the example we've been using. The final cause of a house is to provide shelter for inhabitants. However, this idea becomes more complex when applied to things in nature, such as plants and animals. According to Aristotle, all such things, including human beings, have ends or goals—that is, they are *for something*.

In order to understand something fully, *Aristotle explains, we need to understand why the thing is the way it is—that is, what its "causes" are. According to Aristotle, there are four basic causes.*

XIV. LEONARDO AND THE RENAISSANCE PORTRAIT

BEFORE THE ADVENT of photography, portraiture served as a key repository of memory. During the Middle Ages, portraits were mostly found on tomb monuments, carved from death masks. By the early fifteenth century, however, one begins to find more painted portraits, such as those of the patrons in Masaccio's *Trinity*. Still appearing in a religious context, these figures transformed the donors into perpetual supplicants, remaining eternally in a state of piety even after their living bodies had perished.

As the fifteenth century progressed, portraits began to appear in secular contexts as well. No longer simple facial-recognition devices, these works became sophisticated documents recording dynastically important events. For example, bridal portraits of this era typically featured not only the bride's wedding dress but also the jewelry included in her dowry (the financial component of the marriage arrangement). Thus, portraits served as records of possessions as well as likenesses of the sitters.

Leonardo's *Mona Lisa* would thus have surprised contemporary viewers because its subject wore neither a fancy dress nor elaborate jewelry. But these omissions are among the least of its marvels. Most portraits of the time were painted in profile, but Leonardo placed his subject on a balcony (as though in profile) and then pivoted her upper body so that her face and shoulders turned obliquely toward the viewer. Thus, rather than adornment, it is the Mona Lisa's gaze that commands the attention of the viewer, suggesting a psychological interaction.

The portrait also makes full use of Leonardo's revolutionary *sfumato* (meaning "smoky") technique. The standard practice among Renaissance artists was to outline the forms in their compositions with strong contours and then fill in the spaces with color. Leonardo, however, composed the *Mona Lisa* by transferring a drawing onto a prepared panel, then defining the forms with monochromatic paints (lights and shadows), and only then applying multiple thin layers of colored glaze. In the absence of strong line, the subtle blendings of

Leonardo da Vinci, *Mona Lisa* (1506)

the translucent colors give the *Mona Lisa* the depth and three-dimensionality that make it so difficult to tell whether or not she is smiling.

The sitter is most often identified as Lisa dei Gherardini, the wife of a Florentine merchant. But her precise identity is a matter of dispute, in part because Leonardo never delivered the portrait to its patron, instead choosing to keep it for himself.

Leonardo's *Mona Lisa* revolutionized *the genre of the independent portrait, which by the mid-fifteenth century had become quite popular.*

XIV. DRIFT AND EPISTASIS

WHEN FISHER LOOKED AT A SPECIES, he saw a population that was, for all practical purposes, infinitely large. Wright, on the other hand, saw a population that was highly subdivided—containing many more, much smaller groupings. This difference in vision had a profound effect on the two men's respective thinking.

In Fisher's world of infinitely large populations, where migration and genetic drift mattered little, natural selection was clearly the most important evolutionary force. Wright disagreed. He studied inbreeding, and he was particularly interested in the way that inbreeding behaves in small, isolated populations. It was Wright's contention that, within small inbred populations, the effect of genetic drift can be significant. Specifically, he demonstrated that small sample size greatly increases the likelihood that random chance will alter allele frequency and thus increase the rate of evolution (as defined by population genetics).

Consider the following two experiments: Flip a fair coin four times and calculate the ratio of heads to tails. Then flip the same coin four hundred times and calculate the same ratio. Now repeat both experiments one hundred times each and plot the resulting data points, creating a distribution curve for each sampling strategy. While the average ratio in both cases should approximate 1:1, you will find a much wider distribution of data points on the small-sample (4x) curve than in the large-sample (400x) curves. This reflects the statistical realization that small populations are much more likely than large populations to deviate from expectations.

Another key concept in early population genetics was that of gene interactions. In order to sort out the different variables involved in small-population inbreeding, Wright studied guinea pigs, especially their coat color. He found, importantly, that coat color isn't determined by the simple interaction of two alleles of a single gene but by the interaction of several alleles from different genes.

While Fisher continued to hold the nineteenth-century view that individual genes evolve independently, Wright insisted that more often they evolve in combination, so that a great deal of complexity can result from a relatively small number of genes. Eventually, Wright's viewpoint came to be embodied in the idea of epistasis. An epistatic effect is one that results from the interaction of several different genes. According to Wright, it is the accumulation of epistatic interactions among different alleles and different genes that constrains the evolution of most traits.

Out of Wright's debate with Fisher *over the nature of the genetic landscape emerged the idea of epistasis, which suggested that evolutionary forces are constrained by gene-to-gene interactions.*

XIV. THE EMERGENCE OF CHRISTIANITY

AFTER ANNEXING JUDAEA IN 64 BCE, the Romans exploited the Jewish people, taxing them severely and producing the dark times during which Jesus of Nazareth preached his message of hope and deliverance. The rise of Christianity, however, needs to be understood not only within this historical context but also within the religious debates of the Second Temple period. Initially, Jesus's followers were thoroughly Jewish and addressed themselves directly to the burning (Jewish) theological questions of the day. Only later, perhaps as late as 100 CE, did the Christian movement begin to take on a non-Jewish character and split from the Jewish mainstream.

Although much of the New Testament is historically unreliable, reflecting rival claims made by authors competing to promote their own interpretations of the meaning of Jesus's life, the Gospels do reveal an important dichotomy in early Christianity. The Synoptic Gospels (Mark, Matthew, and Luke) present Jesus primarily as a messiah, recalling and yet significantly reinterpreting the original Jewish concept. During Jesus's lifetime, most Jews would have understood *messiah* to mean a divinely chosen, worldly king of Davidic ancestry. His coming would have signified the end of Israel's oppression and the restoration of its political independence. Jesus's followers, however, promoted a different interpretation of *messiah*. They argued that the coming of the messiah meant not the redemption of Jews *in* the world but the *end* of the world altogether and the rebirth of the Jewish people as part of an entirely new order.

An eleventh-century text of the Gospel of Luke.

The Gospel of John, however, places much less emphasis on Jesus as messiah. Instead, it presents the Jesus movement primarily as an immortality cult: Through faith in Jesus, the Son of God, the believer participates in the Resurrection and thereby achieves eternal salvation. This Jesus doesn't redeem Israel but instead acts as an intermediary between God and the individual believer. Because this interpretation proved far more congenial to non-Jewish believers in Christ, it eventually came to dominate in the Christian church.

When the final schism between the proto-Christians and the rest of the Jewish community took place, the precipitating cause probably wasn't the claim that Jesus was the Messiah. More likely, it was the proto-Christian belief that Jesus was actually divine—an assertion that would have been unacceptably blasphemous to most traditional Jews.

The proto-Christianity that emerged in Judaea *during the Roman period began as a thoroughly Jewish movement and only later split from the Jewish mainstream.*

XV. THE CULTURAL REVOLUTION

DURING THE MID-1960S, experiencing a decline in his health and feeling threatened by party rivals, the seventy-two-year-old Mao became increasingly radical in his characterization of CCP bureaucrats as conservative and self-interested. While making these public accusations, Mao also targeted privately several potential threats to his

A poster from the Cultural Revolution showing young people rallying to Mao.

hold on power—notably Lin Biao (whose suspicious death may have been a Mao-ordered assassination) and Deng Xiaoping. Supporting Mao were intellectuals, especially students, who felt passed over in favor of contemporaries with strong party connections, especially the children of important bureaucrats.

In May 1966, Mao began a purge within the Ministry of Culture. Angry university students joined in the action, became radicalized, and took to the streets wearing red armbands and waving copies of the ubiquitous "little red book" containing quotations from Mao. These Red Guards became the actuating force of the Great Proletarian Cultural Revolution. Anyone they considered counterrevolutionary or anti-Mao was subjected to vigilante justice; and once it became clear that their violence would go unchecked, the Red Guards went on a murderous rampage.

During the fall of 1966, Mao and the other leaders of the Cultural Revolution, especially the Gang of Four, called for attacks on the "four olds"—specifically "old customs, old habits, old culture, and old thinking." (The members of the Gang of Four were Mao's third wife, former actress Jiang Qing, and three of her Shanghai cronies.) In response to the Gang of Four's incitement, the Red Guards began wiping out symbols of China's prerevolutionary past. Buddhist temples were burned; museums and their treasures were destroyed, Meanwhile, children turned against parents, husbands turned against wives, and prominent government officials were paraded through the streets wearing dunce caps or placards stating their counterrevolutionary crimes. After being denounced, many such people were beaten to death.

Although the worst of the violence ended in early 1967, the harsh ideological movement spawned by the Cultural Revolution persisted until Mao's death in 1976. Meanwhile, seven hundred thousand people were persecuted and an estimated four hundred thousand died while countless national treasures were lost.

Determined to maintain *his hold on power, an aging Mao incited disaffected intellectuals to attack his political rivals, thereby unleashing the Cultural Revolution.*

XV. ARISTOTLE'S CONCEPT OF THE SOUL

THUS FAR, in discussing the distinction between form and matter, we've concentrated exclusively on examples of artifacts, such as tables and houses. Aristotle, however, didn't limit his investigations to manufactured things. He applied the same analytical tools to things that occur naturally—such as plants, animals, and rocks.

Among the earliest Greek philosophers were the Presocratics, who are today considered materialists because they believed that in order to exist, a thing had to be material (in the sense of taking up space). Therefore, in their view, the soul, too, had to be material. Some Presocratics conceived of it as a kind of air or breath; others supposed it to be a special kind of fire or heat; still others thought it was composed of very fine "atoms." Plato, however, as discussed earlier, was a dualist. He conceived of the soul as an immortal, immaterial substance joined to a mortal, material body.

In *On the Soul*, Aristotle attempts to steer a course between Presocratic materialism and Platonic dualism. For instance, he carefully avoids suggesting that the soul can do anything without the body. After all, most of the things an organism does—seeing, hearing, digesting, and so on—require both. Without a stomach, there can be no digestion, just as without eyes there can be no sight. A soul is also required for these activities because, in the ancient Greek sense, a body without a soul is inanimate, like a corpse. In an especially memorable passage from *On the Soul*, Aristotle explains that one shouldn't ask whether the soul and body are one any more than whether wax and an imprint in wax are one.

When Aristotle applies the form–matter distinction to human beings, the result seems simple enough: The body is the matter, which is *potentially* alive; and the soul is the form—which, when added to the body, makes it *actually* alive. But this analysis breaks down when one considers the body without the soul. Does the body just lie there, only potentially alive, until the soul comes along and animates it?

There are two immediate problems with this interpretation. First, it sounds a lot like the dualism that Aristotle wants to reject. Second, this is not how human beings, in fact, become alive. Except in *Frankenstein*, one doesn't see bodies that are potentially alive (or were formally alive) suddenly coming to life. Aristotle's application of the form–matter distinction to body and soul is actually much more subtle.

In applying the form–matter distinction to human beings, *Aristotle tries to take a middle course between Presocratic materialism, which understands the soul as a physical substance, and Platonic dualism.*

XV. THE SHIFT TO ROME

IN 1309, because of political unrest in Rome, the papal capital was moved to Avignon, France. Meanwhile, lacking papal leadership and church investment, the city of Rome deteriorated badly. Even after the papacy returned in 1377, the political situation remained difficult for another forty years. As a result, after stability finally returned in 1417 and for the rest of the fifteenth century, nearly all of the church patronage in Rome went toward the intensive rebuilding of the city's infrastructure. The first indication that enough of this work had been completed for the church to begin considering decorative projects came during the reign of Sixtus IV (1471–84), who improved the papal palace with a new set of apartments and also a new chapel (the Sistine).

In 1503, Sixtus IV's nephew Giuliano della Rovere became Pope Julius II. Julius's ten-year reign was marked by an extensive territorial expansion of the papal states and an intensive rebuilding of the papal properties. It was Julius, for example, who reinvigorated the campaign to build a vast new basilica on the site of the fourth-century church of St. Peter's, which had itself been built by the Roman emperor Constantine on the site of the first pope's tomb. During Julius's tenure, the walls of this earlier church were torn down, and Donato Bramante (1444–1514) was called upon to design a new seat for the Catholic Church. Bramante envisioned the structure

Maerten van Heemskerck, *St. Peter's Basilica* (ca. 1535)

as square in form, with an imposing central dome and a variety of *all'antica* (in the manner of the antique) architectural elements. The latter were borrowed from classical temple facades, supposedly as a reference to the biblical Temple of Solomon, and also from Roman secular buildings such as baths.

Bramante didn't invent the idea of a centrally planned church—that is, a church whose outer walls are equidistant from its center (as in a circle or a + sign, as opposed to a cruciform). Already, the concept had been explored as a revival of ancient form, but no one had yet applied it on such an imposing scale. Unfortunately, Bramante's design in the end proved impractical, both from an engineering standpoint and because of the papacy's considerable processional needs. As a result, the basilica that was ultimately built bore little resemblance to his original plans.

Once Pope Julius II decided to rebuild St. Peter's *and remodel the papal palace, Rome quickly became a center of new opportunity for artists and architects.*

XV. FITNESS AND FITNESS LANDSCAPES

IN 1864, British sociologist Herbert Spencer coined the phrase *survival of the fittest* to describe Darwin's theory of natural selection. Spencer's Malthusian point was that in the struggle for life, "favored races" are preserved. Sixty years later, Haldane used a similar concept to quantify just how well a particular organism survives relative to other organisms from the same population.

The genetic endowment passed on to an organism by its parents is called its genotype. (*Genotype* can refer either to the total genetic endowment or to discrete parts.) In order to quantify the relative value of a specific genotype with regard to survivability, Haldane introduced the concept of fitness, which he defined as the reproductive success of a particular genotype relative to other genotypes in the same population. The way that he assigned fitness values was simple: the greater the number of offspring produced by a genotype, the greater its fitness value.

However, Wright's research into the evolutionary effects of gene interactions complicated matters. While Fisher held that natural selection acting on single gene mutations is the primary factor in evolutionary change, Wright argued that the fitness of a mutation can only be determined within the context of other genes.

To visualize these and other theories, Wright developed a three-dimensional model called a fitness (or adaptive) landscape, whose *x*- and *y*-axes display different combinations of genotypes. Typically, each axis represents a gene and its allelic combinations. The coordinates (2,2,10) and (2,3,5) would thus represent two genotypic combinations in which the *x*-axis genotype remains constant while the *y*-axis genotype changes by a single allele. The *z*-axis in these models indicates fitness value. In this case, the first genotype has a higher fitness than the second genotype.

When plotted, these graphs take on the characteristics of physical landscapes, with various peaks and valleys corresponding to advantageous and disadvantageous combinations, respectively. As drawn by Fisher, with his focus on large populations and single genes, these fitness landscapes show very tall peaks (usually only one) toward which all the organisms in the population gravitate. By contrast, Wright's small-population, epistatic approach yields fitness landscapes with multiple peaks of varying height. In these landscapes, forces such as genetic drift can push organisms off stable adaptive peaks, thereby making it possible for natural selection to drive these organisms toward new adaptive peaks.

Extending Haldane's concept of fitness, *Wright developed fitness landscapes to model his theory that the fitness of a given mutation depends on the influence of other genes.*

XV. RABBINIC JUDAISM

IN 66 CE, provoked by the Romans and agitated by the Zealots, the Jewish people finally rebelled. Politically, the revolt was a disaster, and it left Jerusalem in ashes. The climax came in 70 CE, when the Temple was burned, never to be rebuilt. Decades passed before the Jewish community recovered. Of the various sects in circulation before the war with Rome, only two survived: the Christians and the Pharisees.

In many ways, the Pharisees were uniquely placed to lead the postwar Jewish population. Even if the Zealots hadn't been wiped out in the fighting, the terrible destruction wrought by their counsel would have discredited them. The Essenes, who never sought popular leadership and simply wanted to be left alone to await the End Times, were also annihilated by the Romans. The Sadducees, meanwhile, lost their raison d'être when the Second Temple was destroyed. Only the Pharisees, with their strong emphasis on individual observance and study of the Torah, endured to assume postwar leadership. This was appropriate because activities associated with home and synagogue made much more sense for the new Jewish reality than ritual practice in a Temple that no longer existed.

The religious movement that ultimately emerged was created by the rabbis, who were the heirs of the Pharisees and whose title derives from the Aramaic word for "teacher." According to tradition, the early leaders of the rabbinic movement established academies for the teaching of the Torah. At the Council of Jamnia (or Yavneh) held in 76 CE, the rabbis are said to have canonized the authoritative books of the Hebrew Bible and to have collectively rejected all sectarians, especially the Christians. At about the same time, according to Christian tradition, the early church left the Holy Land and fled to Pella in Transjordan. The split symbolized by these events is sometimes referred to as the Parting of the Ways.

Although scholars have questioned almost every aspect of this account, it seems indisputable that the Hebrew Bible attained its standard canonical form shortly after the war with Rome and certainly by the early second century CE. On the other hand, the boundaries between Judaism and Christianity almost certainly didn't solidify until decades, if not centuries, later. Recent scholarship has demonstrated that even if the spokesmen of the rabbinic and early Christian movements *claimed* that their two faiths were separate and wholly inimical, minority groups continued to hold beliefs intermediate between them for several generations.

After the disastrous war with Rome, *the rabbinic movement, based on the teachings of the Pharisees, emerged to lead the decimated Jewish people.*

XVI. CHINA OPENS TO THE WEST

IRONICALLY, WHILE THE LATER STAGES of the Cultural Revolution still roiled China's domestic politics, its international relations became increasingly normalized. In October 1970, Canada became the first Western nation to extend recognition to the PRC as the sole legitimate representative of the Chinese people (as opposed to the ROC government on Taiwan), and this "one China" policy gained momentum at the UN. The Taiwanese government's principal patron, the United States, responded with a "two Chinas" resolution that would have conferred equal legitimacy on Beijing and Taipei; but it failed when Chiang refused to accept limitations on the Nationalists' claim to the mainland. Finally, in October 1971, the UN General Assembly voted, 76–35, to end its recognition of the ROC and seat the PRC instead.

Meanwhile, the administration of the famously anticommunist US president Richard M. Nixon began holding secret talks with the PRC. The potential benefits of improved relations were obvious to both sides: The United States had a clear Cold War interest in furthering the Sino-Soviet split, while the PRC wanted to reestablish bilateral trade (banned since the Korean War) and step out of the USSR's shadow. In April 1971, as a gesture of goodwill, China invited the US Ping-Pong team to visit the mainland, which had previously been closed to Americans. (Not even Chinese Americans with family there had been able to visit or send money.) Thus began the era of "Ping-Pong diplomacy," and three months later US national security adviser Henry Kissinger traveled secretly to Beijing to make arrangements for a state visit.

President Nixon's historic February 1972 to China included a meeting with Mao in Beijing. Later, during a stop in Shanghai, the two nations issued a joint communiqué enumerating US and Chinese positions on several potentially explosive issues, such as the role of the US military in Vietnam and China's commitment to a "one China" policy. Although the statement contained a great deal of disagreement, it nevertheless affirmed the two sides' intention to disagree peacefully and expressed their desire to improve bilateral relations by increasing trade and exchanging diplomats,

Mao greets Pres. Richard Nixon in Beijing.

scientists, athletes, and journalists. According to sinologist Jonathan Spence, the Nixon visit was "a remarkable moment in diplomatic history."

President Nixon's surprise trip to China *in February 1972 ended decades of PRC isolation from the West.*

XVI. POTENTIALITY AND ACTUALITY

EXPANDING HIS EXPLANATION of how the form–matter distinction can be applied to the body–soul dichotomy, Aristotle distinguishes in *On the Soul* between two kinds of actuality in order to establish three stages of being: potentiality (I), first actuality (II), and second actuality (III). First actuality is analogous to being asleep or possessing (but not using) knowledge. Second actuality is being awake or using one's knowledge.

For example, you are (I am assuming) only potentially fluent in ancient Greek— that is, you are at Stage I. You are thus different from a rock, which will never become fluent in ancient Greek. Because I am fluent in ancient Greek, I am at Stage II. However, because I am now writing and thinking in English, my knowledge of ancient Greek is "asleep." If I were to start reading or speaking ancient Greek, then I would be utilizing my knowledge and thus be at Stage III.

Looked at another way, my first actuality (knowing ancient Greek) is also a second potentiality—namely, the potentiality to start reading or speaking ancient Greek at any time. This is important because the soul, according to Aristotle, occupies a similar position. It is a first actuality, because it makes the body actually alive, and also a second potentiality, because it gives the body the additional potentiality of doing something.

But, Aristotle points out, the only body that is *potentially* alive (i.e., at Stage I) is a body that is already *actually* alive (i.e., at Stage II). For example, if an egg really has the potentiality to grow into a chicken, then it must already be actually alive and not just potentially alive. This is because, as even a cursory study of biology shows, living things come only from other living things. There is never a moment when "dead" matter comes to life.

Thus we see that the soul, as the form of a living organism, is nothing but the capacity of the body to actually do what it does. For Aristotle, what makes an eye an actual eye is its capacity to see, which is something that only a "living" eye (that is, an eye belonging to an ensouled body at Stage II) can do. The eye of a corpse is no longer, strictly speaking, an eye, because it has (as far as Aristotle is concerned) irrevocably lost its capacity to function as an eye.

Making a distinction between knowing (first actuality) *and doing (second actuality), Aristotle shows that the soul is merely the capacity of a living body to do what it does.*

XVI. THE SISTINE CHAPEL CEILING

AWARE OF MICHELANGELO'S SUCCESSES with the *Pietà* and the *David*, Pope Julius II lured him to Rome in 1505 with the promise of a commission to construct a monumental marble tomb for Julius himself, to be installed in the new St. Peter's. Shortly after Michelangelo's arrival, however, the funds for this grandiose project were diverted into the pope's military campaign to expand the papal territories. In its place, Michelangelo was given the more economical task of frescoing the vaulted ceiling of the Sistine Chapel.

Typically, church ceilings were decorated to resemble heaven, with broad blue expanses and golden stars; but this wasn't Michelangelo's plan. Instead, he created a program of scenes so complex that scholars believe he must have worked with a theological adviser from the papal staff.

The core of the decoration, occupying the ceiling's central axis, consists of nine scenes from Genesis, beginning with the Creation and ending with Noah. These alternate in size, with the five smaller scenes framed by seated nudes (angels). Around these scenes, Michelangelo placed Old

The Sistine Chapel ceiling.

Testament prophets and, as female counterparts, pagan sibyls who function as foreseers of Christ. Within triangular frames between these prophets (and in lunettes below), Michelangelo placed family groupings depicting Christ's ancestors.

Its complexity notwithstanding, the real innovation of this vast pictorial program is its architectonic structure. Although done entirely in fresco, it mimics several other media. The massive prophets, for example, are nestled in what appear to be three-dimensional stone niches, framed on either side by figures of infant boys seemingly sculpted from marble. These reach up to support cornices, which in turn support the seated nudes around the smaller biblical scenes.

It took Michelangelo four years (1508–12) to complete the ceiling, which he painted in reverse narrative order—that is, he began at the far end of the chapel with the Noah scenes and ended near the altar with God the Father separating light from darkness. As the work progressed, he became more ambitious; thus, the figures become increasingly daring as one moves toward the altar. The difference can be easily seen if one compares the depiction of Zachariah above the chapel entrance with the much more monumental and fully foreshortened image of Jonah above the altar.

The pictorial program that Michelangelo created *for the ceiling of the Sistine Chapel in Rome was unprecedented in its scope and content.*

XVI. THE MODERN EVOLUTIONARY SYNTHESIS

THE RECONCILIATION OF NATURAL SELECTION on continuous traits with Mendelian genetics—accomplished by Fisher, Wright, and Haldane during the 1920s—made possible the leap in thinking that took place during the late 1930s and early 1940s. This breakthrough, known as the modern evolutionary synthesis, combined ideas from several different disciplines into a unified theory of evolution that has come to be accepted by most working biologists.

Theodosius Dobzhansky, trained as both a laboratory geneticist and a field naturalist, was among the first biologists to study the genetics of natural populations (that is, populations living in the wild). Dobzhansky studied natural populations of *Drosophila pseudoobscura* (fruit flies), and in the course of his work he discovered that these populations harbor much more variation than had been predicted by the theoretical models of the early population geneticists. This finding, presented in Dobzhansky's 1937 book *Genetics and the Origin of Species*, strongly supported the role of natural selection as the primary agent of evolutionary change, because it demonstrated the abundance of real-world variation on which natural selection could operate.

Meanwhile, Ernst Mayr's 1942 book *Systematics and the Origin of Species* contributed to the synthesis by redefining the concept of species. (Systematics is the study of species classification.) Although Darwin hadn't placed much emphasis on the distinction between a population and a species, Mayr believed that the difference was meaningful. In his view, species were distinct units in space and time. Specifically, he defined them as groups of interbreeding (or potentially interbreeding) populations reproductively isolated from all other populations. Mayr saw the natural world as composed of many populations, and he believed that speciation occurred when one of these populations became geographically isolated and developed along a different evolutionary path.

George Gaylord Simpson also contributed to the modern evolutionary synthesis with *Tempo and Mode in Evolution* (1944), in which he reconciled evolutionary concepts such as adaptation and common descent with modern paleontology. The changes in morphology present in the fossil record had persuaded paleontologists of Simpson's generation that evolution was linear and predictable (in the sense of the *scala naturae* and Lamarckian determinism). Simpson, however, showed that under close scrutiny this interpretation falls apart and that the evidence actually shows evolution to be irregular and nondirectional, just as natural selection predicts.

The modern evolutionary synthesis *reconciled Darwinian theory with empirical biology and other disciplines to create a new unified theory that still prevails today.*

XVI. THE MISHNAH

THE RABBINIC MOVEMENT succeeded because it offered the Jewish people a way to perpetuate monotheism, the covenant, and the observance of the Torah in a world with no Temple. At the core of this bold reinterpretation of Judaism was a stringent code of ethics, purity, and ritual.

The inspiration for the rabbinic vision came from Exodus 19:6, in which God declares to the Israelites, "You shall be a kingdom of priests and a holy nation to me." This verse was interpreted to mean that all Jews, and not merely a priestly elite, were responsible for the fulfillment of Israel's covenantal obligations. While it would be an exaggeration to say that the rabbis didn't mourn the loss of the Temple, an important innovation of rabbinic thought was its emphasis on the equality of all observances and commandments (and of all Jews) in God's eyes.

Another key rabbinic innovation was the doctrine of the Oral Torah. According to rabbinic tradition, God revealed the Torah to Moses in both written and oral form. The written form was preserved in the Pentateuch, while the oral form was handed down from Moses through dozens of generations until it ultimately reached the Pharisees, who passed it on to the rabbis, at which point it became the basis of rabbinic law. Therefore, although rabbinic law actually had little in common with the laws of the Torah, it was generally understood to have the same divine source and authority.

After the war with Rome, the rabbis became concerned that this oral tradition might not survive in a world of dispersed Jewry, so they decided to write it down. The resulting document, the Mishnah, was compiled about 220 CE. It organized rabbinic law into six "orders" (*sedarim*), each of which presented rabbinic thought on such practical matters as ritual purity, diet, observance of the Sabbath, civil law, and so on.

Along with the Mishnah, other collections of rabbinic tradition were compiled (*midrashim*), which attempted to show that a direct relationship existed between the laws of the Mishnah and the laws of the Torah. This exercise often required radical contortions of the text. Thus, one well-known rabbinic tradition claims that the biblical penalty of "an eye for an eye" actually means that the person whose eye is put out should receive financial compensation.

The innovative rabbinic doctrine *of the Oral Torah helped transform Temple-centered Judaism into a religion focused on personal piety and the observance of religious law.*

XVII. CHINA AFTER MAO

ON JULY 18, 1976, an earthquake leveled the city of Tangshan, killing a quarter of a million people. Although by then nearly three decades of Marxist indoctrination had eradicated nearly all imperial tradition, many elderly Chinese still remembered that, according to tradition, the ends of dynasties were presaged by natural disasters. To these people at least, the earthquake suggested that the Communists had lost the Mandate of Heaven. Then, on September 9, another shock hit China: Mao was dead.

To the surprise and dismay of the Gang of Four, Mao had chosen as his successor Hua Guofeng, who moved quickly to arrest Jiang Qing and her three associates. Accusing them of corrupting Mao's vision of continuous revolution, Hua and his allies began reversing the Cultural Revolution and repairing some of the damage done.

In July 1977, Deng Xiaoping made yet another comeback, winning back the post of vice premier after being purged a year earlier for being a "rightist." (At the time, Hua was serving both as party chair and as head of state.) Together, Hua and Deng returned to the agenda of modernization that Mao had abandoned. At the National Science Conference held in March 1978, they identified several key technological areas for development—including computers, high-energy physics, and aerospace. Toward this end, they announced a commitment to reforming China's educational system, sending more students abroad, and importing more Western technology.

Although Hua and Deng worked together to modernize China, they remained rivals for power, and Deng surreptitiously exploited Hua's identification with Mao.

Deng Xiaoping in Washington, DC, with Pres. Jimmy Carter in January 1979.

As Mao's handpicked successor, Hua couldn't easily separate himself from Mao's legacy, so he embraced it with his "two whatevers" policy: Obey whatever Mao had said, and ensure that whatever Mao had decided was done. During the late 1970s, however, in large part because of Deng's maneuverings, Mao's actions during the Cultural Revolution came under increasing scrutiny.

Especially as more "rightists" were rehabilitated— nearly three million by 1980—Deng's faction took on and ultimately supplanted Hua's "whatever" faction. In September 1980, one of Deng's protégés, Zhao Ziyang, replaced Hua as premier; and in June 1981, another Deng protégé, Hu Yaobang, succeeded Hua as CCP chair. Meanwhile, Deng ruled from behind the scenes as chair of the Military Affairs Commission. The spell of Mao's personality cult was broken, and China moved off in a new direction.

Within five years of Mao's death, *the victims of the Cultural Revolution had reemerged to put China on a path toward modernization and economic reform.*

XVII. HAPPINESS

AS NOTED EARLIER, Aristotle believes in teleology, which is the doctrine that all natural phenomena have ends or goals. For example, the end or goal of a bunny rabbit would be to lead a flourishing bunny life—eating carrots, escaping foxes, making baby bunnies, and so on. The end or goal of a human life is similarly to live well and do well as a human being. People who flourish in this way embody what Aristotle calls happiness. Therefore, when Aristotle poses the central question of his *Nicomachean Ethics*—*What is human happiness?*—he really wants to know *What does it mean for a human being to live and do well?*

Aristotle's conception of happiness is thus somewhat different from our own. While the word *happiness* is often used in modern parlance to describe a positive feeling about oneself and one's life, Aristotle thinks of happiness as much more than a feeling. For him, it means literally living and doing well, flourishing as a human being. Someone under the influence of a drug, for example, may feel happy and say that he is happy, but he may actually be in a miserable condition (say, gravely ill). No one would call such a person happy in the Aristotelian sense.

All human beings would agree that they want to be happy and do well. Yet, as Aristotle points out, disagreement arises when people begin to define more specifically what they think happiness is. Aristotle wonders whether there might not be some activity characteristic of human beings—that is, something especially appropriate to our nature—which, if engaged in, would be living and doing well as a human being (and thus produce happiness). Simply being alive and growing is insufficient, Aristotle says, because this is an activity that human beings share with plants, not something unique to the human condition. For similar reasons, he rejects perceiving and feeling, because other animals do this as well. What is unique and particularly appropriate to human beings, he concludes, is our capacity to think and reason.

For Aristotle, however, activity always trumps mere capacity. If the function of a hammer is to drive nails, then a good hammer drives nails well. A good human being, it follows, engages in the activity of reason well—or excellently, in accordance with virtue. What is central to human happiness, then, is the exercise of reason in accordance with virtue.

In the *Nicomachean Ethics*, *Aristotle focuses on happiness, which he defines not as a positive feeling about oneself and one's life but as living and doing well.*

XVII. THE STANZA DELLA SEGNATURA

SOON AFTER MICHELANGELO returned to Rome, Raphael followed him there in the hope of winning the commission for the Sistine Chapel ceiling. When this assignment went to Michelangelo, Raphael was put to work by Julius II painting the library in the new papal apartments that had been constructed by Julius's uncle Sixtus IV.

The decoration of the papal library (later known as the Stanza della Segnatura) is a summa of learning as it had evolved through the early Renaissance. Frescoes on each of the four walls celebrate a different intellectual discipline: theology, justice, poetry, and philosophy. Perhaps the most remarkable is the fresco dedicated to philosophy, which focuses not on Christian thinkers but their ancient Greek and Roman predecessors. The two central figures are Plato and Aristotle.

The vast architectural space of the painting is carefully rendered, both in its perspective and in its references to classical motifs. Yet the structure seems in some places incomplete—the central dome, for instance, through which one glimpses the sky. For this reason, many scholars believe that Raphael's vast hall was meant to prefigure the new St. Peter's, already under construction and strongly backed by Raphael's patron Julius II. It's also no accident that Raphael's attention to architectural detail and fictive sculpture reflects the innovation of Michelangelo's work in the nearby Sistine Chapel.

Raphael,
The School of Athens (1509–11)

In bisecting his composition, Raphael clearly intended to separate two distinct tenets of thought. On the left, Plato points upward, symbolizing his metaphysical belief in the realm of the unseen. In contrast, Plato's pupil Aristotle gestures outward, his palm parallel to the ground, representing a philosophy that is pointedly earthbound. Other notable figures in *The School of Athens* fresco include Plato's own teacher, Socrates (dressed in light green and enumerating several points on his hand); Pythagoras (in the foreground drawing diagrams in a book); and Euclid (also in the foreground drawing a geometrical proof on a tablet). Raphael thus brings together an impossible gathering of historical personages—impossible because they lived in many different places and times— to summarize the status of learning at the start of the sixteenth century. As a comment upon the rising status of the artist at the time, Raphael even pictures himself standing on the stairs above Euclid. He is one of the few figures in the fresco looking out at the viewer.

With skill matched only by his ambition, *Raphael won the commission to decorate Julius II's library, a challenge complicated by Michelangelo's presence in the Sistina.*

XVII. GENE-CENTRIC SELECTION

BEGINNING WITH DARWIN and continuing for more than a century, evolutionary theorists considered the individual and its unique combination of genes to be the primary unit of natural selection. In 1966, however, about a decade after the discovery and elucidation of the structure of DNA, G. C. Williams published *Adaptation and Natural Selection*, in which he proposed a gene-centric view of evolutionary change.

The prevailing orthodoxy in 1966 was that individuals are selected for the beneficial traits they harbor. But Williams countered that the individual is an unsatisfactory unit for selection because individual organisms reproduce haphazardly. An individual selected for the beneficial features of its genotype will pass on, Williams pointed out, only half of its alleles to its progeny. "Meiosis and recombination," he wrote in *Adaptation and Natural Selection*, "destroy genotypes as surely as death."

During the cellular process of meiosis, the number of chromosomes in a diploid cell is reduced by half in order to form a haploid gamete. Fertilization subsequently restores the normal diploid gene content by combining this haploid gamete with another produced by a second parent. The newly formed individual, of course, contains a combination of alleles that may or may not be as well adapted as the traits originally selected. Furthermore, as genes come together during fertilization, they often recombine, shuffling their content.

A much better choice than the individual for the primary unit of selection, Williams argued, is the gene, because it harbors the benefit and replicates as a unit with fidelity. According to Williams, the true evolutionary struggle for survival doesn't take place among competing individuals but among competing genes. The most fit genes are, therefore, those that produce traits that, in turn, promote the gene's propagation.

Williams's gene-centric approach highly influenced a scientific field known as sociobiology (after entomologist E. O. Wilson's 1975 treatise of the same name). Sociobiology is the study of social behavior among animals from the point of view of natural selection. In other words, sociobiologists attempt to explain social behaviors in terms of the evolutionary advantages and/or disadvantages of the genes that affect those behaviors. This approach makes sense, for example, of the altruistic behavior of worker bees. Although worker bees don't pass on any of their own genes directly (because they don't reproduce), the altruism they show toward the colony as a whole promotes the survival of the *copies* of their genes carried by members of the colony that do reproduce.

In contrast with Darwin's emphasis on the individual *as the primary unit of selection, G. C. Williams proposed a gene-centric view of selection and evolution.*

XVII. THE TALMUDS

WHILE WORK CONTINUED on the *midrashim*, rabbis also began to comment on the Mishnah itself. During this long process, every precept, principle, and maxim in the Mishnah was subjected to minute scrutiny. The results of these complex examinations of rabbinic law, which took place over several centuries, were eventually collected into two titanic works known as the Talmuds. The teachings of the rabbis of Palestine (a Greek name meaning "land of the Philistines") were compiled in the Jerusalem Talmud (*Yerushalmi*), while those of the rabbis of Babylonia were compiled in the Babylonian Talmud (*Bavli*).

Of the two works, the Jerusalem Talmud is the shorter and less thorough, possibly because it was produced under much more difficult circumstances. During the early centuries CE, relations between Jews and Christians in Palestine (and elsewhere) became increasingly acrimonious. Once the Roman Empire became Christianized early in the fourth century, Jews under Roman rule began to experience both legal discrimination and outright persecution. Not surprisingly, this situation contributed to a gradual decline of the rabbinic academies in the Holy Land.

In Babylonia, however, where the Sasanians of Iran now ruled, the situation was completely reversed. Under Sasanian protection and patronage, the Babylonian Jews flourished both commercially and culturally. Later, in the seventh century, the Muslim caliphate conquered the Sasanian Empire, but the Jews of Babylonia continued to be treated with tolerance, and they continued to thrive.

As a result, the Babylonian academies rose to great prominence within the Jewish community, and Jews throughout the Diaspora world began to call upon the leaders of these academies to provide guidance regarding Jewish law and custom. Even after the decline of the Babylonian academies during the tenth century, it was the teachings of the Babylonian rabbis, codified in the Babylonian Talmud, that preserved the core of rabbinic thought.

Judaism would continue to evolve throughout the Middle Ages, as new academies emerged in Palestine, North Africa, Spain, and central Europe—and also as Jews responded dynamically to changing political, social, and cultural conditions in these regions. Nevertheless, until modern times, it was the rabbinic Judaism preserved in the Talmuds that gave the overwhelming majority of world Jewry its sense of Jewish identity. Not until the nineteenth century did alternative understandings of Judaism come to be widespread. Until then, rabbinic authorities acted as the unchallenged guides of the Jewish people, and daily Jewish life was suffused with rabbinic law and custom.

The Jerusalem and Babylonian Talmuds *compiled extensive rabbinic commentaries on every precept, principle, and maxim in the Mishnah.*

XVIII. TIANANMEN AND BEYOND

FREEDOM OF THOUGHT was so limited during the Cultural Revolution that when the bottle of reform was opened, the genie of dissent flew out with a force that left even Deng bewildered. In December 1978, twenty-eight workers from the rural southwest traveled to Beijing's Tiananmen Square to protest poor conditions in their region. In January 1979, thousands more assembled in Tiananmen to demand human rights and democracy. Similar demonstrations took place in Shanghai, Hangzhou, and Guangdong. Although Deng had encouraged freer discourse, these challenges to party authority were more than he could tolerate, and he used the police power of the state to suppress them.

This brief flirtation with free speech and democracy was repeated during the winter of 1986–87, when thousands of university students attended protest rallies in Hefei, Wuhan, Shanghai, and Beijing. More arrests took place; and CCP general secretary Hu Yaobang, accused of being too sympathetic to the students' cause, was forced to resign.

When Hu died in April 1989, thousands of students gathered in Tiananmen Square for an impromptu tribute that spawned a new movement. A list of seven demands was presented to the government, ranging from the rehabilitation of Hu to freedom of the press. When the government rejected these demands, the movement became radicalized, and some students began calling for an end to Communist rule. On May 4, one hundred thousand people marched through the streets of Beijing, and thousands occupied Tiananmen Square, staging highly public hunger strikes.

As the unrest spread, government leaders debated what to do. CCP general secretary Zhao Ziyang was willing to talk with the students; but Deng, backed by Premier Li Peng and a chorus of octogenarians, insisted on a hard line. On May 19, the military was ordered to clear Tiananmen Square. However, when the army transports arrived in Beijing, they found their way blocked by two million ordinary citizens. On June 3, the military returned with tanks, armored personnel carriers, and orders to use deadly force, if necessary. Fighting their way through the crowds, the troops cleared the square with overwhelming force, killing several thousand.

Since the Tiananmen Square Massacre, economic reform has proceeded rapidly in China, with Special Economic Zones in Shenzhen and other coastal cities fostering a rather unbridled form of capitalism. Yet political reform hasn't kept pace, and the government continues to suppress, sometimes brutally, calls for more openness and democracy.

Deng's reform movement unleashed, *especially among students, a popular desire for freedom of speech and democratic change for which the government wasn't prepared.*

XVIII. VIRTUE

AT THE BEGINNING OF BOOK II of the *Nicomachean Ethics*, Aristotle makes an important point about human beings: He says that we are, by nature, capable of acquiring habits. Thus, we have two natures: one that we are born with (including, for example, the ability to see or digest) and a second nature that we acquire through habituation. If you throw the same rock up in the air a thousand times, it will never acquire the "habit" of moving upward; however, if you exercise a thousand days in a row, you will acquire the habit of exercising, and exercising will become second nature to you.

According to Aristotle, habituation is also how we acquire character traits. A person becomes just by acting justly, brave by acting bravely, and so forth. A person's upbringing is important to the sort of person he becomes because it determines whether or not he acquires good or bad habits of character. Children who cheat on tests begin to acquire the habit of cheating, and gradually the momentum builds. The more a person cheats, the more he is a cheater; and the more he is a cheater, the more likely he is to cheat in the future.

Our conduct is important, in Aristotle's view, because we are what we do. Nevertheless, there is more to virtuous action than simply what is done. If I help an elderly person across the street, I may seem to be acting virtuously. But what if I had read earlier in the day that this person rewards helpers generously? Helping an elderly person across the street remains a good thing, but once you learn *why* I did what I did, your assessment of *what* I did changes. For an action to be truly virtuous in Aristotle's view, it must be not only *what* a virtuous person would do but also *done as* a virtuous person would do it. A truly virtuous person, for example, performs virtuous acts for their own sake, not for the sake of what follows from them.

According to Plato, Socrates spent his entire life inquiring into the nature of virtue and how best to live one's life. Aristotle's discussions of happiness and virtue are direct descendants of this project, which Socrates began and Plato continued. Although Plato and Aristotle disagreed about many things, both would have agreed with Socrates that, for human beings, the unexamined life is not worth living.

According to Aristotle, *virtue is acquired through habituation. For an action to be truly virtuous, however, it must be not only what a virtuous person would do but also done as a virtuous person would do it.*

XVIII. THE IMPORTANCE OF BIOGRAPHY

AMONG THE MANY YOUNG ARTISTS who flocked to Florence to study the work of Michelangelo was a sixteen-year-old from Arezzo named Giorgio Vasari (1511–74). By the late 1540s, Vasari had moved to Rome to take up a commission from Pope Paul III. Also at work there on papal commissions were Michelangelo and the Venetian painter Titian. In fact, all three artists were working on different aspects of the same vast decorative program intended to honor the Farnese family, of which Paul III was a member. Because the program's emphasis was biographical, it may have been Vasari's work on this project, along with his continuing observation of Michelangelo, that gave him the idea to write and publish biographies of important Italian artists.

The first edition of *Lives of the Artists* appeared in 1550. By 1568, however, Vasari had revised and expanded the book to include 103 individual biographies—beginning with the thirteenth-century artist Cimabue and ending with the still-living Michelangelo. In light of this accomplishment, Vasari is generally considered the first modern art historian. Certainly, *Lives of the Artists* contains more than a few myths, especially concerning artists who were long dead by Vasari's time; but the book is nonetheless highly regarded and constantly mined for information.

A portrait of Michelangelo from Vasari's *Lives of the Artists* (1568).

One of Vasari's most important goals was to make sense of the changes in style that had led to the Renaissance. His premise was that Giotto had begun the process by resurrecting aspects of the artistic perfection achieved during antiquity but lost in the Dark Ages. Masaccio built upon Giotto's achievements by utilizing Brunelleschi's system of linear perspective. Then, according to Vasari, the "modern age" began with Leonardo, who "besides the force and boldness of his drawing and the extreme subtlety wherewith he counterfeited all the minutenesses of nature exactly as they are…may be truly said to have endowed his figures with motion and breath." Vasari's highest praise, though, was reserved for Michelangelo, who completed the stylistic circle by returning art to its classical perfection. For Vasari, Michelangelo "surpasses and excels not only all those moderns who have almost vanquished nature, but even those most famous ancients who without a doubt did so gloriously surpass her."

Giorgio Vasari bestowed for the first time the honor of *written biography upon the practitioners of the visual arts, elevating them to the lofty rank of philosophers and poets.*

XVIII. THE NEUTRAL THEORY

UNDER THE MODERN EVOLUTIONARY SYNTHESIS, natural selection is considered to be the driving force of evolutionary change, and the genetic variation found in nature is assumed to have either positive (advantageous) or negative (deleterious) fitness consequences. Natural selection acts on this variation, promoting the advantageous variants and purging the deleterious ones.

Given such a model, one would expect to find a relatively low number of variants within a population. Yet, during the 1960s, when technical advances in molecular biology made closer inspection possible, geneticists found quite the opposite. New techniques such as gel-electrophoresis and protein sequencing allowed researchers to quantify for the first time the precise amount of genetic variation in a given population, and much more was found than had been expected. This begged the question: If natural selection is such a powerful force, why hasn't genetic variation been reduced?

Another important discovery was that the amino acid sequences that make up particular proteins in different species were found to evolve at the same constant, clocklike rate. In other words, in tracking a specific protein common to several species, researchers found that the number of differences among them correlated to the evolutionary time separating them. This was unexpected because natural selection was supposed to be species-specific. Therefore, the rate of evolution should have varied from species to species as natural selection acted upon each independently. This begged the question: If these proteins are not evolving in a species-specific manner, what evolutionary force is most responsible for driving their divergence?

In 1968, in response to these empirical observations, Japanese botanist and mathematician Motoo Kimura proposed the neutral theory of molecular evolution. According to Kimura, the vast majority of molecular differences that have evolved among species are "selectively neutral," meaning that they have no fitness advantage or disadvantage. This theory explains why natural selection has failed to act on so much variation, but it also leads to another conundrum: If natural selection acts only on variation that impacts fitness, and most variation doesn't impact fitness, then how important can natural selection be?

The neutral theory of molecular evolution doesn't deny that natural selection plays a role in adaptive evolution, but it does suggest that random processes play a much greater role in guiding an organism's evolutionary trajectory than previously thought—at least on the molecular level. As a result, biologists currently believe that Darwinian evolution is the product of both selection and random (stochastic) change.

The discovery of much more genetic variation *than had been expected prompted Kimura to offer the neutral theory as an alternative to Darwinian natural selection.*

XVIII. MODERN JEWISH IDENTITY

BECAUSE OF THE INFLUENCE OF THE BABYLONIAN TALMUD, Jewish life prior to the modern era was defined exclusively by adherence to the Torah and rabbinic law. In nineteenth-century Europe, however, this understanding began to change.

After suffering through centuries of legal discrimination and forced isolation in urban ghettos, European Jews finally began to move into the cultural mainstream as the internalization of Enlightenment ideas led to the gradual lifting of long-standing restrictions. A major consequence of this so-called Jewish Emancipation, especially in Germany, was the assimilation of Jews into the lifestyles of the Christian majority.

Associated with this trend toward assimilation was a new branch of Judaism, the Reform movement, which conceived of Jewishness primarily as ethical and cultural and thus downplayed Judaism's more ritualistic elements. In other words, the rabbinic focus on Torah observance began to weaken in favor of a more diffuse understanding of what it meant to be a Jew. However, not all Jews accepted this reorientation. Among American Jews, for example, the Orthodox and Conservative movements rejected this looser attitude and held to the rabbinic view of Judaism as strongly, if not exclusively, defined by observance.

Meanwhile, most Jews continued to subscribe to the idea that Jewishness is an ethnically determined identity inherited from one's forebears. During the early twentieth century, anti-Semites exaggerated this idea into the doctrine of Jewish racialism that underlay the destructive teachings of the Third Reich. However, recognition of Jewishness as a matter of birth and heritage does not imply the anti-Semitic idea that Jews constitute a distinct (and presumably inferior) "race."

Another important development in the evolution of modern Jewish identity has been the reemergence of the idea of Jewishness as an identity based on citizenship in a sovereign Jewish state. Zionism, the name given to the movement for an autonomous Jewish homeland, emerged during the late nineteenth century in direct response to anti-Semitism in supposedly progressive Western Europe. According to movement founder Theodor Herzl, Jews could never be truly free or truly safe as long as they remained a vulnerable minority within majority Christian

A Jewish newspaper headline reports the creation of the state of Israel.

states. Eventually, after decades of struggle—not all of it peaceful—the Zionists achieved their goal in 1948 with the creation of the state of Israel.

Although the religious, *cultural, and ethnic aspects of Jewishness continue to be debated, the shared history of Israel provides an enduring basis for Jewish identity.*

FURTHER READING

REVOLUTIONARY BOSTON

Bailyn, Bernard. *The Ideological Origins of the American Revolution.* Cambridge, MA: Belknap Press, 1992.

Maier, Pauline. *From Resistance to Revolution.* New York: W. W. Norton, 1992.

Middlekauff, Robert. *The Glorious Cause: The American Revolution, 1763–1789.* New York: Oxford University Press, 2007.

THE ANATOMY OF THE INTERNET

Berners-Lee, Tim. *Weaving the Web: The Original Design and Ultimate Destiny of the World Wide Web.* New York: Collins Business, 2000.

Gralla, Preston. *How the Internet Works.* Indianapolis: Que, 2006.

Hafner, Katie, and Matthew Lyon. *Where Wizards Stay Up Late: The Origins of the Internet.* New York: Simon & Schuster, 1998.

THE ARMORY SHOW

Brown, Milton. *The Story of the Armory Show.* New York: Abbeville Press, 1988.

Homer, William Innes. *Alfred Stieglitz and the American Avant-Garde.* Boston: New York Graphic Society, 1979.

Mellow, James R. *Charmed Circle: Gertrude Stein and Company.* New York: Henry Holt, 2003.

Zurier, Rebecca, Robert W. Snyder, and Virginia M. Mecklenburg. *Metropolitan Lives: The Ashcan Artists and Their New York.* New York: W. W. Norton, 1995.

SIGMUND FREUD

Gay, Peter. *Freud: A Life for Our Time.* New York: W. W. Norton, 2006.

Kahn, Michael. *Basic Freud.* New York: Basic, 2002.

Schwartz, Joseph. *Cassandra's Daughter: A History of Psychoanalysis.* New York: Penguin, 2001.

Stafford-Clark, David. *What Freud Really Said: An Introduction to His Life and Thought.* New York: Schocken, 1997.

Storr, Anthony. *Freud: A Very Short Introduction.* New York: Oxford University Press, 2001.

SHAKESPEARE'S TRAGEDIES

Booth, Stephen. *King Lear, Macbeth, Indefinition, and Tragedy.* New Haven, CT: Yale University Press, 1983.

Bradley, A. C. *Shakespearean Tragedy.* New York: Penguin, 1991.

Nuttall, A. D. *Why Does Tragedy Give Pleasure?* New York: Oxford University Press, 2001.

Steiner, George. *The Death of Tragedy.* New Haven, CT: Yale University Press, 1996.

THE RENAISSANCE IN FLORENCE

Brucker, Gene. *Florence: The Golden Age, 1128–1737.* Berkeley: University of California Press, 1998.

Martines, Lauro. *Power and Imagination: City-States in Renaissance Italy.* Baltimore: Johns Hopkins University Press, 1988.

Najemy, John M. *A History of Florence, 1200–1575.* Malden, MA: Wiley-Blackwell, 2008.

Najemy, John M., ed. *Italy in the Age of the Renaissance, 1300–1550.* New York: Oxford University Press, 2005.

THE STOCK MARKET

Graham, Benjamin, and Jason Zweig. *The Intelligent Investor.* New York: HarperBusiness Essentials, 2003.

Lefèvre, Edwin. *Reminiscences of a Stock Operator.* New York: Wiley, 2006.

Surowiecki, James. *The Wisdom of Crowds.* New York: Anchor, 2005.

LITERATURE OF THE JAZZ AGE

Hemingway, Ernest. *A Moveable Feast.* New York: Scribner, 1996.

Hutchinson, George, ed. *The Cambridge Companion to the Harlem Renaissance.* New York: Cambridge University Press, 2007.

Lewis, David Levering. *When Harlem Was in Vogue.* New York: Penguin, 1997.

ELECTRICITY AND MAGNETISM

Carlowicz, Michael J., and Ramon E. Lopez. *Storms from the Sun: The Emerging Science of Space Weather.* Washington, DC: Joseph Henry Press, 2002.

Ford, R. A. *Homemade Lightning: Creative Experiments in Electricity.* New York: McGraw-Hill/TAB Electronics, 2001.

Jago, Lucy. *The Northern Lights: The True Story of the Man Who Unlocked the Secrets of the Aurora Borealis.* New York: Knopf, 2001.

Jonnes, Jill. *Empires of Light: Edison, Tesla, Westinghouse, and the Race to Electrify the World.* New York: Random House, 2004.

Mahon, Basil. *The Man Who Changed Everything: The Life of James Clerk Maxwell.* New York: Wiley, 2004.

Verschuur, Gerrit L. *Hidden Attraction: The History and Mystery of Magnetism.* New York: Oxford University Press, 1996.

THE EPICS OF THE TROJAN WAR

Havelock, Eric A. *Preface to Plato.* Cambridge, MA: Harvard University Press, 1963.

Homer. *The Iliad of Homer.* Trans. Richard Lattimore. Chicago: University of Chicago Press, 1961.

Lombardo, Stanley. *The Essential Homer: Selections from the Iliad and the Odyssey.* Indianapolis: Hackett Publishing, 2000.

Virgil. *Aeneid.* Trans. Stanley Lombardo. Indianapolis: Hackett Publishing, 2005.

THE PROTESTANT REFORMATION

Hsia, R. Po-Chia. *The World of Catholic Renewal, 1540–1770.* New York: Cambridge University Press, 1998.

Jacob, Margaret C. *The Cultural Meaning of the Scientific Revolution.* New York: Random House, 1988.

Kaplan, Benjamin J. *Divided by Faith: Religious Conflict and the Practice of Toleration in Early Modern Europe.* Cambridge, MA: Harvard University Press, 2007.

Levack, Brian. *The Witch-Hunt in Early Modern Europe.* New York: Longman, 2006.

Tracy, James D. *Europe's Reformations, 1450–1650: Doctrine, Politics, Community.* Lanham, MD: Rowman and Littlefield, 2006.

Wiesner-Hanks, Merry. *Women and Gender in Early Modern Europe.* New York: Cambridge University Press, 2008.

ISSUES IN FEMINISM

Davis, Angela Y. *Women, Race, and Class.* New York: Vintage, 1983.

Feinberg, Leslie. *TransLiberation: Beyond Pink or Blue.* Boston: Beacon, 1999.

hooks, bell. *Feminism Is for Everybody: Passionate Politics.* Cambridge, MA: South End Press, 2000.

Smith, Barbara, Gloria Steinem, Gwendolyn Mink, Marysa Navarro, and Wilma Mankiller, eds. *The Reader's Companion to U.S. Women's History.* New York: Houghton Mifflin, 1999.

Sullivan, Nikki. *A Critical Introduction to Queer Theory.* New York: New York University Press, 2003.

THE ROOTS OF THE COLD WAR

Gaddis, John Lewis. *The Cold War: A New History.* New York: Penguin, 2006.

Kennedy, David M. *Freedom from Fear: The American People in Depression and War, 1929–1945.* New York: Oxford University Press, 2001.

Rhodes, Richard. *The Making of the Atomic Bomb.* New York: Simon & Schuster, 1995.

GAME THEORY

Dixit, Avinash K., and Barry J. Nalebuff. *Thinking Strategically: The Competitive Edge in Business, Politics, and Everyday Life.* New York: W. W. Norton, 1993.

Dixit, Avinash K., and Susan Skeath. *Games of Strategy.* New York: W. W. Norton, 2004.

http://www.gametheory.net

Shelling, Thomas C. *The Strategy of Conflict.* Cambridge, MA: Harvard University Press, 2007.

METEOROLOGY AND CLIMATE

Chaston, Peter R. *Weather Maps: How to Read and Interpret All the Basic Weather Charts.* Kearney, MO: Chaston Scientific, 2002.

Dessler, Andrew E., and Edward A. Parson. *The Science and Politics of Global Climate Change: A Guide to the Debate.* New York: Cambridge University Press, 2006.

Lyons, Walter A. *The Handy Weather Answer Book.* Canton, MI: Visible Ink Press, 1996.

Stommel, Henry, and Elizabeth Stommel. *Volcano Weather: The Story of 1816, the Year Without a Summer.* Newport, RI: Seven Seas Press, 1983.

Williams, Jack. *The Weather Book: An Easy-to-Understand Guide to the USA's Weather.* New York: Vintage, 1997.

MODERN CHINA

Fairbank, John King, and Merle Goldman. *China: A New History.* Cambridge, MA: Belknap Press, 2006.

Hsu, Immanuel C. Y. *The Rise of Modern China.* New York: Oxford University Press, 1999.

Murphey, Rhoads. *A History of Asia.* New York: Longman, 2008.

Spence, Jonathan D. *The Search for Modern China.* New York: W. W. Norton, 1999.

PLATO AND ARISTOTLE

Ackrill, J. L. *Aristotle the Philosopher.* New York: Oxford University Press, 1981.

Annas, Julia, *Plato: A Very Short Introduction.* New York: Oxford University Press, 2003.

Barnes, Jonathan. *Aristotle: A Very Short Introduction.* New York: Oxford University Press, 2001.

Barnes, Jonathan, ed. *The Complete Works of Aristotle.* Princeton, NJ: Princeton University Press, 1995.

Cooper, John M., and D. S. Hutchinson, eds. *Plato: Complete Works.* Indianapolis: Hackett Publishing, 1997.

Irwin, Terence. *Classical Thought.* New York: Oxford University Press, 1988.

ITALIAN RENAISSANCE ART

Beck, James H. *Italian Renaissance Painting.* New York: Könemann, 1999.

Paoletti, John T., and Gary M. Radke. *Art in Renaissance Italy.* New York: Prentice Hall, 2005.

Turner, A. Richard. *Renaissance Florence: The Invention of a New Art.* New York: Harry N. Abrams, 1997.

Vasari, Giorgio. *The Lives of the Artists.* Trans. Julia Conway Bondanella and Peter Bondanella. New York: Oxford University Press, 1998.

DARWINIAN EVOLUTION

Huxley, Julian. *Evolution: The Modern Synthesis.* London: Allen & Unwin, 1974.

Kimura, Motoo. *The Neutral Theory of Molecular Evolution.* New York: Cambridge University Press, 1985.

Provine, William B. *The Origins of Theoretical Population Genetics.* Chicago: University of Chicago Press, 2001

Wilson, Edward O. *Sociobiology: The New Synthesis.* Cambridge, MA: Harvard University Press, 2000.

THE ORIGINS OF JUDAISM

Coogan, Michael D., ed. *The Oxford History of the Biblical World.* New York: Oxford University Press, 2001.

Dever, William G. *Who Were the Early Israelites and Where Did They Come From?* Grand Rapids, MI: Eerdmans, 2006.

Fredriksen, Paula. *Jesus of Nazareth, King of the Jews.* New York: Vintage, 2000.

Friedman, Richard Elliott. *Who Wrote the Bible?* New York: HarperOne, 1997.

————. *The Bible with Sources Revealed.* New York: HarperOne, 2005.

Holtz, Barry, ed. *Back to the Sources: Reading the Classic Jewish Texts.* New York: Simon & Schuster, 1986.

Schiffman, Lawrence H. *From Text to Tradition: A History of Second Temple and Rabbinic Judaism.* Jersey City, NJ: Ktav Publishing House, 1991.

ACKNOWLEDGMENTS

The Agincourt Press team that created this book included Julia Rubel (photo research), Laura Jorstad (proofreading), Abigail Rubel (indexing), and Jon Glick and Miwako Nishizawa (design and production).

ABOUT THE CONTRIBUTORS

Denise Budd (ITALIAN RENAISSANCE ART) is a lecturer in art history at Columbia University, where she specializes in the work of Leonardo da Vinci and other fifteenth- and sixteenth-century Florentine artists. She is also the director of ArtWatch International, which monitors and campaigns for better practices in the conservation of artwork.

Lynn Catterson (ITALIAN RENAISSANCE ART) is a lecturer at Columbia University, where she coordinates the summer session in art history. Her research focuses on fifteenth-century Italian sculptors.

Art DeGaetano (METEOROLOGY AND CLIMATE) is Professor of Earth and Atmospheric Sciences at Cornell University, where he directs the Northeast Regional Climate Center (NRCC).

After serving as a navigator in the air force, Margaret M. DeGaetano (METEOROLOGY AND CLIMATE) taught earth science, biology, and mathematics in the middle and high schools. She currently teaches meteorology at Tompkins Cortland Community College.

Caroline Fisher (THE RENAISSANCE IN FLORENCE) earned a doctorate in European history from Brandeis University, where her dissertation chronicled the transition of the Florentine government from a medieval commune into an early modern state through the records of the government agency that served as a guardian for orphaned children.

Delano Greenidge-Copprue (LITERATURE OF THE JAZZ AGE) is a professor of humanities at the Manhattan School of Music. After a brief minor-league baseball career, he earned his doctorate from Columbia University, where his dissertation concerned the jazz cadence of nineteenth- and twentieth-century American literature from Herman Melville to Toni Morrison. He continues to write about the interdisciplinary nature of jazz.

Daniel Gremmler (THE EPICS OF THE TROJAN WAR) is a lecturer at the State University of New York at Albany, where he completed his dissertation on Greek tragedy. His other areas of scholarly interest include Aegean prehistory, comparative mythology, and the Elizabethan stage.

Walter E. Grunden (THE HISTORY OF MODERN CHINA) is Associate Professor of History at Bowling Green State University, where he teaches courses on modern Chinese and Japanese history. He is the author of *Secret Weapons & World War II: Japan in the Shadow of Big Science* (2005) and numerous articles on the history of nuclear weapons.

Martha Hadley (SIGMUND FREUD) is an adjunct professor at the Smith College School for Social Work, where she supervises doctoral students in the clinical program. She also maintains a private psychotherapy practice in New York City. She is executive editor of the journal *Studies of Gender and Sexuality*.

Kirsten Jensen (THE ARMORY SHOW) is an art historian specializing in nineteenth- and twentieth-century American art and architecture. She has worked at the Andrew W. Mellon Foundation, the National Academy of Design, and Yale University. She currently chairs the curatorial committee at the Thomas Cole National Historic Site.

William Kavaler (THE STOCK MARKET) has worked in the securities industry for over twenty years as a market maker, portfolio manager, and trader in stocks, bonds, options, and commodities.

David W. Krumme (THE ANATOMY OF THE INTERNET) is Emeritus Associate Professor of Computer Science at Tufts University, where he has taught courses in computer architecture, operating systems, compilers, parallel computing, and C++. He is also a principal in Airbits Wireless, an Internet service provider in Estes Park, Colorado.

Rob J. Kulathinal (DARWINIAN EVOLUTION) is an evolutionary geneticist at Harvard University, where he teaches a full-year course on Darwinian evolution. He began studying the genetics of speciation using the model organism *Drosophila* while completing his doctorate at McMaster University. He has continued this line of research as a biocurator at the gene database FlyBase.

Jesse M. Lander (SHAKESPEARE'S TRAGEDIES) is Associate Professor of English at the University of Notre Dame. His research focuses on Renaissance drama, the history of books, and post-Reformation religious culture. He is the author of *Inventing Polemic: Religion, Print, and Literary Culture in Early Modern England* (2006) and is currently working on a book about staging the supernatural in Shakespearean England.

Ramon E. Lopez (ELECTRICITY AND MAGNETISM) is Professor of Physics at the University of Texas at Arlington. He is a Fellow of the American Physical Society and in 2002 was awarded the Nicholson Medal for Humanitarian Service to Science. He leads a research group that is working in both space physics and science education. His current research focuses on solar wind–magnetosphere coupling and the interpretation of scientific visualization. He is the author or coauthor of more than one hundred publications, including *Storms from the Sun* (2002).

Charles H. Parker (THE PROTESTANT REFORMATION) is Associate Professor of History at Saint Louis University. His research interests focus on the religious and cultural history of early modern Europe with an emphasis on the Low Countries during the sixteenth and seventeenth centuries. His publications, which specifically address issues in the history of Calvinism and Catholicism, include *Faith on the Margins: Catholics and Catholicism in the Dutch Golden Age* (2008) and *The Reformation of Community: Social Welfare and Calvinist Charity in Holland, 1572–1620* (1998).

Michael Pregill (THE ORIGINS OF JUDAISM) is Distinguished Emerging Scholar and Assistant Professor of Religious Studies at Elon University. He has previously taught at Hofstra, Columbia, and NYU. His area of specialization is the Quran and Islamic exegetical literature. His current research focuses on Muslim perceptions and portrayals of Jews in the early Islamic period, as well as on the cross-cultural ramifications of prophecy in late antiquity.

A. Rez Pullen (ISSUES IN FEMINISM) is a doctoral candidate in the Women's Studies Department at Emory University, where she has taught introductory classes in women's studies. Her areas of specialization include queer theory, transgender studies, intersex studies, and feminist theory. Previously, she earned a master's degree in theological studies at Harvard University.

David Rubel (REVOLUTIONARY BOSTON, THE ROOTS OF THE COLD WAR) is the author of more than a dozen book of American history. His recent books include *The Coming Free: The Struggle for African-American Equality* (2005) and *The Story of America: Freedom and Crisis from Settlement to Superpower* (2002), coauthored with Archivist of the United States Allen Weinstein.

Theodore Turocy (GAME THEORY) is Assistant Professor of Economics at Texas A&M University, where he has taught since completing his PhD in managerial economics and decision sciences at Northwestern University. In addition to game theory, his research interests include behavioral, experimental, and computational economics. He also maintains the Gambit software package, which computes the Nash equilibria of games among other game-theory applications.

Iakovos Vasiliou (PLATO AND ARISTOTLE) is Associate Professor of Philosophy at the City University of New York Graduate Center and Brooklyn College. He has published numerous articles on Plato, Aristotle, and Wittgenstein, and is the author of *Aiming at Virtue in Plato* (2008). He has also taught at Johns Hopkins University and Georgia State University.

Dow, Charles, 179
Dow Jones Industrial Average (DJIA), 179
Drag King Dreams (Feinberg), 286
dreams, 44, 54, 59, 84
Dreier, Katherine, 83
"Drenched in Light" (Hurston), 180
Du Bois, W. E. B., 160, 190
dualism, 323, 363
Duchamp, Marcel, 58, 68, 88, 98
Duchamp-Villon, Raymond, 68
Dunbar, Paul Laurence, 175
Duomo, 143, 168, 299, 309, 314, 319, 344, 349
Dutch Revolt, 260
dynamo theory, 151
dynastic cycle, 292

Eakins, Thomas, 28
Earth,
    energy budget of, 214
    magnetic field of, 146, 151
East India Company, 66, 71
Edict of Nantes, 255
Edict of Worms, 220, 230
Edison, Thomas, 141
Edward VI of England, 240
efficient cause, 358
ego, 89
Ego and the Id (Freud), 89
Egoist, 130
Egypt, Jewish sojourn in and exodus from, 311,
    316, 321
Eight, The, 28, 38, 43, 73
Einstein, Albert, 99, 208, 232
Eisenhower, Dwight D., 227
electricity, *see* Syllabus II *passim*
electromagnetic spectrum, 191
electromagnetism, 156, 161, 176, 181, 186, 191, 196
electrons, 111, 131, 136, 146, 156, 181
Eliot, T. S., 130, 150, 195
Elizabeth I of England, 240, 265
Ellington, Duke, 115
Ellison, Ralph, 130
Elpenor, 177, 182, 197
email, 17, 42, 47, 57, 62, 67, 82, 87
Emmy von N., 54
Emperor Jones (O'Neill), 155
Empress Dowager, *see* Cixi
encryption, 102
    public-key, 72
energy,
    heat, 136, 191
    kinetic, 121, 126, 136
    mechanical, 171
    potential, 126, 131
English Reformation, 240
Enlightenment, 250, 300, 381
Enloe, Cynthia, 236
entrainment, 259
environmentalism, 300, 330
epic poetry, *see* Syllabus II *passim*
epistasis, 360, 365
Epistemology of the Closet (Sedgwick), 281
Equal Rights Association (ERA), 216, 221
equestrian statues, 344, 354

equilibrium,
    Hardy-Weinberg, *see* Hardy-Weinberg
        equilibrium
    Nash, *see* Nash equilibrium
Erasmus, Desiderius, 205, 230
Eris, 122, 127
error-correcting codes (ECCs), 67
Esau, 311
Essay on the Principle of Population (Malthus), 315
Essenes, 356, 366
essentialism, 280, 295, 300, 330
Euclid, 374
Euripides, 25, 303
European Recovery Program (ERP), *see* Marshall
    Plan
Euthyphro (Plato), 308
evolution, 248, *see also* Syllabus IV *passim*
Evolution and the Theory of Games (Smith), 248
expressionism, 98
Ezekiel, 336

Fall of Princes (Lydgate), 30
Faraday's Law, 166
Faulkner, William, 125, 140, 195
fauvism, 33, 38, 48, 58, 63, 68, 78, 83, 88, 98
Feinberg, Leslie, 286
Feminine Mystique (Friedan), 226
feminism, *see* Syllabus III *passim*
    global, 261
    liberal, 231, 236
    radical, 231, 236
    socialist, 236
    transnational, 261
feminist disability studies, 266, 271
Ferdinand II (Holy Roman emperor), 270
Ferdinand II of Aragon, 245
Fergusson, John Duncan, 83
Fermi, Enrico, 232
ferromagnetic materials, 156, 161, 176
fin de siècle, 24
final cause, 358
First Continental Congress, 71, 76
First Opium War, 297
First Sino-Japanese War, 327
First Temple, 326, 331, 336, 364
First United Front, 322
first wave, *see* women's suffrage movement
Fisher, R. A., 350, 355, 360, 365, 370
Fisher, Rudolph, 165
fitness, *see* genetics, fitness
Fitzgerald, F. Scott, 120, 125, 140, 145, 150,
    155, 185
Fitzgerald, Zelda, 145, 150
Five Books of Moses, *see* Torah
Five-Year Plans,
    in China, 352, 357
    in Soviet Union, 207
Florence, Renaissance in, *see* Syllabus II *passim*,
    Syllabus IV *passim*
forced loans, 138, 143
foreshortening, 319
formal cause, 353, 358, 363, 368
forms, Platonic theory of, 295, 328, 338, 343, 353
Fort Ticonderoga, 101

Helen, 122, 132, 157, 167
Hellenism, 346, 351, 356
Hemingway, Ernest, 125, 130, 135, 140, 150, 195
Henri, Robert, 28, 73, 83
Henry II of France, 255
Henry III of France, 255
Henry IV of France, 255
Henry VIII of England, 193, 240
Henry of Guise, 255
Henry of Navarre, *see* Henry IV of France
Henslow, John Stevens, 305
Hephaestos, 157
Hera, 122, 192
heredity, *see* genetics, heredity
Hermes, 152, 177, 187, 192
Herodotus, 112, 128
heroic ideal, 142
Herzl, Theodor, 381
Hesiod, 117
Higgins, Eugene, 73
Hippocrates, 303
Hiss, Alger, 277, 282
Hitler, Adolf, 99, 207, 212, 227
Hobbes, Thomas, 275
Holy Roman Empire, 210, 220, 230, 270
Home to Harlem (McKay), 190
Homer, 112, 117, 128, 142, 167, 172, 293
homology, 305
homosexuality, *see* lesbianism, same-sex attraction
Hong Xiuquan, 307
Hooker, Joseph Dalton, 320
Hope, F. W., 305
Hopkins, Harry, 217
House Un-American Activities Committee (HUAC), 277
Howe, Julia Ward, 221
Howe, William, 96, 101
HTML (hypertext markup language), 32, 42
Hu Yaobang, 372, 377
Hua Guofeng, 372
Hughes, James, 175
Hughes, Langston, 165, 175, 190
Huguenots, 255
humanism, 108, 123, 128, 304, 324; *see also* Christian humanism, civic humanism
humidity, *see* relative humidity
hurricanes, 254
Hurston, Zora Neale, 180
Hussites, 200
Hutchinson, Thomas, 36, 51, 61, 76
Huxley, Thomas Henry, 325
hyperlinks, 32, 87
hypnosis, 34, 39, 49
hysteria, 34, 39, 44, 74, 99

id, 90
Iliad (Homer), 112, 117, 127, 132, 142, 147, 152, 177, 192, 293
impressionism, 18, 23, 28, 53
In Search of Our Mother's Gardens (Walker), 251
induction, 111, 166, 171, 176
indulgences, 205, 215, 220
Industrial Revolution, 17, 297
Inferno (Dante), 197

information,
 analog, 22
 digital, 22
 perfect and incomplete, 283, 288
information revolutions, 17, 22
initial public offerings (IPOs), 119
Innocent VIII (pope), 205
insider trading, 134
Institutes of the Christian Religion (Calvin), 235
insulators, 136
"Integrating Disability, Transforming Feminist Theory" (Garland-Thomson), 266
Interim Committee, 237, 247
International Exhibition of Modern Art, *see* Armory Show
Internet, *see* Syllabus I *passim*
Internet bubble, 119, 194
Internet Corporation for Assigned Names and Numbers (ICANN), 42
Internet Protocol (IP), 47, 82
 addresses, 27, 32, 37, 42, 47, 57, 82
Internet service providers (ISPs), 37, 77
Interpretation of Dreams (Freud), 54, 89
intersectionality, 246, 251, 256, 261, 276
intersex studies, 271
Intolerable Acts, 71
inversions, 259
Iphigenia, 167
Isaac, 311
 sacrifice of, 299, 306, 316, 321
Isabella I of Castile, 245
Isaiah, 331
Ishmael, 306
isobars, 234
isotopes, 274
Israel, *see also* Syllabus IV *passim*
 Jacob renamed as, 311
 kingdom of, 296, 331
 modern state of, 296, 381
 ten "lost" tribes of, 331, 336, 341
 Twelve Tribes of, 311, 331
Italian Renaissance art, 163, *see also* Syllabus IV *passim*

Jacob, 311, 316, 321
James I of England, 265
James II of England, 265
Japan,
 introduction of Christianity to, 285
 relations with China, 317, 332, 337, 342, 347, 352
jazz, 110, 115, 130
Jazz Age, literature of, *see* Syllabus II *passim*
Jeroboam, 331
Jerusalem Talmud, *see* Talmud, Jerusalem
Jesuits, 245, 270, 285
Jesus of Nazareth, 200, 361
jet streams, 239, 249
Jewish Emancipation, 24, 381
Jews, *see* Syllabus IV *passim*
 assimilation of, 24, 381
Jiang Qing, 362, 372
Johnson, James Weldon, 110, 155, 170, 185, 190
Jonathan, 326